Read SAP PRESS online also

With booksonline we offer you online access to leading SAP experts' knowledge. Whether you use it as a beneficial supplement or as an alternative to the printed book – with booksonline you can:

- Access any book at any time
- Quickly look up and find what you need
- Compile your own SAP library

Your advantage as the reader of this book

Register your book on our website and obtain an exclusive and free test access to its online version. You're convinced you like the online book? Then you can purchase it at a preferential price!

And here's how to make use of your advantage

1. Visit www.sap-press.com
2. Click on the link for SAP PRESS booksonline
3. Enter your free trial license key
4. Test-drive your online book with full access for a limited time!

Your personal **license key** for your test access including the preferential offer

j45g-96rz-2vi7-s3uq

Maximizing SAP® ERP Financials Accounts Receivable

SAP PRESS is a joint initiative of SAP and Galileo Press. The know-how offered by SAP specialists combined with the expertise of the Galileo Press publishing house offers the reader expert books in the field. SAP PRESS features first-hand information and expert advice, and provides useful skills for professional decision-making.

SAP PRESS offers a variety of books on technical and business related topics for the SAP user. For further information, please visit our website: *www.sap-press.com*.

Naeem Arif, Sheikh Tauseef
Integrating SAP ERP Financials
2010, app. 380 pp.
978-1-59229-300-1

Vincenzo Sopracolle
Quick Reference Guide to SAP ERP Financials Financial Accounting
2010, app. 650 pp.
978-1-59229-313-1

Paul Theobald
Transitioning to IFRS in SAP ERP Financials
2009, 209 pp.
978-1-59229-319-3

John Jordan
100 Things You Should Know About Controlling with SAP ERP Financials
2010, 300 pp.
978-1-59229-341-4

Manish Patel

Maximizing SAP® ERP Financials Accounts Receivable

Bonn • Boston

Galileo Press is named after the Italian physicist, mathematician and philosopher Galileo Galilei (1564–1642). He is known as one of the founders of modern science and an advocate of our contemporary, heliocentric worldview. His words *Eppur se muove* (And yet it moves) have become legendary. The Galileo Press logo depicts Jupiter orbited by the four Galilean moons, which were discovered by Galileo in 1610.

Editor Stephen Solomon
Copyeditor Julie McNamee
Cover Design Jill Winitzer
Photo Credit iStockphoto.com/Maica
Layout Design Vera Brauner
Production Editor Kelly O'Callaghan
Assistant Production Editor Graham Geary
Typesetting Publishers' Design and Production Services, Inc.
Printed and bound in Canada

ISBN 978-1-59229-303-2

1st Edition 2010

Library of Congress Cataloging-in-Publication Data
Patel, Manish.
Maximizing SAP ERP financials accounts receivable / Manish Patel. — 1st ed.
p. cm.
Includes bibliographical references and index.
ISBN-13: 978-1-59229-303-2 (alk. paper)
ISBN-10: 1-59229-303-4 (alk. paper)
1. SAP ERP. 2. Accounts receivable — Data processing. 3. Accounts receivable — Computer programs. I. Title.
HF5681.A3P38 2010
658.15'244 — dc22 2009052657

Contents at a Glance

Contents

Preface

It may not come as a surprise to anyone who has been involved with SAP that numerous implementations do not harness full power of the SAP system. Of course, there are number of valid, justifiable, and practical reasons for not enabling or using certain system functionalities. However, if one of the reasons is that those who use, implement and support SAP system aren't aware of available features and functionalities, this book is an attempt to fill that void. The focus of this book is on Accounts Receivable processes.

The following sections will outline target audience, structure and coverage for this book.

Target Audience

Business users as well as technical professionals can benefit from the information presented in this book.

As a business user, you can read through this book to identify new processes that can be incorporated in your existing SAP system landscape. You can also use information from this book to fine tune your existing SAP processes. For example, you may encounter more efficient ways of processing cash applications, or you may choose to implement enhanced authorizations so that you can more confidently use temporary help during busy times.

As a technical professional, this book will provide you with a business context for configuration activities. I have provided menu paths for configuration activities in the same section as corresponding business process explanation. Additionally, at the end of each chapter is a technical reference section where you can find technical reference information for the specific subject area.

Chapter Organization

Information in all chapters of this book is presented and structured based on business processes. For example, the chapter on customer master data presents information according to different levels of master data, and the chapter on processing incoming payments presents information based on the different steps of processing cash applications. Menu paths and transaction codes for different activities are embedded in the explanation for easy reference. All configuration activities that can impact the business process are also introduced in the same section, along with corresponding configuration menu paths. I have included as many screenshots as possible in these sections to make it easy for you to relate to the process explanation or configuration details. Where applicable, I have also included a separate section in a chapter to provide details of other relevant supporting and reporting transactions.

At the end of each chapter, I have included technical reference for the subject matter discussed in that chapter. I will repeat here the important note that I have also repeated in every chapter.

Note

Considering the large number of technical objects available in an SAP system, the technical information presented at the end of each chapter should only be considered a starting point for analysis, not the sum total of available information.

In general, the technical information includes the following:

- **OSS Notes**: This section provides a sample list of relevant OSS notes. I have focused on consulting, advanced development and similar types of notes applicable for ECC 6.0 system. This list does not include any "program error" OSS notes because you are bound to stumble upon them while trying to implement that business process.
- **Transactions**: This section provides a single point of reference for transactions relevant for that subject. This section usually includes transactions that are explained in detail in that chapter, or other supporting and reporting transactions.
- **Authorization Objects**: This section provides a sample list of authorization objects used by the transactions discussed in that chapter. This section does not

list authorization objects used for standard and common tasks such as ALV reporting, spool processing, batch processing or printing. Appendix B provides details on authorization concepts.

- **Tables and Structures**: This section provides quick reference to important SAP tables and structures that store information presented in that chapter. For the most part, the focus of this section is on business data. So you may not find in this section any tables and structures that store configuration details.
- **BTEs (Business Transaction Events)**: This section provides a list of available Business Transaction Events for the subject area discussed in that chapter. The list includes both types of BTEs: Publish and Subscribe BTEs and Process BTEs. You can refer to Appendix A for more details on BTEs and their implementation.
- **Enhancements**: This section provides a list of enhancements, corresponding function module exits accompanied by brief description of their intended usage. Appendix A provides more details on enhancements and their implementation.
- **BAdIs (Business Add-Ins)**: Business Add-Ins provide different approach for application enhancements. This section provides a list of available BAdIs for the topic discussed in corresponding chapter. You will also find a list of available methods for each BAdI, so you can quickly ascertain whether that BAdI will be useful for your intended implementation. Appendix A provides more details on BAdIs and their implementation.
- **BAPIs (Business APIs)**: This section provides a list of available BAPIs for the SAP business object discussed in corresponding chapter. The section consists of a list of methods available for a business object, corresponding function module, and a brief description of the BAPI method. You can refer to Appendix A for more details on BAPIs and their implementation.

As should be evident, every chapter provides enough food for thoughts for business users as well as for technical professionals.

Topic Coverage

In this book, I have decided to focus on the core processes of Accounts Receivable. Undoubtedly, some processes are more relevant for your business than others. The chapters are not sequential, so you can read it in any order that you choose.

However, if this is your first interaction with SAP, I would suggest first reading Chapter 1 and Chapter 2 before reading any other chapters.

Following is a quick reference for the chapters in this book.

- **Chapter 1:** This chapter focuses on **Customer Master Data**. Topics covered in this chapter include organization of customer master data in an SAP system, detailed explanation of every field on every screen of customer master data, SAP transactions for customer master data maintenance, and associated configuration activities.
- **Chapter 2:** This chapter focuses on **AR transactions** – i.e. customer transactions posted in Accounts Receivable. The chapter provides an overview of key ERP Financials document concepts, AR transactions and document posting aids and processing tools.
- **Chapter 3:** Focus of this chapter is on **Customer Billing** process. This chapter provides information about organizational framework and customer master data in SD component. You will find information about key configuration activities relevant for billing process, and the SAP transactions used to process standard customer billing.
- **Chapter 4:** This chapter builds upon the information presented in Chapter 3. It provides business reference and configuration details for **Additional Billing** topics such as down payments, billing plans, resource related billing and other billing processes.
- **Chapter 5:** This chapter focuses on processing **Incoming Payments**. The chapter is divided into logical steps of entering basic data, selecting customer items, processing customer items, processing payment differences, and posting cash application documents.
- **Chapter 6:** This chapter discusses **Dunning** functionality in SAP system. You will find detailed explanation of different dunning parameters that impact the dunning process, the dunning run and other supporting transactions.
- **Chapter 7:** This chapter focuses on the **Credit Management** functionality available in a standard SAP system. In this chapter, you will learn about the credit management master data, simple credit check and advanced credit monitoring.
- **Chapter 8:** This chapter takes you into the world of **Tax Processing** in SAP systems. The chapter focuses on tax procedure configuration, tax calculation in FI and SD transactions, and on the system interface with external tax calculation solutions.

- **Chapter 9:** This chapter focuses on **Revenue Recognition** functionality. It tackles revenue recognition from different angles such as periodic revenue recognition, event based revenue recognition and revenue recognition along with billing plans.
- **Chapter 10:** This chapter explains typical transactions that are part of **Periodic Processing** such as account clearing, accrual processing, currency revaluation, interest calculation and month end closing.
- **Chapter 11:** This chapter on **AR Reporting** provides an overview of some useful AR and SD reports available in a standard SAP system. It also provides information about reporting tools such as Drilldown reporting, AR evaluations and SAP Query.
- **Chapter 12:** This chapter provides a reference and overview for **SAP Financial Supply Chain Management**. In particular, you will get an overview of advanced functionality and sophisticated features available in FSCM components of credit management, dispute management and collections management.

I hope that you find this book a useful reference, and that you enjoy reading it as much as I enjoyed writing it. Feel free to reach out to me with your feedback.

Manish Patel
Sr. SAP Solutions Consultant
January 2010

This chapter focuses on the maintenance of customer master data in SAP systems. Not only order to cash business transactions make use of data elements from customer master; but in SAP systems, different flags and settings in the customer master also influence the behavior and outcome of customer business transactions.

1 Customer Master Data

In this chapter, we'll first discuss the organization of SAP customer master data and details of important data fields in customer master. Then we'll discuss common transactions and reports available for processing customer master data, followed by technical reference details relevant for customer master data in SAP.

1.1 Organization of Customer Master Data

Through the entire order to cash process, people from different functional areas of your company such as sales, shipping, receivables, and collection need to interact with customer master data. These groups need to have access and influence over different parts of customer information. Also, if a customer transacts with multiple locations of your company, possibly in different countries, then each location of your company also requires the ability to maintain their own customer-specific information. The SAP system manages these requirements by maintaining customer master data at three levels.

Three-Level Master Data

For every customer, you can manage general data, *company code* data, and *sales area* data in the SAP system.

A company code in the SAP system typically represents an organization unit for which you prepare a complete set of financial statements. Accounting entries for AR are posted to a customer account into a specific company code. Your SAP system may have multiple company codes, for example, if your company operates in multiple countries. On the other hand, a sales area in the SAP system represents an organization unit responsible for sales-related activities. Typically, if your company has several distribution channels or several product divisions, your SAP system will contain multiple sales areas.

Figure 1.1 shows an example of customer master data in a SAP system for a customer that transacts with your company locations in the United States and the United Kingdom, and places orders with two sales organizations — standard sales and online sales.

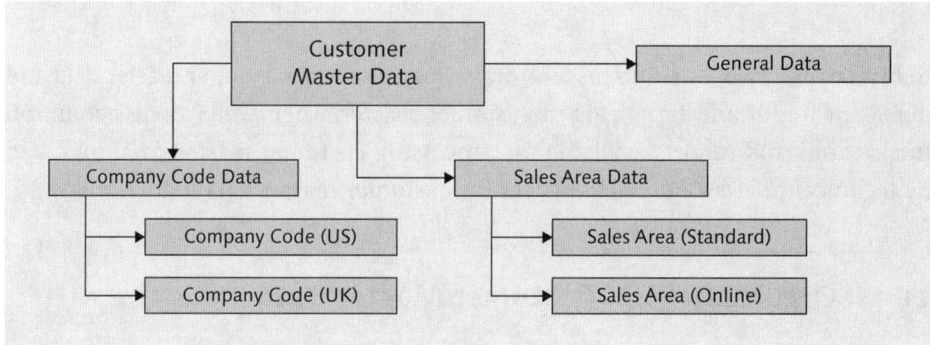

Figure 1.1 Organization of Customer Master Data

A company code can be associated with more than one sales area, but a sales area can be linked to only one company code. Depending on your organizational structure, you may have to maintain different levels of customer master data.

It's possible to create a customer master in SAP systems that only contain general data and company code data. You'll be able to post accounting entries for these customers but won't be able to process any sales transactions. This can be useful for your non-trade receivables, for example, receivables from tenants for which you don't create sales orders.

Similarly, it's possible to create a customer master in SAP systems that only contain general data and sales area data. You'll be able to post sales transactions to such customers but won't be able to post any accounting entries. This can be useful for maintaining different customer locations, as will be evident in the next paragraph. Another aspect of customer master creation in SAP system is the customer account group.

Customer Account Group

In this complex world of business relationships, not all customers are created equal. Business requirements defer depending on legal status (individuals versus corporations), business volume (whether and how much business you may do with them again), business relationship (trade customer or non-trade customer), or any similar criteria. Also, a customer may place an order from one location, require goods delivery to a different location, expect to be invoiced at a third location, and make payment from an entirely different location. Even though you require visibility to such business relationships, your information requirement for each location is different.

A *customer account group* is used to group customer accounts in SAP that share similar business criteria. Depending on your requirements, a customer account group can be used to group customers into domestic customers, foreign customers, franchisees, distributors, wholesalers, and so on. You can even create separate customer account groups for your competitors to maintain and track competitor data. Customer account groups in SAP systems control the following important parameters:

- Number range for the customer numbers
  - This range determines the upper and lower limits of customer numbers.
  - This determines whether numbers for new customers are assigned manually or internally by the SAP system.
  - Multiple customer account groups can share the same customer number range.
- Whether an account group represents one-time customer accounts
  - A one-time customer account represents business transactions with a group of customers. This is useful when you don't anticipate your company to do repeat business with these customers.
  - For one-time accounts, customer data such as address and bank data isn't maintained in the customer master. Instead, this data is entered as necessary when posting individual documents.

- Which fields are ready for input, required to be filled, or hidden during customer master data maintenance
  - This can hide unused fields to simplify screens or ensure that required information must be entered before new customers are saved in the SAP system.
  - As discussed in Section 1.6, Configuration Activities, it's possible to override these field settings for a specific company code or for a specific transaction.

The SAP system provides a large number of predefined customer account groups (Table 1.1). Customer account groups are maintained under IMG • FINANCIAL ACCOUNTING • ACCOUNTS RECEIVABLE AND ACCOUNTS PAYABLE • CUSTOMER ACCOUNTS • MASTER DATA• PREPARATIONS FOR CREATING CUSTOMER MASTER DATA • DEFINE ACCOUNT GROUPS WITH SCREEN LAYOUT (CUSTOMERS).

Account Group	Name	Purpose
0001	Sold to Party	Customer accounts responsible for which sales orders are created
0002	Goods Recipient	Accounts corresponding to customer locations where goods delivery is made
0003	Payer	Customer accounts responsible for making payments against invoices
0004	Bill-to Party	Customer accounts where invoices are sent
0005	Prospective Customers	Potential customer leads, for example, created from your CRM system
0006	Competitors	Customer accounts corresponding to competitors — maintained for competitive advantage
0007	Sales Partners	Business partners collaborating in operational aspects of sales processes
0012	Hierarchy Node	Accounts corresponding to nodes of a customer hierarchy (discussed later in this chapter)
CPD	OTA (int.)	One-time customer accounts with internal number assignment
CPDA	OTA (ext.)	One-time customer accounts with external number assignment

Table 1.1 Customer Account Groups

When you want to create a new customer or extend an existing customer in the SAP system, you have to specify the Account Group, Company Code, and Sales Area to maintain corresponding data. Figure 1.2 shows first screen of customer master creation.

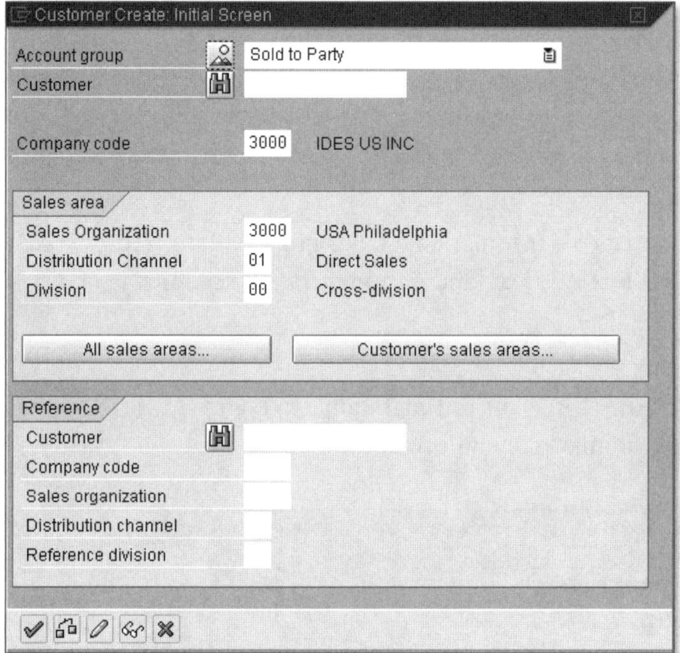

Figure 1.2 Create Customer Master

In the next section, we'll discuss the fields available in the customer master, starting with the general data view. For the purpose of illustration, this section uses an account group for which most fields in the customer master are enabled for data entry. Screens on your system may look different depending on the configuration of your system and the account group you selected.

1.2 General Data View

General data view in a customer master maintenance consists of the following tab pages.

- Address
- Control Data
- Payment Transactions
- Marketing
- Unloading Points
- Export Data
- Contact Person

1.2.1 Address

The Address tab page consists of customer data fields grouped into Name, Search Terms, Street Address, PO Box Address, and Communication sections.

Name

In the NAME section (Figure 1.3), you can maintain TITLE and up to four lines (NAME 1 – NAME 4) of customer name information.

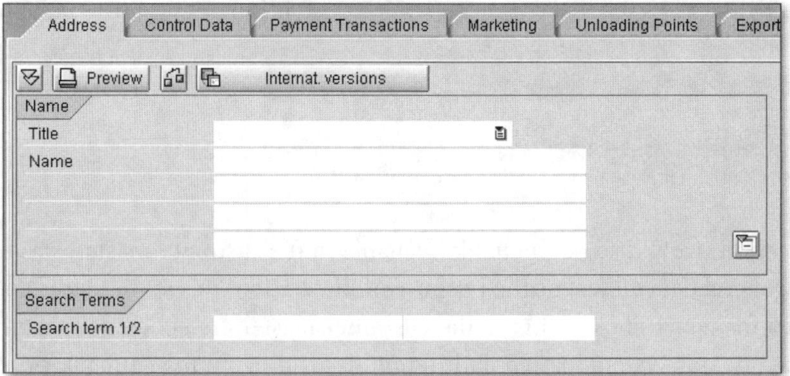

Figure 1.3 General Data – Address – Name and Search Terms

SAP introduced the Business Address Services (BAS) component in SAP R/3 version 4.5 to cater to country- and culture-specific norms for names and addresses. Check IMG • SAP NETWEAVER • APPLICATION SERVER • BASIS SERVICES • ADDRESS MANAGEMENT • FORMS OF ADDRESS AND NAME COMPONENTS. Here you can maintain forms of address, academic titles, name prefixes, name formatting rules such as whether first name should be displayed before or after last name, and so on.

Search Terms

Figure 1.3 also shows the SEARCH TERM 1/2 fields where you can assign meaningful, logical phrases to easily find this customer account number during operational processes. If a customer account represents a company, the search term can be an abbreviation of the company name. If a customer account represents an individual, it can be a combination of first initial + last name. Of course, to effectively use this functionality, consistent guidelines should be followed for determining search terms for new customers.

Street Address

Figure 1.4 shows an expanded view of the ADDRESS tab in the customer master. By clicking on the "–" icon, you can collapse this section so that only the most commonly used address fields are displayed on the screen. In its most detailed form, you can enter the customer address containing up to four lines of street address, Building Code number, Room number, Floor number, Street Number, House Number, District, Postal Code/City, Country, and Region.

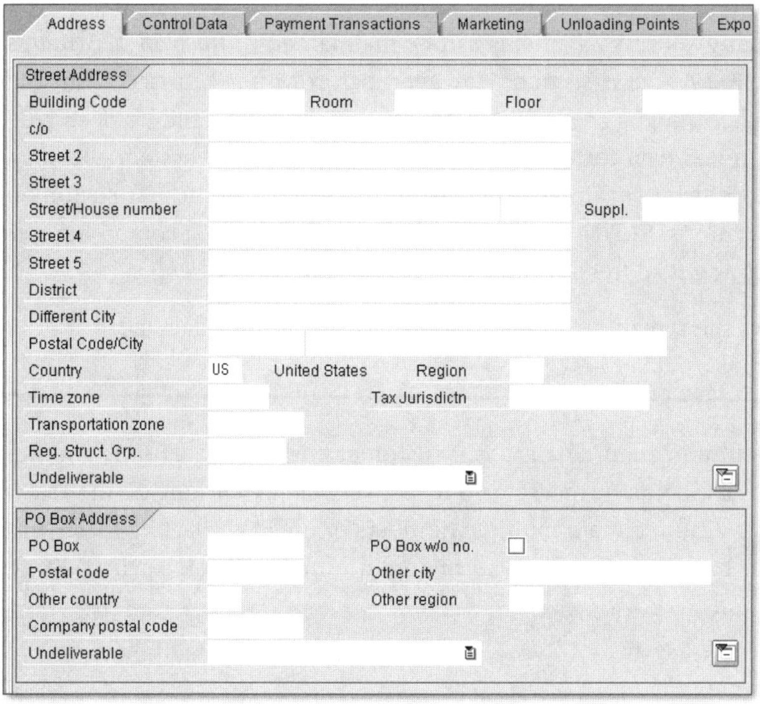

Figure 1.4 General Data – Address – Street and PO Box

Additionally, you can maintain Time Zone, Transportation Zone, Tax Jurisdiction, and other reference fields related to the customer address. We'll discuss some of these fields later in this chapter.

If you need to maintain international address versions (e.g., Japanese addresses in U.S. format), or influence how address fields are displayed on data entry screens, you can find relevant configuration activities under IMG • SAP NetWeaver • Application Server • Basis Services • Address Management • International Settings.

PO Box Address

If the customer address contains a PO Box, you can maintain it in this section of the dialog box. As the expanded view shows in Figure 1.4, several other fields are available to meet special requirements. These fields can be useful for country-specific requirements such as when the PO box address is different from the normal address, or the customer organization has its own postal code. This section also provides you with a field to maintain reasons for non-delivery of communication. This can be used later for data cleanup.

As is evident, many address data fields can be maintained in the Street Address section and PO Box Address section. However, before you get carried away and maintain all of these fields, ensure that you have operational bandwidth to continue to maintain this data for all customers and that your SAP system is configured to use this information in all relevant forms, reports, and other customer-facing communications. SAP Note 35931 is a great reference for a comprehensive list of SAP Notes about address printing and formatting.

Figure 1.5 shows the remaining Communication fields on this data tab.

Communication

Contact and communication details for a customer such as Telephone, Mobile Phone, Fax, and Email can be maintained in this section. By clicking on the arrow next to a field, you can maintain multiple numbers or emails. Selecting the Other communication button enables you to maintain other numbers such as Telex, Tele-fax, Pager, and so on.

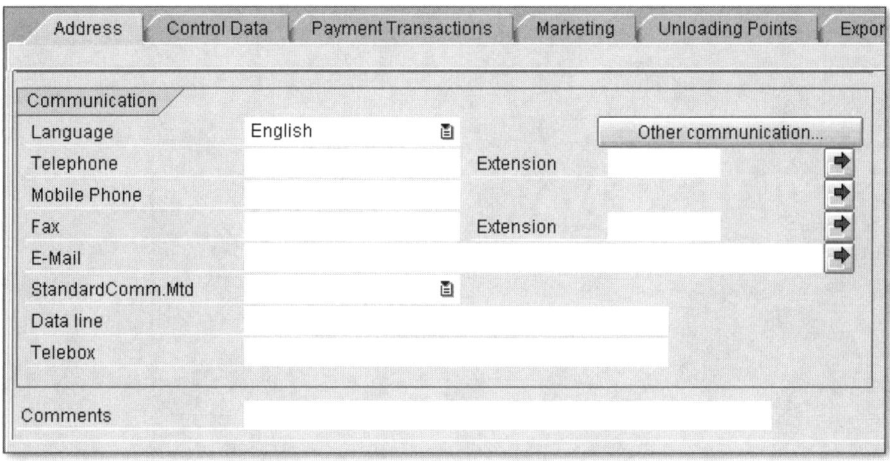

Figure 1.5 General Data – Address – Communication

StandardComm.Mtd is used to maintain the customer's preferred communication method. Subsequently at the time of generating customer correspondence, corresponding programs can check this value for the appropriate delivery method.

Keep in mind, however, that these communication details are for the customer business location. Contact details of individuals working at the customer business location are maintained on a separate screen.

The next tab page in the general data view is Control Data.

1.2.2 Control Data

The Control Data page (Figure 1.6) consists of three data sections: Account Control, Reference data/area, and Tax information.

Account Control

If this customer is also a vendor for your business, then you can maintain the corresponding vendor account number in the Vendor field. This link helps you in analysis of combined activities of both accounts in Accounts Receivable (AR) operational transactions.

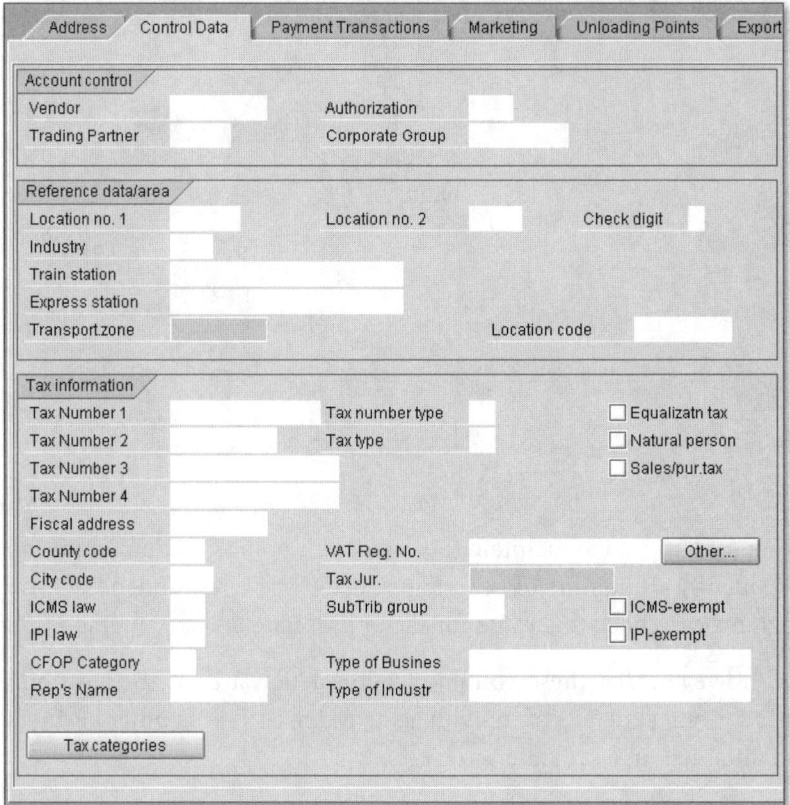

Figure 1.6 General Data – Control Data

The AUTHORIZATION field provides you with additional control over access to this customer master data. Later in this book, we'll discuss SAP authorization concepts in detail, but suffice it to say that using this field, you can restrict access to a group of customer master records only to selected users.

TRADING PARTNER is used by SAP Consolidation Module for elimination of inter-company activities. For the purpose of consolidation, each company code is assigned unique Company ID using IMG • ENTERPRISE STRUCTURE • ASSIGNMENT • FINANCIAL ACCOUNTING • ASSIGN COMPANY CODE TO COMPANY. Subsequently, the company code is created as a 'customer' in all partner company codes, and corresponding Company ID is entered in this field. This assignment ensures that all accounts receivable activities for this 'customer' are recorded accurately as inter-company activities.

CORPORATE GROUP is a freely definable code that can be used to group customers based on business-specific criteria. For example, if your company transacts with multiple subsidiaries of the same corporate group, you can assign the same value to corresponding customer accounts. Subsequently, this field can be used in AR reporting and analysis.

Reference Data/Area

This section contains fields such as LOCATION NO 1 and TRAIN STATION that are more relevant for shipping and order delivery processes. They don't have any influence on AR processes.

Tax Information

TAX NUMBER 1 to TAX NUMBER 4 fields are used for maintaining customer tax numbers. For many countries, there is a recommended usage for each of these four fields. For example,

- Hungary/Italy – (1) Tax Number
- United States – (1) SSN, (2) EIN
- Bulgaria – (1) United Identification Code, (2) Tax Number, (3) SSN
- Russia – (1) INN, (2) OKPO Code, (3) KPP Number, (4) OFK Number

Online help (F1 key) for each Tax Number field lists the recommended usage for different countries. If the country you are looking for doesn't have any specific recommendation, after careful evaluation, it's safe to use that Tax Number field for your discretionary usage.

VAT REG NO field is used for VAT number for customers based in European countries. If a customer has VAT registration numbers in other European countries, those numbers can be maintained by selecting OTHER.

TAX JURISDICTION CODE is relevant mainly in North America, where it uniquely identifies tax authorities that influence tax-relevant transactions. Due to large numbers of ever-changing tax jurisdictions, typically SAP Partner Software, such as Vertex, Taxware, and Sabrix, is integrated with the SAP system to determine tax jurisdiction codes. When a customer address is entered, the integrated software automatically determines and proposes the tax jurisdiction code.

However, if you choose to maintain tax jurisdiction codes within SAP, you can find relevant configuration activities under IMG • FINANCIAL ACCOUNTING • FINANCIAL ACCOUNTING GLOBAL SETTINGS • TAX ON SALES/ PURCHASES • BASIC SETTINGS • DEFINE TAX JURISDICTIONS. In addition, COUNTY CODE and CITY CODE fields are also useful for U.S. tax calculation. These codes can be maintained under IMG • SALES AND DISTRIBUTION • BASIC FUNCTIONS • TAXES • DEFINE REGIONAL CODES.

The remaining fields in this section are relevant only for customer accounts in specific countries. You can maintain values for fields such as TAX NUMBER TYPE, ICMS LAW, IPI LAW, TYPE OF BUSINESS in the configuration. IMG • FINANCIAL ACCOUNTING • FINANCIAL ACCOUNTING GLOBAL SETTINGS • TAX ON SALES/PURCHASES • BASIC SETTINGS includes several country-specific configuration activities for tax calculation. The next section discusses the Payment Transactions tab in the general data view.

1.2.3 Payment Transactions

The Payment Transactions tab (Figure 1.7) includes bank information and other data relevant for payment transactions. This can be useful, for example, if customers have given direct debit authorization for payments. These fields are discussed in more detail in Chapter 5, Customer Payments.

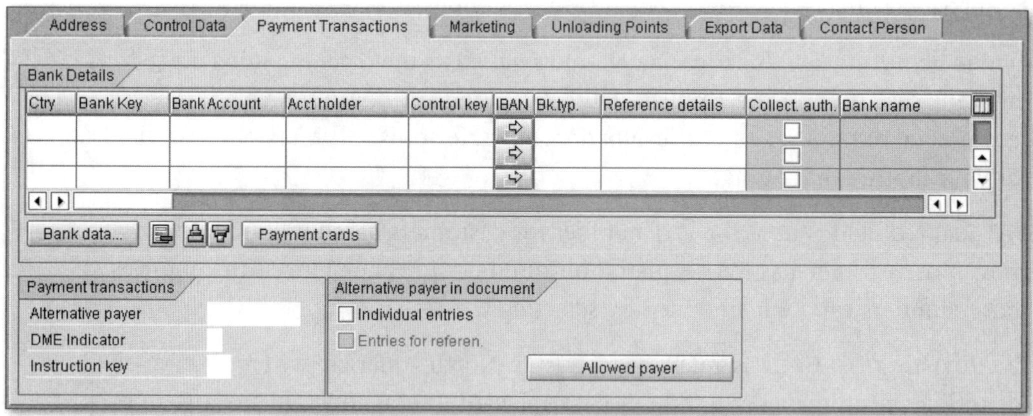

Figure 1.7 General Data – Payment Transactions

In the SAP system, COUNTRY and BANK KEY fields uniquely identify a bank. These bank details can be maintained by selecting BANK DATA on this screen. You may want to consider loading the entire bank directory in your SAP system. Typically, the central bank of a country provides such a directory in electronic format. Corresponding configuration is under IMG • CROSS-APPLICATION COMPONENTS • BANK DIRECTORY • BANK DIRECTORY DATA TRANSFER.

The BANK ACCOUNT field on this screen is used for entering the bank account number, and the ACCT HOLDER field is useful if the account holder name is different from the customer name.

IBAN (International Bank Account Number) is widely used in banking system of European countries. The SAP system provides comprehensive support for IBAN, including country-specific checks to ensure the validity of entered IBANs and automatic generation of IBANs based on information entered for the bank account. SAP Note 392091 provides useful information on the use of IBAN for customers and vendors.

BK.TYP refers to the bank type, which is a freely definable, unique identifier for bank accounts in the customer master. Because these bank details are maintained in the general data view, they aren't assigned to any specific company code. If the customer master contains multiple bank accounts, and you want to ensure that payment is collected from a specific bank account, you can reference Bank Type from this field in the transactional entries to ensure that the appropriate bank account is selected.

The COLLECT AUTH flag should be set for all bank accounts for which you have received collection authorization from the customer. Any additional information such as the collection authorization number can be maintained in the field REFERENCE DETAILS.

ALTERNATIVE PAYER and INDIVIDUAL ENTRIES fields are useful for customer accounts for whom payment is to be collected from an alternative customer account. The account number entered in ALTERNATIVE PAYER is applicable for all customer transactions across all company codes. If the alternative customer account can be different for different transactions, then you should select the INDIVIDUAL ENTRIES field. You can control customer accounts that can be entered as alternative payers in transactions by specifying them using ALLOWED PAYER.

The PAYMENT CARDS button lets you maintain customer credit card numbers. The SAP system provides encryption and controlled access to sensitive credit card information.

Let's now discuss the fields available on the Marketing tab.

1.2.4 Marketing

The MARKETING tab (Figure 1.8) enables you to maintain customer master data useful for marketing. These fields don't have any impact on AR processes. However, you can use these fields for analytic reports and comparisons such as sales by industry, receivables by customer classification, sales per employee evaluations, and so on.

Address | Control Data | Payment Transactions | Marketing | Unloading Points | Expor

Classification

Nielsen ID		Regional Market	
Customer class.		Hierarchy assignment	
Industry			
Industry Code 1			

Key figures

Annual sales		in	
Employees		in	
Fi.Year Variant			

Sales prospecting

Legal status	

Figure 1.8 General Data – Marketing

NIELSEN ID is used to maintain the regional classification of customer locations according to categories created by the A.C. Nielsen Company. CUSTOMER CLASSIFICATION is a freely definable customer grouping for marketing purposes. The INDUSTRY field can be used to assign customer industry codes based on internal classifications used by your company, whereas, INDUSTRY CODES 1-5 are typically used to assign customer industries based on external classification such as Standard Industry Code (SIC).

Values for these fields are maintained in configuration under IMG • SALES AND DISTRIBUTION • MASTER DATA • BUSINESS PARTNERS • CUSTOMERS • MARKETING.

The next tab on in the general data view is Unloading Points.

1.2.5 Unloading Points

Information entered on the Unloading points tab (Figure 1.9) in the customer master data is used by delivery and shipping processes of the order to cash business process.

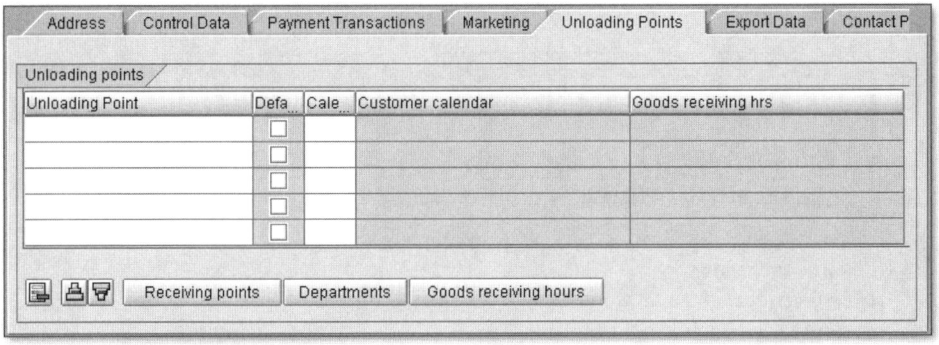

Figure 1.9 General Data – Unloading Points

A quick review of Figure 1.9 shows that you can maintain multiple Unloading point locations where goods are delivered for the customer, one of which can be indicated as the Default location. Each unloading point is assigned a factory calendar that helps determine workdays when goods can be delivered to that location.

Additionally, for each unloading point, you can assign specific Goods receiving hours, Departments, and Receiving points such as floor number, room number, and so on. Values maintained on this tab don't have any direct influence on AR processes.

The next tab on the general data view maintains information relevant for export transactions.

1.2.6 Export Data

As is evident from Figure 1.10, this tab is useful for export compliance and monitoring. Even though these values don't have direct influence on AR processes, customer sales subject to these compliance regulations can increase risk on collections.

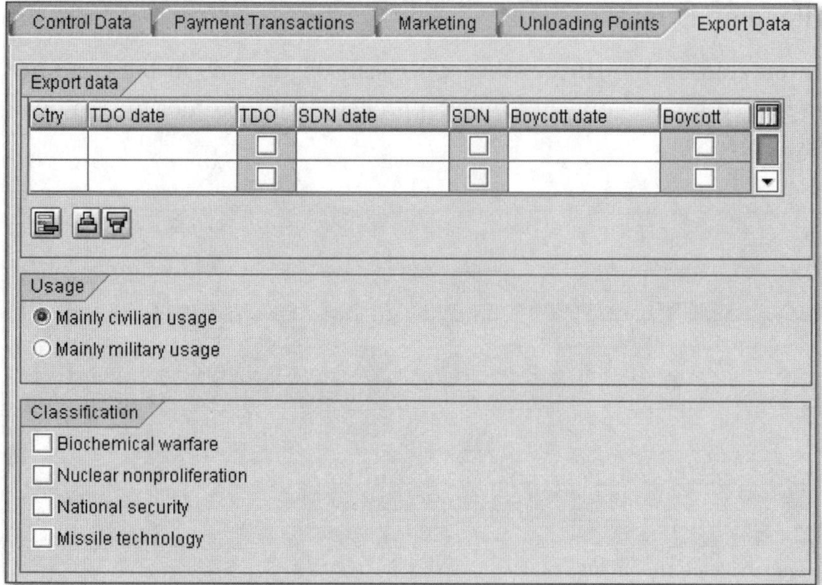

Figure 1.10 General Data – Export Data

For every country that has potential export control validations for this customer, you should maintain an entry in this tab. For each country, you can validate the customer against three lists – Table of Denial Orders/Denied persons list (TDO), specially designated persons list (SDN), and internally maintained BOYCOTT LIST. The last date of review for each list indicates whether the customer account needs another review.

The last tab in the general data view is used for maintaining details of contact persons.

1.2.7 Contact Person

Figure 1.11 shows the CONTACT PERSON tab for the customer master, where you can maintain information about different contact persons associated with a customer account. Primarily, this information is useful for sales and marketing purposes, but it can also be used to maintain contacts relevant for AR processes.

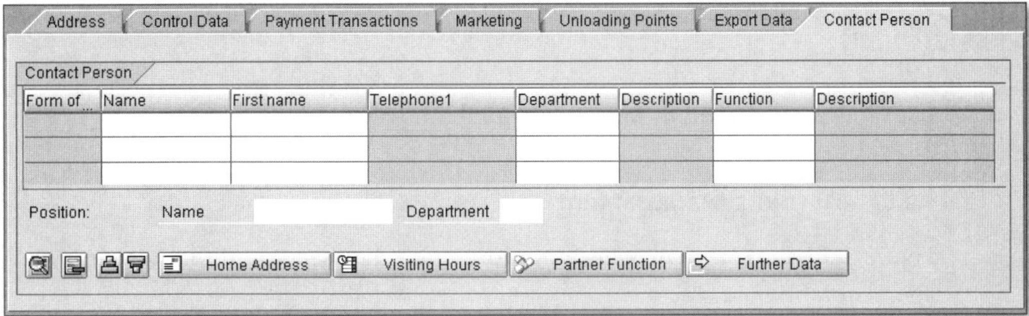

Figure 1.11 General Data – Contact Person

Obviously, the SAP system provides you with the ability to maintain common information such as first name, last name, department, job function, home address, and visiting hours for a contact. However, depending on your business relationship, you can also maintain more detailed contact information.

For example, by selecting FURTHER DATA, you can maintain up to 10 attributes for a contact. These attributes can be used for information such as hobbies, religious affiliation, group memberships, and so on. By double-clicking on a contact name, you can maintain even more details such as their buying habits, preferred call frequency, personal information, and other communication details. Relevant field values for this tab can be configured in IMG • SALES AND DISTRIBUTION • MASTER DATA • BUSINESS PARTNERS • CONTACT PERSON.

Now that we've gone through different tabs in the general data view, it's time to move on to the company code data view for a customer.

1.3 Company Code Data View

The company code data view is used to maintain customer data for a company code. So if multiple company codes in your SAP system transact with this customer, you'll need to maintain this data view for each company code. Company code data view consists of the following tab pages, which in turn consist of fields grouped into sections.

- Account Management
- Payment Transactions

- Correspondence
- Insurance

Let's look at the Account Management tab in detail.

1.3.1 Account Management

Figure 1.12 shows the Accounting Information data section of the Account Management tab.

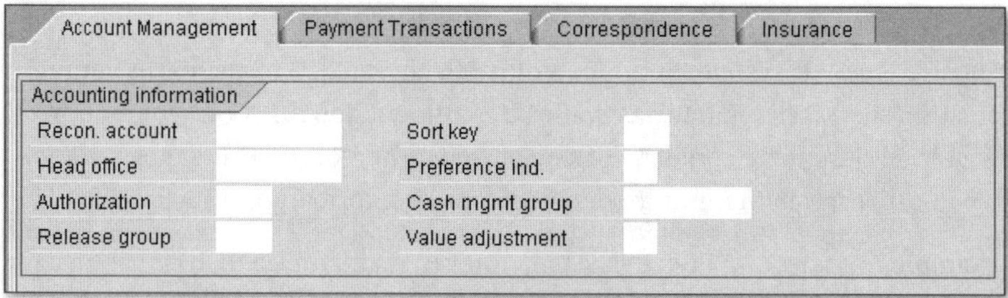

Figure 1.12 Company Code – Account Management – Accounting Information

Accounting Information

RECONCILIATION ACCOUNT is a control GL account in the chart of accounts. All customer transactions that have an accounting impact are posted to the customer account as well as to this control account. Thus, at any given time, the reconciliation account balance shows net receivables for all associated customers.

You may choose to have different reconciliation accounts for different groups of customers such as domestic, foreign, government, and so on. Multiple reconciliation accounts can provide better visibility in AR reporting and can ease the month-end reconciliation process.

SORT KEY is useful in determining the sort sequence of customer line items. When posting AR entries, you can populate the ALLOCATION field manually or let the SAP system automatically populate it based on the definition of a Sort Key. For example, you can enter the customer agreement number in the document header text, and using the Sort Key field, you can make sure that the agreement number is copied to the allocation field. This can help you sort customer items in a report by customer agreement number.

The HEAD OFFICE field in the customer master lets you manage customer relationships where you transact with the customer head office as well as branch locations. In the SAP system, you can maintain the customer account number for the head office in the HEAD OFFICE field of the customer accounts for branch offices. Subsequently, all transactions with branch offices are automatically posted to the head office customer account. This can be useful, for example, if invoices are to be sent to branch offices, but consolidated payment is received from the head office.

Previously, we discussed the authorization group in the Control Data tab of the general data view. If you need to maintain such authorizations separately for each company code, you use the AUTHORIZATION field displayed earlier in Figure 1.12.

CASH MANAGEMENT GROUP is only relevant if you are using the Cash and Liquidity Management component in the SAP system. For the purpose of cash and liquidity planning, you can group customers into different Cash Management groups such as domestic and foreign customers, low risk and high risk customers, and so on. You can define these groups using IMG • FINANCIAL SUPPLY CHAIN MANAGEMENT • CASH AND LIQUIDITY MANAGEMENT • CASH MANAGEMENT • MASTER DATA • SUBLEDGER ACCOUNTS • DEFINE PLANNING GROUPS.

RELEASE GROUP is used by the SAP workflow functionality for routing AR documents for approval. You can define these groups under IMG • FINANCIAL ACCOUNTING • ACCOUNTS RECEIVABLE AND ACCOUNTS PAYABLE • BUSINESS TRANSACTIONS • INCOMING INVOICES/CREDIT MEMOS • CARRY OUT AND CHECK SETTINGS FOR DOCUMENT PARKING • DEFINE RELEASE APPROVAL GROUPS FOR PARKING DOCUMENTS. Note that even though the preceding menu path indicates the definition of RELEASE GROUP under incoming invoices/credit memos, these groups can also be used for other types of AR documents.

The VALUE ADJUSTMENT field is used to revalue AR balances. This may be required, for example, if you need to prepare your financial statements per different accounting standards (U.S. GAAP versus IFRS). You can find configuration activities for the valuation process, including the definition of value adjustment keys, under IMG • FINANCIAL ACCOUNTING • ACCOUNTS RECEIVABLE AND ACCOUNTS PAYABLE • BUSINESS TRANSACTIONS • CLOSING • VALUATE • VALUATIONS.

Figure 1.13 shows other fields on this tab page under the Interest Calculation and Reference Data sections.

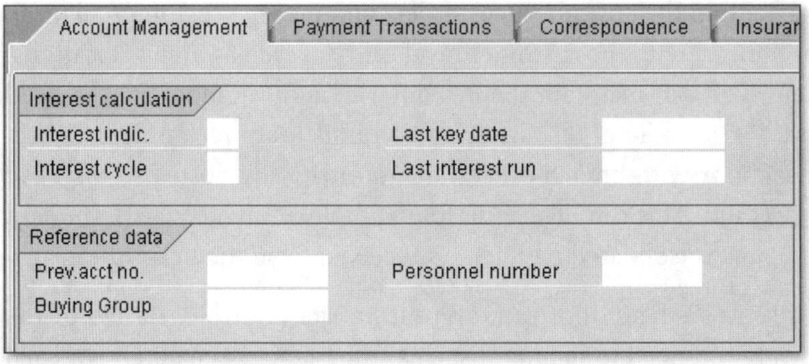

Figure 1.13 Company Code – Account Management – Interest, Reference Data

Interest Calculation

Fields in this section are useful if your company needs to carry out interest calculation on accounts receivables. The SAP system supports comprehensive functionality for different types of interest calculation. For example, the INTEREST INDIC. field specifies whether interest is calculated on the net account balance, or whether it's calculated separately on individual transactions posted to the customer account. INTEREST CYCLE specifies the frequency of interest calculation such as monthly, quarterly, and so on.

You can maintain parameters for the interest calculation process along with the Interest Indicator and Interest Cycle in IMG • FINANCIAL ACCOUNTING • ACCOUNTS RECEIVABLE AND ACCOUNTS PAYABLE • BUSINESS TRANSACTIONS • INTEREST CALCULATION • INTEREST CALCULATION GLOBAL SETTINGS. The other two fields in this section LAST KEY DATE and LAST INTEREST RUN are automatically updated by the interest calculation process.

Fields in the next data section (Figure 1.13) are mainly used for reference and reporting purposes.

Reference Data

Typically, new numbers are assigned to existing customers during SAP implementation projects. In such implementations, you can use the PREV ACCT NO field to store customer numbers from your previous system. However, because there is only one field in the SAP system, you'll have to choose which number to store in this field if you consolidate customer master data from multiple legacy systems, each with their own customer numbers.

Personnel number corresponds to employee number in the SAP Human Resources application. This field should be used only for its intended purpose after careful consideration of its impact and usage in your SAP Human Resources implementation.

If a customer is a member of a buying group or consortium, then you can create a customer account in SAP corresponding to the buying group or consortium and maintain that account number in the Buying Group field of its member customers. Subsequently, the buying group can be used for reporting and analysis such as creating customer statements, analyzing sales volume, and so on.

The next tab in the company code data view is Payment Transactions.

1.3.2 Payment Transactions

This tab contains company code parameters that influence customer payment transactions. These fields are grouped into Payment Data (Figure 1.14), Automatic Payment Transactions, and Payment Advice Notes Data section.

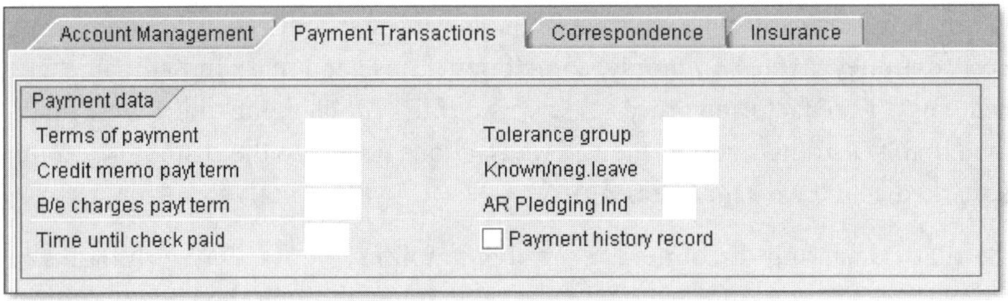

Account Management | Payment Transactions | Correspondence | Insurance

Payment data

Terms of payment — Tolerance group
Credit memo payt term — Known/neg.leave
B/e charges payt term — AR Pledging Ind
Time until check paid — Payment history record

Figure 1.14 Company Code – Payment Transactions – Payment Data

Payment Data

In Terms of Payment and Credit Memo Payment Term fields, you can specify default payment terms for customer invoices and credit memos. These payment terms are defaulted when these transactions are posted directly in AR without reference to sales order. Payment terms are defined in IMG • Financial Accounting •

Accounts Receivable and Accounts Payable • Business Transactions • Incoming Invoices/Credit Memos • Maintain Terms of Payment.

Using Tolerance group, you can specify upper limits for customer transactions and tolerance limits for underpayments and overpayments. Any payment differences within tolerance limits are written off, whereas payment differences over tolerance limits are posted back to the customer account. Tolerance groups are defined in IMG • Financial Accounting • Accounts Receivable and Accounts Payable • Business Transactions • Incoming Payments • Manual Incoming Payments • Define Tolerances (Customers).

Known/negotiated leave can be useful if a customer has negotiated a leave period during which the customer won't be invoiced or dunned for arrears. In such a situation, all AR activities such as invoicing, dunning, and collection need to factor in this time period while calculating invoice due dates. Note that at the time of writing this book, this functionality is still under development, and the SAP system doesn't provide any report and process to automatically consider negotiated leave in AR transactions. This field in SAP is useful as a reference, but any impact of negotiated leave on AR transactions needs to be handled outside of the SAP system.

The AR Pledging Indicator field is useful in business arrangements called factoring, where a company sells its accounts receivables at a discount for immediate access to money. More commonly, companies choose and mark individual receivable items for the factoring process. However, if the AR Pledging Indicator is maintained in the customer master, then all transactions posted to the customer account are marked as relevant for factoring.

Note that calculating discounted receivable amounts, transacting with banks or third parties, and tracking customer receivable items through the entire factoring process isn't yet completely supported in the SAP system. The AR Pledging Indicators can be defined in IMG • Financial Accounting • Accounts Receivable and Accounts Payable • Customer Accounts • Master Data • Preparations for Creating Customer Master Data • Define Accounts Receivable Pledging Indicator.

If the Payment history record field is selected, the SAP system stores several variables such as number of payments, payment volume arrears in days, and so on.

These variables are calculated and stored for each month and can later be used for reporting and analysis.

We'll discuss most of these fields in considerable detail in Chapter 5, Customer Payments. For now, let's look at the data fields in the next section as shown in Figure 1.15.

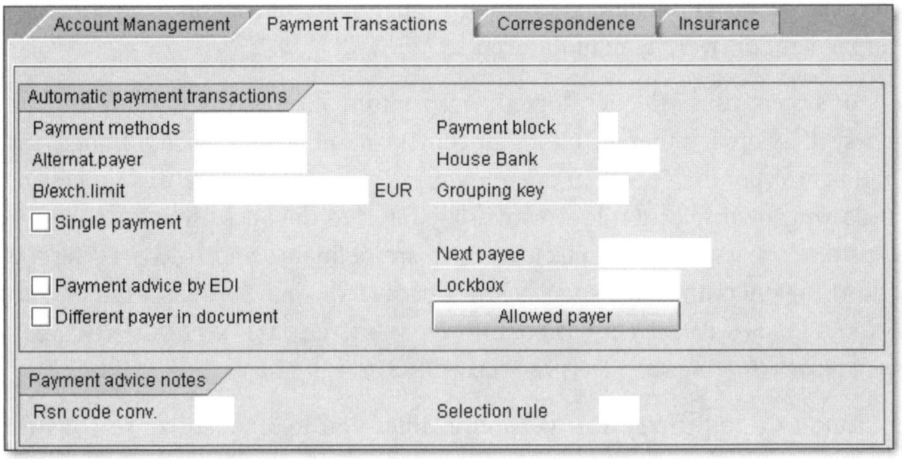

Figure 1.15 Company Code – Payment Transactions – Automatic Payment

Automatic Payment Transactions

Most fields in this section are relevant if you carry out automatic payment processes in accounts receivables, such as automatic collections from customer bank accounts. From that perspective, the Payment methods, House bank, and Payment block fields are self-explanatory. In Section 1.2.3, Payment Transaction Tab, earlier in this chapter, we discussed how an alternate payer can be used to enable payment receipts from alternate customers. Alternative Payer, Different payer in document, and Allowed payer in Figure 1.13 (shown earlier) enable you to make those specifications for each company code.

If customer payments are to be sent to different addresses, then the customer account corresponding to that "remit to" address is maintained in the Next Payee field. Similarly, if your company has established multiple lockboxes for receiving customer payments, then you can assign the corresponding code in the Lockbox field, which in turn can be printed on customer invoices.

Similar to the previous section, we'll discuss most of these fields in detail in Chapter 2, Accounts Receivable Transactions.

Payment Advice Notes

When incoming payments from customers are processed, the SAP system generates payment advice documents that contain information to identify customer open items, to assign incoming payment to identified items, and to process any underpayment or overpayment differences.

The SAP system uses selection logic to map information received from the customer such as order number, billing document number, reference number, and so on to corresponding fields in open invoices. You can influence this process by creating your own selection logic and assigning it to the SELECTION RULE field in the customer master. These selection rules are defined using IMG • FINANCIAL ACCOUNTING • ACCOUNTS RECEIVABLE AND ACCOUNTS PAYABLE • BUSINESS TRANSACTIONS • INCOMING PAYMENTS • INCOMING PAYMENTS GLOBAL SETTINGS • PAYMENT ADVICE NOTES (INCOMING) • DEFINE SELECTION RULES.

The REASON CODE CONVERSION version enables you to standardize reasons for underpayments and overpayments. It's used to convert reasons received from customers to standardized payment difference reasons determined by your company. These versions are defined using IMG • FINANCIAL ACCOUNTING • ACCOUNTS RECEIVABLE AND ACCOUNTS PAYABLE • BUSINESS TRANSACTIONS • INCOMING PAYMENTS • INCOMING PAYMENTS GLOBAL SETTINGS • OVERPAYMENT/UNDERPAYMENT • DEFINE REASON CODE CONVERSION VERSION.

The next tab in the company code view is the Correspondence tab.

1.3.3 Correspondence

The CORRESPONDENCE tab shown in Figure 1.16 consists of fields grouped into Dunning Data, Correspondence, and Payment Notices To sections.

Dunning Data

Here we'll provide only a brief overview of the different concepts and parameters, as Chapter 6, Dunning, provides comprehensive details for dunning processes in the SAP system.

Dunning Procedure controls almost all dunning parameters such as dunning limits, dunning amounts, dunning forms, and so on. You may want to use different dunning procedures for different groups of customers such as domestic or foreign customers, high-risk or low-risk customers, and so on.

Dunning Block lets you block all items posted to a customer account from dunning. If you want only specific customer items to be excluded from the dunning process, you should set the dunning block in respective customer items.

Dunning Recipient specifies the customer account number that receives dunning notices. It's useful if dunning notices are required to be sent to a different customer account than the customer who owes payment.

In the Legal Dunning Procedure field, you enter date from when the legal dunning process was initiated for the customer. Entering this date influences future dunning activities. For example, open items that are blocked for dunning or marked for automatic payment are also printed on dunning notices, specific, legal verbiage can be printed on dunning notices, and so on.

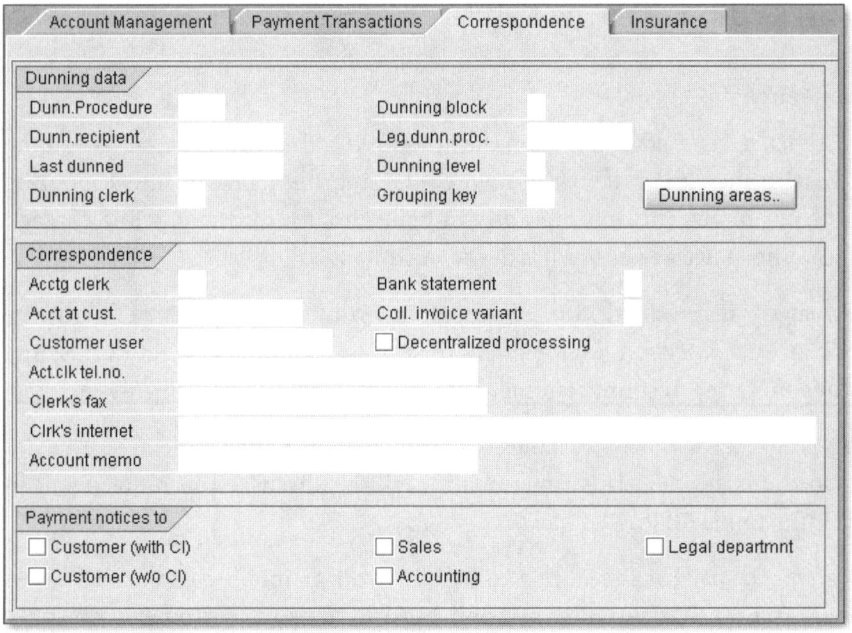

Figure 1.16 Company Code Data – Correspondence

The LAST DUNNED field indicates the date when the last dunning notice was generated, with the corresponding dunning level updated in the DUNNING LEVEL field. Both of these fields are automatically updated by the dunning procedure.

DUNNING CLERK corresponds to an employee responsible for carrying out dunning for this customer. This field can be useful if specific employees are assigned to carry out dunning for a group of customers.

Using GROUPING KEY, you can prepare separate dunning notices for customer items grouped based on specific criteria. Without any grouping key, all customer items to be dunned are included in a single dunning notice.

By clicking on DUNNING AREA, you can maintain multiple dunning areas and corresponding parameters. This is useful only if multiple dunning groups in your company area responsible for dunning the same customer.

Configuration activities for the dunning process can be carried out using IMG • FINANCIAL ACCOUNTING • ACCOUNTS RECEIVABLE AND ACCOUNTS PAYABLE • BUSINESS TRANSACTIONS • DUNNING.

Let's look at the data fields available in the Correspondence section.

Correspondence

ACCT AT CUSTOMER is used to maintain the account number of your company at the customer, with the CUSTOMER USER field containing the name of the accounting clerk at the customer. This information can be useful, for example, while contacting the accounts payable (AP) group at the customer.

A somewhat confusing field, BANK STATEMENT, on this tab actually refers to the frequency at which account statements are sent to customers. We'll discuss the process of generating account statements in Chapter 10, Periodic Processing.

COLLECTIVE INVOICE VARIANT specifies the frequency at which collective invoices are sent to the customer. This functionality will be discussed in more detail in Chapter 3, Customer Billing.

The DECENTRALIZED PROCESSING flag is useful if you maintain customer accounts with Head Office – Branch Office relationships. By default, customer correspondence for branch accounts is sent to the head office. However, if you want to maintain Head Office – Branch Office relationships of customer accounts for information and reporting purposes only, you should set this indicator in the head office customer account. If this indicator is set, then branch account correspondence is sent to individual branch locations.

Other information in this section, such as accounting clerk, accounting clerk telephone number, clerk's fax, and clerk's Internet refer to contact information for the accounting clerk at your company responsible for managing this customer account. You can print this information on customer-facing correspondence as "contact information." It's important to remember, however, that if there are frequent changes at your company, information in this section can quickly become outdated.

Finally, different flags under the Payment Notices to section identify business instances and departments for which payment notices are created in the SAP system.

The last tab in company code data view is Insurance.

1.3.4 Insurance

For longer-term receivables from foreign customers, you may choose to get export credit insurance. Insurance details of this policy are maintained in the Insurance tab (Figure 1.17).

Account Management | Payment Transactions | Correspondence | Insurance

Export credit insurance
Policy number
Institution number
Amount insured EUR
Valid To
Lead months
Deductible %

Figure 1.17 Company Code – Insurance

The insurance policy (Policy Number) covers open receivables from this customer up to an insured amount (Amount insured). You can also maintain other policy information such as validity date (Valid To), deductible percentage (Deductible), and number of months for which open receivable items are covered (Lead months) on this tab.

Next, we'll focus on the sales data view of the customer master.

1.4 Sales Data View

The sales data view is used to maintain customer data for a sales area. As discussed previously, a sales area in the SAP system uniquely identifies a combination of sales organization, distribution channel, and division. These three elements enable you to organize and differentiate your sales processes by geography, by sales channel, and by production groups, respectively. Depending on your organizational structure, you may have multiple sales areas for which you need to maintain master data for one customer.

In the SAP system, the customer billing process is organized under sales processes, so it's useful for those involved in using and implementing SAP AR to be familiar with sales-related data in the customer master. The sales data view consists of the following tab pages, which in turn consist of fields grouped into sections:

- Sales
- Shipping
- Billing Documents
- Partner Functions

In the following sections, we'll look at fields on these data tabs. Our primary focus will be on fields that influence AR processes or are useful for customer analytics and reporting. We'll start with the Sales tab.

1.4.1 Sales

This tab contains customer master fields relevant for sales order, pricing, customer hierarchies, and agency business. Figure 1.18 shows the sales order fields on this tab.

Sales Order

Using the Sales District, Sales Office, and Sales Group fields, you can divide your sales organization into lower level areas of sales responsibility. The organizational hierarchy can be represented as Sales Organization → divided into Sales Districts → divided into Sales Offices → divided into Sales Groups → consisting of sales employees.

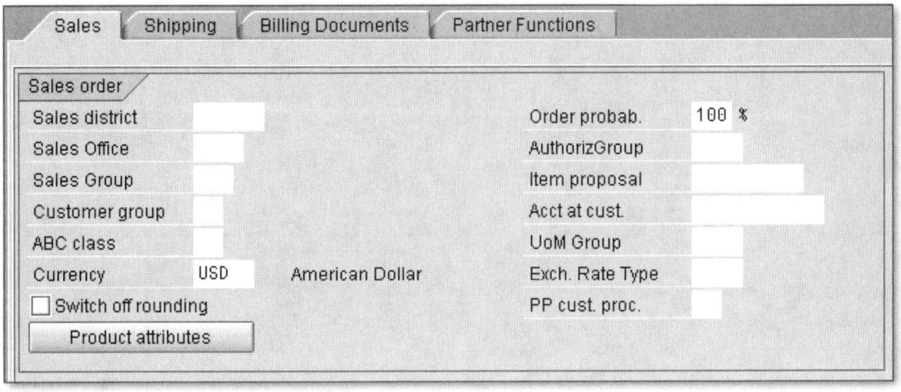

Figure 1.18 Sales Area – Sales – Sales Order

Authorization Group enables you to control access to a customer's sales area data using authorizations. This functionality is similar to what we discussed previously about controlled access to general data and company code data of a customer.

Account at Customer serves a similar purpose as the field with the same name on the Correspondence tab of the company code data view. However, this field can also be maintained for customer accounts for which company code data doesn't exist, such as ship-to locations, goods recipients, sales partners, and so on.

Customer Group is a freely definable field that can be used by your company to group customers for reporting, pricing, or similar sales processes. Available customer groups can be defined using IMG • Sales and Distribution • Master Data • Business Partners • Customers • Sales • Define Customer Groups.

The Currency field represents the currency in which orders from this customer are processed and settled. Currency translation in order processing is carried out based on currency exchange rates maintained in the SAP system. You can influence the selection of the exchange rate by specifying Exchange Rate Type. This is useful if your SAP system contains multiple exchange rates, such as average rate, current rate, intrastate rate, and so on, for the same currency pair. Remaining fields on this tab are shown in Figure 1.19

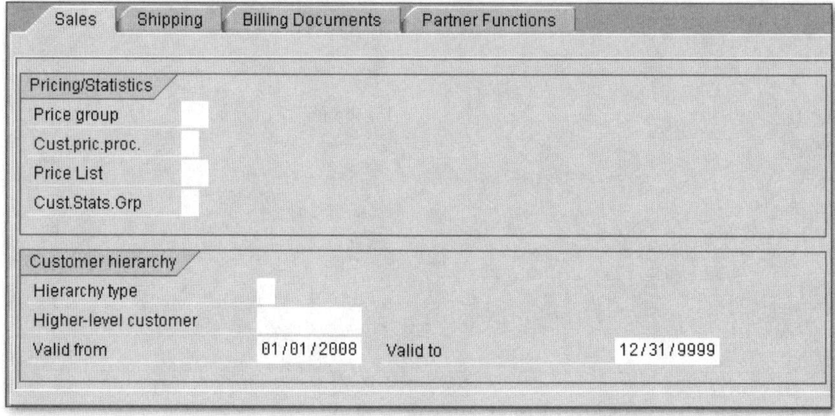

Figure 1.19 Area – Sales – Pricing and Hierarchy

Pricing/Statistics

Fields available in this section influence customer pricing. However, it's important to remember that the SAP system provides a large number of configuration options to influence customer pricing. It's a fairly involved topic that falls in the domain of your colleagues and consultants in the SAP Sales and Distribution area.

Price Group enables you to group customers that have similar pricing requirements such as bulk buyer, occasional buyer, or new customer, whereas Price List lets you specify the price list to be used for customer pricing. For example, you may have different price lists for different groups of customers, such as wholesale, retail, government, or non-profit. Both these fields can be configured using IMG • Sales and Distribution • Basic Functions • Pricing • Maintain Price-relevant Master Data Fields.

Customer Pricing Procedure specifies the customer classification used for determining the pricing procedure that calculates the net selling price based on different pricing elements such as base price, discounts, surcharges, delivery charges, and taxes. Configuration for this classification, along with other pricing procedure parameters is carried out using IMG • Sales and Distribution • Basic Functions • Pricing • Pricing Control • Define and Assign Pricing Procedures.

Customer Statistics Group is relevant if you're using Logistics Information System (LIS) in the SAP system. LIS is a group of totally customizable information systems focused on SAP logistics components such as Purchasing, Inventory, and

Plant Maintenance. Using Customer Statistics Group, you can determine what – if any – information for this customer is updated in the LIS repository. These groups can be defined using IMG • LOGISTICS – GENERAL • LOGISTICS INFORMATION SYSTEM (LIS) • LOGISTICS DATA WAREHOUSE • UPDATING • UPDATING CONTROL • SETTINGS: SALES • STATISTICS GROUPS • MAINTAIN STATISTICS GROUPS FOR CUSTOMERS.

Customer Hierarchy

If your customer accounts include large numbers of locations that are part of a multi-level organization hierarchy (e.g., store locations and offices of a national retailer), then you can set up customer hierarchies in the SAP system. Customer hierarchies provide you with a hierarchical structure of customer accounts that can be used for sales activities, shipping, delivery, pricing negotiations, and reporting.

In Figure 1.19, HIERARCHY TYPE specifies the purpose of the customer hierarchy, such as reporting or pricing, and HIGH-LEVEL CUSTOMER specifies the customer account of the higher-level node in the hierarchy. Using VALID FROM and VALID TO dates, you can specify the duration for which this hierarchy assignment is valid.

Configuration for customer hierarchies is carried out using IMG • SALES AND DISTRIBUTION • MASTER DATA • BUSINESS PARTNERS • CUSTOMERS • CUSTOMER HIERARCHY.

The next tab in the customer master sales data view is the Shipping tab.

1.4.2 Shipping

Information maintained on the Shipping tab (Figure 1.20) is mainly relevant for shipping and goods delivery processes.

Shipping

Selecting the ORDER COMBINATION flag indicates that it's okay to combine multiple customer orders in a single delivery. In the DELIVERY PLANT field, you can maintain the default plant of your company from where goods delivery to this customer is made.

POD (Proof of Delivery) related fields can have an impact on the customer invoicing process. As we'll discuss in Chapters 3, Customer Billing, and 4, Advanced Billing, by default, the customer is invoiced for the quantity per delivery document. Any quantity discrepancies are subsequently processed through credit memos.

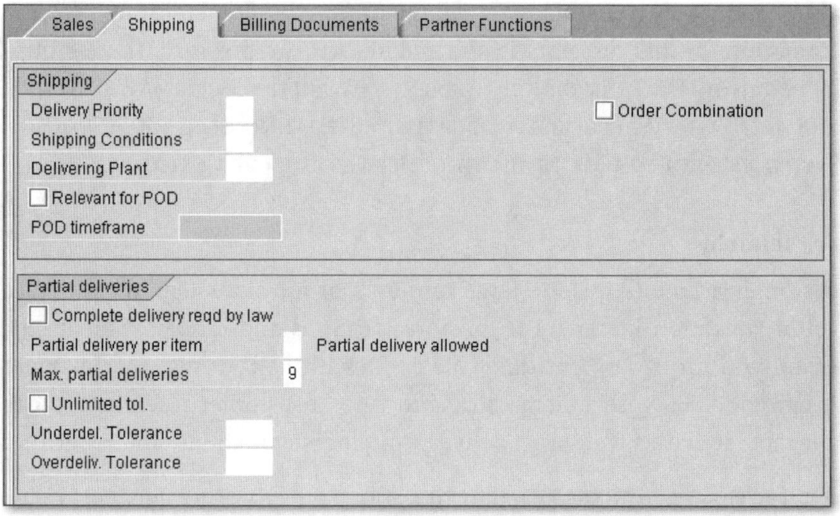

Figure 1.20 Sales Area – Shipping

If the RELEVANT FOR POD flag is selected, the customer sends confirmation for the received quantity, and the customer invoice is generated based on the received quantity regardless of the quantity in the delivery document. The difference in quantity can be due to any reason such as theft or spoilage. POD confirmation can include reasons for quantity discrepancies, which can be analyzed further to improve operational efficiency.

If the Relevant for POD flag is selected, you can also enter a POD TIMEFRAME that specifies the number of days in which proof of delivery is expected. After that time interval has passed, delivery is automatically confirmed.

Note that this isn't the only place where you can set the POD relevance of a sales process. You can set a POD relevance flag in the sales order, or you can specify delivery item types as POD relevant in the configuration settings. You'll find POD-related configuration activities under IMG • LOGISTICS EXECUTION • SHIPPING • DELIVERIES • PROOF OF DELIVERY.

Partial Delivery

This section (Figure 1.20) contains fields that influence the partial delivery of items. The COMPLETE DELIVERY REQUIRED BY LAW flag specifies whether partial deliveries for an order are allowed per law. If partial deliveries are allowed for a sales order, you can further specify whether partial deliveries are allowed for an order item by using the appropriate setting in Partial Delivery per item field. Using the Maximum number of partial deliveries field, you can restrict the maximum number of deliveries into which an order item delivery is split.

You can maintain over- and under tolerance limits acceptable to the customer in the fields Underdel tolerance and Overdel tolerance. These limits are specified as a percentage of the quantity specified in the order item. If the customer has indicated no such restrictions, you can select Unlimited Tolerance.

The Shipping tab on the sales area view also includes a Transportation section (not shown in Figure 1.20) that contains transportation-relevant fields such as transportation zone, train station for regular delivery, and train station for express delivery of goods. Let's now look at the fields in the Billing Documents tab.

1.4.3 Billing Documents

Billing Documents (Figure 1.21) is one of the most important data tabs in the customer master for AR processes. It contains several fields that directly influence postings in Financial Accounting.

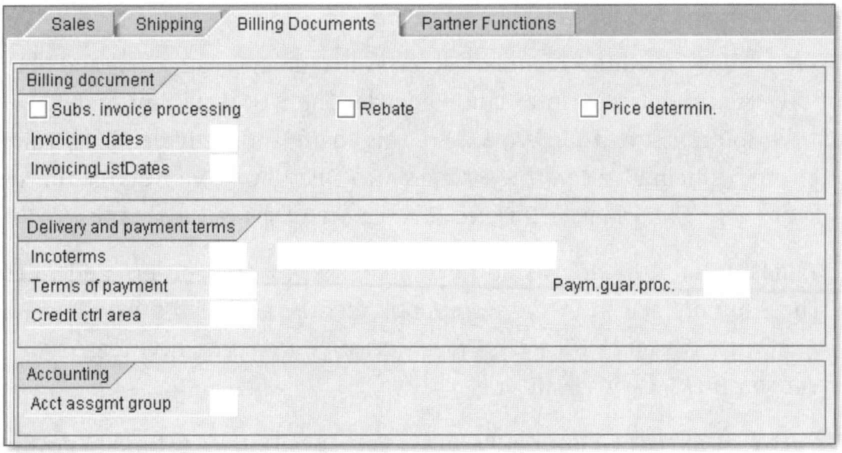

Figure 1.21 Sales Area – Billing Documents

Billing Document

The Rebate flag on this tab indicates that this customer may be granted a rebate. The SAP system can support considerably complex rebate arrangements with customers based on sales amount, sales quantity, and several other criteria. You can find corresponding configuration activities under IMG • Sales and Distribution • Billing • Rebate Processing.

The Price determination flag is relevant if this customer is part of a customer hierarchy and you want to maintain pricing for this customer. For example, this customer may represent the district or regional office that negotiates prices for a group of retail stores.

Invoicing Dates specifies the schedule of billing dates for the customer. This schedule is determined based on specifications of the factory calendar assigned to this field. You can maintain the factory calendar specifications using IMG • SAP NetWeaver • General Settings • Maintain Calendar • Factory Calendar.

In the Invoice List Dates field, you can specify the factory calendar that specifies the schedule for generating invoice lists. Using invoice lists, you can prepare a list of customer billing documents and then periodically send that list for settlement or collection.

Delivery and Payment Terms

Incoterms refer to international commercial terms that define costs, risks, and obligations of buyers and sellers in international trade. The SAP system provides several standard incoterms such as Ex Works, Free on Board, and Delivered Duty Paid. These terms can be maintained in IMG • Sales and Distribution • Master data • Business Partners • Customers • Billing Document • Define incoterms.

Payment Terms entered in this section are defaulted to sales orders and sales invoices. These are defined in IMG • Financial Accounting • Accounts Receivable and Accounts Payable • Business Transactions• Incoming invoices/credit memos • Maintain terms of payment.

In the Payment Guarantee Procedure field, you specify the customer-specific component of the payment guarantee procedure. A payment guarantee can take the form of a credit card authorization, a letter of credit, or any such similar guarantee. Configuration activities for payment guarantee procedures are carried out under IMG • SALES AND DISTRIBUTION • FOREIGN TRADE/CUSTOMS • DOCUMENTARY PAYMENTS • RISK MANAGEMENT FOR FINANCIAL DOCUMENTS • DEFINE AND ASSIGN PAYMENT GUARANTEE SCHEMA.

The CREDIT CONTROL AREA field specifies the organizational unit in your company responsible for credit management of this customer account. It's possible to override this credit control area in sales orders. We'll discuss credit control area and credit management functionality in Chapter 7, Credit Management.

Accounting

ACCOUNT ASSIGNMENT GROUP in the customer master is used as one of the criteria to determine GL accounts that are posted during customer invoice processing. For example, when customer revenue is posted to the general ledger (GL), you can post revenue from different types of customers to different GL accounts. Customer account assignment groups are maintained in IMG • SALES AND DISTRIBUTION • BASIC FUNCTIONS • ACCOUNT ASSIGNMENT/COSTING • REVENUE ACCOUNT DETERMINATION • CHECK MASTER DATA RELEVANT FOR ACCOUNT ASSIGNMENT • CUSTOMERS: ACCOUNT ASSIGNMENT GROUPS. We'll revisit this functionality in Chapter 3, Customer Billing.

The Billing tab in the sales data view also includes fields for sales tax (Figure 1.22).

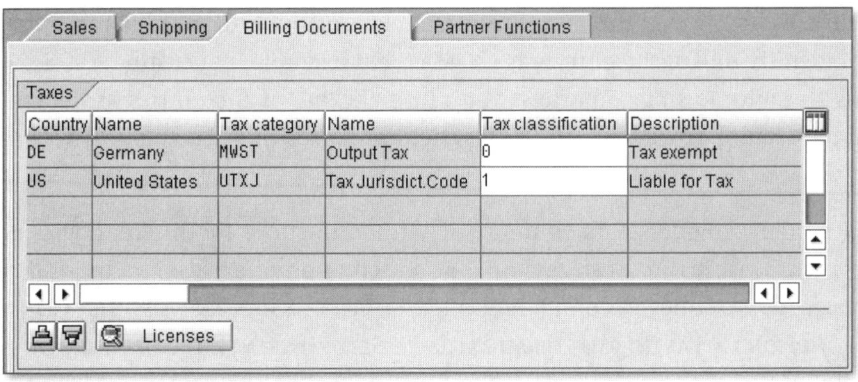

Figure 1.22 Sales Area – Billing Documents – Taxes

Taxes

In this section, you need to maintain Tax Classification of a customer in every country where customer delivery can originate. Tax classification of a customer can indicate whether the customer is tax-exempt, liable for full tax payment, or eligible for partial tax credit. The list of countries and available tax classifications displayed on this tab depends on sales tax configuration in your SAP system.

If a customer is liable for taxes but carries a tax-exempt certificate, you can maintain the tax-exempt certificate number and validity dates by selecting the Licenses option on the screen. We'll discuss tax configuration and processes in Chapter 8, Tax Processing.

In the next section, we'll discuss the last tab in the sales area data view: Partner Functions.

1.4.4 Partner Functions

The Partner Functions tab on the customer master is used to manage business relationships of the customer with other customer accounts. A customer can play different roles in different business relationships. For example, customer A can be a goods recipient for customer B and a payer for customer C. In the SAP system, such different business relationships are managed with the help of a partner function.

In Figure 1.23, Partner Function specifies the business relationship of the customer account entered in the Number field with the customer account being maintained. If a customer has the same business relationship with multiple partners, you can identify one of the entries as Default. For example, if a customer is associated with multiple ship-to parties, you can mark one of the entries as default. During transaction processing, the SAP system proposes that account as a default ship-to party.

The SAP system provides a large number of partner functions for different types of business relationships. You can review the configuration of existing partner functions or create new ones in configuration under IMG • Sales and Distribution • Basic Functions • Partner Determination • Setup Partner Determination • Partner Functions.

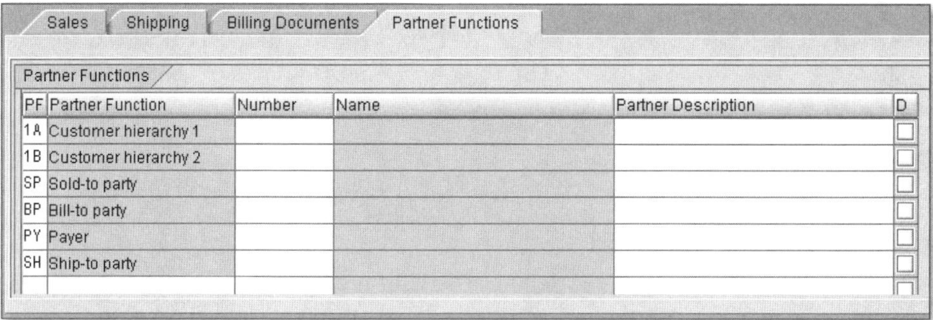

Figure 1.23 Sales Area – Partner Functions

Now that we've covered the most commonly used fields in the customer master, let's go through the common transactions and reports available for the customer master.

1.5 Transactions

As you may have already experienced based on your interaction with SAP so far, there can be multiple menu paths to access the same transaction and multiple reports that may give you the same information presented in different ways. Presented in this section are the most common menu paths and transactions.

1.5.1 Master Data Maintenance

Previous sections in this chapter described the customer master fields on these screens, so we won't go into field level details in this section. Table 1.2 shows the transactions available for customer master data maintenance for AR, sales and centralized maintenance.

Following are the menu paths corresponding to the transactions mentioned in Table 1.2:

- For AR: SAP MENU • ACCOUNTING • FINANCIAL ACCOUNTING • ACCOUNTS RECEIVABLE • MASTER RECORDS
- For sales: SAP MENU • LOGISTICS • SALES AND DISTRIBUTION • MASTER DATA • BUSINESS PARTNER • CUSTOMER
- For central maintenance: SAP MENU • ACCOUNTING • FINANCIAL ACCOUNTING • ACCOUNTS RECEIVABLE • MASTER RECORDS • MAINTAIN CENTRALLY

Transaction Codes	Create	Change	Display
AR ▸ General data view ▸ Company code data view	FD01	FD02	FD03
Sales ▸ General data view ▸ Sales data view	VD01	VD02	VD03
▸ Central maintenance ▸ All three data views	XD01	XD02	XD03

Table 1.2 Customer Master Maintenance Transactions

In the next section, we'll discuss change management of customer master data.

1.5.2 Change Management

The SAP system records all changes made to customer master data in *change records*. A CHANGE RECORD stores all relevant details of the change. Figure 1.24 shows change records and details of changes made to the YEAR field on the Marketing tab of the general data view.

Customer 0000001400 A.I.T.

Date	Field	New	Old
01/03/06	Year no. given for	1995	1993
11/07/04	Year no. given for	1993	0000

Details

Details	
Date	01/03/06
Time	09:47:11
User	CRANA
Field	Year no. given for (KNA1-JMJAH)
from	1993
to	1995

Figure 1.24 Change Records for Customer Master

However, for important customer data such as customer addresses and bank details, you may want to ensure that a second person reviews the changes before these changes become effective. For this purpose, the SAP system provides you with dual control for change management. If any field on the customer master is changed that is identified for dual control, all payment transactions to that customer are blocked.

You can specify fields relevant for dual control using IMG • FINANCIAL ACCOUNTING • ACCOUNTS RECEIVABLE AND ACCOUNTS PAYABLE • CUSTOMER ACCOUNTS • MASTER DATA • PREPARATIONS FOR CREATING CUSTOMER MASTER DATA • DEFINE SENSITIVE FIELDS FOR DUAL CONTROL (CUSTOMERS).

Following transactions are relevant for change management purposes:

- FD04: Display changes for one customer account (for AR)
- VD04: Display changes for one customer account (for sales)
- XD04: Display changes for one customer account (centralized)
- OV51: Display changes for multiple customer accounts
- FD08: Confirm changes made to one customer account
- FD09: Confirm changes made for multiple customer accounts

Also, from any transactions mentioned in Section 1.5.1, you can use ENVIRONMENT • ACCOUNT CHANGES to review customer account changes.

In the next section, we'll look at blocking and deleting customer master.

1.5.3 Customer Block and Deletion Indicators

A customer account in the SAP system can be blocked for accounting entries, sales order processing, delivery processing, processing of billing documents, and sales support such as sales activities and mailing campaigns. As shown in Figure 1.25, these customer account blocks can be set for a specific company code, a specific sales area, all company codes, or all sales areas.

Figure 1.25 Customer Master Blocks

To define blocks for sales and distribution processes, you use the following:

- Sales order blocks: IMG • SALES AND DISTRIBUTION • SALES • SALES DOCUMENTS • DEFINE AND ASSIGN REASON FOR BLOCKING • DEFINE BLOCKING REASONS
- Delivery blocks: IMG • LOGISTICS EXECUTION • SHIPPING • DELIVERIES • DEFINE REASONS FOR BLOCKING IN SHIPPING • DELIVERY BLOCKS
- Billing blocks: IMG • SALES AND DISTRIBUTION • BILLING • BILLING DOCUMENTS • DEFINE BLOCKING REASON FOR BILLING • BILLING: BLOCKING REASONS

If no customer transactions are posted, you can delete customer master data completely or for a specific company code or a sales area. If customer transactions are already posted, then those customer accounts can only be removed from your SAP system using the data archiving process.

Following are relevant transactions for functionality discussed in this section:

- FD05: Block/unblock customer accounts for posting
- VD05: Block/unblock customer accounts for sales processes
- XD05: Block/unblock customer accounts (centrally)

- FD06: Set deletion indicator (AR)
- VD06: Set deletion indicator (sales)
- XD06: Set deletion indicator (centrally)
- OBR2: Delete customer master data

In the next section, we'll look at available reports for customer master data.

1.5.4 Reports

Following are some of the customer master reports available in the standard SAP system:

- S_ALR_87012179: Customer master list
- S_ALR_87012180: Customer address list
- S_ALR_87012195: List of customers created in sales but not in finance, or list of customers created in finance but not in sales
- VC/2 – Sales Summary: Customer partner information with sales data
- VDH2: Display customer hierarchy

1.6 Configuration Activities

In this section, we'll focus on additional configuration activities relevant for setting up customer master data. You'll find these configuration activities under IMG • Financial Accounting • Accounts Receivable and Accounts Payable • Customer Accounts • Master Data • Preparations for creating Customer Master Data. For brevity, we'll refer to this menu path as Customer master IMG in this and the following section. Let's first look at the configuration of Customer Account Groups.

1.6.1 Customer Account Groups

We discussed the significance of customer account groups in Section 1.1, Organization of Customer Master Data. These groups are maintained using Customer master IMG • Define Account Groups with Screen Layout (Customers). Figure 1.26 shows a screen where you can maintain status of various fields for customer account group 0001 in the company code data view, Account Management tab (discussed in Section 1.3.1, Account Management).

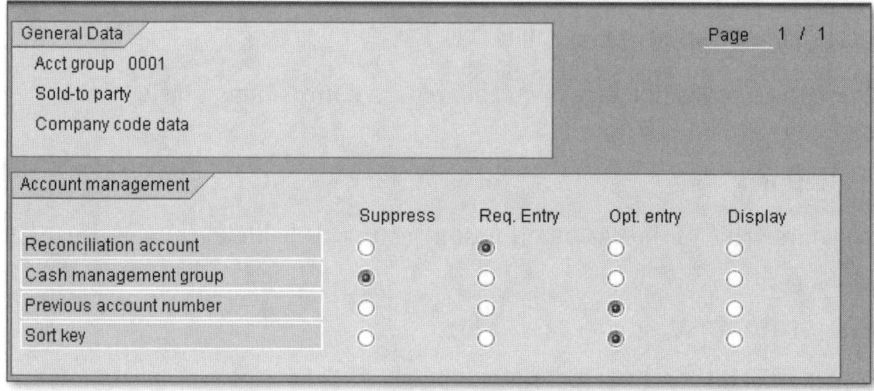

Figure 1.26 Customer Account Group – Field Status Group

As Figure 1.26 shows, you can set the status of any field on customer master maintenance as display, optional entry, required entry, or suppressed. This provides you with considerable flexibility on the layout of customer master maintenance screens. Two additional configuration activities with this respect are relevant: screen layout per company code and screen layout per activity. These two configuration activities are especially relevant because they let you modify screen layouts of corresponding SAP transactions without any development.

Screen Layout Per Company Code and Activity

Using screen layout per company code, you can specify different screen layouts for customer master maintenance for different company codes. This configuration activity can be carried out under Customer master IMG • Define Screen Layout per Company Code (Customers).

On the other hand, screen layout per activity enables you to set different screen layouts for the following activities:

- Create, change, and display customer (accounting)
- Create, change, and display customer (sales)
- Create, change, and display customer (centrally)

As you may have noticed, these activities have one-to-one correspondence with customer master maintenance transactions mentioned in Section 1.5.1, Master Data Maintenance. This configuration activity can be carried out under CUSTOMER MASTER IMG • DEFINE SCREEN LAYOUT PER ACTIVITY (CUSTOMERS).

The next configuration activity is maintenance of customer number ranges.

1.6.2 Customer Number Range

Using CUSTOMER MASTER IMG • CREATE NUMBER RANGES FOR CUSTOMER ACCOUNTS (Figure 1.27), you can define customer account number ranges. If the EXT flag is selected, the number range is interpreted as an external number range.

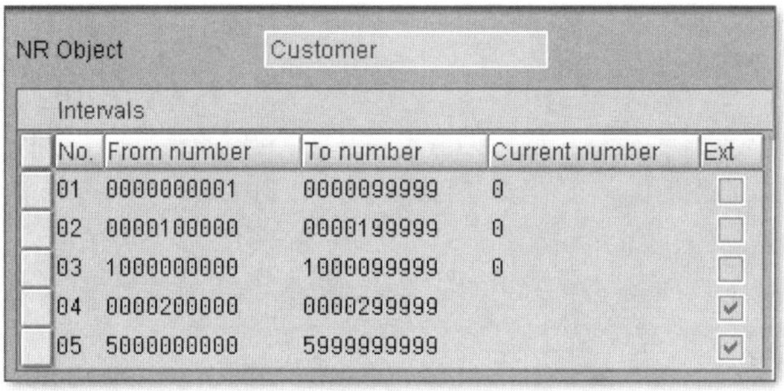

NR Object: Customer

Intervals

No.	From number	To number	Current number	Ext
01	0000000001	0000099999	0	☐
02	0000100000	0000199999	0	☐
03	1000000000	1000099999	0	☐
04	0000200000	0000299999		☑
05	5000000000	5999999999		☑

Figure 1.27 Customer Number Range

These number ranges in turn are assigned to customer account groups using CUSTOMER MASTER IMG • ASSIGN NUMBER RANGES TO CUSTOMER ACCOUNT GROUPS.

The next section discusses maintenance of customer master texts.

1.6.3 Customer Master Texts

Customer master texts in the SAP system help you maintain texts or notes for a customer account. The size of these text notes can be practically unlimited, so you can preserve older customer notes while entering as much new information as necessary. Not only that, you can also maintain different notes for different purpose such as marketing, shipping, receivables, dunning, and so on. In configuration, you define types of customer master texts using the following activities:

- Customer master IMG • Define Text IDs for Central Texts (Customers)
- Customer master IMG • Define Text IDs for Accounting Texts (Customers)

You can display and maintain these texts (Figure 1.28) by selecting Extras • Texts. This menu can be accessed from any customer master maintenance transaction discussed in Section 1.5.1, Master Data Maintenance.

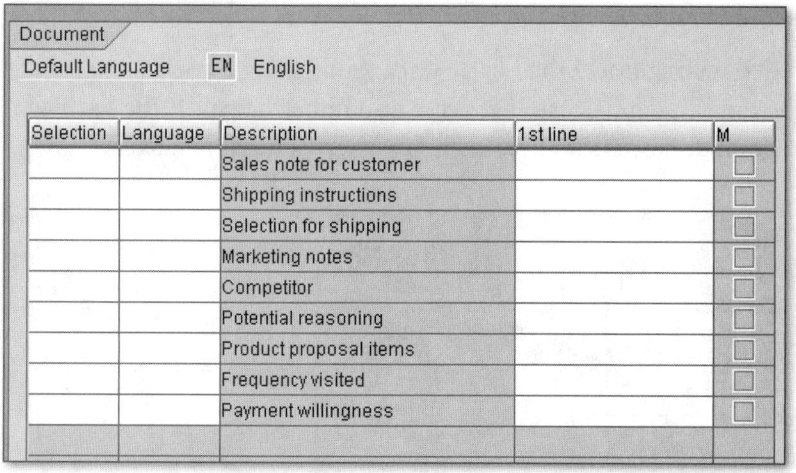

Document

Default Language EN English

Selection	Language	Description	1st line	M
		Sales note for customer		☐
		Shipping instructions		☐
		Selection for shipping		☐
		Marketing notes		☐
		Competitor		☐
		Potential reasoning		☐
		Product proposal items		☐
		Frequency visited		☐
		Payment willingness		☐

Figure 1.28 Customer Master Texts

Let's now look at message control for customer master maintenance.

1.6.4 Customer Message Control

While interacting with SAP transactions, you'll encounter numerous messages. These messages can be of different types such as information messages (I), warning messages (W), or error messages (E) depending on default settings. You can influence this message type using Customer Master IMG • Change Message Control for Customer Master Data.

For example, per the default SAP settings, the message "Customer is marked for deletion" (F2 131) is issued as an information message. You may want to keep this message as an information message for batch input processing but issue it as a warning or as an error message for a specific business user. On the other hand, you may also choose to completely suppress this message by selecting the (-) option. Figure 1.29 shows examples of these message control settings.

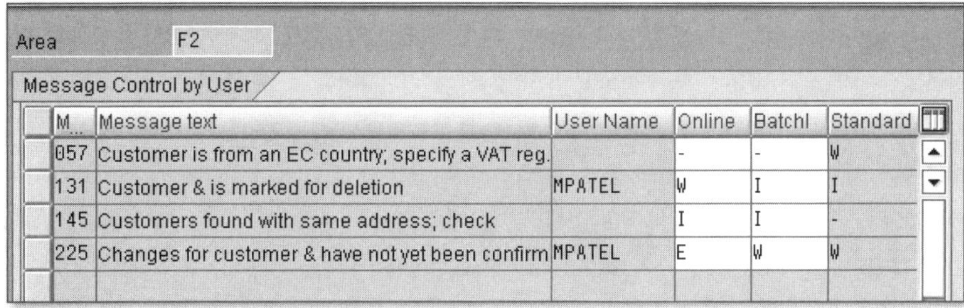

Figure 1.29 Customer Master Message Control

Beginning with the next section, we'll discuss the technical details.

1.7 Technical Reference

This section provides technical reference material for customer master maintenance. Considering the large number of technical objects available in a SAP system, this information should only be considered as a starting point for analysis. You'll find more details about using this information in later chapters of this book.

1.7.1 SAP Notes

With large number of SAP Notes available for any particular topic in the SAP system, it's impossible and somewhat counter-productive to list all available notes. The list of SAP Notes in Table 1.3 is just a sample list.

OSS Note	Relevance
0000117557	Which fields of the address are printed where
0000035931	Collective note for printing/formatting addresses
0000491546	Generation of IBAN for European countries
0000639188	Customer searches do not check authorizations
0000503396	Mass generation of IBAN for multiple customer accounts
0000850365	Connecting FI-AR and FI-AP to SAP BusinessObjects Global Trade Services
0000548278	Workflow FAQ – release group from customer master

Table 1.3 Customer Master Maintenance – SAP Notes

OSS Note	Relevance
0000023850	Customer payment history is not updated
0000064842	Management of export credit insurance
0000548716	Customer hierarchy FAQ
0000789876	Change of validity period in customer hierarchy
0000867678	POD, delivery and billing document
0000881094	PO box and company postal code
0000163554	Tax number checks in customer master: General
0000171048	Search for customer based on old account number
0000380507	SD partner determination: FAQ for functions
0000009272	Customer master authorization for sales area data
0000075340	Archiving of customer accounts with SD dependencies
0000015509	Change documents for changes to bank data
0000384462	Import, change, and distribution of master data and addresses

Table 1.3 Customer Master Maintenance – SAP Notes (Cont.)

In the next section, we'll look at authorization objects available for customer master maintenance.

1.7.2 Authorization Objects

The topic of SAP system authorizations is discussed in a later chapter.. Table 1.4 lists authorization objects to be considered with respect to transactions discussed in this chapter.

Object	Description
B_BUPA_RLT	Business Partner: BP Roles
B_BUPR_BZT	Business Partner Relationships: Relationship Categories
F_BNKA_MAN	Banks: General Maintenance Authorization
F_KNA1_AEN	Customer: Change Authorization for Certain Fields
F_KNA1_APP	Customer: Application Authorization

Table 1.4 Authorization Objects – Customer Master Maintenance

Object	Description
F_KNA1_BED	Customer: Account Authorization
F_KNA1_BUK	Customer: Authorization for Company Codes
F_KNA1_GEN	Customer: Central Data
F_KNA1_GRP	Customer: Account Group Authorization
F_SKA1_KTP	GL Account: Authorization for Charts of Accounts
S_SCD0	Change Documents
V_KNA1_BRG	Customer: Account Authorization for Sales Areas
V_KNA1_VKO	Customer: Authorization for Sales Organizations

Table 1.4 Authorization Objects – Customer Master Maintenance (Cont.)

Note

Table 1.4 and similar other lists of authorization objects in this book don't include objects required for reports or for carrying out common activities such as for file access, printing, and navigating in the SAP system.

1.7.3 Tables and Structures

Table 1.5 lists tables and structures for customer master data maintenance.

Table	Relevance
KNA1	Customer master – general data
KNB1	Customer master – company code data
KNVV	Customer master – sales data
ADDR1_VAL	Address data
KNBK	Customer master – bank details
KNVP	Customer master – partner functions
KNVK	Customer master – contact person details
KNB5	Customer master – dunning data

Table 1.5 Customer Master Tables and Structures

The next section provides information about available technical modifications.

1.8 Enhancements and Modifications

This section provides list of available enhancements, BTEs, BAdIs, and BAPIs, which are relevant for customer master maintenance in the SAP system.

1.8.1 Enhancements

Using customer master enhancements, you can add custom logic to carry out additional validations and custom business processing, such as validating payment terms offered to a group of customers or making sure that at least one contact person is entered.

- SAP Enhancement – SAPMF02D (User exits: customer master data)
  - Function Module exits – EXIT_SAPMF02D_001 (Customers: user exit for checks prior to saving)

You can access this enhancement in configuration using CUSTOMER MASTER IMG • DEVELOP ENHANCEMENTS FOR CUSTOMER MASTER DATA.

1.8.2 Business Add-Ins (BAdIs)

Using Business Add-Ins configuration under CUSTOMER MASTER IMG • ADOPTION OF CUSTOMER'S OWN MASTER DATA FIELD, you can add custom fields to the SAP customer master. For example, you can add custom fields to meet country-specific, industry-specific, or business-specific requirements.

Following BAdIs are available for customer master processing:

- CUSTOMER_ADD_DATA_CS
  - This BAdI is used to integrate custom fields into standard screen display of customer master maintenance transactions.
  - Methods available for this BAdI can be used to carry out tasks such as data transfer for set data and get data, transfer of function codes to add-on tab pages, and hiding add-on tab pages.
- CUSTOMER_ADD_DATA
  - This BAdI is used to process data entered in custom fields.

  - Methods available for this BAdI can be used to carry out final checks, to save data outside of a standard save, to read add-on data, to read change documents, and so on.
- CUSTOMER_ADD_DATA_BI
  - This BAdI is used to process data entered in custom fields during batch input processing and ALE distribution process.
  - Methods for this BAdI can be used to fill ALE segments with custom data, to pass on customer defined segments, to check a data row during batch input processing, and similar activities.

The next section discusses available BAPIs for managing customer master data.

1.8.3 BAPIs

Table 1.6 lists some of the available methods in the SAP system for customer master data maintenance. These methods are available for the "customer" object.

Method	Function Module	Description
Create	BAPI_CUSTOMER_ CREATE	Create Customer Master
Edit	BAPI_CUSTOMER_ EDIT	Change Customer Master
Display	BAPI_CUSTOMER_ DISPLAY	Display Customer Master
Delete	BAPI_CUSTOMER_ DELETE	Delete Customer Master
ExistenceCheck	BAPI_CUSTOMER_ EXISTENCECHECK	Check whether Customer Account exists
Find	BAPI_CUSTOMER_ FIND	Find Customer Using Matchcode
GetContactList	BAPI_CUSTOMER_ GETCONTACTLIST	List of Customer Contact Persons
GetSalesAreas	BAPI_CUSTOMER_ GETSALESAREAS	Read Customer Sales Areas

Table 1.6 BAPIs Available for Customer Master Maintenance

Method	Function Module	Description
AddHierarchyNodes	BAPI_CUSTOMER_ HIERARCHIE_INS	Create Nodes in SD Customer Hierarchy
ChangeHierarchyNodes	BAPI_CUSTOMER_ HIERARCHIE_UPD	Change Nodes in SD Customer Hierarchy

Table 1.6 BAPIs Available for Customer Master Maintenance (Cont.)

1.9 Summary

In this chapter, we focused on maintenance of customer master data in three data views – general data, company code data, and sales area data. Throughout this book, we'll make reference to concepts discussed in this chapter as applicable.

In the next chapter, we'll discuss the concepts related to accounting documents.

In this chapter, you'll find details on accounting documents processing and supporting functionalities in the SAP system. We'll also look at some of the most commonly used accounts receivable documents such as customer invoices and credit/debit memos. Functionalities discussed in this chapter aren't unique to accounts receivable, so you'll be able to use much of this information in accounts payable, general ledger, or any other SAP component that generates or processes accounting documents.

2 Accounts Receivable Transactions

In this chapter, we'll start with a discussion of the basic concepts and attributes of accounting documents in the SAP system. These attributes aren't unique to accounts receivable (AR). However, if the AR component is your first or only interaction with the SAP system, then knowledge of these attributes is essential. Then we'll discuss how to process some commonly used AR documents. For example, you'll see that in the SAP system, customer invoices posted in Financial Accounting are distinctly different from customer invoices posted in the Sales component. We'll mainly focus on AR documents that are manually created in the SAP system. Other chapters of this book discuss automatically generated AR documents generated during the order to cash processes. Finally, we'll discuss utilities that can improve efficiency, especially for manual entries.

2.1 Basic Concepts

An accounting document in the SAP system refers to a document that affects balances of general ledger (GL) accounts. This also includes documents posted in subledger systems such as AR, accounts payable (AP), and asset accounting. This is because integration of the SAP system ensures that any document posted to a subledger account is automatically and simultaneously posted to the corresponding reconciliation account in GL. In this section, we'll discuss core attributes of an accounting document such as ledger, document type, document number, document dates, posting period, and posting key.

2.1.1 Ledger

All accounting documents are posted to one or more ledgers. The New GL functionality in SAP ERP Central Component 6 allows you to designate one ledger as a leading ledger and several other ledgers as non-leading ledgers. Typically, the leading ledger follows the same accounting principle as that of your consolidated financial statements, whereas non-leading ledgers are used to prepare financial statements in different currencies or to meet different accounting principles.

Tip

The default leading ledger in an SAP system is designated `0L`. Even if your SAP system doesn't have multiple active ledgers, you may have to use this value while running some standard reports in the SAP system.

Configuration settings determine the ledgers to which automatically generated accounting documents are posted. You can also use separate transactions to make adjustment postings only to specific ledgers. We won't go into detail about using multiple ledgers in this book. However, if you want to explore the use of multiple ledgers for AR processes, you'll find configuration settings under SAP IMG • Financial Accounting • Financial Accounting Global Settings • Ledgers • Ledger.

Let's now look at document types.

2.1.2 Document Type

Document types in the SAP system help to distinguish between different types of business transactions. SAP provides more than 40 document types for different business transactions in receivables, payables, asset accounting, inventory accounting, and payroll. Table 2.1 shows some of the document types available for customer transactions.

Even though it's recommended to use these document types as is for their intended purpose, you can choose to create your own document types, modify existing ones, or use them for a different purpose than recommended. How to use document types to distinguish different transactions is largely a business decision. Figure 2.1 shows configuration details behind a commonly used document type – DR (Customer invoice posted directly in FI).

Document Type	Typical Usage
RV	Customer invoice (based on billing document posted in Sales)
DR	Customer invoice (posted directly in AR)
DG	Customer credit memo
DZ	Customer payment (incoming)
ZP	Customer payment (outgoing)
DA	Customer document (e.g., adjustment postings)
DB	Customer recurring entry document
SA	Customer document posted directly in GL
AB	Reversal of document posted directly in GL

Table 2.1 Document Types

Document Type DR Customer invoice

Properties
Number range 18
Number range information
Reverse DocumentType DR
Authorization Group

Account types allowed
☐ Assets
☑ Customer
☐ Vendor
☐ Material
☑ G/L account

Special usage
☐ Btch input only

Control data
☐ Net document type
☑ Cust/vend check
☐ Negative Postings Permitted
☐ Inter-company postgs
☐ Enter trading partner

Default values
Ex.rate type for forgn crncy docs

Required during document entry
☑ Reference number
☐ Document header text

Joint venture
Debit Rec.Indic
Rec.Ind. Credit

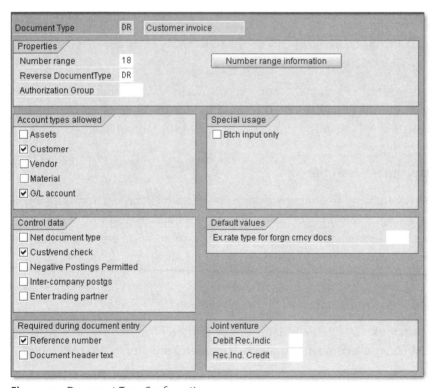

Figure 2.1 Document Type Configuration

Following are some of the important attributes controlled by the document type:

- **Number Range**: This value determines document numbering. We'll discuss this further later in this chapter.
- **Reverse Document Type**: Document type used for posting reversal of document.
- **Account Types Allowed: Customer, GL Account**: Selecting these flags allows you to post to customer accounts and to GL accounts.
- **Cust/Vend Check**: If this flag is selected, you can enter only one customer account per document. You can post multiple entries to the same customer account, but you can't use the document type to post transfers between two customer accounts.
- **Reference Number**: If this flag is selected, you have to enter a reference number in the document header before a document can be posted.

You'll find configuration settings for DOCUMENT TYPE under SAP IMG • FINANCIAL ACCOUNTING • FINANCIAL ACCOUNTING GLOBAL SETTINGS • DOCUMENT • DOCUMENT HEADER • DEFINE DOCUMENT TYPES.

Other fields control whether the entry of document header text is mandatory, and whether this document type can be used to post to vendor accounts or asset accounts. Let's now look at the Number Range value in more detail.

2.1.3 Document Number

In the SAP system, a number range assigned to a document type determines document numbering. Even though technically it's possible to assign multiple document types to the same number range, you may want to do so only for document types that are used for similar purposes. Figure 2.2 shows the definition of document number ranges.

Following are important points to observe in Figure 2.2:

- Number ranges are uniquely defined for each company code. This is to be expected because a company code represents a legal entity in the SAP system.
- If the Ex flag is selected, document numbers have to be generated externally (e.g., number range 02 and 04). If this flag isn't selected, document numbers are automatically generated (e.g., number range 01 and 03).

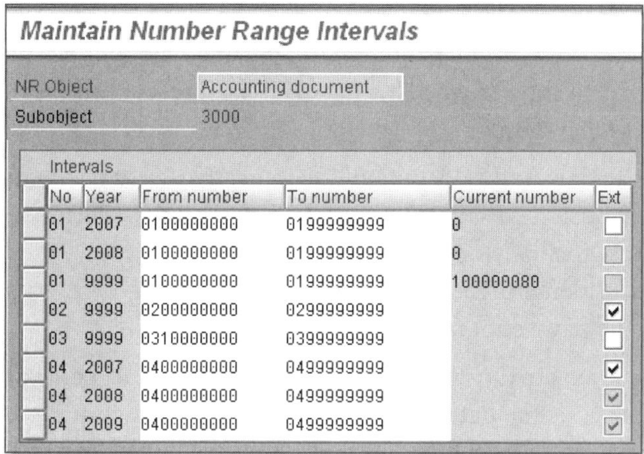
Maintain Number Range Intervals

NR Object: Accounting document
Subobject: 3000

Intervals

No	Year	From number	To number	Current number	Ext
01	2007	0100000000	0199999999	0	☐
01	2008	0100000000	0199999999	0	☐
01	9999	0100000000	0199999999	100000080	☐
02	9999	0200000000	0299999999		☑
03	9999	0310000000	0399999999		☐
04	2007	0400000000	0499999999		☑
04	2008	0400000000	0499999999		☑
04	2009	0400000000	0499999999		☑

Figure 2.2 Document Number Range

- The field Year determines the fiscal year *up to* which the number range is valid. For example, in the preceding figure, documents with number range 01 will start from 0100000000 for fiscal year 2007 and 2008, and then will continue the same numbering up to year 9999.

Tip

The SAP system provides utilities to copy number range definitions across company codes or across fiscal years.

The next important attribute of an accounting document is document dates.

2.1.4 Document Dates

You'll come across the following dates while working with accounting documents:

- Entry Date: This is the system date on which the document was entered in the SAP system. Every document is automatically updated with the system date and timestamp. You can't change this date.
- Document Date: This is the date on which the document was issued. For example, the document date for a customer invoice entered by you will be the same as the entry date, whereas for documents received from customers, the document date can represent the date when the documents were issued.

- Posting date: This is the date on which GL account balances are updated. For example, for documents received from customers, the posting date will be the date when they are entered in the system. This date can also be used to make post-dated entries in the SAP system.
- Baseline date: This date is relevant for document line items that carry payment terms, such as line items posted to customer or vendor accounts. This date refers to the date based on which payment discount terms are calculated. Based on configuration settings, it defaults to the document date, posting date, or a different date, including the payment grace period.
- Value Date: This date is relevant for document line items posted to bank or cash flow accounts. It represents the date on which cash flow will be impacted, and it's calculated based on configuration settings. For example, after the check is deposited to a bank account, it may take few days for the funds to be available.

Posting Date mentioned in the preceding list also determines the posting period of a document as described next.

2.1.5 Posting Period

Each company code in the SAP system is associated with a fiscal year that consists of posting periods for which financial statements are prepared. A fiscal year in the SAP system can follow the calendar year (Jan – Dec) or can be different from the calendar year (Apr – Mar). It can consist of posting periods that correspond to calendar months, or you can define posting periods based on the 4/4/5 convention.

When documents are posted in the AR component, the SAP system automatically determines the posting period based on posting date (discussed previously) and fiscal year, so you don't need to manually calculate and update posting period. However, familiarity with the concept of posting period versus calendar month is extremely important while working with accounting documents in the SAP system.

Definition of fiscal year and posting periods is carried out under SAP IMG • Financial Accounting • Financial Accounting Global Settings • Fiscal year • Maintain fiscal year variant. Figure 2.3 shows the definition of a non-calendar fiscal year (July – June). It also shows the definition of how calendar month, last day of a calendar month, and posting period are linked with each other. The next section discusses the definition and use of posting keys.

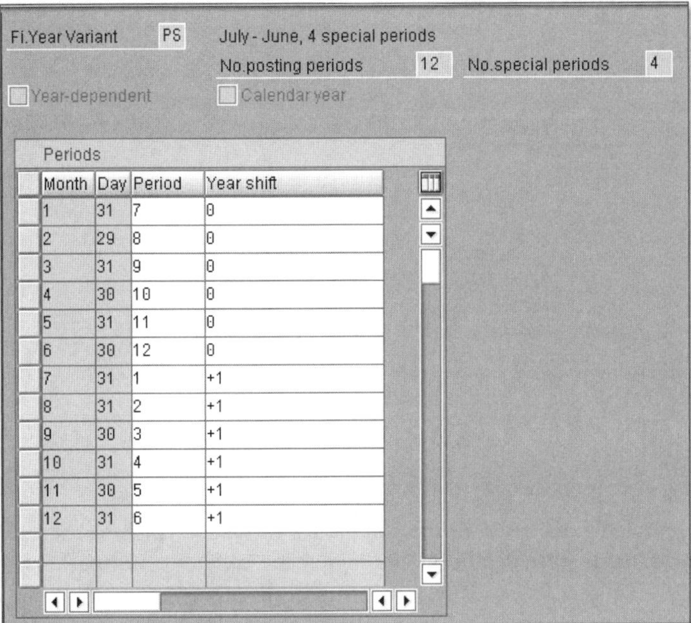

Month	Day	Period	Year shift
1	31	7	0
2	29	8	0
3	31	9	0
4	30	10	0
5	31	11	0
6	30	12	0
7	31	1	+1
8	31	2	+1
9	30	3	+1
10	31	4	+1
11	30	5	+1
12	31	6	+1

Figure 2.3 Fiscal Year Variant

2.1.6 Posting Key

Posting keys in SAP are two-digit codes that determine two main attributes of every line item in an accounting document: 1) whether the line item is a debit or a credit, and 2) whether the line item posts to a GL account, customer account, vendor account, asset account, or an inventory account. Many GL reports include posting keys, and a few of the posting transactions also require posting keys, so it helps to be familiar with some that are the most commonly used as shown in Figure 2.4.

You'll find configuration of posting keys under SAP IMG • Financial Accounting • Financial Accounting Global Settings • Document • Line Item • Controls • Define posting keys. You may notice that there are multiple posting keys that debit a customer account or that credit a customer account. You can use many of these interchangeably, as long as you use them consistently.

01	Invoice	Debit	Customer
04	Other receivables	Debit	Customer
11	Credit memo	Credit	Customer
15	Incoming payment	Credit	Customer
21	Credit memo	Debit	Vendor
25	Outgoing payment	Debit	Vendor
31	Invoice	Credit	Vendor
39	Special G/L credit	Credit	Vendor
40	Debit entry	Debit	G/L account
50	Credit entry	Credit	G/L account
70	Debit asset	Debit	Asset
75	Credit asset	Credit	Asset
89	Stock inwrd movement	Debit	Material
99	Stock outwd movement	Credit	Material

Figure 2.4 Posting Keys

Tip

Many AR document templates delivered in the standard SAP system, such as a customer statement, have a predefined definition and legend for different posting keys. You may want to keep that in mind if you choose to use posting keys in a non-standard way.

So far, we've discussed the core attributes of an accounting document in the SAP system. Now we're ready to look at some of the most common AR transactions. It's important to note that in the SAP system, a customer invoice or credit memo directly posted in AR is different from a customer invoice or credit memo generated based on billing activity in Sales and Distribution (SD). SD customer invoices are for trade receivables that correspond to sales of goods and services, whereas FI documents are for non-trade receivables such as invoicing subtenants for office rent. It's advisable to use different document types and different numbering ranges for FI documents and for SD documents posted to AR. One of the benefits of this SAP functionality is that you don't have to create "dummy" sales orders in the SAP system just to generate customer invoices.

Other chapters in this book are devoted to AR documents generated in SD. But in this chapter, we'll only focus on customer documents generated in FI. Let's start with the original, general interface for entering customer documents.

2.2 AR Transactions – General Interface

These transactions use the original, general interface in which one data entry screen refers to one document line item. Examples of transactions that use this interface are given here:

- **Customer invoice**: Accounts Receivable Menu • Document entry • Invoice – general (Transaction F-22)
- **Customer credit memo**: Accounts Receivable Menu • Document entry • Credit memo – general (Transaction F-27)

2.2.1 Initial Screen

Figure 2.5 shows the first screen of the invoice entry transaction with the general interface. It's divided into two sections: document header and first line item.

We've already discussed some of the fields shown in the document header section of this transaction, such as Document Date, Posting Date, Document Type, and Posting Period. Other fields such as Document Header Text and Document Reference are self-explanatory. Currency fields are relevant if you want to process foreign currency documents.

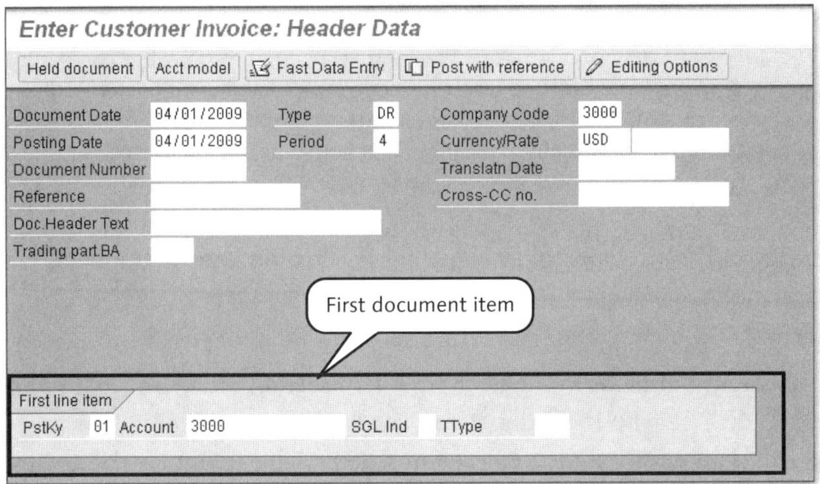

Figure 2.5 Invoice Entry – Initial Screen

Foreign Currency Documents

This seems an appropriate place to discuss the processing of foreign currency documents in the SAP system. You can enter a transactional document in the SAP system in any currency, called document currency, to any company code — as long as the corresponding configuration settings are maintained. These settings are maintained under SAP IMG • SAP NETWEAVER • GENERAL SETTINGS • CURRENCIES. Some of the commonly used configuration activities are listed here:

- Set decimal places for the document currency, for example, zero for Japanese Yen.
- Maintain exchange rate types, for example, average, current.
- Define translation ratios for currency translation between document currency and company code currency. Company code currency is also referred to as local currency or functional currency.
- Maintain valid exchange rates for the combination of document currency and exchange rate type.

Additional configuration activities provide you with the advanced functionality of maintaining reference exchange rates and maintaining exchange rate spreads. However, those activities aren't relevant for the purpose of this discussion.

> **Note**
>
> If you enter a document currency in field Currency that is different from the company code currency, the SAP system uses the latest exchange rate maintained in the system and exchange rate type "M" to calculate balances in the company code currency. You can use fields Rate or Translation Date to ensure the balance calculation using a specific exchange rate or using an exchange rate of a specific date.

The bottom part of the screen provides fields for the first document line item.

First Line Item

The two most important fields in the First Line Item section of Figure 2.5 are the Posting Key and the Account. In Section 2.1.6, Posting Key, we explored how posting keys determine the type of an account and whether the account is debited or credited. By entering a posting key that debits customer account (e.g., 01) and a customer account number, you indicate that the first line item of the document debits a customer.

One of the confusing aspects of this document entry interface is that even though the transaction title indicates that it's for entering a customer invoice, practically it can be used to enter any type of transaction to any type of account. For example, by choosing a credit posting key for a customer, you can use this transaction to post a customer credit memo. Depending on the configuration settings of the document type, you can use this transaction to even post a vendor invoice or a vendor debit memo by using the appropriate posting key and a vendor account.

Tip

While using this type of interface for document entry, instead of focusing on which SAP transaction code was used to start the interface, focus on what is entered in the DOCUMENT TYPE, POSTING KEY, and the ACCOUNT fields.

When you press Enter, you'll be taken to the next screen.

2.2.2 Subsequent Screens

Figure 2.6 shows the subsequent screen where you can enter more document line item details.

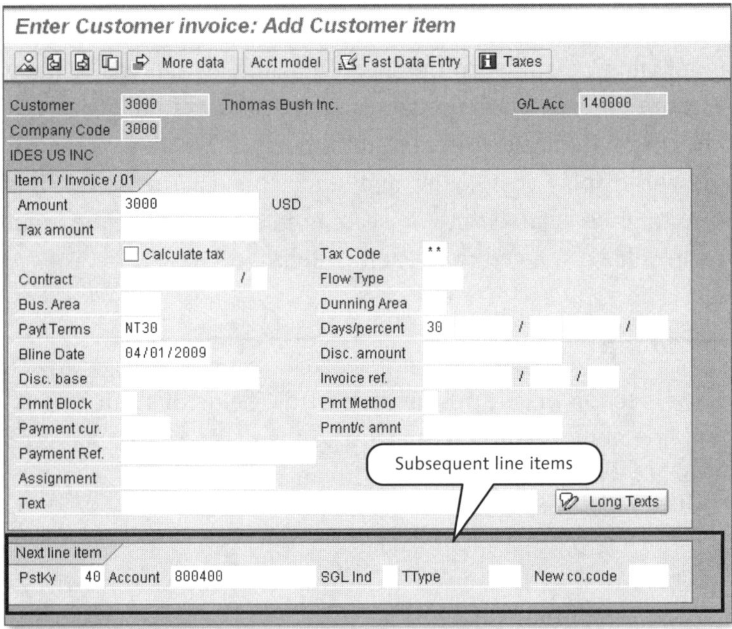

Figure 2.6 Invoice Entry – Subsequent Screen

As shown in the figure, the upper part and center part of this screen refers to the information for the current document item, whereas the bottom part of this screen refers to the next document item. So, for example, the upper part of this screen contains information entered on the previous screen such as CUSTOMER ACCOUNT, CUSTOMER RECONCILIATION ACCOUNT, COMPANY CODE, and a POSTING KEY.

The bottom part of the screen contains POSTING KEY and ACCOUNT fields for the next document line item, and when you press Enter, a screen similar to the one shown in Figure 2.6 is displayed. For entering more document items, you can continue to enter the posting key and account at the bottom of the screen and more details about the document line item on the next screen.

Tip

To expedite data entry in transactions that use the general interface, you can configure fast-entry screens that help you enter multiple line items on one screen. A GL fast-entry screen uses line item layouts that can be configured to only include relevant document fields. Configuration activity for defining GL fast-entry layouts can be accessed using Transaction O7E6.

However, the center part of the screen displayed in Figure 2.6 is where you enter most of the details about a document line item. It contains common document item fields such as AMOUNT, ASSIGNMENT, and LINE ITEM TEXT, as well as additional fields. The layout and availability of these additional fields can vary widely depending on the account entered on the previous screen. For example, a screen for customer account items will display discount term fields, whereas a screen for entering GL accounts will display cost center and similar fields. The field status group configuration settings associated with an account make up one of the main factors determining the fields displayed for each line item.

2.2.3 Field Status Group

Field status group is a collection of settings for all possible fields that can be processed for a document line item. As shown in Figure 2.7, you can set the status of each document item field as suppress, required entry, or optional entry.

Additional account assignments

	Suppress	Req. Entry	Opt. entry
Settlement period	◉	○	○
Material number	◉	○	○
Cost center	○	◉	○
CO/PP order	○	○	◉
WBS element	○	○	◉
Sales order	◉	○	○
Personnel number	◉	○	○

Figure 2.7 Field Status Group

Every GL account in a chart of accounts is assigned a field status group. When you enter a document line item for a GL account, the field status group associated with that GL account determines the fields available on the next screen. For document items that correspond to a customer account or a vendor account, the field status group associated with their GL reconciliation account makes this determination.

The SAP system delivers several preconfigured field status groups that you can use with different types of GL accounts such as reconciliation accounts, bank accounts, asset accounts, material accounts, expense accounts, and so on. You can configure field status groups using SAP IMG • FINANCIAL ACCOUNTING • GENERAL LEDGER ACCOUNTING • BUSINESS TRANSACTIONS • G/L ACCOUNT POSTING • MAKE AND CHECK DOCUMENT SETTINGS • DEFINE FIELD STATUS VARIANTS • DEFINE FIELD STATUS GROUPS.

Even though this interface may not seem user-friendly for the manual entry of documents, it provides considerable technical flexibility and maneuverability. Hence, transactions with this interface are widely used for development efforts that require programmatically loading customer documents into the SAP system. For manual entry of AR documents, you may want to use Enjoy transactions.

2.3 AR Transactions – Enjoy Interface

These transactions use an interface where you can enter multiple document line items on a single screen. Examples of transactions that use this interface are listed here:

- **Customer invoice**: Accounts Receivable Menu • Document entry • Invoice (Transaction FB70)
- **Customer credit memo**: Accounts Receivable Menu • Document entry • Credit Memo (Transaction FB75)

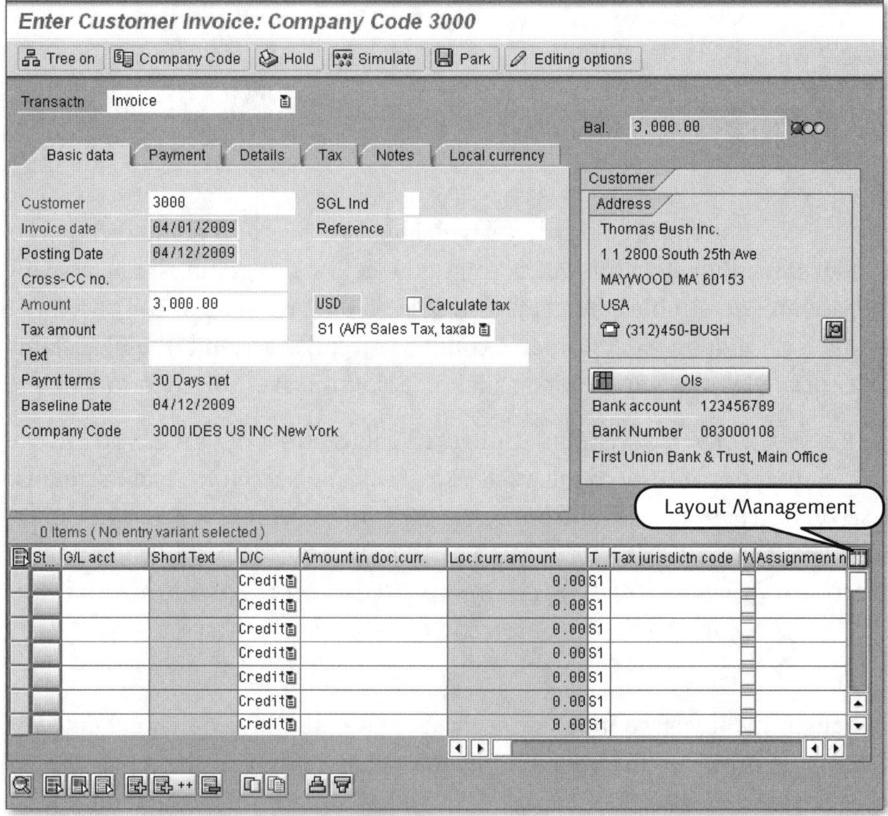

Figure 2.8 Invoice Entry – Enjoy Transaction

Figure 2.8 shows an example of an invoice entry that uses the Enjoy interface. The screen can be divided into document header and document line items.

2.3.1 Document Header

The Basic Data tab on the document header corresponds to the entry of most commonly applicable fields such as Customer Account, Invoice Date, Posting Date, and Invoice Amount. Other details such as customer address, payment terms, and customer bank account are automatically displayed based on data maintained in the customer master. Other tabs in the document header are listed here:

- **Payment**: This tab contains additional fields for payment details such as payment method, payment currency, discount terms, and bank information.
- **Details**: This tab contains fields to maintain additional details such as three reference fields, header text, and other dunning parameters.
- **Tax**: Tax information on this tab is automatically copied from customer master data. If necessary, you can change this information.
- **Notes**: This tab enables you to maintain long text, description, or any notes associated with the customer document that you're entering.
- **Local Currency**: This tab lets you change the default amounts calculated in the company code ledger.

One of the advantages of this Enjoy interface is that you don't need to navigate to additional tabs unless you want to change or maintain specific document data. Most common and useful document fields are all entered on the first header tab and are always visible while you enter document line items.

2.3.2 Document Line Items

In the line items section of the Enjoy interface, you can enter document items that debit or credit a GL account. You can double-click on a document line item to enter most common fields such as the amount, cost center, and line item text for a document item. Alternately, you can use the horizontal scroll bar to view additional columns and enter necessary information for a document item. You may notice a column for the company code, which you can use to post cross-company code transactions. Let's look at that option in more detail.

Cross-Company Transactions

You can post cross-company code documents by entering a different company code in a document line item. Let's continue with the example shown in Figure 2.8 for a customer invoice for $3,000. Let's say that out of this total receivable amount, $2,000 was for company code 3000, and the remaining $1,000 was to be posted to the same GL account but in company code 1000. You can enter two document line items, each with the appropriate amount in a different company code, and the invoice transaction will automatically generate intercompany document entries.

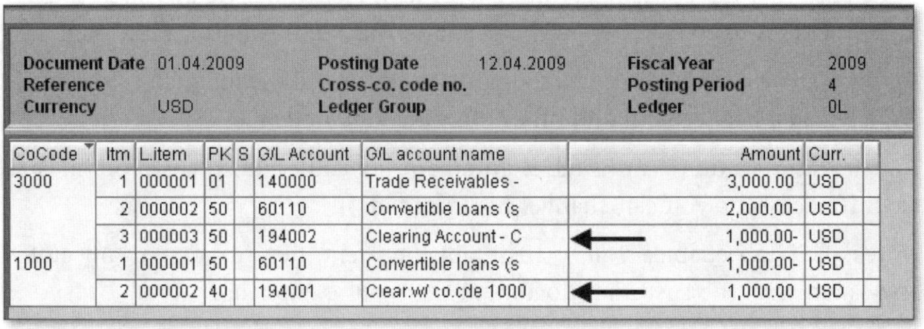

Document Date	01.04.2009	Posting Date	12.04.2009	Fiscal Year	2009
Reference		Cross-co. code no.		Posting Period	4
Currency	USD	Ledger Group		Ledger	0L

CoCode	Itm	L.item	PK	S	G/L Account	G/L account name		Amount	Curr.
3000	1	000001	01		140000	Trade Receivables -		3,000.00	USD
	2	000002	50		60110	Convertible loans (s		2,000.00-	USD
	3	000003	50		194002	Clearing Account - C	←	1,000.00-	USD
1000	1	000001	50		60110	Convertible loans (s		1,000.00-	USD
	2	000002	40		194001	Clear.w/ co.cde 1000	←	1,000.00	USD

Figure 2.9 Cross-Company Code Transaction

As you can see in Figure 2.9, the document entry in company code 3000 automatically generates a separate document in company code 1000 containing intercompany entries. You can use this functionality to even post to several other company codes simultaneously. The posting transaction will automatically generate a separate document in each company code along with appropriate intercompany entries. Individual documents in each company code that result from such intercompany posting are linked with each other by a common cross-company code document number.

Tip

In the document entries using the general interface discussed in the previous section, you can post cross-company transactions by entering a different company code in the Next Line Item section as shown earlier in Figure 2.6.

This interface is obviously more user friendly compared to the general interface discussed in the previous section. However, the line item section of this transaction interface consists of almost 80 fields, whereas for all practical purposes, you require far fewer fields than that! Instead of having to scroll through multiple columns for each line item, you can use the layout management functionality.

2.3.3 Layout Management

Figure 2.10 shows layout management in more detail. When you select the layout management option in Figure 2.8, the Table Settings window is displayed.

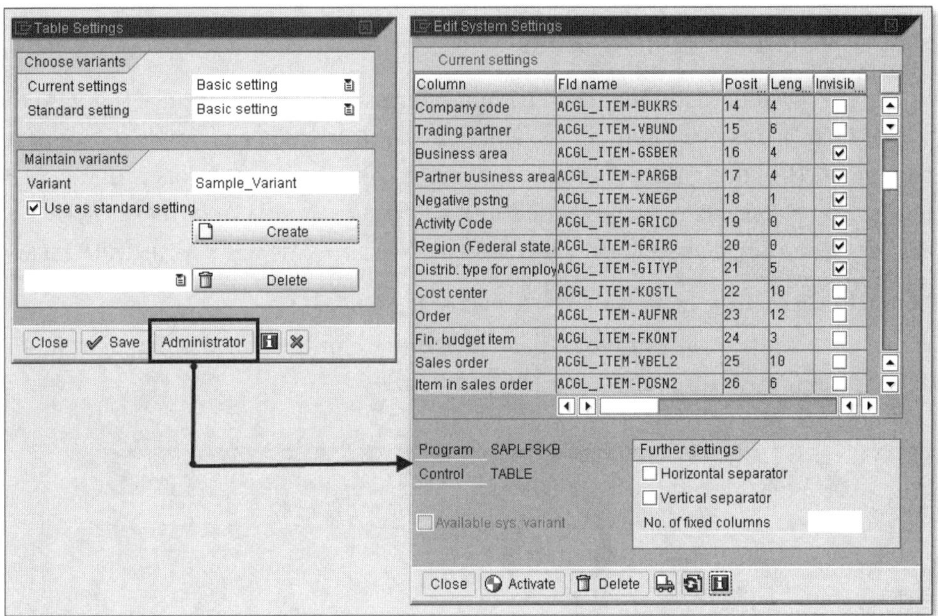

Figure 2.10 Layout Management

The Table Settings window provides the initial interface where you determine whether you want to create, change, or delete an existing layout. When you select the Administrator option, you're presented with the second window where you can set the status of fields. Fields with the invisible status aren't displayed in the line item layout. So in Figure 2.10, six fields marked with invisible status won't be displayed when a user selects the SAMPLE_VARIANT layout.

Tip

When deciding to configure line layouts and field status, you should take into account not only manual document entry but also automatically generated documents from other SAP components, such as Sales or Customer Service.

In the next section, we'll look at other AR transactions and functionalities.

2.4 Other AR Transactions

In this section, we'll discuss commonly used AR transactions and functionalities such as maintaining payment terms, document change, and document reversal.

2.4.1 Maintain Payment Terms

In the SAP system, maintenance of payment terms is a configuration activity, so to add or manage new payment terms, you'll need the assistance of your SAP support personnel. The configuration activity for maintaining payment terms is under SAP IMG • FINANCIAL ACCOUNTING • ACCOUNTS RECEIVABLE AND ACCOUNTS PAYABLE • BUSINESS TRANSACTIONS • OUTGOING INVOICES/CREDIT MEMOS • MAINTAIN TERMS OF PAYMENT.

Figure 2.11 shows an example of payment term definition for net payment in 45 days but with cash discounts for early payments.

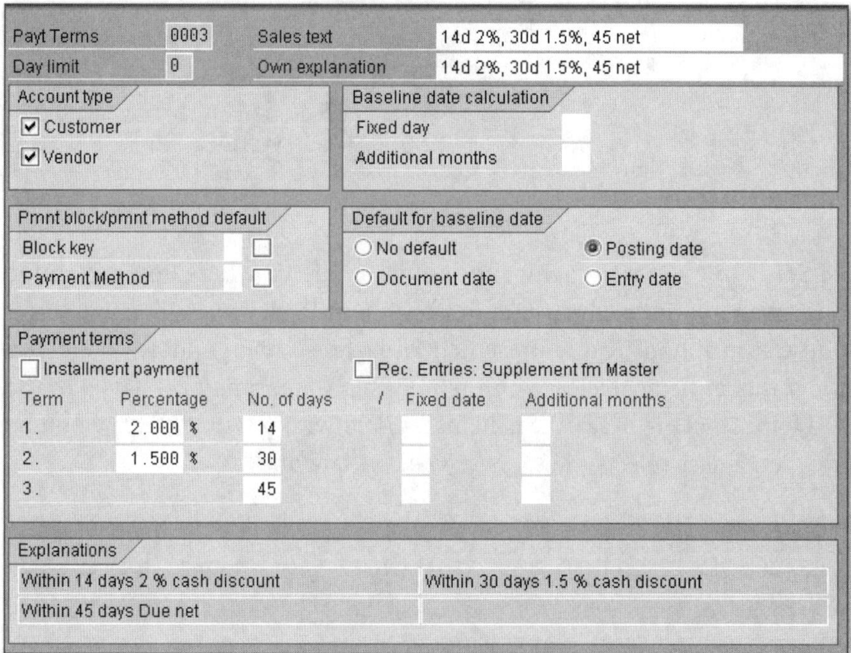

Figure 2.11 Payment Term Configuration

As is evident from the figure, a payment term definition consists of several attributes:

- **Sales Text**: This is an automatically generated description of payment terms based on its parameters.
- **Own Explanation**: If you want to use a payment term description different from the sales text, you can enter it in this field.
- **Account Type**: This attribute controls whether this payment term can be used for vendor accounts and customer accounts.
- **Default for Baseline Date**: Determines whether discount baseline date in a document requires manual entry or it's defaulted as entry date, document date, or posting date. We discussed these dates in Section 2.1.4, Document Dates.
- **Baseline Date Calculation**: Allows you to further influence calculation of the baseline date by replacing the day or by adding the number of months to the default baseline date.

Example

Let's say the discount baseline date is determined as 04/08/2009.

- If Fixed Day = 15, baseline date = 04/15/2009.
- If Additional Month = 1, baseline date = 05/08/2009.
- If Fixed Day = 20 and additional month = 1, baseline date = 05/20/2009.

- **Payment Block**: A payment block is proposed for all documents in which this payment term is entered. This provides you with an opportunity to review the document and its payment terms before releasing it for further processing.
- **Payment Method**: A payment method is proposed for all documents in which this payment term is used. This provides you with an opportunity, for example, to propose that all payment terms with large discounts are paid by electronic payments.
- **Payment Term Percentage**: Specifies the discount percentages as follows:
  - A payment term consists of three segments, from which up to two segments can have discount percentages for early payment. The last segment always corresponds to the net payment without any discount.

- You can specify a fixed date or additional months for each segment of the payment term. The example cited with calculation of baseline date shows how these parameters influence the calculation of dates.

The flag INSTALLMENT PAYMENT indicates that the current payment term is an installment payment term, as explained next.

Installment Payment Term

An installment payment term is useful if a payment is to be made in several installments — each with its own payment terms. The configuration activity for maintaining payment terms is under SAP IMG • FINANCIAL ACCOUNTING • ACCOUNTS RECEIVABLE AND ACCOUNTS PAYABLE • BUSINESS TRANSACTIONS • OUTGOING INVOICES/ CREDIT MEMOS • DEFINE TERMS OF PAYMENT FOR INSTALLMENT PAYMENTS.

Terms of Payment for Holdback/Retainage

Terms of Pay...	Inst	Percent	Pmnt term
0017	1	30.000	0002
0017	2	40.000	0004
0017	3	30.000	0005
JP03	1	50.000	JP01
JP03	2	50.000	JP02
MF01	1	50.000	0002
MF01	2	30.000	0004
MF01	3	20.000	0005
R001	1	40.000	ZR01
R001	2	30.000	ZR02
R001	3	30.000	ZR03

Figure 2.12 Installment Payment Terms

As shown in Figure 2.12, the definition of an installment payment term consists of multiple installments. For each installment, you specify the installment percentage and corresponding payment terms. For example, payment term MF01 consists of three installments: first installment of 50% with payment term 0002, second installment of 30% with payment term 0004, and third installment of 20% with payment term 0005. The definition of payment terms 0002, 0004, and 0005 determine any individual cash discount percentages.

Let's now look at other AR transactions such as document change or display.

2.4.2 Document Change, Display

You'll find transactions to display and change accounting documents under SAP MENU • ACCOUNTING • FINANCIAL ACCOUNTING • ACCOUNTS RECEIVABLE • DOCUMENT • CHANGE (Transaction FB02) or DISPLAY (Transaction FB03). The display document transaction doesn't require any elaborate explanation, so we'll mainly focus on the change document transaction.

After accounting documents are already posted, you can only change information or reference fields such as document header text, reference document number, line item text, or line item assignment field. For unpaid invoices, you can also change payment-related fields such as payment terms or payment methods. System configuration settings determine the conditions under which each document field can be changed. You'll find these settings under SAP IMG • FINANCIAL ACCOUNTING • FINANCIAL ACCOUNTING GLOBAL SETTINGS • DOCUMENT • DOCUMENT HEADER/LINE ITEM • DOCUMENT CHANGE RULES, DOCUMENT HEADER/LINE ITEM.

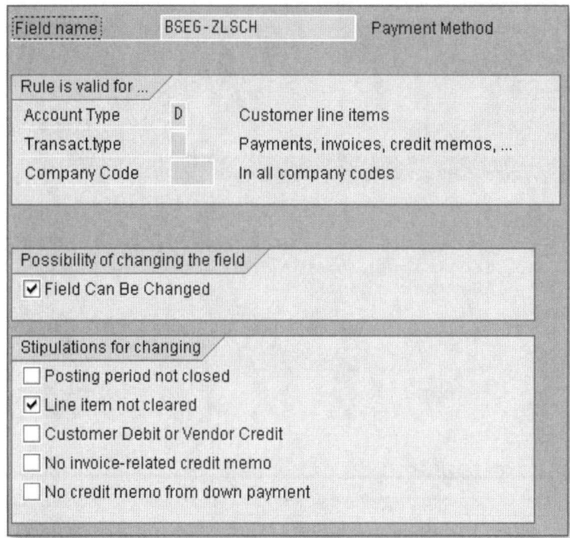

Figure 2.13 Document Change Rule

Figure 2.13 shows an example of document change rules for the Payment Method field in document line items. As shown in the figure, you can set document change rules separately for documents based on ACCOUNT TYPE, TRANSACTION TYPE, or even by COMPANY CODE. Additionally, you can specify different stipulations under which a field value can be changed. The example shown in the figure specifies that you can change the Payment Method field in a document line item only if it hasn't been cleared, for example, by a customer payment. The SAP system provides document change rules that can be used as is for almost all fields of an accounting document.

Another common business requirement is to post a document reversal.

2.4.3 Document Reversal

You'll find transactions to post a document reversal under the menu path SAP MENU • ACCOUNTING • FINANCIAL ACCOUNTING • ACCOUNTS RECEIVABLE • DOCUMENT • REVERSE • INDIVIDUAL REVERSAL (Transaction FB08) or MASS REVERSAL (Transaction F.80).

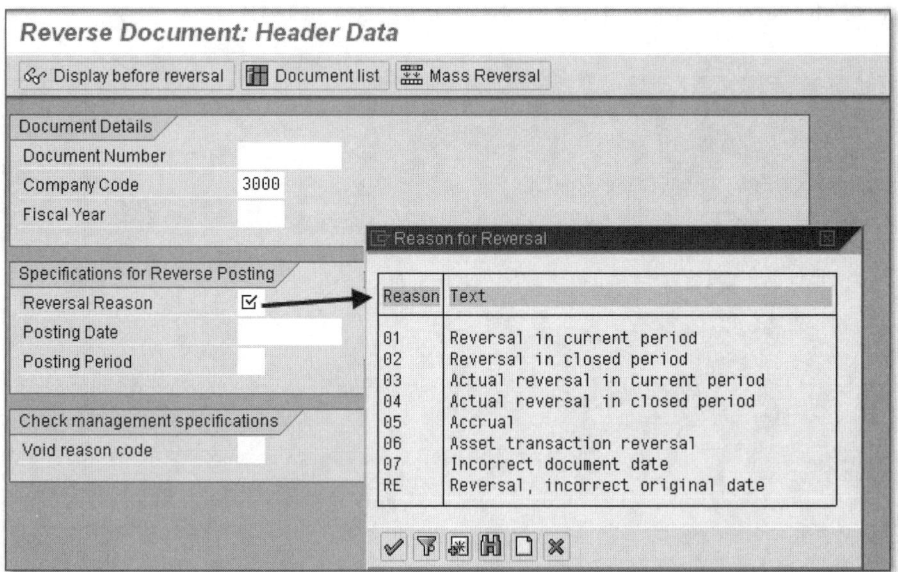

Figure 2.14 Reverse Document

Figure 2.14 shows a screen for the transaction used to reverse a single document. You use reversal reason codes to classify reasons for document reversals so that you can differentiate between, for example, reversal documents due to incorrect postings and reversal documents for month-end accruals. You can configure reversal reason codes using SAP IMG • FINANCIAL ACCOUNTING • ACCOUNTS RECEIVABLE AND

ACCOUNTS PAYABLE • BUSINESS TRANSACTIONS • ADJUSTMENT POSTINGS/REVERSAL • DEFINE REASONS FOR REVERSAL.

The mass reversal transaction is useful if you want to reverse multiple documents that meet one or more criteria. The mass reversal transaction provides large numbers of criteria for document selection such as document type, posting date, entry date, reference number, and user id. After specifying the appropriate selection criteria, the transaction will reverse all documents that meet the criteria. You can use this program to even reverse cross-company code documents discussed in Section 2.3.2, Document Line Items.

Another very useful functionality is to post a document with reference.

2.4.4 Post with Reference

This functionality is available only through the general interface discussed in Section 2.2, AR Transactions – General Interface. To access this functionality, you select Post with Reference from the initial screen of any transaction that uses the general interface.

Figure 2.15 shows different options available to you after you select the POST WITH REFERENCE option.

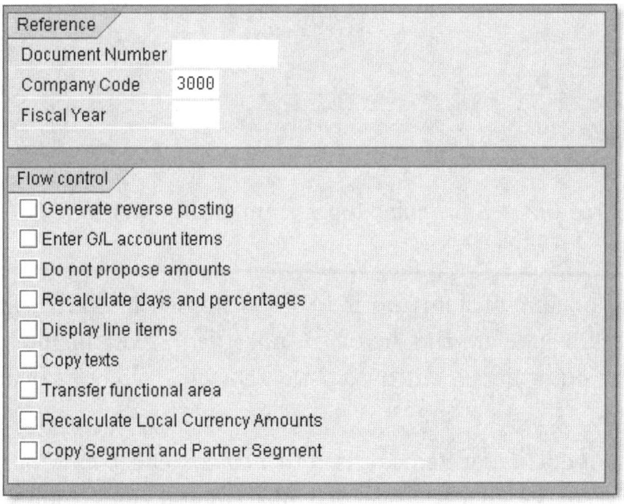

Figure 2.15 Post with Reference

You can use this functionality to post new documents that share some or all details with existing documents.

In the next section, we'll discuss how to display line items posted to customer accounts.

2.4.5 Customer Line Items (FBL5N)

This is one of the most commonly used and extremely versatile transactions in the AR component. Figure 2.16 shows a partial selection screen of this transaction.

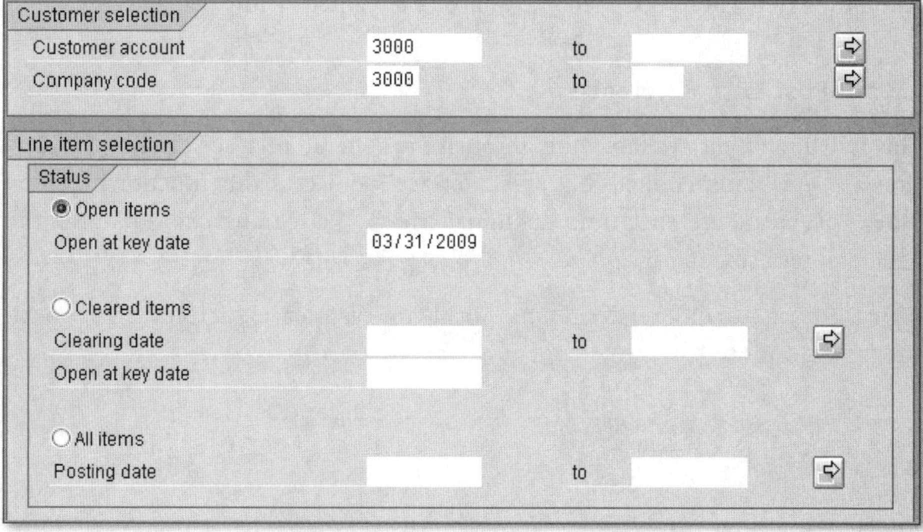

Figure 2.16 Customer Line Items

This transaction provides three options for selecting document line items posted to customer accounts:

- Open Items: Displays all document items posted to a customer account that aren't yet cleared. These include unpaid invoices, unsettled credit memos, down payments, and any other document posted to a customer account that isn't yet cleared.
- Cleared Items: Displays all document items posted to a customer account that were cleared between the specified clearing dates. Unlike the previous option,

you can even display document items that were open as of a specified key date but have been cleared since then.

- ALL ITEMS: Displays all document items posted to a customer account regardless of its clearing status.

The resulting document item list provides a large number of options to customize the content and format the output. We introduced this transaction in this chapter to provide you with a quick reference. We'll revisit it in much more detail in the chapter in this book that explains different reporting and information transactions in the AR component. For now, let's focus on other document processing aids available in the SAP system.

2.5 Document-Processing Aids

In this section, we'll explore document-processing aids such as validations, substitutions, fast entry, account assignment layouts, and recurring entries. These functionalities are available for all types of accounting documents, not just the documents posted in AR.

2.5.1 Validation/Substitutions

Document validations and substitutions provide you with an ability to validate and substitute document data before accounting documents are posted in the SAP system. For example, using validations, you can ensure that document lines containing a certain range of GL accounts are always posted with a cost center. Similarly, using substitutions, you can substitute a default value for a cost center before a document is posted.

You configure document validations and substitutions using transactions available under the SAP IMG • FINANCIAL ACCOUNTING • FINANCIAL ACCOUNTING GLOBAL SETTINGS • DOCUMENT • DOCUMENT HEADER or LINE ITEM configuration area. Figure 2.17 shows an example of a validation rule to ensure that all document line items posted to GL account 470400 contain a cost center. An error message is displayed if a document line item is entered without a cost center, and the user has to enter the valid cost center before the document can be posted. The following list provides an overview of validation functionalities:

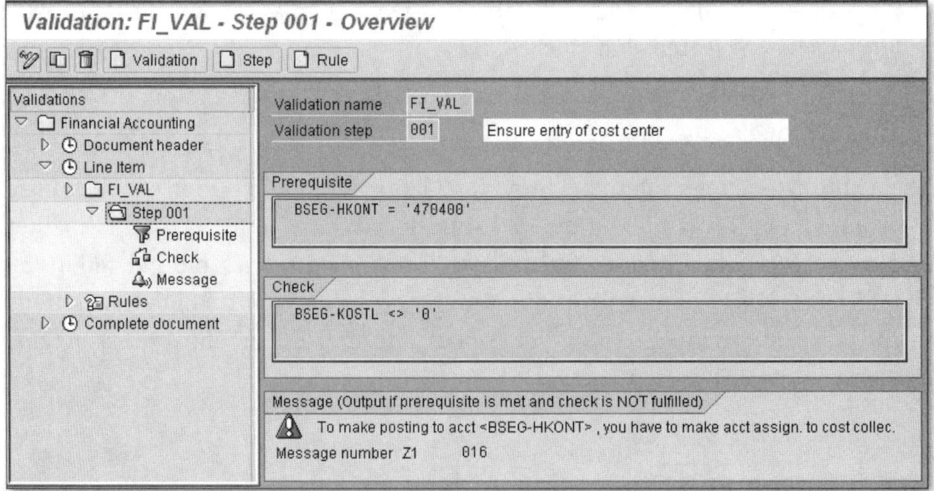

Figure 2.17 Validation Configuration

- You can create document validations for three call-up points: document header, document line item, and complete document. A validation for a complete document can validate values entered in multiple line items.
- A validation consists of one or more validation steps. Each validation step consists of PREREQUISITE conditions, CHECK conditions, and MESSAGE definition.
  - Validation MESSAGE is only issued when conditions specified in the PREREQUISITE are met, but conditions specified in the CHECK fail.
- While specifying conditions for PREREQUISITE or for CHECK, you can use any of the following values:
  - Field value from the document header
  - Field value from the document line item
  - Value of the system fields such as transaction code, user ID, and system date
  - Value returned by predefined conditions grouped into reusable rules
  - Value returned by custom development such as user exits
- You can configure the message display as information, warning, error, or abort messages.

On the other hand, document substitution rules provide you with the following functionalities:

- You can create document substitutions for four call-up points: document header, document line item, complete document, and, if applicable for your installation, cost of sales accounting.
- A substitution consists of one or more substitution steps. Each substitution step consists of PREREQUISITE conditions and SUBSTITUTION logic:
  - Substitution logic is only processed if conditions specified in the PREREQUISITE are met.
- Condition definition for substitution prerequisite and validation prerequisite are similar
- You can use any of the following logic for substituting the value of a field:
  - Constant value
  - Value of another document field
  - Value returned by custom development such as user exits

Tip

You can assign only one validation and one substitution for each combination of a company code and a call-up point. Because of this, prerequisite conditions of validation and substitution steps should be unique enough to ensure that they are processed only for intended business scenarios.

In the following section, we'll discuss document parking.

2.5.2 Document Parking

You use the document parking functionality to enter and park accounting documents that aren't yet complete because, for example, all necessary information isn't available. The advantage of using document parking is that when necessary information is available, you can retrieve the parked document, enter the missing information, and then post it into the system. Not only that, you can also include parked documents in most reports, forms, statements, and tax returns, as well as use them to create additional documents such as payment requests.

Both types of interfaces discussed in Sections 2.2, AR Transactions – General Interface, and 2.3, AR Transactions – Enjoy Interface, provide you with functionality so that instead of posting a document, you can save it as a parked document.

Alternatively, you can use the dedicated document parking transactions available under Accounts Receivable SAP MENU • Document entry • Document Parking. Similar to post document transactions, this menu area contains transactions to park customer invoice and credit memo documents using both the general interface and the Enjoy interface.

You'll find transactions to process parked accounting documents under Accounts Receivable SAP MENU • Document • Parked Documents. Following are some of the follow-up activities for parked documents:

- Post or delete a parked document (FBV0)
- Change a parked document (FBV2)
- Display a parked document (FBV3)
- Change header information of a parked document (FBV4)
- Display changes made to a parked document (FBV5)
- Refuse a parked document (FBV6)

The last transaction in particular is useful if your SAP system has been configured to use SAP Business Workflow. Due to space constraints, we won't discuss workflow settings for parked documents in detail. However, you can configure SAP Business Workflow in the SAP system so that after a parked document is entered by an employee, it gets automatically forwarded to the appropriate people who can review it, release it for posting, or reject it. The forwarding and release procedure can be conditional upon user-defined criteria. You'll find configuration settings for setting up the workflow for parked documents under SAP IMG • Financial Accounting • Accounts Receivable and Accounts Payable • Business Transactions • Outgoing Invoices/Credit Memos • Carry out and Check Settings for Document Parking.

Next, we'll discuss account assignment models.

2.5.3 Account Assignment Models

An *account assignment model* provides default values for one or more document lines that can be used as a reference while posting new documents.

PK	CoCd	G/L	Tx	Jurisdictn Code	Cost Ctr	Amount
40	3000	420000			11000	
40	3000	420000			11010	
40	3000	420000			11021	
40	3000	431000			11000	
40	3000	431000			11010	
40	3000	431000			11021	
40	3000	472000	V0		11000	
40	3000	472000	V0		11010	
40	3000	472000	V0		11021	
50	3000	399999	V0			

Account Assignment Model Items

Figure 2.18 Account Assignment Model

For example, accounting entries for recording travel expenses typically use the same GL accounts, similar descriptions, and maybe the same cost centers. Figure 2.18 shows an account assignment model that can potentially represent such an example. It includes possible combinations of GL accounts and cost centers for the intended purpose, in this case, recording travel expenses. Subsequently, a user who is posting a document in the SAP system can simply reference this account assignment model, enter expense amounts in the appropriate line items, and post the document! Thus, carefully designed account assignment layouts can greatly speed up the entry of documents of the same type.

You define account assignment models using SAP ACCOUNTS RECEIVABLE MENU • DOCUMENT ENTRY • REFERENCE DOCUMENTS • ACCOUNT ASSIGNMENT MODELS (Transaction FKMT). To use account assignment models while entering documents using the general interface or the Enjoy interface, you use menu path EDIT • SELECT ACCOUNT ASSIGNMENT TEMPLATES.

The account assignment model can be used in AR transactions that use the general interface or the Enjoy interface.

The next section discusses processing recurring entries in the SAP system.

2.5.4 Recurring Entries

Recurring entries are commonly used to process periodic documents such as posting rent invoices, month-end accruals, and adjustments. In the SAP system, you set up recurring entries by first setting up a recurring entry master, and subsequently running recurring entry process to post recurring entries.

Master Document

You access the setup of the recurring entry master document by using ACCOUNTS RECEIVABLE SAP MENU • DOCUMENT ENTRY • REFERENCE DOCUMENTS • RECURRING ENTRY DOCUMENT (Transaction FBD1). Figure 2.19 shows the initial screen for entering a recurring entry master document.

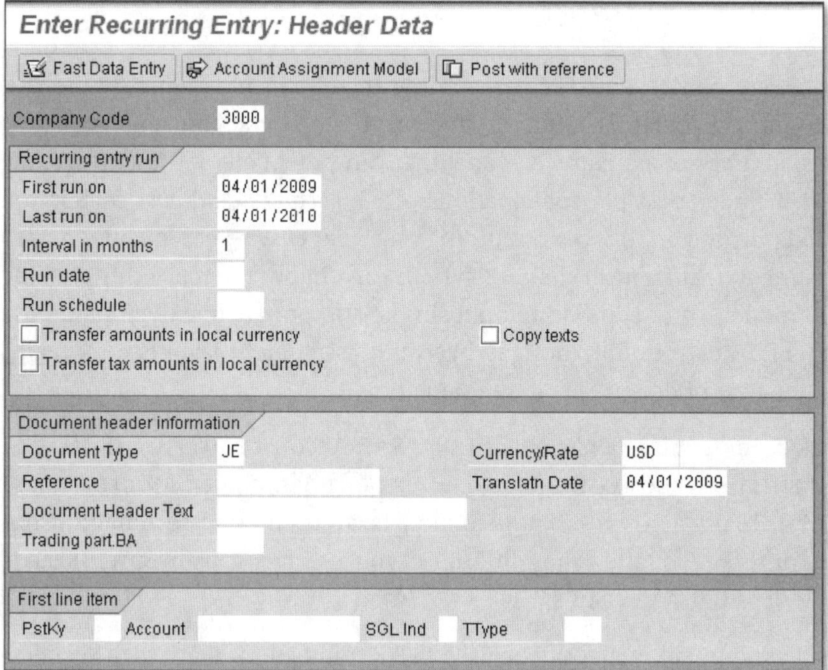

Figure 2.19 Recurring Entry Document Master

The following list provides details of fields under the RECURRING ENTRY RUN section.

- **First Run On**: This is the date from which the first recurring entry is to be carried out.
- **Last Run On**: This is the date up until which the final recurring entry is to be carried out.
- **Interval in Months**: This field specifies periodicity of recurring entries. Value of 1 specifies monthly, 3 specifies quarterly, and so on.
- **Run Date**: The calendar day on which the recurring entry is posted. For the example shown in Figure 2.19:
  - If this field is blank, recurring entries are posted on the 1st, which is the day entered in First Entry On.
  - If this field carries a different value (e.g., 10), recurring entries are posted on the 10th day of a month.
- **Run Schedule**: A Run Schedule lets you specify exact dates for posting recurring entries. If recurring entry postings don't confirm to set periodicity, you use this field instead of specifying Interval in Months.
  - Configuration of the run schedule and corresponding run dates is carried out using SAP IMG • Financial Accounting • Financial Accounting Global Settings • Document • Recurring Entries • Define Run Schedules and Enter Run Dates.

The three indicators Copy Texts, Transfer Amounts in Local Currency, and Transfer Tax Amounts in Local Currency determine whether values from the master document are copied to recurring entries. The indicators for local currency are especially relevant for recurring documents in foreign currency. For example, depending on the type of business transaction, you may want local currency amount to be either copied from the master document or recalculated based on the applicable exchange rate.

Tip

By default, the payment term from the master document is copied into recurring entries. However, if you select Rec Entries: Supplement from Master flag in the payment term definition (refer to Figure 2.11), the payment term in recurring entries are copied from the customer master data. It helps you take into consideration the possibility of any changes to the customer payment terms.

The area menu to display, change, or delete recurring entry master document is ACCOUNTS RECEIVABLE SAP MENU • DOCUMENT • REFERENCE DOCUMENTS.

In next section, we'll see how to post recurring entries.

Post Recurring Entries

To process recurring entries, you access ACCOUNTS RECEIVABLE SAP MENU • PERIODIC PROCESSING • RECURRING ENTRIES • EXECUTE (Transaction F.14).

The transaction provides you with several selection criteria such as document type, posting date, and entry date. Other relevant features of this transaction are listed here:

- You can run recurring entry transaction several times a month or once every few months.
- During each run, this transaction creates a batch session for all pending recurring entries for the specified settlement period.
- To post these recurring entries, you follow the standard process of executing a batch session in the SAP system. To process a batch session, select SYSTEM • SERVICES • BATCH INPUT • SESSIONS from any screen, select the session name, and choose PROCESS.

We've gone through several transactions and functionalities in this chapter. The next section provides an easy reference for transactions discussed in this chapter.

2.5.5 List of Transactions

Table 2.2 lists some of the transactions discussed in this chapter.

Transaction	Usage
F-22/F-27	Customer invoice/credit memo – general
FB70/FB75	Customer invoice/credit memo – Enjoy
FB02/FB03	Change/display accounting document
FB08	Reversal of a document
F.80	Mass reversal of documents

Table 2.2 AR Transactions

Transaction	Usage
FBL5N	Display customer line items
FKMT	Set up account assignment model
OBB8	Configure payment terms
OBB9	Configure installment payment terms
OB28	Configure validations for accounting documents
OBBH	Configure substitutions for accounting documents
FV70/FV75	Park/edit invoice/credit memo
F-64/F-67	Invoice/credit memo parking – general
FBV0	Post/delete parked document
FBV2/FBV3	Change/display parked document
FBV6	Refuse parked document
FBD1	Set up recurring document master
FBD2/FBD3	Change/display recurring document master
F.14	Process recurring entries
F.15	List recurring entries

Table 2.2 AR Transactions (Cont.)

In next section, we'll look at the technical objects available for AR transactions.

2.6 Technical Reference

This section lists the technical objects such as SAP Notes, authorization objects, and tables and structures relevant for processing AR transactions. Considering the large number of technical objects available in the SAP system, this information should only be considered a starting point for analysis.

2.6.1 SAP Notes

Table 2.3 is a list of SAP Notes relevant for AR transactions.

SAP Note	Relevance
0000546889	FAQ: Screen variants in FI Enjoy transactions
0000863267	FAQ: Validations in Enjoy transactions
0000111989	Reversal of a reversed document
0000042615	Substitution rules in FI documents
0000984305	Line item display – definition of special fields
0000842318	FAQ: Maintenance of validations and substitutions
0000971193	Mass deletion of parked documents
0001346425	FI: Fast-entry screens corrupted after upgrade
0001249223	FI: Problems when posting parked documents
0000322636	Cross-company code posting with Acct Assignment Model
0000827413	Changeability of fields in FI documents
0000335608	Translation of 2nd/3rd local currency from 1st/Trx currency
0000099775	Mass change of posting date/fiscal year in parked documents
0001070629	FAQ: New general ledger migration
0000161922	Excluding users from releasing parked documents
0000210706	Parked documents with logical database BRF

Table 2.3 SAP Notes for AR Transactions

In the next section, we'll look at authorization objects available for AR transactions.

2.6.2 Authorization Objects

Table 2.4 lists some of the authorization objects to be considered for transactions discussed in this chapter.

Object	Description
F_BKPF_BED	Accounting Doc: Account Authorization for Customers
F_BKPF_BEK	Accounting Doc: Account Authorization for Vendors
F_BKPF_BES	Accounting Doc: Account Authorization for GL Accounts

Table 2.4 Authorization Objects – AR Transactions

Object	Description
F_BKPF_BLA	Accounting Doc: Authorization for Document Types
F_BKPF_BUK	Accounting Doc: Authorization for Company Codes
F_BKPF_BUP	Accounting Doc: Authorization for Posting Periods
F_BKPF_KOA	Accounting Doc: Authorization for Account Types
F_FAGL_LDR	General Ledger: Authorization for Ledger
F_SKA1_BUK	GL Account: Authorization for Company Codes
F_SKA1_KTP	GL Account: Authorization for Chart of Accounts
F_IT_ALV	Line item display: Change and save layout
F_KNA1_APP	Customer: Application Authorization
F_KNA1_BED	Customer: Account Authorization
F_KNA1_BUK	Customer: Authorization for Company Codes
F_KNA1_GEN	Customer: Central Data
F_KMT_MGMT	Account Assignment Model: Maintenance and Use
G_ADMI_CUS	Central Administrative FI-SL Tools
G_GB90_	Validation/Substitution/Rules: Rules
G_GB93_	Validation/Substitution/Rules: Validation

Table 2.4 Authorization Objects – AR Transactions (Cont.)

The next section provides a list of tables and structures.

2.6.3 Tables and Structures

Table 2.5 lists tables and structures relevant for processing AR transactions.

Table	Relevance
BKPF	Accounting document: header
BSEG	Accounting document: details
BSID	Secondary index for customer documents
BSAD	Secondary index for customer documents – cleared items
BSIK	Secondary index for vendor documents

Table 2.5 AR Transactions – Tables and Structures

Table	Relevance
BSAK	Secondary index for vendor documents – cleared items
VBKPF	Parked documents – header
VBSEGD	Parked documents – customer segment
VBSEGK	Parked documents – vendor segment
VBSEGS	Parked documents – GL account segment
VBSET	Parked documents – taxes
KMKPF	Account assignment models – header
KMZEI	Account assignment models – items
BKDF	Recurring entries – document header supplement

Table 2.5 AR Transactions – Tables and Structures (Cont.)

Now we'll look at the objects and functionality available for enhancing and modifying the functionality of processing AR transactions.

2.7 Enhancements and Modifications

This section provides a list of available BTEs, enhancements, BAdIs, and BAPIs relevant for AR transactions. These are used to enhance and modify the standard functionality available in the SAP system.

2.7.1 Business Transaction Events (BTE)

Using BTEs, you can attach additional function modules and custom logic to the standard SAP system. The list of BTEs available for AR transactions is too big to be included in this chapter, so Table 2.6 provides only a partial list of publish and subscribe (P/S) and process BTEs available for AR transactions.

Type	BTE	Event/Process
P/S	00000900	Fill customer fields before line item display
P/S	00001005	Check posting key or account
P/S	00001011	Post document: Check at line item level

Table 2.6 AR Transactions – List of BTEs

Type	BTE	Event/Process
P/S	00001020	Post document: Prior to final checks
P/S	00001025	Post document: After final checks
P/S	00001040	Reverse document: After processing standard doc
P/S	00001041	Reverse document: Before reversing clearing doc
P/S	00001110	Change document: Save the standard data
P/S	00001120	Change document: GUI call up at line item
P/S	00001610	Line item display: GUI call up
P/S	00001630	Line item display: Prior to first list
P/S	00001650	Line item display: Add to data per line
Process	00001100	Document posting: Adjust baseline date and discount terms
Process	00001110	Document posting: Check invoice duplication
Process	00001120	Document posting: Field substitution header/items
Process	00001130	Document posting: (SAP-Internal) country- or industry-specific field substitution
Process	00001150	Open FI: Get offsetting account
Process	00002210	Document parking: Amount release
Process	00002211	Document parking: Account assignment approval
Process	00002212	Document parking: Determine accounting clerk
Process	00002213	Document parking: Check if posting is allowed
Process	00002214	Document parking: Determine release approval path
Process	00002220	Document parking: Determine person with release authorization

Table 2.6 AR Transactions – List of BTEs (Cont.)

The next section discusses Business Add-Ins available for AR transactions.

2.7.2 Business Add-Ins (BAdIs)

Business Add-In implementations are enhancements to the standard SAP system. Most BAdIs provided by the SAP system accommodate industry-specific or country-specific requirements. However, you can also use BAdI implementations to meet any unique requirements for your business. Following are some of the BAdIs available for AR transactions:

- FI_LIMIT_CURCONV
  - This BAdI can be used to define restrictions in the specific company code definition of local currencies.
  - This BAdI provides a method CHECK, to check entries before saving to Table V_T001A.
- FI_LIMIT_PROCESS
  - This BAdI enables you to prevent the execution of specific processes such as transactions or reports. It's called up at the start of each process.
  - This BAdI provides one method CHECK, to determine whether a process should be executed.
- BADI_PRKNG_NO_UPDATE
  - This BAdI can be used to disable the processing of parked documents.
  - It provides one method, PARKING_NO_UPDATE, to deactivate the update of parked documents.

The next section takes a look at available BAPIs.

2.7.3 BAPIs

Table 2.7 lists some of the available methods in the SAP system for AR transactions. These methods are available for the object "ARAccount" (Customer Account).

Method	Function Module	Description
GetBalancedItems	BAPI_AR_ACC_ GETBALANCEDITEMS	Read clearing entries and the items they cleared for a customer account in a given period.
GetCurrentBalance	BAPI_AR_ACC_ GETCURRENTBALANCE	Read customer balance (standard and Special GL transactions) for the current year.
GetKeyDateBalance	BAPI_AR_ACC_ GETKEYDATEBALANCE	Read customer balance (standard and Special GL transactions, noted items) at a given key date.

Table 2.7 AR Transactions – List of BAPIs

Method	Function Module	Description
GetOpenItems	BAPI_AR_ACC_ GETOPENITEMS	Read customer open items (including noted items) at a given key date.
GetPeriodBalances	BAPI_AR_ACC_ GETPERIODBALANCES	Read customer's current balance for the current fiscal year, together with transactions and sales per period.

Table 2.7 AR Transactions – List of BAPIs (Cont.)

2.8 Summary

In this chapter, we discussed the most common customer transactions posted in the AR component. It's important to note that regardless of the SAP component in which the original document is posted, all entries that impact GL account balances are always posted as FI documents. As mentioned before, the utilities and posting aids discussed in this chapter are applicable to any type of accounting document.

In this chapter, you'll find concepts and configuration activities that influence SAP billing processes. If you're interested in the SAP billing process asa business user, you may want to skim through the sections on configuration activities and only focus on sections dealing with billing transactions. The next chapter provides details on billing functionalities that build upon the details discussed in this chapter. The chapter begins with an overview of master data and organizational data relevant for billing process. Subsequently, we'll get into more configuration details of the billing type and account determination. Lastly, we'll discuss the most commonly used billing transactions.

3 Customer Billing

In the previous chapter, we discussed AR documents such as customer invoices directly posted in AR. In this chapter, we'll focus on customer billing document generated based on sales documents. We'll start with a brief overview of the sales process to put the billing process in a larger context. Then we'll look at the activities involved in the configuration of the billing processes, followed by detailed discussion of the billing process itself. The advanced topics such as billing plans, retroactive billing, and self-billing are discussed in the next chapter. However, you should read this chapter before reading the advanced topics because this chapter provides the foundation of concepts and functionalities of billing process.

Tip

In the SAP system, the billing document and the corresponding accounting document are two separate documents, each with different document numbers, different document types, and different sets of processing transactions. For example, you can't use programs or forms used for processing customer billing documents to process customer invoices directly posted in AR, and vice versa.

A large part of this chapter deals with developing concepts and explaining configuration activities that are important in the customer billing process. Information presented in this chapter may be too technical if your primary involvement in SAP billing processes is only as a business user. In that case, you may want to browse through sections that explain configuration activities and focus more on sections that explain billing transactions. Also, the next chapter discusses billing process more from a business user viewpoint. However, if you're involved in the implementation of SAP billing processes, you should go through this entire chapter to understand the relevant configuration activities.

The first section gives an overview of the underlying organizational data, master data, and pricing procedure for billing processes.

3.1 Master Data and Pricing Procedures

The billing process in the SAP system is influenced by several parameters, attributes, and criteria associated with customers, products, sales organizations, plants, and other master data. In this section, we'll start with a high level overview of organizational data, master data, and the all-important pricing procedure.

3.1.1 Organizational Structure

In Chapter 1, Customer Master Data, we looked at customer master data maintenance for company codes and sales organizations. This section provides a brief introduction to common organizational elements relevant for billing processes. It's unlikely that these organizational elements will be configured specifically based on AR processes. More commonly, organization-wide processes determine the SAP organizational structure, which in turn impacts billing processes.

Table 3.1 provides a quick reference for SAP organizational elements.

Organizational Unit	Description
Company code	▸ Company codes represent the smallest organizational unit in Financial Accounting for which you prepare financial statements for external, statutory reporting. ▸ Legal and tax requirements influence the company code structure in the SAP system. ▸ Customer AR entries are posted to the company code.

Table 3.1 Organizational Units in the SAP System

Organizational Unit	Description
Sales organization	▸ Sales organizations typically represent business units or geographical areas that are responsible for independently managing sales activities. ▸ Every sales organization is assigned to a company code. Multiple sales organizations can be assigned to a company code. ▸ Billing document processing is done at the level of sales organizations.
Distribution channel	▸ Distribution channels represent different means through which goods and services are sold, for example, retail, wholesale, OEM, or online. ▸ Every distribution channel is assigned to a sales organization.
Division	▸ Divisions represent groupings of products, services, and different lines of businesses within an organization. ▸ Every division is assigned to a sales organization.
Sales area	▸ Sales areas represent *valid* combinations of sales organization, distribution channel, and division. ▸ All sales documents such as sales orders are entered and processed in a sales area.
Plant	▸ Plants in the SAP system represent organizational units responsible for the production, procurement, sale, or maintenance of goods and services. ▸ Every plant is assigned to a company code. Combinations of sales organization and distribution channel are assigned to one or more plants. ▸ The SAP system uses this assignment to default to the plant from which order deliveries are made.

Table 3.1 Organizational Units in the SAP System (Cont.)

You can find this information for a billing document in the display billing document transaction (VF02) under GOTO • HEADER • HEADER • GENERAL INFORMATION. To validate the definition and assignment of organizational units, check configuration areas via SAP IMG • ENTERPRISE STRUCTURE • DEFINITION or ASSIGNMENT.

The following is a simplified and summarized version of the details just mentioned.

- Sales documents are entered and processed in sales areas.
- Product deliveries and returns are processed from plants.
- Customer billing documents are processed in sales organizations.
- AR entries for billing documents are posted to company codes.

In the next chapter, you'll see how the preceding logic is relevant in different types of business transactions such as intercompany billing or third-party processing.

In addition to the organizational data, you also have to maintain master data that influence the billing process.

3.1.2 Master Data

In this section, we'll focus on important master data that impact billing calculations and billing processes. Let's start with the document partner functions.

Partner Functions

In Chapter 1, Customer Master Data, we looked at the functionality of customer partner functions. Partner functions maintained in the customer master are defaulted to every sales order. However, these values can be changed in individual sales orders. So for the purpose of billing process, only the partner functions assigned to a sales order are important. The following list provides an overview of different partner functions and their impact on different billing processes.

- **Sold-to party**: This is the customer account that places the sales order. Attributes of this customer account impact several aspects of the billing process such as pricing calculation, receivables posting, tax calculation, and GL account determination.
- **Payer**: This is the customer account that makes payment for billing documents sent to customers. If the payer account is different from the sold-to party, then its attributes impact the processes of GL account determination, receivables posting, and cash application.
- **Bill-to party**: This is the customer account that receives billing documents. If the bill-to party account is different from the payer or sold-to party account, then its attributes impact the output determination process that prints or sends billing documents.

- **Ship-to party**: This is the customer account that receives goods or services. If the ship-to party account is different from the sold-to party, its attributes impact the process of tax calculations.
- **Sales representatives**: This is an optional partner function. However, if relevant, attributes of sales representative accounts have an impact on commission calculations.

The details just mentioned should give you a general idea of the impact of different partner functions. These partner functions play an especially important role in special types of sales transactions such as intercompany sales, export sales, or third-party shipments. The second important aspect of the billing process is customer pricing data.

Customer Pricing Data

In Section 1.4.1, Sales, of Chapter 1, we looked at the pricing parameters maintained in customer master data. You may want to read that section if you haven't already. We won't repeat the information presented in that chapter here.

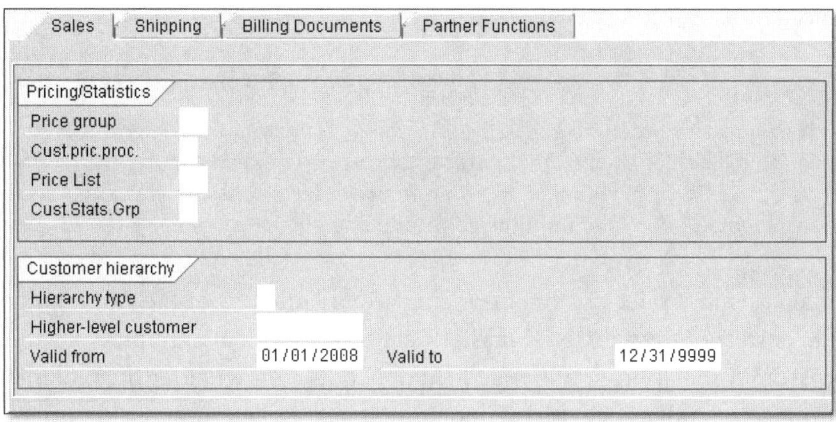

Figure 3.1 Customer Pricing Data

For a quick reference, Figure 3.1 is reproduced from Chapter 1 to show pricing attributes available for customer master data. The values maintained in the Price Group, Price List, and Customer Pricing Procedure fields influence pricing calculation in customer billing. Also, keep in mind that these values are taken from the sold-to party account associated with the sales transaction. Next, let's look at the relevant information in the material master data.

Material Master Data

The material master in the SAP system contains an extremely detailed and comprehensive set of master data and attributes that are relevant for a range of business processes such as sales, procurement, production, maintenance, storage, accounting, and costing. We've seen how customer master data is maintained at three levels: general data, company code data, and sales data. Similarly, material master data is maintained on multiple levels such as general data, sales organization, purchasing organization, plant, and storage location. At each level, the material master contains information relevant for the corresponding business processes. For example, data for sales processing is maintained for each sales organization, whereas data for production and costing is maintained at the plant level.

In this section, we'll primarily focus on two groups of material attributes: the attributes that are relevant for pricing calculation and the attributes that are relevant for GL account determination. Figure 3.2 shows two data tabs of material master maintenance (Transaction MM02).

> **Note**
>
> Material costs in a sales order are generally obtained directly from the material master. However, in the billing documents, the source of pricing can be different depending on the business transaction. For example, in a third-party order processing, material costs in billing document are obtained from the corresponding purchase order.

The material costs in a sales document pricing are obtained from the Accounting 1 tab of the corresponding material master data. Pricing calculation picks up the material cost from the appropriate price field depending on whether the material Price Control is S (standard price) or V (moving average price). Another important field is the Price Unit field, which specifies whether the price maintained in the material master is for 1 unit, 10 units, 100 units, and so on. For relatively simple business models, you can maintain these prices manually, or you can use the elaborate and complex functionality of product costing to automatically calculate cost estimates and update the costs in the material master.

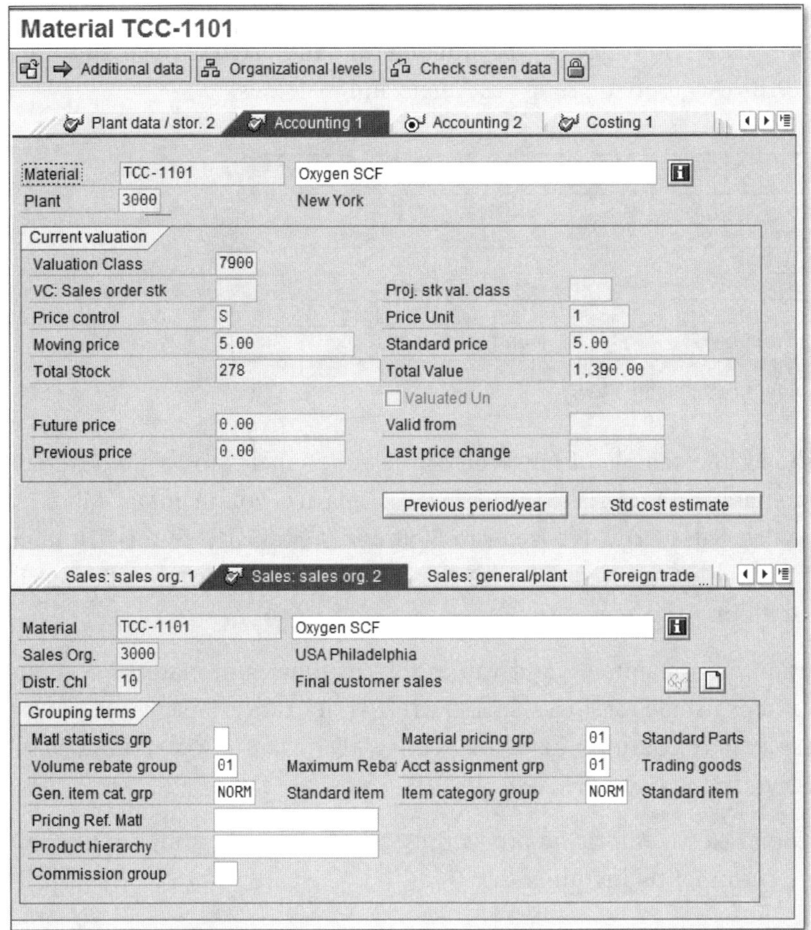

Figure 3.2 Material Master Data

The Sales: Sales Org 2 tab of the material master contains few fields that are relevant for sales pricing. You can use the Material Pricing Grp field to group materials for sales pricing. Alternatively, you can maintain Pricing Ref Material so that pricing components relevant for the reference material are also applied to this material. The Account Assignment Group field is discussed in the next section.

Account Assignment Groups (AAG)

We'll discuss GL account determination in Section 3.3.1, GL Account Determination, later in this chapter. You can use different criteria for GL account determination such as sales organization, chart of accounts, or document type. However, the two most frequently used criteria for GL account determination are the Customer AAG and the Material AAG used to group customers and materials.

AcctAssgGr	Description
01	Direct
02	Distributors
03	Resellers
04	OEM

Customer AAG

AcctAssgGr	Description
10	Products
20	Maintenance
30	Consulting
40	Training
50	Outsourcing

Material AAG

Figure 3.3 Account Assignment Groups

Figure 3.3 shows an example of how you can use these fields to group different types of customers and materials. In the material master, you maintain Material AAG on the Sales: Sales Org 2 tab (refer to Figure 3.2). Similarly, in the customer master, you maintain Customer AAG on the Billing Documents tab (Chapter 1, Section 1.4.3, Billing Documents).

In configuration, you maintain valid values for customer and material account assignment groups using SAP IMG • SALES AND DISTRIBUTION • BASIC FUNCTIONS • ACCOUNT ASSIGNMENT/COSTING • REVENUE ACCOUNT DETERMINATION • CHECK MASTER DATA RELEVANT FOR ACCOUNT ASSIGNMENT.

The next section deals with pricing procedures, which is another important component of the customer billing process.

3.1.3 Pricing Procedures

A *pricing procedure* provides a framework for calculating pricing components of a sales document. We'll only focus on its functionality pertaining to the integration between billing documents and corresponding accounting documents. However, you should note that pricing procedures in the SAP system provide a highly versatile framework to meet any complex pricing requirements.

You configure pricing procedure using SAP IMG • SALES AND DISTRIBUTION • BASIC FUNCTIONS • PRICING • PRICING CONTROL • DEFINE AND ASSIGN PRICING PROCEDURES. Figure 3.4 shows an example of a pricing procedure configuration.

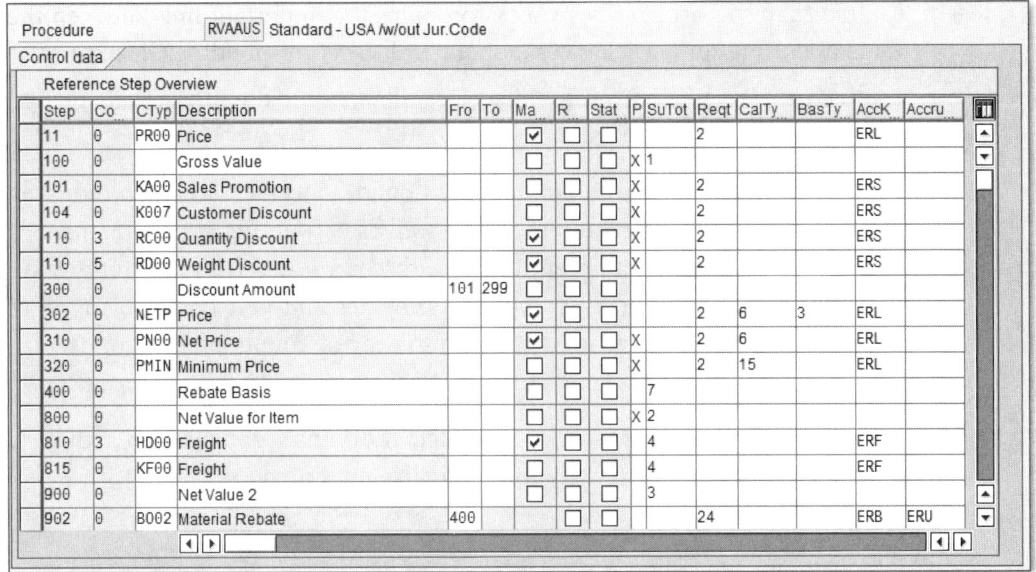

Procedure RVAAUS Standard - USA /w/out Jur.Code

Control data

Reference Step Overview

Step	Co	CTyp	Description	Fro	To	Ma	R	Stat	P	SuTot	Reqt	CalTy	BasTy	AccK	Accru
11	0	PR00	Price			[x]	[ ]	[ ]			2			ERL	
100	0		Gross Value			[ ]	[ ]	[ ]	X	1					
101	0	KA00	Sales Promotion			[ ]	[ ]	[ ]	X		2			ERS	
104	0	K007	Customer Discount			[ ]	[ ]	[ ]	X		2			ERS	
110	3	RC00	Quantity Discount			[x]	[ ]	[ ]	X		2			ERS	
110	5	RD00	Weight Discount			[x]	[ ]	[ ]	X		2			ERS	
300	0		Discount Amount	101	299	[ ]	[ ]	[ ]							
302	0	NETP	Price			[x]	[ ]	[ ]			2	6	3	ERL	
310	0	PN00	Net Price			[x]	[ ]	[ ]	X		2	6		ERL	
320	0	PMIN	Minimum Price			[ ]	[ ]	[ ]	X		2	15		ERL	
400	0		Rebate Basis			[ ]	[ ]	[ ]		7					
800	0		Net Value for Item			[ ]	[ ]	[ ]	X	2					
810	3	HD00	Freight			[x]	[ ]	[ ]		4				ERF	
815	0	KF00	Freight			[ ]	[ ]	[ ]		4				ERF	
900	0		Net Value 2			[ ]	[ ]	[ ]		3					
902	0	B002	Material Rebate	400			[ ]	[ ]			24			ERB	ERU

Figure 3.4 Pricing Procedure Configuration

The following is a very high level overview of pricing procedure configuration:

- You can configure elaborate rules that determine the pricing procedure for a sales transaction. These rules help you determine a pricing procedure based on criteria such as sales organization, distribution channel, and sales document type.
- The figure shows an example of a pricing procedure that consists of different pricing components such as base price, different types of discounts and promotions, freight charges, and rebate amounts.
- As shown in the figure, a pricing procedure provides a spreadsheet-like framework where each line represents a different pricing component such as product price, discounts, freight charges, and rebates.
- This framework allows one pricing component to make a cross-reference to another pricing component. For example, you can configure so that the rebate is calculated as a percentage of the net price.
- A condition type (Ctyp) associated with each line specifies the underlying criteria for calculation. For example, a customer discount may be calculated using the customer number, customer group, customer hierarchy, or any other criteria.

- A three-character account key (AccK) provides the important link between the value calculated for a pricing component and the corresponding GL account.
- The accrual (Accr) field is useful to specify the account key for accruals such as rebate accruals or freight accruals.

In Figure 3.4, notice how combinations of a condition type and an account key are used to satisfy pricing requirements as well as accounting requirements. For example, pricing lines for different types of discounts and sales promotions are assigned different condition types but the same account key. Using this type of configuration, you can calculate different types of discounts based on different criteria and still post to the same GL account.

In the next several sections, we'll go through additional configuration activities, starting with an important activity for configuring billing types.

3.2 Billing Types

It's important to understand that in the SAP system, the concept of *billing type* refers to different types of customer documents. For example, customer billing, pro forma invoice, cash sale, rebate settlement, and intercompany billing are all defined as billing types in the SAP system. In this section, we'll discuss the extremely important functionality of configuration and derivation of billing types.

3.2.1 Billing Type Configuration

Configuration of a billing type is one of the most important activities for the billing process. The SAP system provides preconfigured billing types that can be used as is for many business scenarios. You access billing type configuration using SAP IMG • Sales and Distribution • Billing • Billing Documents • Define Billing Types (Transaction VOFA).

Figure 3.5 shows the upper part of the billing type configuration screen. The example shown is for billing type F2 (Invoice), which is the default billing type assigned to standard sales order type ZOR. Following are the details of the configuration fields relevant for this chapter.

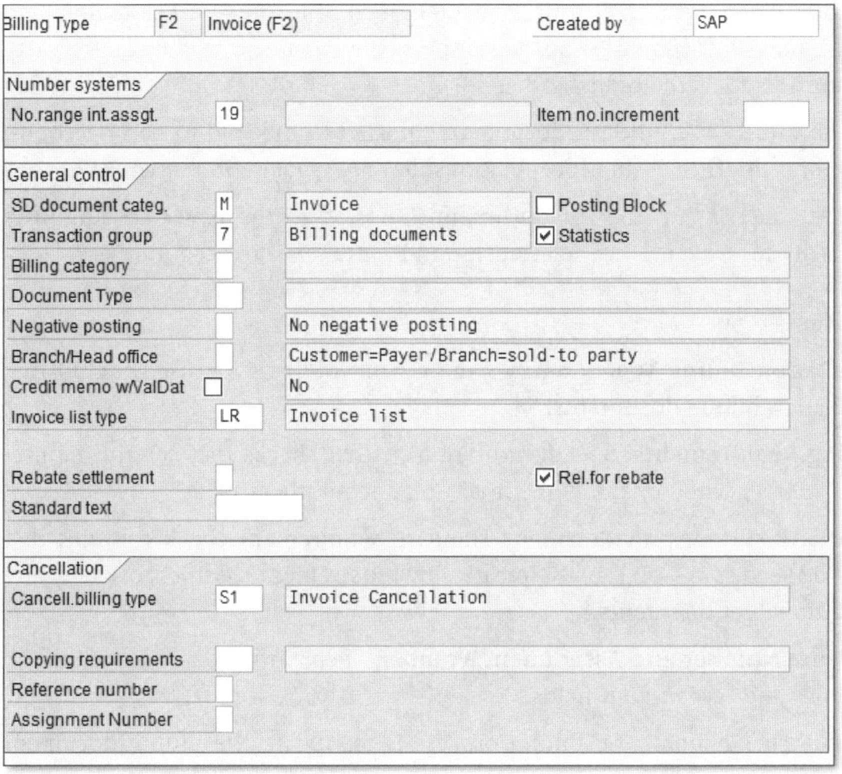

Billing Type	F2	Invoice (F2)	Created by SAP

Number systems

No.range int.assgt.	19		Item no.increment

General control

SD document categ.	M	Invoice	☐ Posting Block
Transaction group	7	Billing documents	☑ Statistics
Billing category			
Document Type			
Negative posting		No negative posting	
Branch/Head office		Customer=Payer/Branch=sold-to party	
Credit memo w/ValDat	☐	No	
Invoice list type	LR	Invoice list	
Rebate settlement			☑ Rel.for rebate
Standard text			

Cancellation

Cancell.billing type	S1	Invoice Cancellation
Copying requirements		
Reference number		
Assignment Number		

Figure 3.5 Billing Type Configuration – I

General Control

- **Number Range Assignment**: Specifies the number range used for generating the billing document number.
    - In some countries, legal requirements dictate the numbering of customer billing documents. Check SAP Notes for applicable solutions.

Tip

You can assign the FI document type in the billing type configuration. If this assignment is left blank, the system uses RV as the default FI document type for all types of billing documents.

- **Branch Office/Head Office**: If payer and sold-to party are different, the value in the Branch Office/Head Office field specifies the customer account to which the accounting document should be posted.

  - If the value is initial, regardless of the branch office/head office maintained in FI, the AR document is posted to the payer account, and the sold-to party is considered as the branch office.
  - If the value is "A," the AR document is posted to the sold-to party account. The branch office/head office relationship in FI is taken into account.
  - If the value is "B," the AR document is posted to the payer account. The branch office/head office relationship in FI is taken into account.

Cancellation

- **Cancellation Billing Type**: Specifies the default billing type used for posting cancellation billing documents.
- **Copying Requirements**: Specifies the routine that checks that certain requirements are met when one document is copied to another.
  - The SAP system provides many standard requirement check routines that can be used as is. You can also create new requirement routines to satisfy any additional requirements.
- **Reference Number and Assignment Number**: Specify the details copied to the Reference and Assignment fields.
  - Default behavior of the billing process is to update the billing document number in the reference number and leave the assignment number field empty.
  - You can use any of the values listed in Table 3.2 to override the default update to Reference and Assignment fields.

Use value ...	... to update the following to reference and assignment field
A	Purchase order number
B	Sales order number
C	Delivery number
D	External delivery number
E	Actual billing document number
F	External delivery number if available, otherwise, delivery number

Table 3.2 Reference and Assignment Fields

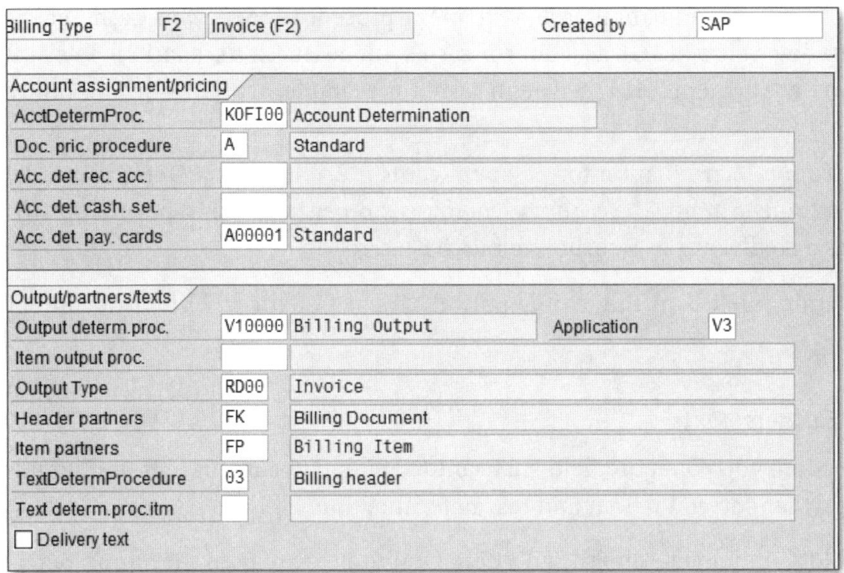

Figure 3.6 Billing Type Configuration – II

Continuing with the discussion of billing type configuration, Figure 3.6 shows the lower part of the billing type configuration screen. This part contains important configuration fields for account assignment and output controls.

Account Assignment/Pricing

This section contains fields for GL account assignments. Later in this chapter, we'll discuss these account determination procedures in more detail.

- The document pricing procedure (Doc. Pric. Procedure) determines the pricing of the document type. We discussed this procedure in Section 3.1.3, Pricing Procedures.
- The account determination procedure (AcctDetermProc.) is used to determine GL accounts for revenues, freight, taxes, and other components of document pricing.
- The account determination reconciliation account procedure (Acc. Det. Rec. Acc.) is used to override the default customer reconciliation account used.
    - The default customer reconciliation account is the account specified in the customer master data in company code data view.

- The account determination cash settlement procedure (Acc. Det. Cash Set.) is used to determine the GL account for cash settlement. This scenario is relevant if customer payments are received in cash, for example, at retail stores or utility companies.
- The account determination for payment cards procedure (Acc. Det. Pay. Cards) is used to determine GL accounts when a customer pays using payment cards such as a credit card or a corporate purchase card.

The remaining fields on this configuration screen pertain to billing document output.

Output/Partners/Texts

In this section, you configure fields relevant for billing document output determination, partner determination, and text determination.

- The fields Output Determ Proc and Item Output Proc are used for output determination for the billing document header and billing document items.
  - Using output determination, you can determine whether a customer billing document output is a printout, a fax, a PDF file, an electronic output, or a combination of those.
  - You can also specify the recipient of the billing output as bill-to party, ship-to party, payer, or any combination of those. We discussed customer partner functions in Chapter 1, Customer Master Data.
  - You configure output determination procedures in the configuration area via SAP IMG • Sales and Distribution • Basic Functions • Output control • Output determination • Output determination using the condition technique • Maintain output determination for Billing Documents.
- The fields Header Partners and Item Partners are used for partner determination for billing document header and billing document items.
  - Using partner determination, you can make sure that necessary partner functions such as bill-to party, ship-to party, payer, sold-to party, and sales representative are associated with billing documents.
  - You configure partner determination procedures in the configuration area via SAP IMG • Sales and Distribution • Basic Functions • Partner Determination • Setup Partner Determination.

Tip

The functionality of partner determination can be helpful, for example, to make sure that billing documents are always entered with the sales representative and sales manager. Subsequently, this information can be used to analyze sales, collection, and commission numbers for sales reps and sales managers.

- The fields Text Determ. Procedure and Text Determ Proc Item are used for text determination for billing document header and billing document items.
  - The text determination procedures help you ensure that consistent text comments and notes are entered and maintained for billing documents.
  - Examples of such comments include product-specific sales notes, delivery-specific notes, and any other notes pertaining to that invoice. For AR, this information can be useful in dispute settlement and collection processes.
  - You configure text determination in the configuration area via SAP IMG • Sales and Distribution • Basic Functions • Text Control.

As is evident, numerous parameters in billing type configuration control and influence different aspects of the customer billing process. As discussed, many of these functionalities have direct and tangible benefits for AR processes such as collections and cash application. The SAP system provides many preconfigured billing types that can be used as is. Table 3.3 provides a list of some commonly used billing types.

Billing Type	Usage
F1, F2	Customer billing
IV	Intercompany billing
L2	Debit memo
G2	Credit memo
F5	Pro forma invoice for order
F6	Pro forma invoice for delivery

Table 3.3 Billing Types

In the next section, we'll look at billing type parameters configured for sales document types.

3.2.2 Billing Type Determination

Billing type determination depends on the configuration parameters of sales document types and sales document items. First let's look at the configuration of sales document types. As is the case with billing types, sales document types in the SAP system correspond to different types of customer documents and not just sales orders. For example in the SAP system, sales document types represent customer orders, inquiries, quotations, and contracts, as well as customer agreements. You carry out sales order type configuration using SAP IMG • SALES AND DISTRIBUTION • SALES • SALES DOCUMENTS • SALES DOCUMENT HEADER • DEFINE SALES DOCUMENT TYPES (Transaction VOV8).

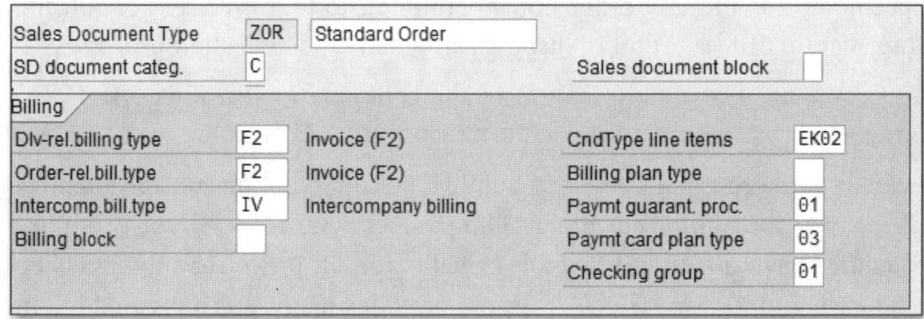

Figure 3.7 Sales Document Type

Figure 3.7 shows a partial screen of the sales document type configuration. Specifically, the figure shows billing-relevant parameters for sales document type ZOR (standard order).

You can configure default billing types for each of the following scenarios:

- Order-related billing type (Order-Rel. Bill type) is proposed for billing scenarios that aren't relevant for deliveries, for example, professional services such as consulting, legal, or maintenance work.
- Delivery-related billing type (Dlv-Rel. Bill Type) is proposed for billing scenarios that are relevant for deliveries, for example, standard orders for delivery of products or maintenance of spare parts.
- Intercompany billing type (Inter-Comp. Bill Type) is proposed for intercompany billing transactions.

- Billing Block provides you with an ability to block a customer invoice from being processed.
  - You may want to evaluate whether your business processes require billing block for a sales order type because it will block all order items from billing. Instead, a common practice is to specify billing blocks for sales document items, which we'll discuss in Section 3.2.3, Billing Type Reference.
- Billing Plan Type specifies the billing plan for the billing document. We'll discuss billing plans in the next chapter.
- Payment Card Plan Type and Checking Group are relevant for billing processes in which the customer has paid using payment cards. These parameters control the settlement process and authorization check process for payment cards.

As is evident from the preceding discussion, configuration parameters of the sales document type provide the default billing types for different business scenarios. However, the actual determination of the billing type depends on the configuration of the sales document item categories.

3.2.3 Billing Type Relevance

Consider a typical business scenario where a customer places an order for the purchase of a machine and corresponding training service. In the sales order, these two components are created as separate order items with different pricing. These components have to be billed differently as well. Billing of the machine is due after it's delivered, whereas billing for training service doesn't include any physical delivery. It's the billing configuration parameters of sales document item types that determine how the billing is carried out.

You configure sales document item categories using SAP IMG • Sales and Distribution • Sales • Sales Documents • Sales Document Item • Define Item Categories (Transaction VOV8). Figure 3.8 shows billing-relevant configuration parameters for a commonly used item category TAN (standard item).

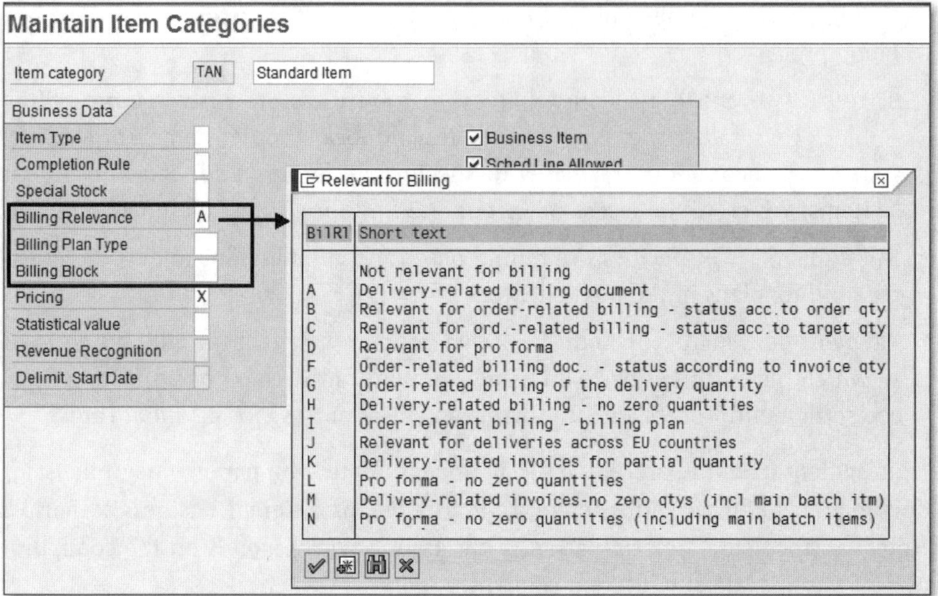

Figure 3.8 Billing Relevance

- We already discussed the use of Billing Block and the Billing Plan Types fields previously. The values defined here are applicable to sales document items instead of the whole document.
  - As you'll see later in this chapter, all eligible customer invoices are automatically proposed and processed during a billing due list process. Even though you have an opportunity to intervene, manual identification of documents is impractical for large processing volume.
  - Instead, you can use the default billing block for relevant sales document types, such as credit returns. This will ensure that all customer credit documents will be blocked from automatic processing until someone verifies the returns and manually removes the billing block.
- However, the Billing Relevance field of a document item category is one of the most important configuration parameters for the billing process.
  - As shown in the figure, the value of the Billing Relevance field determines whether a document item is relevant for billing. If it is, Billing Relevance determines whether it's a pro-forma invoice, order-relevant billing, delivery-relevant billing, or any other type.

The SAP system provides a very large number of preconfigured document item categories. Table 3.4 lists examples of item categories and corresponding billing relevance.

Item Category	Billing Relevance
AFTX – Text item	<initial> – Not relevant for billing
AGE – Service quotation	<initial> – Not relevant for billing
TAN – Standard item	A – Delivery-related billing
TAM – Assembly item	A – Delivery-related billing
BVN – Cash sales item	B – Order-related billing (Order Qty)
TAD – Service item	B – Order-related billing (Order Qty)
TADC – Configurable service item	B – Order-related billing (Order Qty)
TAS – Third-party item	F – Order-related billing (Invoice Qty)
NLC – Interco. stock transport item	D – Relevant for pro forma billing
RLN – Returns order	D – Relevant for pro forma billing

Table 3.4 Item Categories

Note

From a technical and procedural viewpoint, these configuration activities are under the purview of SAP logistics resources. However, it's important for the finance group to work closely with them to ensure that configuration done for sales and billing processes meet their requirements as well.

In the next chapter, we'll revisit the discussion of billing relevance when we discuss billing plans. For now, let's look at other configuration activities.

3.3 Other Configuration

Other configuration activities relevant for the billing process include the GL account determination, cost center assignments, and dunning area assignments. In this section, we'll discuss these configuration activities in detail. However, before continuing further, you may want to familiarize yourself with the pricing procedure configuration (Section 3.1.3, Pricing Procedures) if you haven't already.

3.3.1 GL Account Determination

As you'll see later in this chapter, when a customer billing document is processed, it automatically generates an accounting document. The account determination configuration ensures that all amounts in a billing document post to the correct GL accounts. The most important account determination transaction is the revenue account determination.

Revenue Account Determination

Even though the configuration area may indicate otherwise, this configuration activity is used to configure not only revenue accounts but also all other GL accounts such as discounts, freight, rebates, or taxes. You configure the revenue account determination using SAP IMG • SALES AND DISTRIBUTION • BASIC FUNCTIONS • ACCOUNT ASSIGNMENT/COSTING • REVENUE ACCOUNT DETERMINATION • ASSIGN G/L ACCOUNTS (Transaction VKO8).

Assign G/L Accounts

Table	Description
1	Cust.Grp/MaterialGrp/AcctKey
2	Cust.Grp/Account Key
3	Material Grp/Acct Key
4	General
5	Acct Key

Figure 3.9 Revenue Account Determination

Figure 3.9 shows the initial account determination screen. It shows the sequence in which the billing process carries out the GL account determination. The name of each evaluation option shows the criteria used for GL account determination in addition to the fixed criteria such as sales organization and chart of accounts. The evaluation options and determination sequence are completely customizable. In this example, first the process would try to determine the GL account based on the customer group, material group, and account key. Next the process would try to determine the GL account based on the customer group and account key. This continues until it reaches the last option. If the process can't determine a GL account through any evaluation options, you'll get an error message. Figure 3.10 shows the GL account assignment screen for the first evaluation option.

Cust.Grp/MaterialGrp/AcctKey

Cust.Grp/MaterialGrp/AcctKey

App	CndTy.	ChAc	SOrg.	AAG	AAG	ActKy	G/L Account	Provision acc.
V	KOFK	INT	3000	01	01	ERB	883000	
V	KOFK	INT	3000	01	01	ERF	809000	
V	KOFK	INT	3000	01	01	ERL	800000	
V	KOFK	INT	3000	01	01	ERS	888000	
V	KOFK	INT	3000	01	02	ERB	883000	
V	KOFK	INT	3000	01	02	ERF	809000	
V	KOFK	INT	3000	01	02	ERL	800000	
V	KOFK	INT	3000	01	02	ERS	888000	
V	KOFK	INT	3000	02	01	ERB	883000	
V	KOFK	INT	3000	02	01	ERF	809000	
V	KOFK	INT	3000	02	01	ERL	801000	
V	KOFK	INT	3000	02	01	ERS	888000	
V	KOFK	INT	3000	02	02	ERB	883000	
V	KOFK	INT	3000	02	02	ERF	809000	
V	KOFK	INT	3000	02	02	ERL	801000	
V	KOFK	INT	3000	02	02	ERS	888000	

Figure 3.10 Account Assignment Evaluation

We first discussed account keys in Section 3.1.3, Pricing Procedures. These account keys used for GL account determination are freely definable. You define and assign account keys using SAP IMG • SALES AND DISTRIBUTION • BASIC FUNCTIONS • ACCOUNT ASSIGNMENT/COSTING • REVENUE ACCOUNT DETERMINATION • DEFINE AND ASSIGN ACCOUNT KEYS. Table 3.5 lists some commonly used account keys.

Account Key	Description
ERB	Rebate sales deductions
ERF	Freight revenue
ERL	Sales revenue
ERS	Sales deductions
ERU	Rebate accruals

Table 3.5 Account Keys

Another account determination configuration activity is reconciliation account determination.

Reconciliation Account Determination

In Chapter 1, Customer Master Data, we discussed the concept of the reconciliation account. A customer reconciliation account is a control GL account that reflects real time, net receivables of all associated customer accounts. It's common practice to assign different reconciliation accounts to different customer groups to accurately differentiate and report domestic receivables and international receivables, or government receivables and other trade receivables. Because the reconciliation account is part of the specific company code data, you can assign reconciliation accounts in different company codes so that it most accurately reflects the customer relationship with that company code. However, this may be difficult to manage if a customer has different types of business relationships with different sales organizations of the same company code.

For such business scenarios, you can configure reconciliation account determination. For example, you can set the configuration so that all sales transactions processed for consulting services are always posted to the reconciliation account for consulting receivables, regardless of the reconciliation account assigned in the customer master.

The configuration technique for reconciliation account determination is similar to the one for revenue account determination. You carry out reconciliation account assignment using SAP IMG • Sales and Distribution • Basic Functions • Account Assignment/Costing • Reconciliation Account Determination • Assign G/L Accounts (Transaction OV64).

Note

The standard SAP system provides condition type KOAB and the following evaluation sequences for reconciliation account determination:

8 – Sales Organization/Distribution Channel

4 – Sales Organization

The next section discusses cash account determination.

Cash Account Determination

This configuration activity is relevant for processing customer cash payments. Cash transaction processing requires that the billing process post debit entries to a cash account instead of a customer receivable account. You carry out this configuration using SAP IMG • SALES AND DISTRIBUTION • BASIC FUNCTIONS • ACCOUNT ASSIGNMENT/COSTING • CASH ACCOUNT DETERMINATION • ASSIGN G/L ACCOUNTS (Transaction OV77).

Note

The standard SAP system provides condition type CASH and the following evaluation sequences for reconciliation account determination:

9 – Sales Organization/Distribution Channel/ Division

4 – Sales Organization

We won't discuss the configuration activity for revenue account determination in this section because this book contains a separate chapter (Chapter 9, Revenue Recognition) for revenue recognition processes. The three other types of GL account determination procedures are assigned to the billing type configuration (Section 3.2.1, Billing Type Configuration).

In addition to the GL account assignment, two other relevant configuration activities are cost center assignment and dunning area assignment. In the next section, we'll look at the cost center assignment process.

3.3.2 Cost Center Assignment

Some types of sales transactions such as customer returns, free samples, or promotional materials can be directly expensed. The GL account determination discussed in the previous section takes care of determining the expense account, whereas configuration activity in this section helps you determine the cost center for the expense posting.

Tip

This configuration activity requires the cost center assignment to be the same for a specific combination of characteristics. For more flexibility in cost center assignment, you may want to evaluate using FI substitution rules (Chapter 2, Accounts Receivable Transactions) or user enhancements.

You carry out this configuration activity using SAP IMG • SALES AND DISTRIBUTION • BASIC FUNCTIONS • ACCOUNT ASSIGNMENT/COSTING • ASSIGN COST CENTERS

(Transaction OVF3). Figure 3.11 shows the configuration screen for Cost Center Determination.

Cost Center Determination

Cost Center Determination

SOrg.	DChl	Dv	OrdRs	Description	Cost Ctr	Valid From
3000	10	00	105	Free of charge sample	3100	01/01/2008
3000	10	00	999	Marketing material f. Mailing	3200	01/01/2008
3000	10	6Z	105	Free of charge sample	3100	01/01/2008
3000	10	6Z	999	Marketing material f. Mailing	3200	01/01/2008
3000	10	A1	105	Free of charge sample	3100	01/01/2008
3000	10	A1	999	Marketing material f. Mailing	3200	01/01/2008
3000	10	Z2	105	Free of charge sample	3100	01/01/2008
3000	10	Z2	999	Marketing material f. Mailing	3200	01/01/2008
3000	6Z	00	105	Free of charge sample	3100	01/01/2008
3000	6Z	00	999	Marketing material f. Mailing	3200	01/01/2008
3000	6Z	6Z	105	Free of charge sample	3100	01/01/2008
3000	6Z	6Z	999	Marketing material f. Mailing	3200	01/01/2008
3000	6Z	A1	105	Free of charge sample	3100	01/01/2008
3000	6Z	A1	999	Marketing material f. Mailing	3200	01/01/2008
3000	6Z	Z2	105	Free of charge sample	3100	01/01/2008
3000	6Z	Z2	999	Marketing material f. Mailing	3200	01/01/2008

Figure 3.11 Cost Center Determination

As shown in the figure, cost center 3100 is assigned to all orders that have order reason "Free of Charge Sample," whereas cost center 3200 is assigned to all orders that have order reason "Marketing Material f. Mailing." In the example shown here, the cost center assignment differs only based on order reasons, regardless of the distribution channels or divisions of a sales organization. However, this configuration activity provides enough flexibility to set up very comprehensive cost center assignments that can differ based on combinations of sales organization, distribution channel, division, and order reason.

3.3.3 Dunning Area Assignment

Chapter 6, Dunning, contains an in-depth discussion of the dunning functionality in the SAP system. At that point, you'll be introduced to the concept of the dunning area. For the purpose of the current discussion, it's sufficient to understand a dunning area as an organizational unit within a company code responsible for customer dunning.

Tip

This configuration activity requires the dunning area assignment to be same for a specific combination of characteristics. For more flexibility in the dunning area assignment, you may want to evaluate using FI substitution rules (Chapter 2, Accounts Receivable Transaction) or user enhancements.

You carry out this configuration activity using SAP IMG • SALES AND DISTRIBUTION • BASIC FUNCTIONS • ACCOUNT ASSIGNMENT/COSTING • ASSIGN DUNNING AREAS. Figure 3.12 shows the configuration screen for the dunning area assignment.

Dunning Area

Sales Organizati...	Distr. Chl	Divisi	Dunning Area
3000	01	00	10
3000	01	01	10
3000	01	6Z	10
3000	01	Z2	10
3000	01	Z5	10
3000	10	00	20
3000	10	01	20
3000	10	03	20
3000	10	07	20
3000	10	08	20
3000	10	20	20
3000	10	30	20
3000	10	60	20
3000	10	61	20
3000	10	62	20

Figure 3.12 Dunning Area Assignment

As shown in the figure, dunning area 10 is assigned to all sales transactions in distribution channel 01, whereas dunning area 20 is assigned to sales transactions in distribution channel 10. In this example, dunning area assignment differs based on distribution channel, regardless of the divisions of a sales organization. However, this configuration activity provides enough flexibility to set up very comprehensive dunning area assignments that can differ based on combinations of sales organization, distribution channel, and division.

Lastly, let's see how the billing output is generated using the output determination procedure.

3.3.4 Output Determination

In Section 3.2.1, Billing Type Configuration, we briefly discussed billing output procedures that are used for the determination of billing output. Another relevant concept in understanding billing output is that of an output type. The output type specifies whether output is displayed on the screen, is printed, or is generated electronically. You configure output determination activities in the configuration area via SAP IMG • SALES AND DISTRIBUTION • BASIC FUNCTIONS • OUTPUT CONTROL • OUTPUT DETERMINATION • OUTPUT DETERMINATION USING THE CONDITION TECHNIQUE • MAINTAIN OUTPUT DETERMINATION FOR BILLING DOCUMENTS.

Note

Even though it's possible to generate all of the different output formats mentioned in this section, each output type requires additional technical setup and possibly even additional hardware. You should work with your SAP technical support to evaluate efforts required in implementing different types of output.

In a nutshell, for each billing type, you first assign the output determination procedure and an output type. Secondly, for each output type, you can assign a transmission medium and a partner function. Figure 3.13 shows an example of output control for output determination. Using this configuration, for example, you can specify that a billing document be sent as a printout to a payer and as an email to a bill-to party.

Output Control: Output By Partner Function

Out.	Med	Funct	Name	Name
FUCO	1	SH	Cert. of Origin US	Ship-to party
FUEP	1	SH	Export PackingList	Ship-to party
FUPI	1	BP	Pro forma Invoice US	Bill-to party
FUSD	1	SH	Shipper's ExportDec	Ship-to party
FUSI	1	SH	Shippers Let of Inst	Ship-to party
MAIL	7	ZP	Mail	Mail Partner
RD00	1	BP	Invoice	Bill-to party
RD00	2	BP	Invoice	Bill-to party
RD00	6	BP	Invoice	Bill-to party
RD00	A	BP	Invoice	Bill-to party
RD01	1	BP	Single Invoice List	Bill-to party

Figure 3.13 Output Control

Transmission medium (Med) in Figure 3.13 represents the manner in which billing output is produced for a business partner. Table 3.6 lists transmission mediums available in the standard SAP system.

Transmission Medium	Use
1	Print output
2	Fax
4	Telex
5	External send
6	EDI
7	Simple Mail
8	Special function
9	Events (SAP Business Workflow)
A	Distribution (ALE)
T	Tasks (SAP Business Workflow)

Table 3.6 Transmission Mediums

This completes the discussion of different configuration aspects of a standard billing process. Now we're ready to delve into billing transactions.

3.4 Billing Transactions

In most companies, the AR group is responsible for processing customer billing. However, as discussed before, in the SAP system, billing transactions are part of the Sales and Distribution (SD) component. You'll find billing-related transactions under the menu area SAP MENU • LOGISTICS • SALES AND DISTRIBUTION • BILLING • BILLING DOCUMENT.

In this chapter, we'll focus on three most commonly used billing processes: processing billing documents, canceling billing documents, and releasing blocked billing documents. The next chapter will provide details on other billing transactions such as self-billing and retro-billing.

3.4.1 Processing Billing Documents

We've already discussed that billing documents may be generated based on deliveries, on proof of delivery (POD) status, or on sales orders. As you'll see in the next chapter, billing documents may be generated at a regular interval based on periodic billing plans or based on the completion of specific events. Other processes such as price adjustments, credit memos, and down payments also generate billing documents.

Of course, you can create one billing document at a time based on an individual order, delivery, or reference document. However, more commonly, you'll use a billing due list to generate billing documents.

Billing Due List

The billing due list (Transaction VF04) provides an integrated, interactive interface to review and process all billing documents that are due, regardless of their origin.

Figure 3.14 shows the selection screen of a billing due list process.

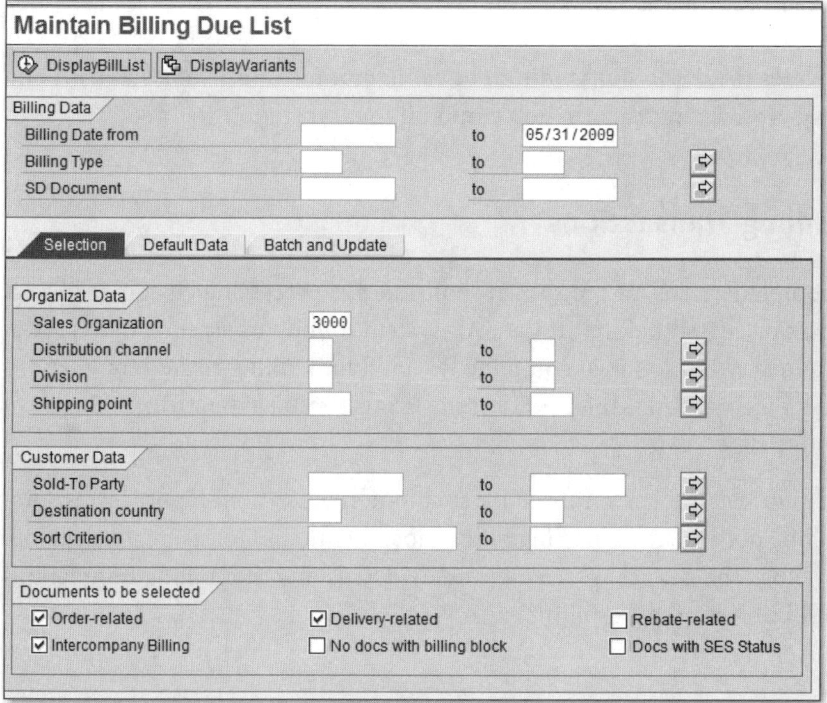

Figure 3.14 Billing Due List – Selection Screen

It contains usual selection criteria such as Billing Date, Billing Type, Sold-To Party, and Sales Organization. However, of particular importance are the selections under the Documents To Be Selected section. Table 3.7 provides the details of the different selection criteria.

Select the following indicator ...	... to include the following in the billing due list.
Order-Related	Billing documents based on sales orders, for example, billing documents for services.
Delivery-Related	Billing documents based on deliveries, for example, billing documents for product deliveries.
Rebate-Related	Credit documents for customer rebates. For more details on this comprehensive customer rebate processing functionality, refer to other SAP PRESS books focused on the SD component.
Intercompany Billing	Intercompany billing documents. These documents are discussed in Chapter 4.
No Docs with Billing Block	Only billing documents without billing block. You have two options to process billing documents with billing blocks. Either don't select this indicator in the billing due list, or use the specific transaction provided for releasing billing documents (Section 3.4.3, Blocked Billing Documents).
Docs with SES Status	Billing documents that aren't relevant for POD process plus the billing documents for which POD status is set as quantity confirmed. We'll discuss the POD process in the next chapter.

Table 3.7 Document Selection Indicators

The fields on the Default Data tab on the selection screen (refer to Figure 3.14) can be used to specify Billing Type, Billing Date, Date of Services Rendered, and the Pricing Date for billing documents. Date of Services Rendered is used for tax calculations in order-based billing. Pricing Date is used to influence billing documents to use pricing as of a specific date.

Specification of these values is optional. If these values aren't specified, the billing process uses built-in default logic to determine the appropriate values. For example, for delivery-based billing, Date of Services Rendered is the date of goods issue, or the delivery date is used as the pricing date.

Figure 3.15 shows an example of a billing list output. This screen lists all billing documents based on the criteria specified on the selection screen. You can customize this list output by selecting the menu path SETTINGS • LAYOUT • CURRENT.

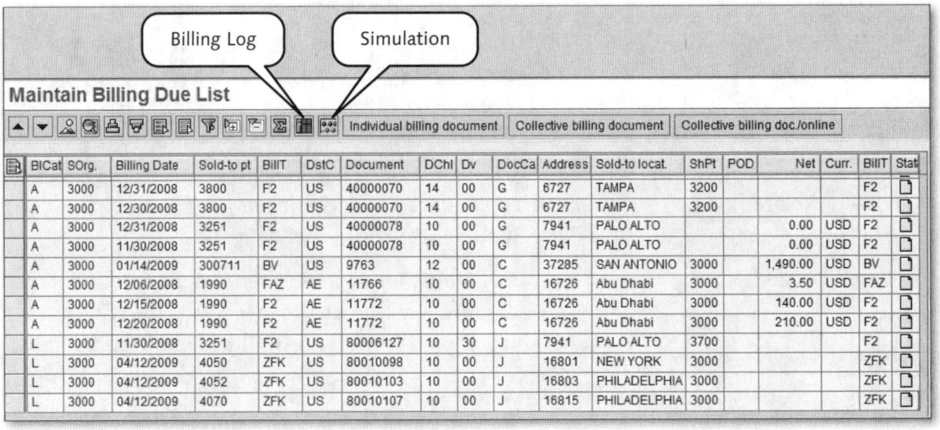

Billing Log

Simulation

Maintain Billing Due List

Individual billing document | Collective billing document | Collective billing doc./online

BlCat	SOrg.	Billing Date	Sold-to pt	BillT	DstC	Document	DChl	Dv	DocCa	Address	Sold-to locat.	ShPt	POD	Net	Curr.	BillT	Stat
A	3000	12/31/2008	3800	F2	US	40000070	14	00	G	6727	TAMPA	3200				F2	
A	3000	12/30/2008	3800	F2	US	40000070	14	00	G	6727	TAMPA	3200				F2	
A	3000	12/31/2008	3251	F2	US	40000078	10	00	G	7941	PALO ALTO			0.00	USD	F2	
A	3000	11/30/2008	3251	F2	US	40000078	10	00	G	7941	PALO ALTO			0.00	USD	F2	
A	3000	01/14/2009	300711	BV	US	9763	12	00	C	37285	SAN ANTONIO	3000		1,490.00	USD	BV	
A	3000	12/06/2008	1990	FAZ	AE	11766	10	00	C	16726	Abu Dhabi	3000		3.50	USD	FAZ	
A	3000	12/15/2008	1990	F2	AE	11772	10	00	C	16726	Abu Dhabi	3000		140.00	USD	F2	
A	3000	12/20/2008	1990	F2	AE	11772	10	00	C	16726	Abu Dhabi	3000		210.00	USD	F2	
L	3000	11/30/2008	3251	F2	US	80006127	10	30	J	7941	PALO ALTO	3700				F2	
L	3000	04/12/2009	4050	ZFK	US	80010098	10	00	J	16801	NEW YORK	3000				ZFK	
L	3000	04/12/2009	4052	ZFK	US	80010103	10	00	J	16803	PHILADELPHIA	3000				ZFK	
L	3000	04/12/2009	4070	ZFK	US	80010107	10	00	J	16815	PHILADELPHIA	3000				ZFK	

Figure 3.15 Billing Due List – Processing Screen

The process of creating billing documents is fairly straightforward:

1. Enter the selection criteria on the billing due list selection screen, and execute the transaction. You can use variants to save predefined selections to speed up this process. If you aren't familiar with variants, they are described in detail in Chapter 11, AR Reporting.
2. The transaction displays the billing due list in ALV format. The ALV format is a spreadsheet-like format that provides standard functionality of selecting, totaling, sorting, and filtering the list output. You select the billing documents that you want to process and select the processing option.
3. The billing due list provides two possible processing options. Depending on sales volume and billing frequency, a billing due list may include several orders and deliveries for each customer. The two options differ in how the billing document is generated from multiple sales documents.
   - If you choose the Individual Billing Document option, the process creates a separate billing document for every sales document.
   - If you choose the Collective Billing Document option, the process creates one billing document for every unique combination of invoice splitting criteria. You can process collective billing documents online or in the background.

Tip

The billing due list process (Transaction VF04) provides an interactive interface to process billing documents. On the other hand, Transaction VF06 provides more advanced options to schedule billing documents processing as a background job. For example, that transaction lets you specify options such as number of jobs, number of customers per job, and target computer servers.

4. For every billing document, the process generates billing output based on output determination, and posts the accounting document in Financial Accounting. Of course, if you've selected the Simulate option, the process carries out checks and validations but doesn't post any accounting entries and doesn't generate billing outputs.
5. At the end, the billing process generates a log detailing success or failure of the process, along with relevant details. You can view the log by selecting the Billing Log option. It's very important to review the log at the end of every billing process to identify any problems.

One point that requires further explanation from this process is that of invoice splitting.

Invoice Splitting

For a collective invoice, the billing process generates one billing document for multiple sales documents based on unique invoice splitting criteria. At the very minimum, the billing process generates separate billing document for each unique combination of customer number, billing type, and sales organization. Also, the billing process generates a separate document if any of the document header fields (e.g., payment terms) are different in the sales documents.

You can configure the system so that a separate billing document is generated based on other specific criteria. However, this is another technical area that is under the purview of SAP SD support, so here we'll only discuss it briefly. You'll need to work with your SAP SD support to implement this functionality. The invoice split functionality makes use of Copy Controls and Requirements routines.

- The Copy Controls routine let you specify information that is copied from one sales document to another, for example, creating a sales order with reference to another sales order, or creating a delivery document with reference to a sales order, or creating a billing document with reference to a sales order or a delivery document.

- The Requirements routine let you add code snippets where you can specify the conditions that are "required" to be fulfilled for a certain activity or step to occur.

If you specify additional criteria to ensure invoice splitting, you should make sure that it works as expected for intercompany billing, retroactive billing, use of customer hierarchy, or any other scenario that is applicable to your business. Several SAP notes address the issue of invoice splitting in different scenarios. SAP Note 0000011162 provides a good overview of possible criteria that influence invoice splitting.

Before moving on to next transaction, let's briefly look at the one-off creation of a customer billing document.

Create a Billing Document

To create an individual billing document based on one or more sales documents, you can use Create Billing Document (Transaction VF01). Figure 3.16 shows the initial screen of this transaction.

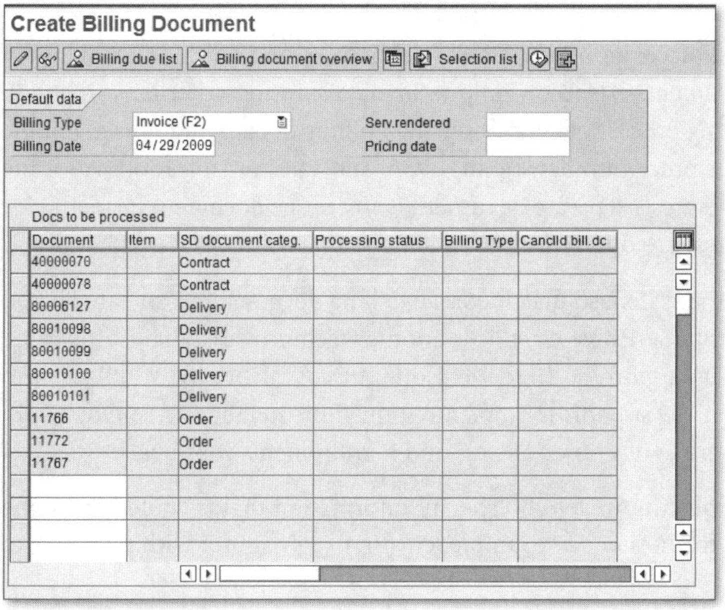

Create Billing Document

Billing due list | Billing document overview | Selection list

Default data

Billing Type: Invoice (F2) | Serv.rendered:

Billing Date: 04/29/2009 | Pricing date:

Docs to be processed

Document	Item	SD document categ.	Processing status	Billing Type	Cancld bill.dc
40000070		Contract			
40000078		Contract			
80006127		Delivery			
80010098		Delivery			
80010099		Delivery			
80010100		Delivery			
80010101		Delivery			
11766		Order			
11772		Order			
11767		Order			

Figure 3.16 Create Billing Document

The data shown in this figure is for illustration purpose only, which is why it uses the same billing type for contracts, orders, and deliveries. More likely, you'll use different types of billing documents for different sales documents. When you execute or save the transaction, it generates billing documents, posts accounting entries, and generates billing outputs.

As you may have already noticed, you can simulate the overview of billing documents or branch to the billing due list screen from this transaction. To display the log of billing creation, you can select the menu path EDIT • LOG.

In the next section, we'll look at the cancellation of billing documents.

3.4.2 Cancellation of Billing Documents

You may have to cancel billing documents due to any number of reasons such as incorrect amounts, incorrect accounts, incorrect timing with respect to product delivery, or any other reason. You can use Cancel Billing Document (Transaction VF11) to cancel one or more billing documents. Figure 3.17 shows the main screen of the cancellation transaction.

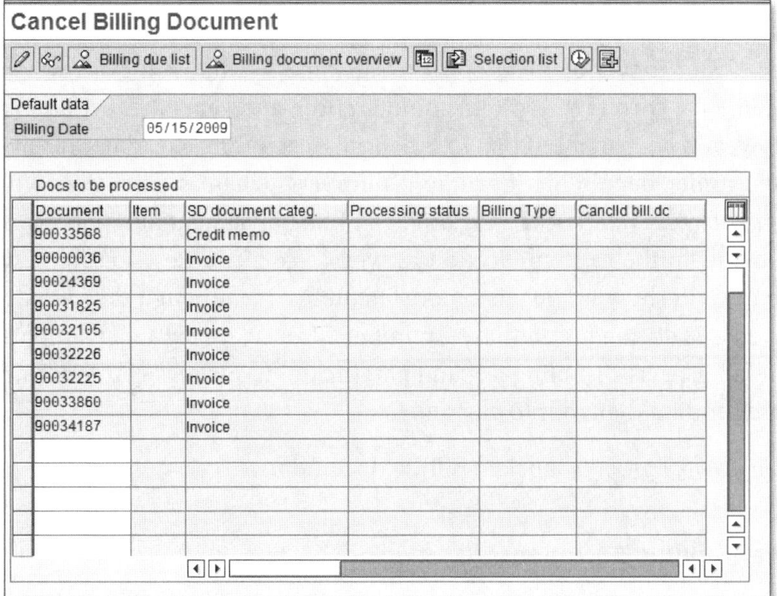

Figure 3.17 Cancel Billing Document

You may notice that the screen for canceling billing documents closely resembles the screen for creating individual documents. You simply enter billing documents that you want to cancel, and choose the Save option to cancel the billing documents. You have access to the same options as in the Create Billing Document transaction. You can branch to Billing Document Overview or Billing Due List from the cancellation screen. Also, you can display a detailed log using the menu path EDIT • LOG.

Tip

You can cancel individual line items of a billing document by using the Change Billing Document transaction (Transaction VF02). After displaying the billing document details, you can use the menu option EDIT • CANCEL ITEM to cancel individual items.

It's common to cancel billing documents for external, customer-relevant reasons such as an incorrect billing amount. However, you should carefully consider the overall impact before canceling billing documents to correct any internal errors. One of the main reasons is that the tight integration between the billing process and Financial Accounting in the SAP system poses some challenges that you may not have encountered in other systems.

Consider the scenario where you realize that billing documents are posted to incorrect GL accounts after they are already sent to customers. Sure, you can reverse the billing documents, correct the system configuration, and generate new billing documents. However, keep in mind that in Financial Accounting, customer receivables are posted under new billing document numbers, whereas customers will send their payments with reference to the original billing document numbers! This can create problems in the cash application as well as collections. Also, the new billing documents will show up on customer statements even though they would not have received any documents with new numbers. Hence, it's extremely important to validate all aspects of billing documents, including Financial Accounting postings, before sending them out to customers.

Finally, let's see how to process blocked billing documents.

3.4.3 Blocked Billing Documents

The transaction discussed in this section is used to process billing documents that could not be completely processed due to incomplete or incorrect data or due to configuration settings. In the SAP system, the process of printing customer billing documents is decoupled from the process of generating accounting entries. So it's not only possible but also fairly common to be able to print customer billing documents even if there were problems in generating corresponding accounting entries. Using the Blocked Billing Documents transaction (Transaction VFX3), you can process such blocked billing documents.

Tip

Preferably, you should run this transaction after every billing run to identify and correct any errors. At the very least, you should include this transaction in month-end activities to process any blocked billing documents.

The transaction offers standard selection criteria such as sales organization, billing type, document number, customer or payer number, creation date, and user. You can also generate an output list of billing documents that are blocked due to specific types of errors. Figure 3.18 shows a sample output of this transaction.

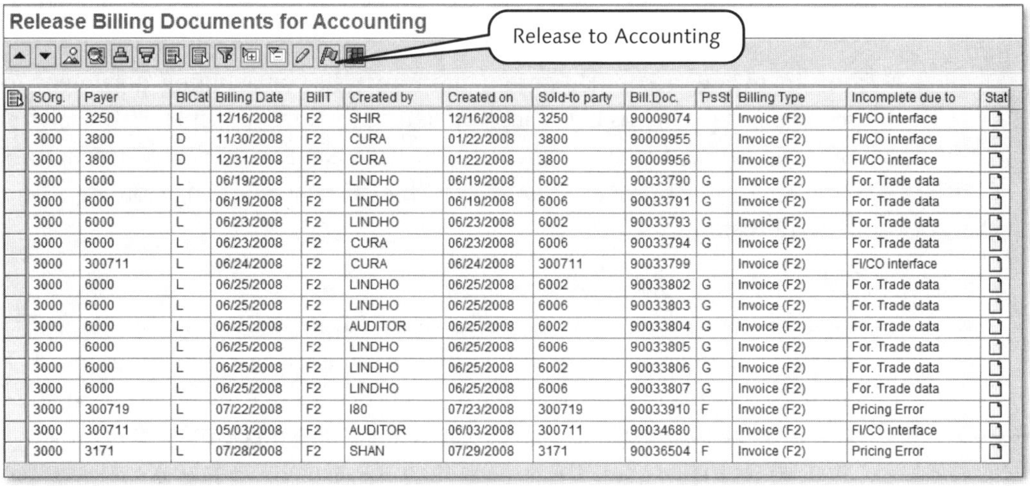

Release Billing Documents for Accounting

Release to Accounting

SOrg.	Payer	BlCat	Billing Date	BillT	Created by	Created on	Sold-to party	Bill.Doc.	PsSt	Billing Type	Incomplete due to	Stat
3000	3250	L	12/16/2008	F2	SHIR	12/16/2008	3250	90009074		Invoice (F2)	FI/CO interface	
3000	3800	D	11/30/2008	F2	CURA	01/22/2008	3800	90009955		Invoice (F2)	FI/CO interface	
3000	3800	D	12/31/2008	F2	CURA	01/22/2008	3800	90009956		Invoice (F2)	FI/CO interface	
3000	6000	L	06/19/2008	F2	LINDHO	06/19/2008	6002	90033790	G	Invoice (F2)	For. Trade data	
3000	6000	L	06/19/2008	F2	LINDHO	06/19/2008	6006	90033791	G	Invoice (F2)	For. Trade data	
3000	6000	L	06/23/2008	F2	LINDHO	06/23/2008	6002	90033793	G	Invoice (F2)	For. Trade data	
3000	6000	L	06/23/2008	F2	CURA	06/23/2008	6006	90033794	G	Invoice (F2)	For. Trade data	
3000	300711	L	06/24/2008	F2	CURA	06/24/2008	300711	90033799		Invoice (F2)	FI/CO interface	
3000	6000	L	06/25/2008	F2	LINDHO	06/25/2008	6002	90033802	G	Invoice (F2)	For. Trade data	
3000	6000	L	06/25/2008	F2	LINDHO	06/25/2008	6006	90033803	G	Invoice (F2)	For. Trade data	
3000	6000	L	06/25/2008	F2	AUDITOR	06/25/2008	6002	90033804	G	Invoice (F2)	For. Trade data	
3000	6000	L	06/25/2008	F2	LINDHO	06/25/2008	6006	90033805	G	Invoice (F2)	For. Trade data	
3000	6000	L	06/25/2008	F2	LINDHO	06/25/2008	6002	90033806	G	Invoice (F2)	For. Trade data	
3000	6000	L	06/25/2008	F2	LINDHO	06/25/2008	6006	90033807	G	Invoice (F2)	For. Trade data	
3000	300719	L	07/22/2008	F2	I80	07/23/2008	300719	90033910	F	Invoice (F2)	Pricing Error	
3000	300711	L	05/03/2008	F2	AUDITOR	06/03/2008	300711	90034680		Invoice (F2)	FI/CO interface	
3000	3171	L	07/28/2008	F2	SHAN	07/29/2008	3171	90036504	F	Invoice (F2)	Pricing Error	

Figure 3.18 Blocked Billing Documents

The output list shows information pertaining to blocked or incomplete billing documents in a default ALV layout. You can modify this layout to add or remove other information fields by using standard ALV functionality. Of particular importance is the column Incomplete Due To, which provides the reason why accounting entries for a billing document were not posted. Following are some of the possible reasons that may be displayed in this column:

- **Accounting Block**
  - This error indicates that billing documents are blocked due to the accounting block set in the billing document type configuration (Section 3.2.1, Billing Type Configuration). Usually this type of billing block indicates an intentional, procedural reason to place billing documents on block, so you should follow appropriate procedure to ensure that it's acceptable to remove the billing block.
  - To remove this type of billing block, you can go to the maintenance transaction of a sales order, a delivery, or a contract and manually remove the billing block.
- **Error in FI/CO Interface**
  - This error can be a result of a range of issues. Some common issues are that the FI posting period may not be open, the GL accounts or cost centers may be blocked for posting, or the GL account determination process may fail to return a GL account for one of the pricing conditions.
  - You can review account determination analysis for a billing document to ascertain any problems in GL account determination. To display this analysis, select GOTO • HEADER • PRICING CONDITIONS HEADER • ENVIRONMENT • ACCOUNT DETERMINATION ANALYSIS in the display or change billing document transaction.
- **Pricing Error**
  - This error indicates a problem in the definition or calculation of the pricing procedure. The error can be in pricing agreements, pricing conditions, or a number of other master data that influence sales pricing. You can analyze pricing calculations using GOTO • HEADER • PRICING CONDITIONS HEADER or GOTO • ITEM • ITEM CONDITIONS, and then selecting the Analysis option at the bottom of the screen.
  - You can check Section 3.1.3, Pricing Procedures, for the configuration path of pricing procedure maintenance. You may also want to check other pricing configuration activities under SAP IMG • SALES AND DISTRIBUTION • BASIC FUNCTIONS • PRICING.

- **Foreign Trade Data**
  - This error means that at least some of the foreign trade data is missing in the corresponding billing document. Check the Foreign Trade/Customs tab in a billing document header and billing document items to validate and maintain missing foreign trade data.
  - As necessary, also validate Check Foreign Trade: Export Data and Foreign Trade: Import Data in the material master maintenance.
  - Also, check the incompleteness schema assignment of the relevant country and import/export transaction. You'll find this configuration activity under SAP IMG • SALES AND DISTRIBUTION • FOREIGN TRADE/CUSTOMS • CONTROL FOREIGN TRADE DATA IN MM AND SD DOCUMENTS • FOREIGN TRADE DATA IN MM AND SD DOCUMENTS.
- **Error in Authorization**
  - You may encounter this error if the user processing the billing due list doesn't have authorization access to one or more components of the accounting entries such as a company code, GL account, or cost center. Your SAP support team that is responsible for system security and authorization can assist you with resolving this error.

After you've identified and corrected the underlying reasons, you can use the Release to Accounting option in this transaction to release billing documents and post corresponding accounting entries. On the other hand, if you want to release a one-off billing document, you can do so by selecting Release to Accounting option in the Change Billing Document (VF02) transaction.

In the next section, we'll see how to view the sales document flow after billing documents are generated and accounting entries are posted.

3.4.4 Document Flow

Document flow provides a one-screen interface to view the entire order-to-cash flow for sales documents. This is an extremely useful functionality for AR personnel because it provides easy access to any document in an order-to-cash cycle. For example, collections personnel can use document flow to answer customer questions about past deliveries or whether order returns have been processed, and cash application personnel can use document flow to identify and verify customer documents for which to post customer payments.

Tip

A document flow screen will show different document types and corresponding document numbers. However, users will need appropriate display authorization to actually view the details of any specific sales document.

Figure 3.19 shows an example of a document flow associated with sales order 11805. As shown, a document flow can provide a one-point, comprehensive look at all relevant transactions, including sales orders, delivery documents, invoices, and even customer returns and associated documents.

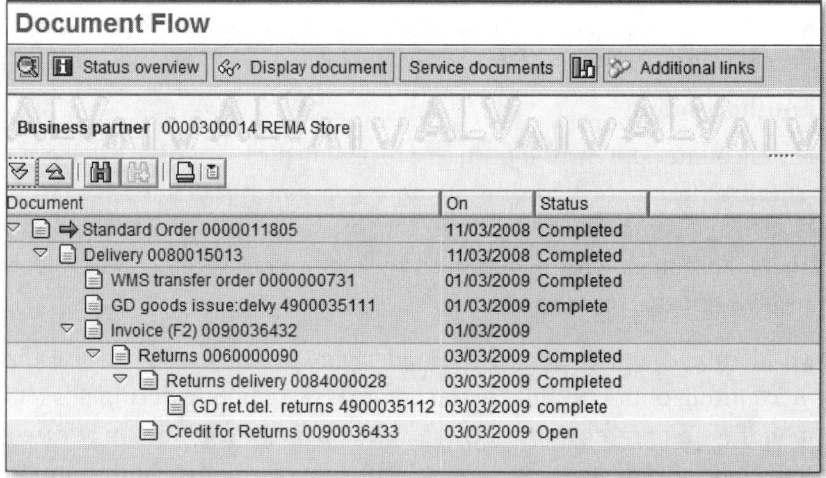
Document Flow

Status overview | Display document | Service documents | Additional links

Business partner 0000300014 REMA Store

Document	On	Status
Standard Order 0000011805	11/03/2008	Completed
Delivery 0080015013	11/03/2008	Completed
WMS transfer order 0000000731	01/03/2009	Completed
GD goods issue:delvy 4900035111	01/03/2009	complete
Invoice (F2) 0090036432	01/03/2009	
Returns 0060000090	03/03/2009	Completed
Returns delivery 0084000028	03/03/2009	Completed
GD ret.del. returns 4900035112	03/03/2009	complete
Credit for Returns 0090036433	03/03/2009	Open

Figure 3.19 Document Flow

You can display the document flow from any of its individual documents. However, you should keep in mind that if you display the document flow from the delivery document of one sales order item, it doesn't display the document flow for any other sales order items. You should use the top-most document in any order-to-cash cycle to view the document flow in its entirety. The following list provides the menu path to display document flow from different types of documents.

- **Sales contract**: In Display Sales Contract (VA43) transaction, select menu path Environment • Display Document flow.
- **Sales Order or Sales Contract**: In Display Sales Order (VA03) transaction, select menu path Environment • Display Document Flow.

- **Delivery Document**: In Display Delivery Document (VL03N) transaction, select menu path Environment • Document flow
- **Billing Document**: In Display Billing Document (VF03) transaction, select menu path Environment • Display Document Flow.
- **Accounting Document**: In Display Accounting Document (FB03) transaction, select menu path environment • Document Environment • Relationship browser.

This concludes our discussion of concepts and configuration of billing processes and commonly used billing transactions. The next section provides a quick transaction list reference.

3.4.5 Transaction List

Table 3.8 provides a list of business transactions discussed in this chapter.

Transaction	Usage
VF04	Process billing due list
VF06	Background processing of billing documents
VF01	Create billing document
VF02	Change billing document
VF03	Display billing document
VF11	Cancel billing document
VFX3	Blocked billing documents
VF31	Collective output from billing documents
XD02	Maintain customer master data
MM02	Maintain material master data
VA43	Display sales contract
VA03	Display sales order
VL03N	Display delivery document
FB03	Display accounting document

Table 3.8 Billing Processes – Transactions

In the next section, we'll look at technical objects available for billing processes.

3.5 Technical Reference

This section lists technical objects such as SAP Notes, authorization objects, and tables and structures relevant for billing processes. Considering the large number of technical objects available in the SAP system, this information should only be considered as a starting point for analysis.

3.5.1 SAP Notes

Table 3.9 is a list of SAP Notes relevant for billing processes.

SAP Note	Relevance
0000892646	Unable to cancel billing document after currency revaluation
0000400000	FAQ: Cancellation of billing documents
0001259505	FAQ: New cancellation procedure in SD
0000339928	New cancellation procedure cannot be deactivated
0000360602	Billing due list issues a blank list screen
0000399041	Create sales order with reference to billing document
0000305011	Create pro forma invoices for internal deliveries
0000445763	Pro forma invoice for intercompany billing
0000180756	Creation of billing document for the closed posting period
0000036353	Summarizing FI documents through AC interface
0001242755	Selection via multiple sales organizations
0000371675	Include pro forma invoices in billing due list
0000864944	Unable to edit/implement billing BAdIs
0000011162	Invoice split criteria in billing document
0000354222	Foreign trade data incompletion error for domestic business
0000145468	Missing check for closed posting period
0000033533	Billing release for sold-to party without accounting data
0000960611	FAQ: Output control in sales and distribution
0000960088	FAQ: Sending SD messages externally
0000454893	Sending sales document output as an email

Table 3.9 SAP Notes for Billing Transactions

SAP Note	Relevance
0000547570	Material cost (VPRS) determination in pricing
0000011916	Combining order and delivery in one billing document

Table 3.9 SAP Notes for Billing Transactions (Cont.)

In the next section, we'll look at authorization objects available for the billing functionality.

3.5.2 Authorization Objects

Table 3.10 lists some of the authorization objects to be considered for transactions discussed in this chapter.

Object	Description
F_BKPF_BED	Accounting Doc: Account Authorization for Customers
F_BKPF_BLA	Accounting Doc: Authorization for Document Types
F_BKPF_BUK	Accounting Doc: Authorization for Company Codes
F_BKPF_BUP	Accounting Doc: Authorization for Posting Periods
F_BKPF_KOA	Accounting Doc: Authorization for Account Types
V_KONH_VKO	Condition: Authorization for Sales Organizations
V_KONH_VKS	Condition: Authorization for Condition Types
V_VBAK_AAT	Sales Document: Authorization for Sales Document Types
V_VBAK_VKO	Sales Document: Authorization for Sales Areas
V_VBRK_FKA	Billing: Authorization for Billing Types
V_VBRK_VKO	Billing: Authorization for Sales Organizations
V_VBSK_STO	Billing: Authorization for Cancellation Collective Runs
F_FAGL_LDR	General Ledger: Authorization for Ledger
F_SKA1_BUK	GL Account: Authorization for Company Codes
F_SKA1_KTP	GL Account: Authorization for Chart of Accounts
F_IT_ALV	Line Item Display: Change and Save Layout

Table 3.10 Authorization Objects – Billing Transactions

The next section lists tables and structures.

3.5.3 Tables and Structures

Table 3.11 lists tables and structures relevant for processing billing transactions.

Table	Relevance
BKPF	Accounting document: header
BSEG	Accounting document: details
BSID	Secondary index for customer documents
BSAD	Secondary index for customer documents – cleared items
VBRK	Billing document: header data
VBRP	Billing document: item data
VBUK	Sales doc: Header status and administrative data
VBUP	Sales doc: Item status and administrative data
VBFA	Sales document flow
VBPA	Sales document: Partner
VBPAPO	Sales document: Item partners
KONV	Sales document conditions
EIKP	Foreign trade: Export/import header data
EIPO	Foreign trade: Export/import item data
VRKPA	SD index: Billing items by partner function
VRPMA	SD index: Billing items per material
VKDFS	SD index: Billing initiator

Table 3.11 Billing Transactions – Tables and Structures

Now we'll look at the objects and functionality available for enhancing and modifying billing processes.

3.6 Enhancements and Modifications

This section provides list of available BTEs, enhancements, BAdIs, and BAPIs relevant for billing functionality. These are used to enhance and modify the standard functionality available in the SAP system.

3.6.1 Business Transaction Events (BTE)

Using BTEs, you can attach additional function modules and custom logic to the standard SAP system. The list of BTEs available for AR transactions is too big to be included in this chapter, so Table 3.12 provides only a partial list of publish and subscribe (P/S) and process BTEs available for billing processes.

Type	BTE	Event/Process
P/S	00501009	Create billing document data
P/S	00501010	Save billing document data
P/S	00501011	Save and update SIS with billing data

Table 3.12 Billing Process – List of BTEs

The billing interface provides additional BTEs, though they are more specific to revenue recognition and SAP CRM. The SAP CRM processes are outside the scope of this book. However, the BTEs for the revenue recognition component are discussed in Chapter 9, Revenue Recognition.

The next section discusses enhancement for AR transactions.

3.6.2 Enhancements

Using enhancements, you can add custom logic to carry out additional validations and custom business processing. Let's look at some of the enhancements that you can use for billing processes.

- Table 3.13 lists a group of enhancements for AC interface, which is the interface that transfers billing documents to accounting. These enhancements can be used to modify or update different components of accounting entries.

Enhancement	Description
SDVFX001	User exit for header line
SDVFX002	User exit for customer line items
SDVFX003	User exit for cash clearing line items
SDVFX004	User exit for GL line items
SDVFX005	User exit for accrual line items

Table 3.13 Enhancements – Billing Process

Enhancement	Description
SDVFX006	User exit for tax line items
SDVFX007	User exit for billing plans (refer to Chapter 4)
SDVFX008	User exit for entire SD-FI transfer structure
SDVFX009	User exit for payment reference (refer to Chapter 5)
SDVFX010	User exit for the customer lines item table
SDVFX011	User exit for account determination structures KOMKCV and KOMPCV

Table 3.13 Enhancements – Billing Process (Cont.)

- **V05I0001:** User exit for billing index
  - Table VKDFS contains the billing index of all documents that are relevant for billing and for which billing hasn't occurred. This enhancement lets you augment the update of the billing index.
  - For example, the enhancement contains the following function modules for order-related and delivery-related billing documents:

    `EXIT_SAPLV05I_001`: Index for order-related billing

    `EXIT_SAPLV05I_002`: Index for delivery-related billing

Additionally, the SD component of the SAP system provides an extremely powerful framework for additional customization. Using this framework (Transaction VOFM), you can specify formulas and routines that control several aspects of the sales process that can impact customer billing. For example, you can control data copied from an order or a delivery to the billing document, or you can specify or augment data based on specific criteria. You can even configure routines that impact pricing calculations. These routines and formulas are extensively used in different configuration activities.

Work with your SAP support team for evaluating whether this framework (Transaction VOFM) can be used to enhance the billing processes in the SAP system to meet your business requirements.

3.6.3 Business Add-Ins (BAdIs)

Business Add-In implementations are enhancements to the standard SAP system. Most BAdIs provided by the SAP system accommodate industry-specific or country-specific requirements. However, you can also use BAdI implementations to meet any unique requirements for your business.

SAP provides BADI_SD_BILLING and BADI_SD_BILLING_ITEMS for the billing process. Each BAdI definition contains several methods that can be used to read, add, change, and check billing documents, or to influence documents before posting them to accounting.

However, these BAdIs are intended only for SAP internal use and industry solutions. Refer to SAP note 0000864944 for more details. Instead of using these BAdIs, you may want to evaluate other enhancements and user exits to implement your business requirements.

The next section takes a look at available BAPIs.

3.6.4 BAPIs

Table 3.14 lists some of the available BAPI methods for the object `ItCustBillingDoc` (Customer Billing Document).

Method	Function Module	Description
`Create`	`BAPI_BILLINGDOC_CREATE`	Create a billing document online
`CreateMultiple`	`BAPI_BILLINGDOC_CREATEMULTIPLE`	Create multiple billing documents based on the information in Table BILLING_DATA_IN
`Edit`	`BAPI_BILLINGDOC_EDIT`	Change a billing document online
`Display`	`BAPI_BILLINGDOC_DISPLAY`	Display a billing document online
`Confirm`	`BAPI_BILLINGDOC_CONFIRM`	Confirm a billing document
`Cancel`	`BAPI_BILLINGDOC_CANCEL1`	Cancel a billing document
`ExistenceCheck`	`BAPI_BILLINGDOC_EXISTENCECHECK`	Check whether a billing document exists

Table 3.14 Customer Billing – List of BAPI Methods

Method	Function Module	Description
GetDetail	BAPI_BILLINGDOC_ GETDETAIL	Get detailed information on a billing document via output structure BILLINGDOC_DETAIL
GetList	BAPI_BILLINGDOC_ GETLIST	Get a list of billing documents that meet the required selection criteria

Table 3.14 Customer Billing – List of BAPI Methods (Cont.)

3.7 Summary

In this chapter, we discussed the concepts and configuration of the billing process in the SAP system. We also looked at the most commonly used billing transactions. The content in this chapter was decidedly more focused on the technical details, which is why we spent most of the chapter looking at the configuration of organizational units, pricing procedures, and billing types. The many configuration settings provide comprehensive functionality to implement billing processes. We also looked at the attributes and parameters maintained in the customer master and material master that have an impact on pricing calculations. Additionally, we looked in detail at the GL account determination functionality. Finally, we discussed the three most commonly used billing processes: creating billing documents, canceling billing documents, and releasing blocked billing documents.

In the next chapter, we'll look at advanced billing functionalities such as billing plans, POD processes, and billing in different types of sales transactions.

The previous chapter discussed the standard customer billing process. In this chapter, we'll go through different business scenarios that require additional, advanced billing functionalities. We'll discuss customer down payments, different types of billing plans, retroactive customer billing, resource-related billing, and billing processes in other business scenarios. Each of these topics is self-contained, so you can directly branch to the section relevant for your business processes.

4 Additional Billing Functionality

In the previous chapter, we discussed concepts and configuration involved in the standard customer billing process. This chapter builds upon the functionality discussed in the previous chapter and goes through additional, advanced billing processes. It will be helpful, though not required, for you to be familiar with the details discussed in the previous chapter. We'll start with the functionality of processing customer down payments, followed by different types of billing plans. We'll go through the details of periodic billing plans as well as milestone billing plans. Subsequent sections cover the functionalities of resource-related billing and retroactive billing. Finally, you'll learn how to process customer billing in different types of business scenarios.

4.1 Down Payments

It's common for businesses to either request or receive payments from their customers as an advance against their orders. This is especially the case in the industries where the sales-to-delivery timeframe is long or the order involves customer-specific manufacturing or development. Regardless of the reasons, processing customer down payments consists of the following steps:

1. Post the down payment request (optional).
2. Process the down payments received from customers.

3. Process customer invoices.
4. Match the down payments with the corresponding customer invoices.

You can process customer down payments in the SAP system either as direct postings in the Accounts Receivable (AR) component or through the sales process in the Sales and Distribution (SD) component.

4.1.1 AR Down Payments

In Chapter 2, Accounts Receivable Transactions, we discussed posting AR documents directly to the customer account. The SAP system provides similar transactions for processing customer down payments. However, to ensure ease of reporting, traceability, and reconciliation, it's important that down payment transactions can be identified separately in a customer account. The SAP system handles this requirement by means of special GL transactions.

Special GL transactions enable you to designate certain AR transactions as special transactions so that you can enter, process, and settle them separately from regular accounts receivables. The SAP system supports many special GL transactions such as down payments, bank guarantees, and letter of credit. For the purpose of the AR down payment process, you'll find corresponding configuration activities under SAP IMG • FINANCIAL ACCOUNTING • ACCOUNTS RECEIVABLE AND ACCOUNTS PAYABLE • BUSINESS TRANSACTIONS • DOWN PAYMENTS RECEIVED.

Special GL transaction balances are updated in separate reconciliation accounts to provide easy visibility, traceability, and reconciliation of entries. Figure 4.1 shows one of the important configuration activities for processing AR down payments. To ensure that special GL transactions are recorded and processed separately, you assign a different reconciliation account for each type of special GL transaction.

To process incoming down payments, you'll use transactions under SAP MENU • ACCOUNTING • FINANCIAL ACCOUNTING • ACCOUNTS RECEIVABLE • DOCUMENT ENTRY • DOWN PAYMENT. These transactions have a similar user interface and processing options as the AR transactions discussed in Chapter 2, Accounts Receivable Transactions:

- Post down payment request (Transaction F-37)
  - Special Transaction Type "F"

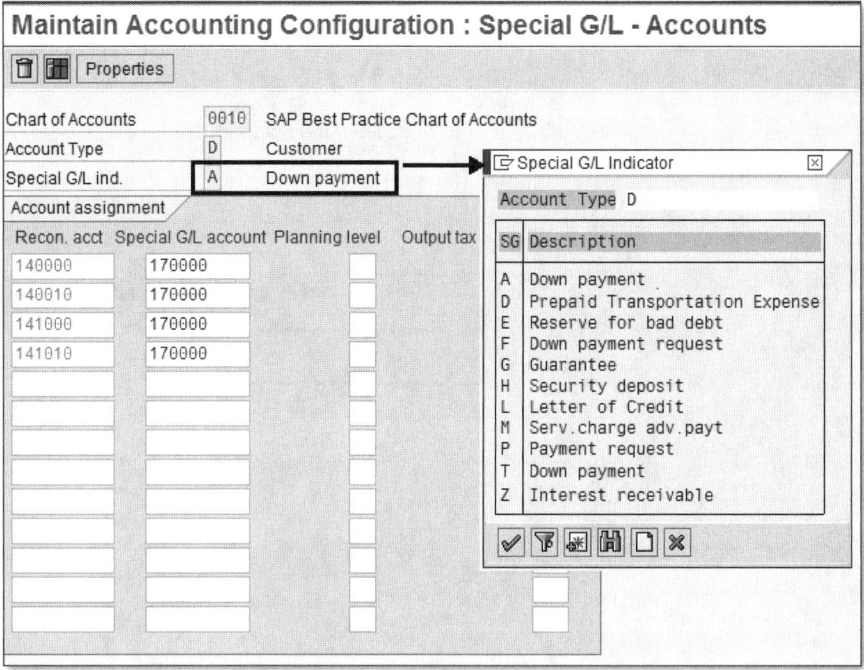

Figure 4.1 AR Down Payments – Configuration

  - This is an optional step in down payment processing. Using this transaction, you can post a down payment request in the SAP system for a customer account. Subsequently, you can generate formal customer communication based on this document to request a down payment.

- Post down payment (Transaction F-29)
  - Special Transaction Type "A"
  - This is the transaction you use to post an incoming down payment to a customer account. The only difference between this transaction and the other AR transactions for incoming payments is that you have to enter a special GL indicator on the initial screen (Figure 4.2).
- Clear down payment (Transaction F-39)
  - You use this transaction to match and clear customer down payments against customer invoices. The customer invoices can be the ones posted using AR invoice transactions (Chapter 2, Accounts Receivable Transactions) or customer billing document transactions (Chapter 3, Customer Billing).

Post Customer Down Payment: Header Data

New item | Requests

Document Date	04/23/2009	Type	DZ	Company Code	3000
Posting Date	04/23/2009	Period	11	Currency/Rate	USD
Document Number				Translatn Date	
Reference				Cross-CC no.	
Doc.Header Text	D/Pymnt for Ord # 1200973				
Trading part.BA					

Customer

Account	3000	Special G/L ind	A
Altern.comp.cde			

Bank

Account	113100	Business Area	
Amount	2100	LC amount	
Bank charges		LC bank charges	
Value date	11/05/2009	Profit Center	
Text		Assignment	

Figure 4.2 AR Down Payments – Posting

- For customer billing documents, you'll be able to match down payments against the accounting documents corresponding to the customer billing document.
- This transaction clears and matches down payments with invoices. It also transfers customer account entries from a special GL reconciliation account to the regular customer reconciliation account.

Tip

If you choose to use AR transactions for processing down payments, ensure that all relevant reports that you use are able to differentiate between standard AR transactions and special GL transactions. This is especially important for custom developed reports because most standard SAP reports have an option to separately select or report special GL transactions.

Let's now consider how to process customer down payments using SD transactions.

4.1.2 SD Down Payments

The SD transactions for processing customer down payments are a little more involved than corresponding AR transactions. There are also restrictions in that you can only use SD down payment transactions for order-relevant billing. These transactions can't be used for delivery-related billing. However, the benefit of using SD transactions is that you can use the same process for customer down payments as the one used for customer invoices and credit memos. The following is a generic sequence of steps you follow to process down payments using SD transactions:

1. Create a milestone billing plan corresponding to the schedule of expected down payments.
   - We'll discuss milestone billing plans later in this chapter (Section 4.2.2, Milestone Billing Plan). For the purpose of this discussion, consider these plans as a collection of one or more deadlines for down payments and the final payment. For example, if for a $50,000 invoice you're expecting three down payments of $5000 each and the final payment of $35000, the first step will be to create a milestone billing plan with four deadlines.
2. Assign billing plan milestones to the relevant sales document.
   - The milestone billing plan can be assigned to the sales order header or separately to individual sales order items.
   - If the schedule of expected down payments is different, you'll need to separately assign milestones for each sales order item.
3. Use the billing due list (Chapter 3, Customer Billing) to generate the down payment request.
   - The deadlines specified in billing plans determine the dates when down payment requests show up in the billing due list for processing.
   - Down payment requests show up in the SD document flow (Chapter 3, Customer Billing). They are also automatically posted to Financial Accounting.
4. Process the customer down payment using the incoming payment transaction.
   - During this process, the SAP system proposes and assigns available down payment requests from the customer account.
5. Process customer invoices using the billing due list process.
   - During this process, the SAP system assigns and applies all of the received down payments to the customer invoice.

Tip

Even if you use SD transactions for processing down payments, you have to configure special GL transactions and separate reconciliation accounts as described in Section 4.1.1, AR Down Payments. You may want to evaluate whether the number of customer down payments processed by your business is worth the additional effort and configuration required in using SD transactions for down payments.

We discussed several billing parameters in Chapter 3, Customer Billing. The SAP system provides the following standard parameters for processing customer down payments using SD transactions:

- Sales document item category: TAO (milestone billing)
- Condition type: AZWR (down payment/settlement)
- Billing document types: FAZ (down payment request) and FAS (cancellation of down payment request)

In the next section, we'll discuss the functionality of billing plans.

4.2 Billing Plans

In many business scenarios, a simple, one-time customer billing isn't sufficient or isn't practical. Delivery of complex projects, combination of deliveries from multiple international partners, and multi-year contracts are all examples of scenarios where customer billing should take place either over a period of time or after specific tasks are completed. Billing plans functionality in the SAP system is useful in such business scenarios. The SAP system supports two types of billing plans:

- **Periodic billing plan**: Allows the billing of predefined amount at a predefined frequency, for example, quarterly billing for an order for equipment rental.
- **Milestone billing plan**: Allows the billing of fixed or variable amounts on predefined dates or after project milestones are completed. For example, milestone billing plans are useful for make-to-order manufacturing or custom development software projects.

Note

It's important to differentiate between installment plans and billing plans. Installment plans allow customers to pay one invoice in installment payments, and they are controlled by installment payment terms. Billing plans provide an ability to generate multiple customer invoices for one order. Payments of individual invoices generated for a billing plan depends on the payment terms associated with each invoice.

You'll find billing plan configuration under SAP IMG • SALES AND DISTRIBUTION • BILLING • BILLING PLAN. We'll refer to the configuration path as Billing Plan IMG for the sake of brevity. Let's look at how to configure each type of billing plan in detail, starting with periodic billing plans.

4.2.1 Periodic Billing Plan

You configure periodic billing plans using BILLING PLAN IMG • DEFINE BILLING PLAN TYPES • MAINTAIN BILLING PLAN TYPES FOR PERIODIC BILLING. Figure 4.3 shows the configuration screen of a 12-month billing plan that generates monthly invoices and derives its dates from a sales contract.

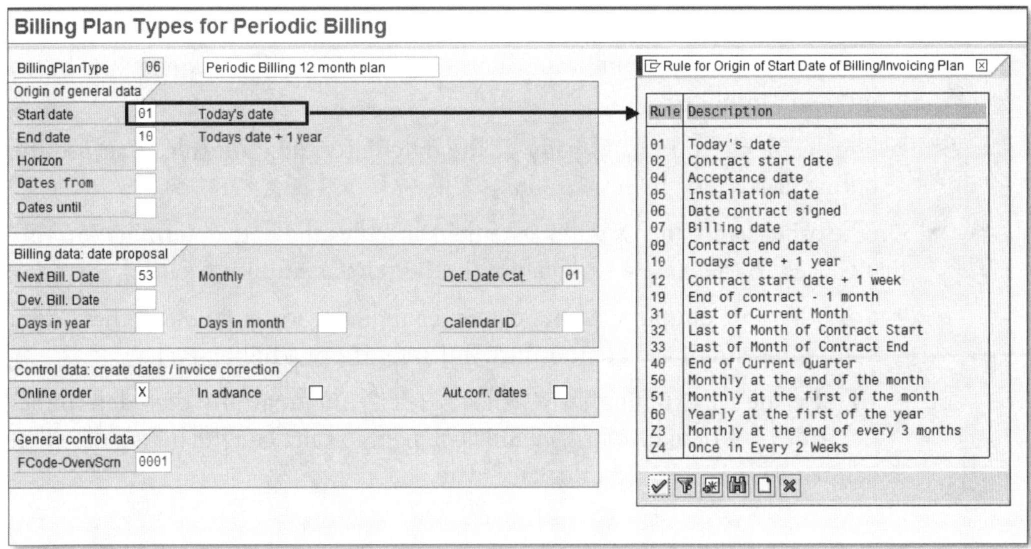

Figure 4.3 Periodic Billing Plan – Configuration

Following are the details of some important fields in this configuration screen.

Origin of General Data

- For the Start Date and the End Date of a periodic billing plan, you can specify date determination rules. You can use one of the many predefined rules provided in the SAP system, or as you'll see later in this section, you can create a new one that meets your business requirements.
- Instead of End Date, you can use the Horizon field to determine the upper end of the currently planned end date.
  - This functionality is useful if the billing end date is far out in the future. For example, for a multi-year contract requiring monthly billing, you can use Horizon to propose the billing dates for one year. Toward the end of the first year, you can use it to propose billing dates for next year, and so on.
  - For calculating Horizon, you can use any of the date determination rules that use the current date as the reference date.

Billing Data: Date Proposal

- Next Billing Date specifies the date determination rule that is used for determining the next billing date.
  - In Figure 4.3, rule 53 indicates that the next billing date is generated based on the monthly rule.
  - For this field, you can use any of the date determination rules that use the billing date as the reference date.
- On the other hand, the Dev Bill Date field specifies the date determination rule that is used to calculate any deviation in the calculated billing date.
  - Consider an example where a customer requests to be invoiced three days before the end of the quarter during the course of a billing plan.
  - You use the Next Billing Date field to specify the quarterly date determination rule, and then use the Dev Bill Date field to calculate the billing date that is three days before the calculated date.

Control Data

This section contains some of the most important fields of this configuration activity. However, the field names don't necessarily convey the far-reaching impact these settings have.

- The Online Order field determines whether billing dates of the billing plan are calculated automatically (X) or entered manually (blank).
- The In Advance indicator specifies the billing period for which the billing document is generated.
  - Consider an example of a monthly billing plan, with the date determination rule as first of the month. For a billing document with the billing date March 1st, if this indicator isn't selected, it corresponds to the month of February; if this indicator is selected, it corresponds to the month of March.
- The Auto Corr. Dates indicator is relevant for business scenarios that have relatively flexible end dates for a billing plan.
  - Consider an example of a monthly billing plan for 12 months, for which 11 billing documents have already been generated. If for any reason the billing plan is changed to 10 months, the customer account should receive a credit memo for one month.
  - If this indicator is selected, the system automatically generates credit memo dates in the billing plan. Otherwise, you have to process credit memos separately and manually.

With the help of these parameters, you can configure almost any type of periodic billing plans. Before we look at the milestone billing plans, let's see the role played by date determination rules in milestone billing plans.

Date Determination Rules

As shown in Figure 4.3 in the previous section, the SAP system provides many predefined date determination rules. However, if you want to create new rules, you can configure them by using Billing Plan IMG • Define rules for determining dates. Figure 4.4 shows an example of a date determination rule configuration.

In the date determination rule configuration, note the following:

- Baseline Date specifies the reference date for the calculation rule. The reference date has to be one of the predefined dates available in the system.

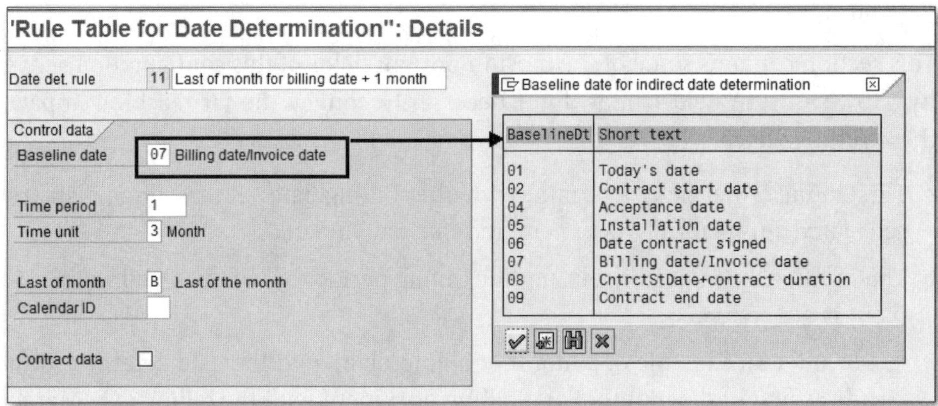

Figure 4.4 Date Determination Rule

> **Tip**
>
> If the Contract Data indicator is selected, the system ignores the reference date specified in the date determination rule. Instead, it calculates the date based on the dates specified in the sales document header.

- Time Period and Time Unit determine the offset for the calculated date.
  - Time Period can be any positive or negative number. A negative time period specifies "prior" dates, for example, one month before contract end date.
  - Time Unit specifies whether the time period specifies days (1), weeks (2), months (3), or years (4).
- Last of the Month specifies whether the calculated date should be kept as is (blank value) or should be modified to be first date of the month (A) or last date of the month (B).

You can configure date determination rules to meet almost any practical requirements by choosing appropriate values for the Time Period and Time Unit fields. Similarly, the field Baseline Date provides most commonly relevant dates for date determination. Table 4.1 lists the dates that can be used as the baseline date in date determination rules.

> **Note**
>
> Even though date categories are discussed in Section 4.2.1, Periodic Billing Plans, they are also used for milestone billing plans.

Baseline Date	Description
01	Today's date
02	Contract start date
04	Acceptance date
05	Installation date
06	Date contract signed
07	Billing date/invoice date
08	Contract Start Date plus Contract duration
09	Contract end date

Table 4.1 Baseline Dates in Date Determination Rules

In the next section, we'll explore the configuration of milestone billing plans.

4.2.2 Milestone Billing Plan

Before we delve into the configuration of milestone billing plans, a little explanation is in order. Milestone billing plans are commonly used in conjunction with another component called SAP Project Systems (PS). The SAP PS component provides comprehensive functionality for planning, scheduling, costing, and execution of projects. These projects can range from relatively simple to extremely complex. All of the projects have in common that they each consist of specific tasks and event milestones. For example, a software development project may have milestones of requirement finalization, coding, testing, and delivery. Obviously, a large project such as construction of a plant can consist of numerous tasks and milestones.

It's a common business practice in such projects to tie customer invoicing to project milestones. That is where milestone billing plans come into picture. These billing plans require an event to trigger or a milestone to be reached before the corresponding customer billing document is generated. This event trigger is automatically provided if milestone billing plans are tied to projects in SAP PS. Otherwise, you can manually enter and manage milestone dates when the customer invoicing should occur.

You configure milestone billing plans using BILLING PLAN IMG • DEFINE BILLING PLAN TYPES • MAINTAIN BILLING PLAN TYPES FOR MILESTONE BILLING. Figure 4.5 shows the configuration screen of a sample milestone billing plan.

Maintaining Billing Plan Types for Milestone Billing
BillingPlanType 10 PS: Milestone Billing
Origin of general data
Start date 01 Today's date
RefBillPlanNo.
Billing data: date proposal
Date category 01
Control data: create dates
Online order X
General control data
FCode-OvervScrn 0003

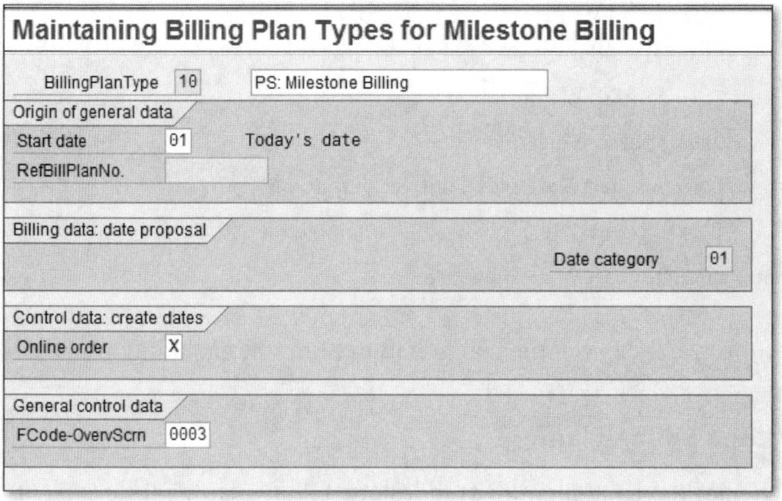

Figure 4.5 Milestone Billing Plan – Configuration

The configuration screen is relatively simple with very few fields to maintain:

- The Start Date field specifies the start of a milestone billing plan.
  - You can use any of the date determination rules discussed in Section 4.2.1, Periodic Building Plans, to derive the start date.
- The Online Order field has the same usage as the one for periodic billing plans.
  - It specifies whether billing dates of the billing plan are calculated automatically (Y) or entered manually (blank).
- Date Category is assigned using a different configuration activity.
  - Date Category determines several important parameters for the billing plan, so let's look at that configuration separately.

The date category assignment to a milestone billing plan is carried out using BILLING PLAN IMG • DEFINE AND ASSIGN DATE CATEGORIES. Figure 4.6 shows an example of date category 01 associated with a milestone billing plan.

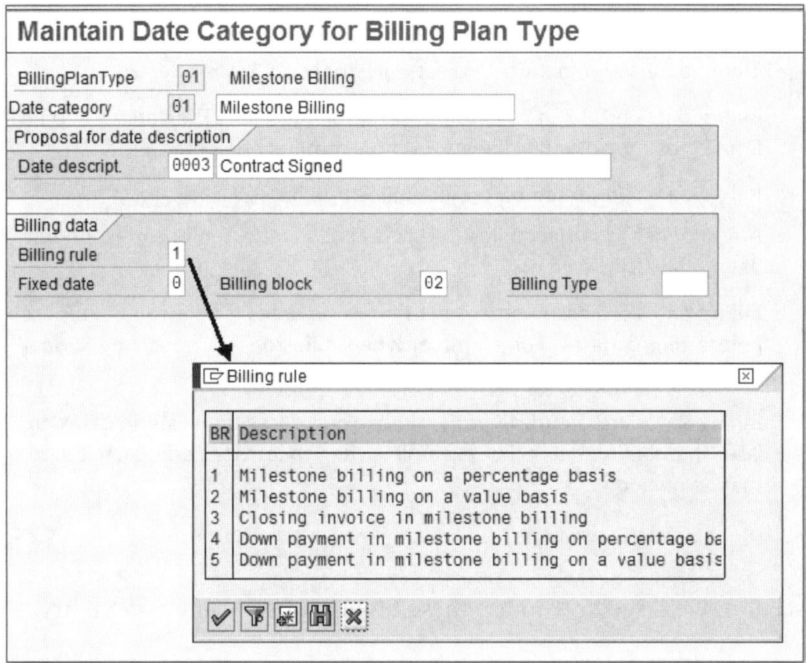

Figure 4.6 Assign Date Category to a Billing Plan

In Figure 4.6, the Billing Block and Billing Type fields are self-explanatory, so let's focus on the other fields.

- The field Date Description specifies a name that will be proposed for a milestone. For example, you can create different date descriptors for a project to correspond to the initial payment, contract signed, 50% delivery complete, 100% delivery complete, and final settlement.
- The field Billing Rule specifies the type of billing for the date category. As shown in the figure, this value determines whether milestone billing is based on fixed amounts or based on percentages of the net item amount. The same field is relevant for milestone billing plans that are used for down payment processing with SD transactions
- The Fixed Date field controls whether billing dates are fixed or are adopted based on planned/actual dates of project milestones. Table 4.2 shows possible options for this field.

Value	Interpretation
Blank	Billing date assignment to project milestones isn't possible/relevant.
0	Billing dates are fixed as entered in the billing plan. They aren't copied from or overwritten by changes in project milestone dates.
1	Billing dates are based on project milestone dates. Any changes to project milestone dates is also reflected in corresponding billing dates.
2	Billing dates are based on project milestone dates if milestone dates are before billing dates. For example, when milestones are reached sooner than expected.
3	Billing dates are based on project milestone dates if milestone dates are later than billing dates. For example, when milestones are reached later than expected.

Table 4.2 Fixed Date in a Date Category

In the next section, we'll see how to use these billing plans during order entry.

4.2.3 Using Billing Plans

One possibility is to assign billing plan types directly to a sales document type. For example, you can assign a periodic billing plan type to a sales contract type used for specific types of business transactions, such as periodic equipment rentals. All items in that sales contract will share the same periodic billing plan. You can assign a billing plan type to a sales document type using BILLING PLAN IMG • ASSIGN BILLING PLAN TYPES TO SALES DOCUMENT TYPES.

Another possibility is to assign billing plan types to an item category. In Chapter 3, Customer Billing, we discussed billing type configuration, item category configuration, and their impact on billing process. If you haven't already, please review relevant sections of Chapter 3. You can assign a billing type to a document item category either in the billing type configuration (discussed in Chapter 3) or using BILLING PLAN IMG • ASSIGN BILLING PLAN TYPES TO ITEM CATEGORIES.

To put together what we discussed so far about billing plans, consider the following:

- Billing plan types assigned to sales document item categories are applicable to individual document items.
- For a periodic billing plan, the billing plan type configuration specifies the date proposal and date determination rules for the start date and end date.
- For a milestone billing plan, the billing plan type configuration specifies the date determination rule for the billing start date.
- Date categories specify the type of billing (percentage or amount) and the type of date proposal (manual or automatic) and date descriptions. Date descriptions can correspond to different milestones of a project.
- At the time of sales order entry, based on relevant configuration parameters, the system determines the type of a billing plan. Depending on the configuration settings, either the system proposes dates automatically or you have to enter the dates manually.

Note

The sales item category or the document type determines the type of billing plan that can be assigned to a sales order item. This is a configuration activity, and it can't be changed at the time of order entry.

Figure 4.7 shows an example of a periodic billing plan as you would see it in a billing document. In this example, the Settlement Date represents the date when the billing document was generated, whereas the other two dates specify the period that billing document corresponds to. The date category discussed here is displayed in a separate column (DCat) along with Bill Value. The Billing Status column shows one of the following values:

- **<blank>:** Not relevant,
- **A:** Not yet processed,
- **B:** Partially processed,
- **C:** Completely processed,

These self-explanatory status values are automatically updated by the billing process. You can reach the screen in Figure 4.7 in a sales order or a billing document by selecting GOTO • HEADER/ITEM • BILLING PLAN.

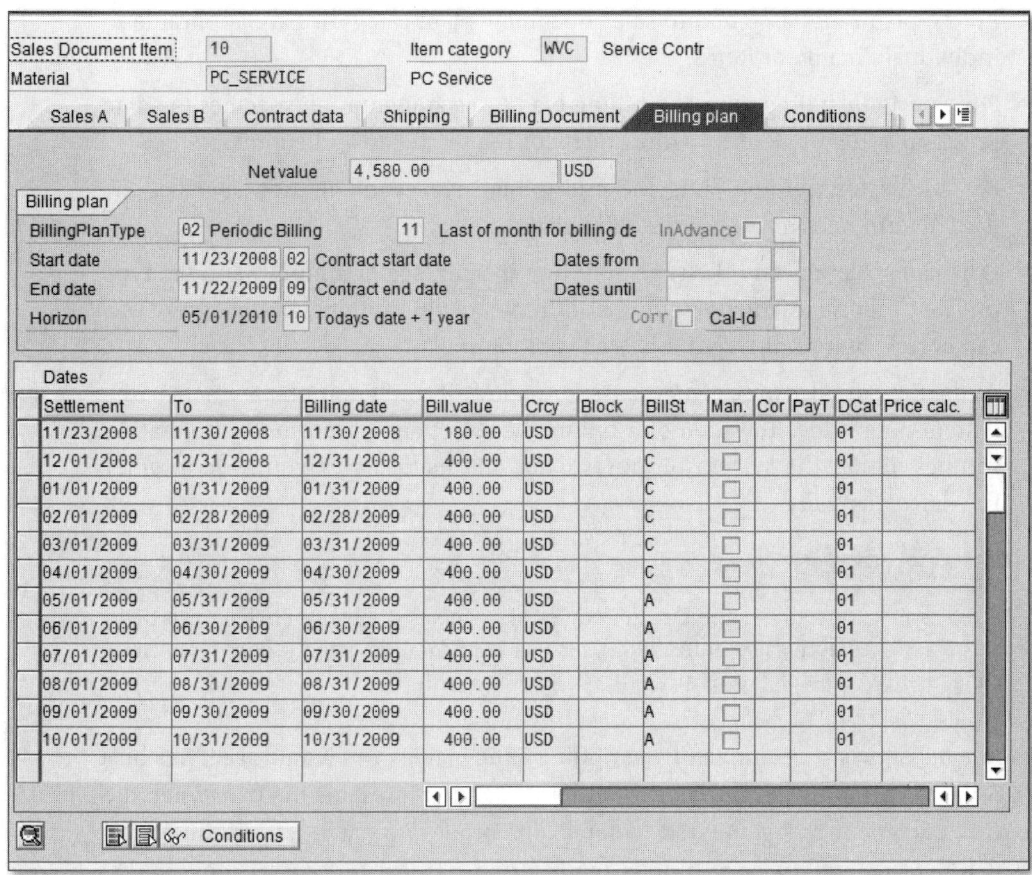

Settlement	To	Billing date	Bill.value	Crcy	Block	BillSt	Man.	Cor	PayT	DCat	Price calc.
11/23/2008	11/30/2008	11/30/2008	180.00	USD		C	☐			01	
12/01/2008	12/31/2008	12/31/2008	400.00	USD		C	☐			01	
01/01/2009	01/31/2009	01/31/2009	400.00	USD		C	☐			01	
02/01/2009	02/28/2009	02/28/2009	400.00	USD		C	☐			01	
03/01/2009	03/31/2009	03/31/2009	400.00	USD		C	☐			01	
04/01/2009	04/30/2009	04/30/2009	400.00	USD		C	☐			01	
05/01/2009	05/31/2009	05/31/2009	400.00	USD		A	☐			01	
06/01/2009	06/30/2009	06/30/2009	400.00	USD		A	☐			01	
07/01/2009	07/31/2009	07/31/2009	400.00	USD		A	☐			01	
08/01/2009	08/31/2009	08/31/2009	400.00	USD		A	☐			01	
09/01/2009	09/30/2009	09/30/2009	400.00	USD		A	☐			01	
10/01/2009	10/31/2009	10/31/2009	400.00	USD		A	☐			01	

Figure 4.7 Periodic Billing Plan – Example

Figure 4.8 shows an example of a milestone billing plan in a sales document. In this example, a billing plan consists of two project-related milestones, with additional stages for down payment and final invoicing. Most information on this screen is self-explanatory. The Billing Status field has the same significance as the one in the periodic billing plan discussed previously.

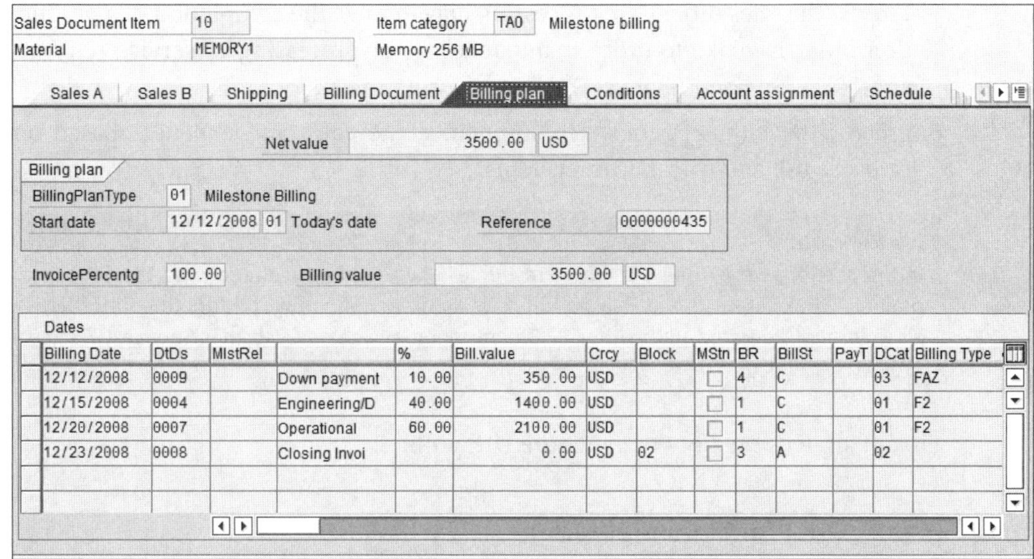

Billing Date	DtDs	MlstRel		%	Bill.value	Crcy	Block	MStn	BR	BillSt	PayT	DCat	Billing Type
12/12/2008	0009		Down payment	10.00	350.00	USD			4	C		03	FAZ
12/15/2008	0004		Engineering/D	40.00	1400.00	USD			1	C		01	F2
12/20/2008	0007		Operational	60.00	2100.00	USD			1	C		01	F2
12/23/2008	0008		Closing Invoi		0.00	USD	02		3	A		02	

Figure 4.8 Milestone Billing Plan – Example

In the next section, we'll look at the more advanced form of billing functionality, called resource-related billing.

4.3 Resource-Related Billing

Resource-related billing functionality is useful when the customer billing is based on resource consumption. For example, a software project is billed based on the number of hours used in project implementation, or a make-to-order product development is billed based on time and materials used for development. In such scenarios, it's impractical, if not impossible, to know the exact price and total billing amount at the time of the sales order. Instead, the SAP system provides the following functionality to process such billing requirements:

1. Configure DIP (Dynamic Item Processor) profiles that specify how the charges are collected, summarized, and processed, and associate them with sales document item categories.
2. Create sales orders that consist of items associated with DIP profiles.

3. Process the sales order. The processing may involve the completion of a production order in make-to-order manufacturing, or processing of service requests and T&E (Time and Expenses) requests for a project.
4. Process the billing requests to summarize the costs and expenses based on resource use and by sales order items.

> **Note**
>
> In this section, we'll discuss a simple resource-related billing scenario from the SD component. However, resource-related billing is an extremely powerful functionality that is also closely integrated with other SAP components such as Customer Service (CS) and Project Systems (PS).

First of all, let's see how to configure DIP profiles.

4.3.1 DIP Profile Configuration

DIP (Dynamic Item Processor) profiles form the core of resource-related billing configuration. These are so named because the billing items are determined dynamically based on resource use. You configure DIP profiles using SAP IMG • Sales and Distribution • Sales • Sales Documents • Customer Service • Service Quotation/Resource Related Billing • Profiles for Resource Related Billing/Quotation Creation. A DIP profile controls usage, characteristics, value sources, and material determination for resource-related billing.

Usage and Characteristics

Figure 4.9 shows configuration screens relevant for usage and characteristics for DIP profile SP000001. This is a template profile delivered in the SAP system for resource-related billing.

In this figure, the upper part shows the usage configuration, and the lower part shows the configuration characteristics.

- A DIP profile can be used for billing and results analysis, or for quotation and sales order pricing. The Usage field indicates the type of configuration.
  - In this section, we'll only focus on the use of DIP profiles for billing.
  - Results analysis is relevant for resource-related billing in project systems.

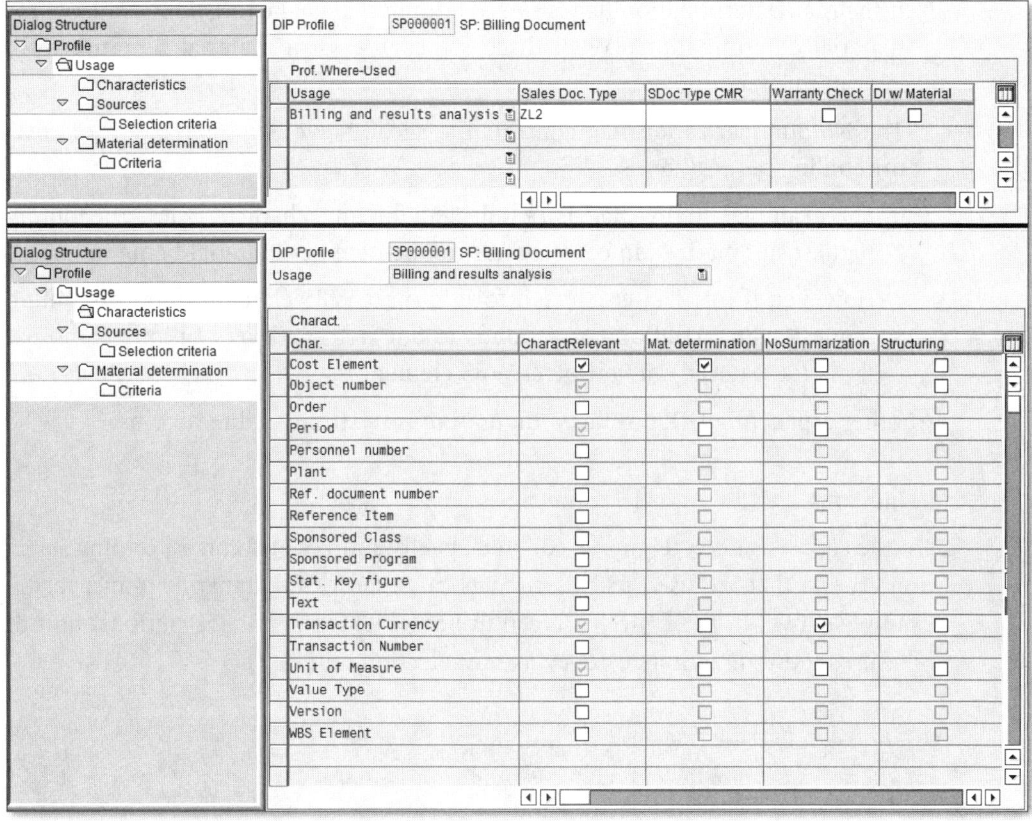

Figure 4.9 Figure 4.9 DIP Profile – Usage

- The fields Sales Doc Type and Sales Doc Type CMR specify the document types used while processing resource-related billing.
  - If only Sales Doc Type is specified, it's used to post debit as well as credit entries in the customer billing request.
  - If both document types are specified, Sales Doc Type is used to post debit entries, whereas Sales Doc Type CMR is used to post credit entries.
- On the Characteristics screen, you can select the relevance of a large number of characteristics. Figure 4.9 shows only a partial list of characteristics.
- If the Charact.Relevant flag is selected, then that characteristic is considered relevant for resource-related billing. For example, if this flag is selected for a work order, project WBS element, and a cost center; costs are summarized by these three characteristics.

- If the Mat.Determination flag is selected, then that characteristic is available for material determination. (We'll discuss the process of material determination later in this section.)
- The No Summarization flag controls the second-level summarization of costs into billing request items.
  - For example, if this flag isn't selected for any characteristics, the billing request summarization corresponds to one item per material being invoiced.
  - However, if this flag is selected for a project WBS element, then the billing request summarization corresponds to one item for every unique combination of a material and a project WBS element.

Another aspect of a DIP profile configuration is to specify value sources.

Value Sources

On the sources screen (Figure 4.10), you specify sources and corresponding selection criteria that are used to collect costs or expenses for dynamic items. In the example shown in the figure, you can use cost elements, posting periods, unit of measure, and transaction currency as the selection criteria.

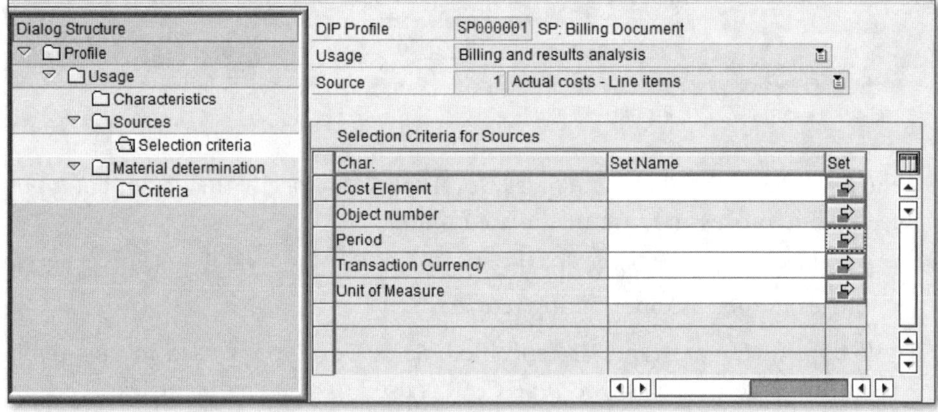

Figure 4.10 DIP Profile – Value Sources

Following are a few points to keep in mind while configuring sources for DIP profiles:

- You can specify multiple value sources for a DIP profile. The preceding example derives 100% of its costs from actual line item costs. However, you can combine data from multiple value sources.
- Table 4.3 lists value sources configured in a DIP profile and the corresponding database table or user exit that provides the values.

Value Source	Database Table/User Exit
Actual costs – Line items	COVP – CO Object line items
Actual costs – Totals records	COSPA – Cost totals for external postings COSSA – Cost totals for internal postings
Statistical ind. – Line items	COVPR – Line items for statistical key figures
Statististical ind. – Totals records	COSRA – Statistical key figure totals
Funds – Line items	V_COFP – Fund flow document lines
Funds – Totals records	FMSUA – Funds management totals records
Planned costs – Totals records	COSPA – Cost totals for external postings COSSA – Cost totals for internal postings
Plan statistical ind – Totals records	COSRA – Statistical key figure totals
Easy Cost Planning	User exit CKF_DIP_CUSTOMER_EXIT
Intercompany – Line Items	COVP – CO Object line items

Table 4.3 Value Sources for DIP Profile

- You can also assign apportionment percentages to each value source. For example, if an R&D project contract stipulates billing of only 60% of actual costs, you can assign 60% to the actual line items value source.

The final step in DIP profile configuration is the material determination.

Material Determination

Of course, the ultimate objective of configuring a DIP profile is to be able to map the costs and expenses to a material that can be invoiced to a customer. You carry out this configuration on the material determination screen (Figure 4.11).

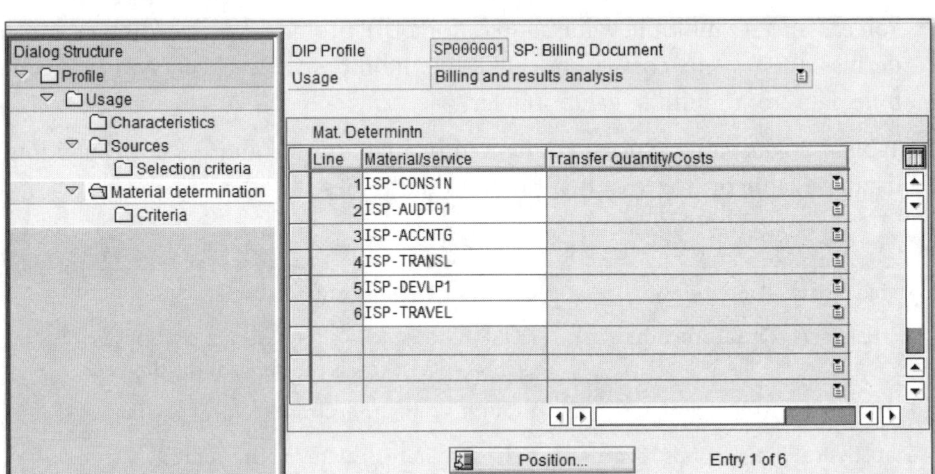

Figure 4.11 DIP Profile – Material Determination

The figure shows an example list of materials corresponding to different services such as consulting, auditing, accounting, and translating. Cost determination and assignment of each material takes place as follows:

- Every material on the material determination screen is assigned a combination of selection criteria.
- The selection criteria consist of characteristics marked as relevant for material determination (refer to the characteristics discussion in DIP profile).
- All costs from value sources that satisfy the selection criteria are allocated to the corresponding material.

Example

Materials ISP-ACCTNG and ISP-TRANSL are assigned the same set of WBS elements and different ranges of cost elements. While evaluating value sources, all costs and expenses posted to the specified WBS elements are allocated to materials ISP-ACCTNG or ISP-TRANSL depending on the cost elements.

The final configuration activity is to assign the DIP profile to the sales document item categories.

Assign DIP Profile

In Chapter 3, Customer Billing, we discussed sales document item categories and the corresponding attributes that impact the billing process. You assign the DIP profile discussed in the previous section to the appropriate item categories as shown in Figure 4.12.

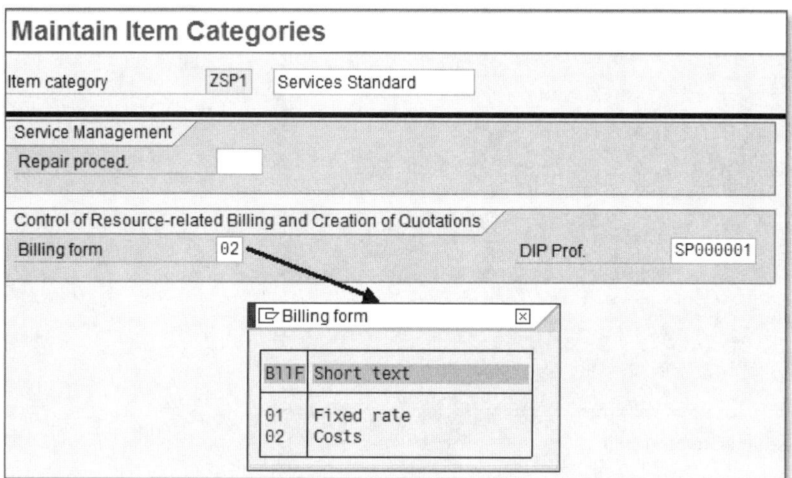

Figure 4.12 DIP profile assignment

As shown in the figure, you assign DIP Profile to a sales document item category along with a Billing Form. To use dynamic items, the billing form should be set to value 02.

Let's now see how to use and process resource-related billing documents.

4.3.2 Using Resource-Related Billing

You can process resource-related billing for an order or a contract, only if it contains document items with the document item categories associated with DIP profiles. To initiate resource-related billing, select SAP MENU • LOGISTICS • SALES AND DISTRIBUTION • SALES • ORDER • SUBSEQUENT FUNCTIONS • RESOURCE-RELATED BILLING DOCUMENT (Transaction DP91).

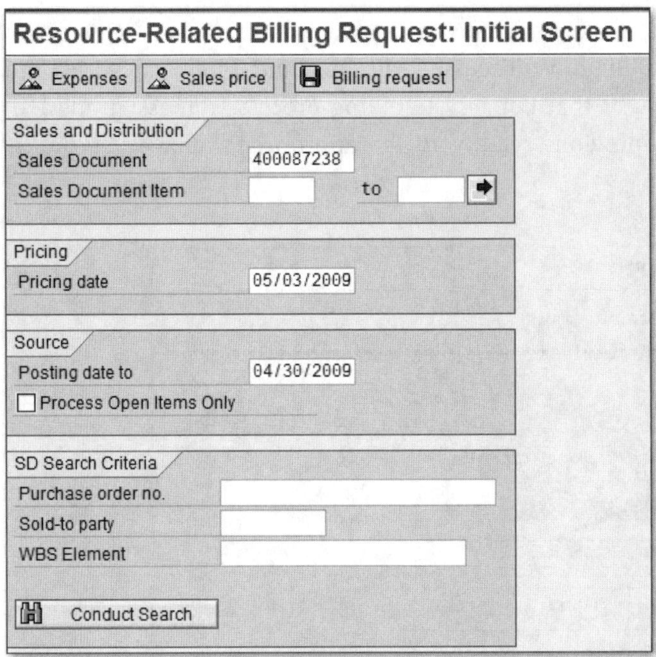

Figure 4.13 Resource-Related Billing

Figure 4.13 shows the initial screen for processing resource-related billing. Following are some relevant points about this transaction:

- The transaction selects sales prices of different resources as of the date specified in the Pricing Date field.
- The Posting Date To field specifies the date up to which postings to value sources are taken into account. In the example shown in the figure, all accounting postings up to 04/30/2009 are evaluated for billing.
- You can choose the Sales Price option to process billing items sorted and combined per SD items, using SD pricing calculations.
  - From this screen, you can branch out to condition maintenance to review or adjust the sales pricing of individual items. We discussed pricing conditions in Chapter 3, Customer Billing.

- You can choose the Expenses option to process billing items sorted and combined per the dynamic items calculated using the DIP profile.
  - From this screen, you can review and validate the cost assignment to the dynamic items. You can also review the default apportionment percentages and modify them as necessary.
- Following is the high-level process flow of this transaction:
  - Select all entries that satisfy the selection criteria based on value sources configured in the DIP profile.
  - Carry out sales pricing evaluation based on the pricing date and resource consumption.
  - Summarize costs and expenses based on the characteristics configuration in the DIP profile.
  - Carry out the cost assignment to materials based on the material determination configuration in the DIP profile.
  - Calculate the net balance of the amount assigned to a material and the amount already billed.
  - Depending on the usage configuration of the DIP profile, either generate one billing request for the net balance of all items, or generate separate billing requests for the debit and credit balances of all items.

After you've reviewed the details, you choose the Billing Request option to post the billing request document. If you want to view the DIP profile associated with a sales document, select DISPLAY SALES ORDER (VA03) • GOTO • ITEM • SALES B tab.

Tip

Transaction DP96 provides collective processing of resource-related billing documents. The transaction provides several selection criteria and pricing calculation options, as well as the option to run it in a test mode.

As mentioned before, resource-related billing functionality is extremely powerful. It can be used in any business scenario that requires or allows the accumulation of costs and revenues by sales orders or sales contracts. Some examples of such business scenarios are sales orders for make-to-order manufacturing, for WBS elements of customer projects, or for maintenance requests or service requests.

4.4 Retroactive Billing

As the name suggests, *retroactive billing* is used to reevaluate older billing documents. This functionality is used most commonly when price revisions are effective retroactively. The SAP system provides a comprehensive retro-billing process to meet this business requirement. However, you should note that this process isn't automatic. In other words, a revised price agreement doesn't automatically create price adjustment documents. You have to manually initiate the retro-billing process.

4.4.1 Retro Billing Process

To initiate the retro-billing process, you select SAP MENU • LOGISTICS • SALES AND DISTRIBUTION • BILLING • BILLING DOCUMENT • RETRO-BILLING (Transaction VFRB).

Figure 4.14 shows the initial screen of the retro-billing process. The figure shows an example of a business scenario in which price revisions occurring in April are effective from the beginning of the year. Most fields on the screen are self-explanatory. However, two fields require detailed explanation.

Retro-billing

Payer	3000		
Sales organization	3000		
Billing date from	01/01/2009		
Billing date to	04/20/2009		
Pricing type	C		
Currency		to	
Sold-to party		to	
Material		to	

☐ Include invoices w/same values

Figure 4.14 Retroactive Billing

First is the indicator Include Invoices w/Same Values. If this indicator is selected, the retro-billing process includes invoices in which the new price after the retro-billing calculation is the same as the current net price.

Example

The original invoice for a widget is for $100. Then the list price was revised to $90, and a retro-billing run created a customer credit memo for $10. However, later the price revision was deemed incorrect, and the list price was changed back to $100. During the subsequent retro-billing run, the process will find that the required new price or current list price ($100) is the same as the net invoice price ($100).

- If this indicator isn't selected, the process won't include the original invoice in the retro-billing process.
- If this indicator is selected, the process will include the original invoice in the retro-billing process. It will take into account the $10 credit memo that is already posted and create a $10 debit memo adjustment.

The next important field in the retro-billing transaction is Pricing Type. This field controls how the system evaluates pricing data while creating adjustment documents. Table 4.4 lists some of the available pricing types and their impact on pricing recalculation. By default, retro-billing uses pricing type C for recalculation.

Pricing Type	Details
A – Copy price components and redetermine scales	Condition values aren't redetermined. Only the scaled prices are redetermined.
D – Copy pricing elements unchanged	Similar to "A," however, instead of redetermining scales, the process redetermines base values.
B – Complete new pricing	Completely new pricing is carried out. Manually entered condition values in the original document are lost.
C – Copy manual pricing and redetermine others	Similar to "B," however, manually entered condition values from the original document are copied to the new document.
G – Copy pricing elements unchanged and redetermine taxes	The process redetermines taxes, cost conditions, and intercompany billing conditions. Other conditions are treated as in pricing type "D"
H – Redetermine freight conditions	The process redetermines delivery costs and freight conditions. Other conditions are treated as in pricing type "D."

Table 4.4 Pricing Types

You can create custom pricing types to differently recalculate condition values and pricing. SAP Note 0000024832 provides detailed information on additional pricing types, as well as details on how to implement custom pricing types.

Another critical aspect of retro-billing is the identification and differentiation of primary and secondary documents.

4.4.2 Primary and Secondary Documents

Let's revisit the example cited in the previous section. The example referred to a $100 invoice for which the first retro-billing process had created a $10 credit memo. Particularly, consider how the process determines that the $100 invoice is the original (primary) document and the $10 credit memo is the subsequent (secondary) document. Also, consider how the process will differentiate this $10 credit memo from another $50 credit memo for damaged goods, which should be evaluated based on the revised price.

The process makes this determination based on the reason code assigned to a sales document. Every order reason is assigned relevancy for retro-billing. This relevancy determines whether the retro-billing document considers a sales document as a primary document or a secondary document. You configure order reasons (Figure 4.15) using SAP IMG • SALES AND DISTRIBUTION • SALES • SALES DOCUMENTS • SALES DOCUMENT HEADER • DEFINE ORDER REASONS.

For every order reason, the value assigned in the Relevance column determines how the document is processed by retro-billing. The following values are possible:

- **<blank>:** Not used for retroactive billing.
- **1:** Credit/debit memo request used for retro-billing.
- **2:** Credit/debit memo to be retro-billed at the price change.

All invoices are always considered as primary documents. Additionally, you assign the value of 2 to all reason codes for primary documents. For example, credit memos for damaged goods should be considered primary documents, and any price revisions to the original invoice should also be reflected in those credit memos.

Sales Documents: Order Reasons

Order reason	R	Description
005		Newspaper advertisement
006		Excellent price
007		Fast delivery
008		Good service
100	1	Price discrepancy: price was too high
101	2	Poor quality
102	2	Damaged in transit
103	2	Quantity discrepancy
104	2	Material ruined
105		Free of charge sample
200	1	Price discrepancy: price was too low
300	2	Service / Repair
310	2	Returns
400		Run schedule header exists
410		Pre-run schedule header exists

Figure 4.15 Order Reason Codes

On the other hand, you assign the value of 1 to all reason codes for secondary documents. For example, the $10 adjustment credit memo discussed in the previous example should be considered as a secondary document. Any price revisions to the original invoice may trigger new adjustments but won't have any effect on that credit memo.

If you find that the retro-billing calculation isn't working as expected, you may want to compare the reason code configuration with the reason codes assigned to the sales documents. For example, you can view the order reason for a sales document by choosing Display Sales Order (Transaction VA03) • Goto • Header • Sales tab.

Finally, in the next section, we'll look at the billing process in different business scenarios.

4.5 Other Scenarios

This section discusses billing processes in different business scenarios such as third-party orders, consignment, free-of-charge delivery, and the POD process.

4.5.1 POD Process

The proof of delivery (POD) process is used in business scenarios where a customer's invoice is issued only after and only for the confirmed quantities delivered. Because it's yet another aspect that can influence the customer invoicing process, let's spend some time understanding it.

Whether a sales transaction is POD relevant depends on several factors:

- **POD relevance configuration of a delivery item**
  - The configuration of delivery items for POD relevance is carried out using SAP IMG • LOGISTICS EXECUTION • SHIPPING • DELIVERIES • PROOF OF DELIVERY • SET POD RELEVANCE DEPENDING ON DELIVERY ITEM CATEGORY.
  - In this transaction you configure its relevance for POD process and its automation level for every delivery item category.
- **POD relevance of ship-to party master data**
  - The POD-relevant master data of a customer is maintained using CHANGE CUSTOMER DATA (Transaction XD02) • SALES AREA DATA VIEW • SHIPPING tab.
  - On this tab, you can specify whether this customer is POD relevant and the time period after which POD status is automatically marked as confirmed.
- **POD relevance of a sales document**
  - You can also directly mark a sales document item as POD relevant. To maintain POD relevance of a sales document item, select DISPLAY SALES ORDER • GOTO • ITEM • SHIPPING TAB.

For the POD-relevant sales transactions, you can issue an invoice only after the POD status is marked as verified or confirmed. More commonly, the POD process involves the electronic exchange of delivery documents and POD confirmations. However, you can also manually set the POD status in delivery documents by using SAP MENU • LOGISTICS • SALES AND DISTRIBUTION • SHIPPING AND TRANSPORTATION • OUTBOUND DELIVERY • CHANGE • SINGLE DOCUMENT (Transaction VL02N).

Note

You may want to keep in mind that POD confirmation doesn't create an entry in the SD document flow discussed in Chapter 3, Customer Billing. You have to check the POD status directly in a delivery document.

On the other hand, you can use a worklist for outbound deliveries to process their POD confirmations and to generate the corresponding billing documents. You access this worklist using SAP MENU • LOGISTICS • SALES AND DISTRIBUTION • SHIPPING AND TRANSPORTATION • PROOF OF DELIVERY • WORKLIST OUTBOUND DELIVERIES FOR POD (Transaction VLPODL). The transaction provides several selection criteria to select delivery documents waiting for POD processing.

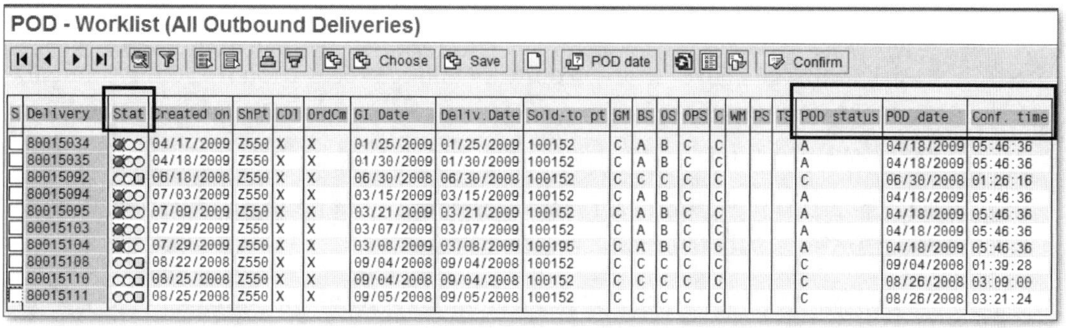

POD - Worklist (All Outbound Deliveries)

Choose | Save | POD date | Confirm

S	Delivery	Stat	Created on	ShPt	CDl	OrdCm	GI Date	Deliv.Date	Sold-to pt	GM	BS	OS	OPS	C	WM	PS	TS	POD status	POD date	Conf. time
	80015034		04/17/2009	Z550	X	X	01/25/2009	01/25/2009	100152	C	A	B	C	C				A	04/18/2009	05:46:36
	80015035		04/18/2009	Z550	X	X	01/30/2009	01/30/2009	100152	C	A	B	C	C				A	04/18/2009	05:46:36
	80015092		06/18/2008	Z550	X	X	06/30/2008	06/30/2008	100152	C	C	C	C	C				C	06/30/2008	01:26:16
	80015094		07/03/2009	Z550	X	X	03/15/2009	03/15/2009	100152	C	A	B	C	C				A	04/18/2009	05:46:36
	80015095		07/09/2009	Z550	X	X	03/21/2009	03/21/2009	100152	C	A	B	C	C				A	04/18/2009	05:46:36
	80015103		07/29/2009	Z550	X	X	03/07/2009	03/07/2009	100152	C	A	B	C	C				A	04/18/2009	05:46:36
	80015104		07/29/2009	Z550	X	X	03/08/2009	03/08/2009	100195	C	A	B	C	C				A	04/18/2009	05:46:36
	80015108		08/22/2008	Z550	X	X	09/04/2008	09/04/2008	100152	C	C	C	C	C				C	09/04/2008	01:39:28
	80015110		08/25/2008	Z550	X	X	09/04/2008	09/04/2008	100152	C	C	C	C	C				C	08/26/2008	03:09:00
	80015111		08/25/2008	Z550	X	X	09/05/2008	09/05/2008	100152	C	C	C	C	C				C	08/26/2008	03:21:24

Figure 4.16 POD Worklist

In the sample list (Figure 4.16) generated by this transaction, note the following:

- The Stat field and POD STATUS field provide the following indicators:
  - **A:** POD status not yet processed (Red)
  - **B:** POD status partially processed but not yet confirmed (Yellow)
  - **C:** POD status completely processed and confirmed (Green)
- The fields POD Date and Conf Time show the POD confirmation date and time for confirmed documents, whereas for the pending documents, these fields propose the system date and time. You can change this value by selecting the POD Date button at the top of the screen.

To create a billing document from this screen, select the documents for which POD processing is confirmed, and choose GOTO • CREATE BILLING DOCUMENTS.

4.5.2 Intercompany Billing

Intercompany transactions refer to scenarios when one company of an organization (ordering company) orders goods from a plant assigned to another company (delivering company) belonging to the same organization. There are two processing options for such intercompany transactions:

- Intercompany sales processing, in which the delivering plant delivers goods directly to a customer
- Intercompany stock transfer, in which the delivering plant delivers goods to a plant assigned to the ordering company

Because both companies prepare their financial statements independently, the delivering company has to invoice the receiving company for such transactions regardless of the processing option used. These invoices are processed in the SAP system with the help of an intercompany billing process. You'll find the configuration for intercompany billing under SAP IMG • SALES AND DISTRIBUTION • BILLING • INTERCOMPANY BILLING.

Under this configuration area, activities corresponding to organizational assignment are especially important.

- The first step is to assign possible combinations of delivering company plants and receiving company sales organizations.
- The next step is to assign an internal customer number to the receiving sales organizations (Figure 4.17).

View for Inter-Company Billing": Overview

Sales org.	Sales Organization	CustInterC	Cust.inter-co.bill.
0001	Sales Org. Germany		
0005	Germany Frankfurt	10000	IDES AG
0006	USA Philadelphia	30000	IDES US Inc.
0007	Germany Frankfurt	10000	IDES AG
0008	USA Philadelphia	30000	IDES US Inc.
1000	Germany Frankfurt		
1020	Germany Berlin		

Figure 4.17 Assign Customer to Sales Organization

The intercompany billing process uses organizational assignments in the configuration to determine the internal customer for which the billing documents are generated.

Tip

Intercompany sales transactions involve the generation of two billing documents: a billing document for the end customer and an intercompany billing document for intercompany billing.

In the standard SAP system, you can use billing types IV (intercompany billing) and IG (intercompany credit memo) for intercompany transactions. The intercompany billing documents are automatically created, and they are processed using the billing due list (Transaction VF04). You may recall from Chapter 3, Customer Billing, that the billing due list selection criteria involves an indicator for Intercompany Billing. You have to select that indicator to process intercompany billing documents.

In the next section, we'll discuss pro forma invoices.

4.5.3 Pro Forma Invoices

Pro forma invoices are the invoices generated on the basis of sales orders or deliveries. Especially in international trades, these invoices are necessary to provide custom authorities evidence of the cost of goods.

The following points differentiate pro forma invoices from standard invoices:

- Goods issue isn't required before you create a delivery-related pro forma invoice.
- Billing status in the sales order or delivery document isn't updated, so you can create as many pro forma invoices as you like for a sales or a delivery.
- Data from pro forma invoices isn't passed on to Financial Accounting, so no AR entries are posted to the customer account.

The standard SAP system provides billing types F5 (for sales orders) and F6 (for deliveries) for pro forma invoice processing.

Tip

The standard SAP system provides one SD document type for intercompany billing and a different one for pro forma invoices. Refer to SAP Note 445763 for details on how to create a new billing type that combines characteristics of pro forma invoices and intercompany billing.

You can use the same transaction to create pro forma invoices as the one used to create individual billing documents. You access this transaction using SAP MENU • LOGISTICS • SALES AND DISTRIBUTION • BILLING • BILLING DOCUMENT • CREATE (Transaction VF01).

Let's now see how to process billing documents for customer orders fulfilled by third-party vendors.

4.5.4 Billing Third-Party Orders

In third-party order processing, you pass along a customer order to a third-party vendor for order fulfillment. The vendor delivers products directly to the customer and invoices you. You generate customer billing based on the invoice received from the vendor. The cost calculation in the billing document is based on the purchase order and the vendor invoices.

Note

For third-party orders, if the vendor sends any subsequent adjustments for third-party transactions that are already billed, the revised costs are automatically updated in customer billing documents.

Similar to billing documents for standard sales orders, billing documents for third-party orders are displayed and processed using the billing due list. However, it's the Billing Relevance of the sales document item category that determines when a billing document for a third-party order shows up in a billing due list.

We discussed Billing Relevance in Chapter 3. This parameter has special significance in third-party order processing.

- **If Billing Relevance is set to "F":** Order-related billing, status accordingly to invoice quantity

  - A customer invoice is included in the billing due list only after the vendor invoice is received or the goods receipt from the vendor is posted.
  - The order is considered completely billed until the next vendor invoice is received.
- **If Billing Relevance is set to "B":** Order-related billing, status according to order quantity
  - A customer invoice is included in the billing due list immediate after the customer order is entered.
  - The order is considered completely billed only when the invoiced quantity equals the order quantity.

Table 4.5 lists other configuration parameters available in the standard SAP system for third-party order processing. Refer to Chapter 3, Customer Billing, for more details on how these parameters influence the billing process.

Sales Item Categories	
ALES	Third-party item (ALE processing)
TAS	Third-party sales order item
TASG	Third-party credit memo item
Billing Type	
G2S	Third-party credit memo

Table 4.5 Standard Billing Parameters for Third-Party Orders

The next section refers to billing for customer consignment processing.

4.5.5 Consignment Billing

The actual billing process for consignment orders isn't very different from the billing process for standard orders. However, let's briefly review the consignment process itself to put this type of billing in proper perspective.

In the consignment process, goods are stored at the customer location as consignment stock, but they are owned by your company until the customer decides to use them. The customer is only billed for the actual quantities of goods after the goods are removed from the consignment stock. At any time, customer has an option to return unused goods. In the SAP system, the inventory in customer consignment stock is identified separately with a Special Stock indicator (W). Without going into too much detail about the logistics business processes, the customer consignment process involves the following main transactions:

- Consignment fill-up: This process augments or fills up the customer consignment stock. No customer billing is required because the inventory is still owned by your company.
- Consignment pick-up: This process removes stock from the customer consignment stock. Again, there is no need to generate a customer credit memo because the inventory was already owned by your company.
- Consignment issue: This process records the customer's usage of consignment stock. These transactions are recorded in the SAP system using sales orders of a specific order type. Customer billing is carried out based on the corresponding delivery documents.
- Consignment return: This process corresponds to the customer returning stock to the consignment stock. You would process this transaction similar to a returns sales transaction. A returns delivery is created based on the returns sales transaction. A customer credit memo is generated based on a returns delivery.

Note

The process for returnable packaging (Special Stock indicator "V") is also very similar to the process described in this section. The only exception is that a customer is invoiced only if the customer doesn't return the packaging within the specified time period. The sales order type used to invoice the customer for returnable packaging is LN.

Processing of consignment billing and consignment credit memos is similar to the standard billing process. So you can use individual billing (Transaction VF01) or the billing due list (VF04) to process these transactions. You can also use the standard Billing Document Type unless there is any specific business requirement to be able to identify consignment billing documents separately.

Table 4.6 lists other configuration parameters available in the standard SAP system for customer consignment processing. Refer to Chapter 3, Customer Billing, for more details on how these parameters influence the billing process.

Sales Order Type	
KB	Consignment fill-up
KA	Consignment pick-up
KE	Consignment issue
CR	Consignment returns
Sales Item Categories	
KEN	Consignment issue
KRN	Consignment returns

Table 4.6 Standard Billing Parameters for the Consignment Process

The next section describes billing for the cash on delivery process.

4.5.6 Cash on Delivery Process

In the standard order to cash process, you generate the customer invoice for the end customer after the goods delivery is completed. However, in the cash on delivery process, you expect the customer to pay immediately upon delivery so that the delivering or the forwarding company collects money on your behalf. For such sales transactions, it's necessary to post accounting entries so that receivables are posted against the forwarding agent instead of the end customer.

In Chapter 1, Customer Master Data, we discussed the concept of partner functions in the SAP system. For the cash on delivery orders, you have to make sure to assign the forwarding agent to the payer partner function (PY).

Tip

Refer to Chapter 3, Customer Billing, for more details on how accounting entries are posted when the sold-to party and payer are different in a billing document.

It's possible to assign the customer account for the forwarding agent directly in an order entry. However, if your company processes a high volume of cash on delivery transactions, you may want to update the configuration to automatically carry out partner determination. You carry out this configuration setting using SAP IMG • Sales and Distribution • Basic functions • Partner Determination • Setup Partner Determination.

Let's now see how to process free-of-charge items.

4.5.7 Free-of-Charge Items

It's common practice for many companies to provide free-of-charge items to their customers as part of a negotiated contract, marketing promotion, or other reasons. The free-of-charge items may be the same items or different items; they may represent items already included in an order or in addition to the ordered quantities. The SAP system supports all these variations of free-of-charge items. Obviously, these items are part of a customer invoice, but the customer isn't charged for those items.

In the SAP system, you can handle free-of-charge requirements in two ways depending on the configuration of the corresponding Sales Item Category.

- You can mark a sales item category as not relevant for pricing.
  - While entering an order, you enter free-of-charge items with the specific sales item category.
  - This assignment will ensure that even though the items are part of a sales order and a billing document, they aren't invoiced.
- You can mark sales item as relevant for pricing but then discount it by 100% in the pricing calculation.
  - This approach is useful if you need to integrate free-of-charge item calculations in other SAP components such as a profitability analysis.

You carry out the configuration for free-of-charge items in configuration area SAP IMG • SALES AND DISTRIBUTION • BASIC FUNCTIONS • FREE GOODS • CONTROL FREE GOODS PRICING. Figure 4.18 shows a screen of configuration activity Control Pricing for Free Goods Activity.

As shown in the figure, the Carry Out Pricing indicator assigned to the sales document item category controls the free-of-charge items calculation. The Standard item category (TANN) provided in the SAP system for this purpose takes the approach of not carrying out pricing. However, you can assign pricing indicatory "B" to an item and then configure the pricing procedure to carry out a calculation for a 100% discount. Refer to Chapter 3, Customer Billing, for more details on pricing calculation.

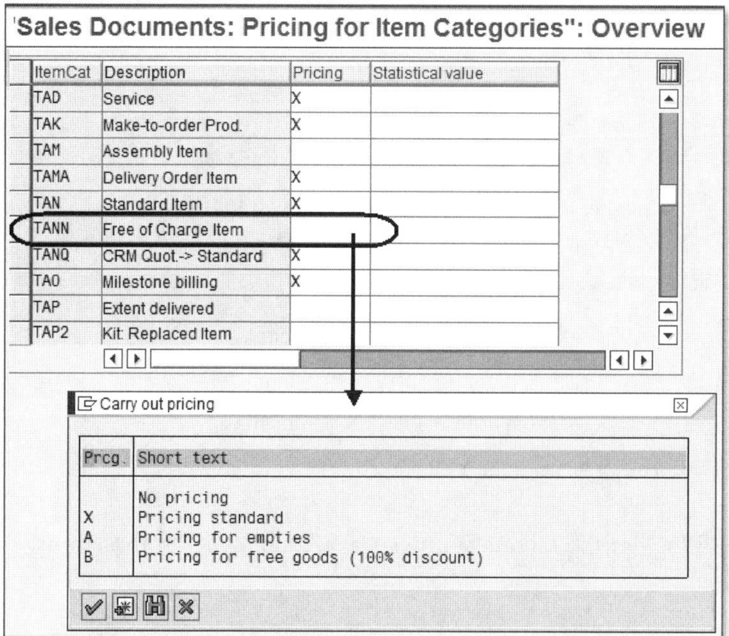

Figure 4.18 Pricing for Item Categories

This concludes the discussion of different business scenarios in this section. The next section summarizes different transactions discussed in this chapter.

4.5.8 List of Transactions

Table 4.7 lists some of the transactions discussed in this chapter.

Transaction	Usage
F-37	Enter down payment request (AR)
F-29	Post customer down payment (AR)
F-39	Clear customer down payment (AR)
VF04	Process billing due list
DP91	Resource-related billing
DP93	Resource-related billing (intercompany)
DP96	Resource-related billing (collective processing)

Table 4.7 Transactions – Advanced Billing

Transaction	Usage
VFRB	Retro-active billing
VL02N	Change outbound delivery
VLPODL	Worklist of outbound deliveries for POD
VLPODF	Worklist of subsequent processing for POD
VLPODQ	Automatic POD confirmation
VF01/VF02/VF03	Create/change/display billing document
VA01/VA02/VA03	Create/change/display sales order
MM01/MM02/MM03	Create/change/display material master
XD01/XD02/XD03	Create/change/display customer master

Table 4.7 Transactions – Advanced Billing (Cont.)

In next section, we'll look at the technical objects available for AR transactions.

4.6 Technical Reference

This section lists technical objects such as SAP Notes, authorization objects, and tables and structures relevant for processing AR transactions. Considering the large number of technical objects available in the SAP system, this information should only be considered as a starting point for analysis.

4.6.1 SAP Notes

Table 4.8 is a list of SAP Notes relevant for AR transactions.

SAP Note	Relevance
0000574517	Partial payment of customer down payment requests
0000186233	Down payment clearing in multiple currencies
0000858702	Down payments in resource-related billing
0000213526	Customizing of down payment processing SD/FI
0000831158	FAQ: Periodic billing plans

Table 4.8 SAP Notes for Advanced Billing

SAP Note	Relevance
0000830097	FAQ: Milestone billing plans (reference)
0000830484	Generating settlement period and billing date in billing plan
0000210123	Manual dates in periodic billing plans
0000973220	Billing plans and canceling billing documents
0000428728	FAQ: Resource-related billing
0000496349	Resource-related billing and credit management
0000512698	Customizing DIP profiles in the productive system
0000537556	Resource-related billing: Costs, currencies, and exchange rates
0000331047	Retroactive billing for intercompany billing
0000338922	Analysis isn't for cross-company transactions
0000038501	Intercompany billing document before customer billing
0000367149	Intercompany billing in foreign currency
0000862582	Performance problems in retroactive billing transaction
0000024832	Pricing rules (pricing type) and their explanations
0001074846	POD maintenance views not available in IMG
0000867678	POD, delivery, and billing documents
0000445763	Pro forma invoices for intercompany billing
0000371675	Include pro forma invoices in list of billing documents (VF05)
0000492831	Customer consignment process and credit management
0000554912	Free-of-charge delivery without reference to order
0000352441	Accumulated cost calculation in main item

Table 4.8 SAP Notes for Advanced Billing (Cont.)

In the next section, we'll look at the authorization objects available for AR transactions.

4.6.2 Authorization Objects

Table 4.9 lists some of the authorization objects to be considered for transactions discussed in this chapter.

Object	Description
F_BKPF_BED	Accounting Doc: Account Authorization for Customers
F_BKPF_BLA	Accounting Doc: Authorization for Document Types
F_BKPF_BUK	Accounting Doc: Authorization for Company Codes
F_BKPF_BUP	Accounting Doc: Authorization for Posting Periods
F_BKPF_KOA	Accounting Doc: Authorization for Account Types
V_VBRK_FKA	Billing: Authorization for Billing Types
V_VBRK_VKO	Billing: Authorization for Sales Organizations
V_VBSK_STO	Billing: Authorization for Cancellation Collective Runs
V_LIKP_VST	Delivery: Authorization for Shipping Points
V_VBAK_AAT	Sales Document: Authorization for Sales Document Types
V_VBAK_VKO	Sales Document: Authorization for Sales Areas
V_VBAK_FAK	Sales Document: Authorization for Billing Block

Table 4.9 Authorization Objects – Advanced Billing

The next section provides a list of tables and structures.

4.6.3 Tables and Structures

Table 4.10 lists tables and structures relevant for processing AR transactions.

Table	Relevance
BKPF	Accounting document: Header data
BSEG	Accounting document: Item data
BSID	Secondary index for customer documents
BSAD	Secondary index for customer documents – cleared items
VBAK	Sales document: Header data
VBAP	Sales document: Item data
VBRK	Billing document: Header data
VBRP	Billing document: Item data
KONV	Conditions – transaction data

Table 4.10 Advanced Billing – Tables and Structures

Table	Relevance
FPLA	Billing plan
FPLT	Billing plan: Dates

Table 4.10 Advanced Billing – Tables and Structures (Cont.)

Now we'll look at the objects and functionality available for enhancing and modifying the functionality of processing AR transactions.

4.7 Enhancements and Modifications

This section provides a list of available BTEs, enhancements, BAdIs, and BAPIs relevant for the billing functionality discussed in this chapter. These are used to enhance and modify the standard functionality available in the SAP system.

4.7.1 Enhancements

Using enhancements, you can add custom logic to carry out additional validations and custom business processing. Let's look at some of the enhancements that you can use for functionalities discussed in this chapter.

1. We discussed how you can use different characteristics to summarize and calculate values in resource-related billing. Table 4.11 lists the available enhancements for resource-related billing.

Enhancement	Description
AD010001	Contains several exits that can be used to change object list and its hierarchy for resource-related billing
AD010002	Contains exits to delimit selection criteria and/or filter data that is determined for resource-related billing
AD010003	Creates user-defined characteristics for RRB dynamic items
AD010005	Creates user-defined sources for user-defined resource-related billing characteristics
AD010007	Changes resource-related billing dynamic item processing information
AD230001	Contains several exits that can be used to modify items, structures, and other outputs in the bill print processor

Table 4.11 Enhancements for Resource-Related Billing

2. **KSDIEX01:** Enhancement for summarizing PO items in resource-related billing
   - This enhancement is relevant for resource-related billing documents in which you can add a summarization level to PO items before they are included in a billing request.
   - It contains function modules `EXIT_SAPLEBBS_001-003`, which can be used to summarize open items and delete unallowed costs from a billing request.
3. **SDVFX007:** User exit for a billing plan in AC interface
   - This is one of the user exits we mentioned in Chapter 3, Customer Billing. It's part of a group of user exits for the interface that transfers billing document to accounting.
   - This user exit can be used to update or modify billing plan information for an item.
4. **V60F0001:** Enhancement to change billing dates in a billing plan
   - Table FPLT contains the dates of a billing plan. Using this enhancement, you can change the billing date to be different from the one calculated by the billing plan.
   - The enhancement contains function module `EXIT_SAPLV60F_001` for editing the proposed billing dates.

The next section provides details of BAdIs available for the functionalities discussed in this chapter.

4.7.2 Business Add-Ins (BAdIs)

Business Add-In implementations are enhancements to the standard SAP system. Most BAdIs provided by the SAP system accommodate industry-specific or country-specific requirements. However, you can also use BAdI implementations to meet any unique requirements for your business. Following are some of the BAdIs available for the billing functionalities discussed in this chapter.

1. BADI_SD_DATE_UPDATE
   - This BAdI can be used to redetermine dates in a billing plan.
   - This BAdI provides a method `DATE_TO_DETERMINATION`, which accesses billing plan Tables FPLA and FPLT for date modifications.

2. BADI_SD_PRICING_TUN
   - This BAdI is useful for performance tuning pricing calculations for SD documents containing a billing plan.
   - This BAdI provides a method called `PRICING_TUNING` that can be used for fine tuning pricing calculation performance.
3. DPBP_INFLUENCE_PROC
   - This BAdI is useful for influencing billing plan and calculations in resource-related billing.
   - This BAdI provides a method called `CONSIDER_DATE_TO`. This method is used to determine the posting date up to which documents are considered in resource-related billing calculations.
4. BADI_SD_V46H0001
   - This BAdI provides customer functions for resource-related billing.
   - This BAdI provides methods to influence resource-related billing functionality at the time of creating an item (`EXIT_SAPLV46H_001`), making changes to partner functions (`EXIT_SAPLV46H_002`), and creating or changing header details (`EXIT_SAPLV46H_003`).

4.8 Summary

In this chapter, we discussed advanced billing functionalities. We started with how to process customer down payments, followed by periodic billing plans, and milestone billing plans. Resource-related billing can be used for billing scenarios that require customer billing based on used resources. An extensive section detailed how you can use the billing process in the SAP system for a wide range of business scenarios. In the next chapter, we'll go into the details of processing customer incoming payments.

This chapter describes the process of posting incoming payments in the SAP system. The primary focus of this chapter is on one SAP transaction that is used to manually process, match, and post incoming payments. You'll discover tips and tricks associated with this transaction that makes it versatile enough to support numerous business requirements. You'll also learn about additional tools and functionalities in the SAP system that assist in processing customer payments efficiently.

5 Incoming Payments

In today's business world, processing incoming payments no longer means simply posting a check received from a customer to a receivables account. The global economy demands that your incoming payments and cash application system support multiple currencies, different payment methods, complex selection and matching criteria, large data volume, and different processing interfaces depending on the tasks at hand. The incoming payments may be received manually or electronically. The SAP system can easily handle all such complexities and much more.

Note

This chapter focuses on the manual processing of incoming payments. The SAP system also provides comprehensive functionality for electronic processing of incoming payments and automatic debit functionalities that aren't part of this chapter.

Logically, the process of applying customer payments in the SAP system can be divided into the following steps and activities:

1. Entering basic information
2. Selecting customer items
3. Processing customer items
4. Processing payment differences
5. Simulating and posting

In this chapter, we'll look at each of these steps in detail, starting with the first step of entering basic information.

5.1 Entering Basic Information

One of the most common transactions used for processing incoming payments is accessed using SAP MENU • FINANCIAL ACCOUNTING • ACCOUNTS RECEIVABLE • DOCUMENT ENTRY • INCOMING PAYMENTS (Transaction F-28). As you'll see later in this chapter, even though this transaction appears under the Accounts Receivable menu; it can be used to process incoming payments from any other business partners such as vendors or employees. Figure 5.1 shows the first screen for processing incoming payments.

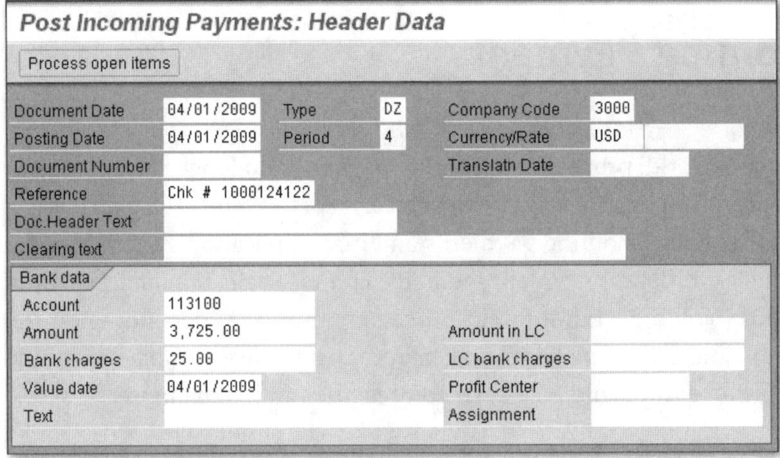

Figure 5.1 Incoming Payment Header Screen

For the purpose of entering basic data, the first two sections of the screen are important because this is where you enter document header data and bank data.

5.1.1 Document Header Data

Entering document header data for incoming payments is done similarly to other accounting documents in the SAP system. We discussed many of these fields, but let's review them here again briefly. Fields such as Document Date, Posting Date, and Document Type are defaulted based on the configuration settings.

The fields Currency, Rate, and Translation Date specify the currency and exchange rate details for the payment document. This helps you process incoming payments in a currency that is different from the functional currency of the company code, or even currencies of customer invoice documents. This functionality can be helpful for multinational companies as well as while working with multinational business partners. For example, in such business relationships, it isn't uncommon to invoice customer subsidiaries in one currency, and receive payments in a different currency from their head office.

Reference is a useful field to enter the customer document number, a check number, an incoming wire transfer number, or similar payment identification.

Tip

In addition to the SAP-generated document number, you can print this reference document number on the customer account statement. This will help your customers to easily identify their documents and any differences.

Clearing Text is another useful field where you can enter a clearing text that is automatically copied to all open items that are cleared with the payment. This text can later serve to provide easy reference for any details associated with incoming payments. After basic details of incoming payment are entered, you have to enter bank-related data.

5.1.2 Bank Data

This data section consists of fields relevant for the debit bank account entry in the accounting document.

The Account Field corresponds to the GL account in the company chart of accounts that corresponds to the main bank account when payment is deposited. Profit Center, Assignment, and Text provide you with account assignments and information fields associated with the bank entry.

The Amount field corresponds to the net amount deposited in the bank, excluding any bank charges. Bank charges are entered separately in the Bank Charges field. For example, companies may elect to receive customer payments electronically, but the banks may deduct processing fees from the incoming payments. Figure 5.1 shows an example in which $25 toward bank charges are deducted from the customer payment of $3,750, so that the net entry to the bank account is $3,725. If the payment currency is different from the functional currency of the company code, corresponding amounts in functional currency are displayed in the fields Amount in LC and LC Bank Charges.

Apart from clearing separating bank charges from the net cash receipt, there is an added advantage of entering bank charges in a separate field as just described. In configuration, you can assign a default GL account for the bank charges using SAP IMG • FINANCIAL ACCOUNTING • ACCOUNTS RECEIVABLE AND ACCOUNTS PAYABLE • BUSINESS TRANSACTIONS • INCOMING PAYMENTS • INCOMING PAYMENTS GLOBAL SETTINGS • DEFINE ACCOUNTS FOR BANK CHARGES (CUSTOMERS) • BANK CHARGES TRANSACTION BSP. The corresponding cost center to collect bank charges is then assigned as the default cost center in the GL account master data. Thus, by maintaining the required settings, you can automatically post the bank charges to the required GL account and cost center.

After the document header data and bank data are entered, you're ready to select open items posted to the customer account.

5.2 Selecting Open Items

You have numerous options available to you for selecting open documents that are to be cleared against incoming payment. If you're posting a payment to a customer account with a low transaction volume, then simply entering the customer account number may be sufficient. However, if you routinely process incoming payments to customer accounts with large transaction volume, you'll certainly appreciate different ways in which you can select open items.

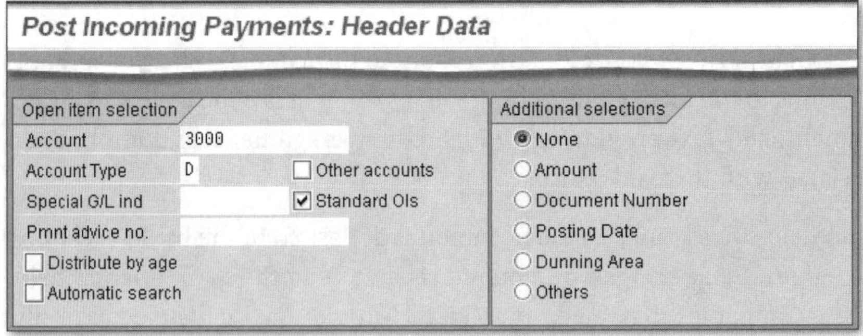

Figure 5.2 Main Selection Options

Figure 5.2 shows selection options available to you on the first screen of the incoming payment transaction. The fields ACCOUNT TYPE and ACCOUNT jointly determine the type of incoming payment you're processing. Table 5.1 shows possible options for the field ACCOUNT TYPE.

Account Type	Account	Use
D	Customer Account	Payment received from customers
K	Vendor Account	Payment received from vendors or (in a typical implementation) employees
S	GL Account	Payment processed directly to GL account

Table 5.1 Account Types for Incoming Payments

Field STANDARD OI indicates that you want to select regular open items. Additionally, you can select special GL transactions by entering the corresponding indicators in field SPECIAL GL IND. These selections may be sufficient for simple payment processing. However, for complicated business scenarios, you can select open items based on other criteria, such as the following:

1. Automatic selection
2. Selecting multiple accounts
3. Selection based on payment advice
4. Selection based on additional criteria

Let's look at these options in more detail.

5.2.1 Automatic Selection

If the account you're processing has a large number of open items, you can use either the Distribute by Age or Automatic Search options to automatically search for items that can be cleared with the incoming payment. You'll find both these indicators in the bottom-left corner of the first screen.

If the DISTRIBUTE BY AGE indicator is selected, the open items are selected according to their number of days in arrears. The process starts with selection of open items with the most days in arrears and continues by selecting open items with fewer days in arrears as long as the remaining balance from the incoming payment amount can be allocated to the next item. Any remaining balance from the payment amount is displayed as not assigned.

On the other hand, if the AUTOMATIC SEARCH indicator is selected, the selection process attempts to find a combination of items whose total matches the payment amount entered on the first screen. An internal algorithm carries out the selection of open items, and it stops and totals the selected items as soon as a good approximation is achieved. Any remaining balance from the payment amount is displayed as not assigned.

Another fairly common business requirement is to select open documents posted to multiple accounts.

5.2.2 Selecting Multiple Accounts

You can choose additional customer and vendor accounts by selecting the OTHER ACCOUNTS flag on the first screen of this transaction. If this indicator is selected, an additional pop-up window is displayed where you can enter additional accounts.

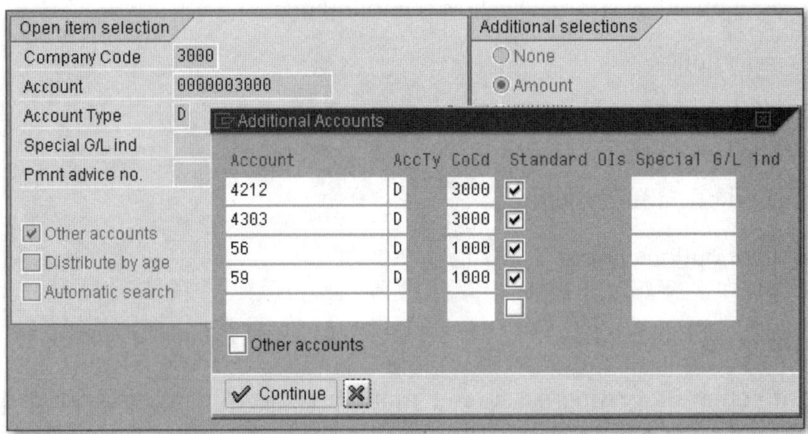

Figure 5.3 Additional Accounts

As Figure 5.3 shows, you can enter as many additional accounts as required. For each account, you enter the account number, account type, standard OI indicator, and special GL indicators. You can add several accounts of any account type from any company code.

Tip

Using other accounts selection, you can choose accounts and thus open documents from other company codes. This functionality helps you process incoming payment in one company code against invoices posted in any other company codes. When the payment document is posted, the payment transaction automatically creates the required intercompany entries.

If these selections aren't sufficient, then you can select documents using any of the additional selections.

5.2.3 Additional Selections

On the bottom-right corner of the first screen (refer to Figure 5.2), you have an option to choose other commonly used selection criteria such as amount, document number, posting date, and dunning area for an open item. By selecting OTHER from the list of selection options, you can open up an even bigger list of criteria based on which you can select open items.

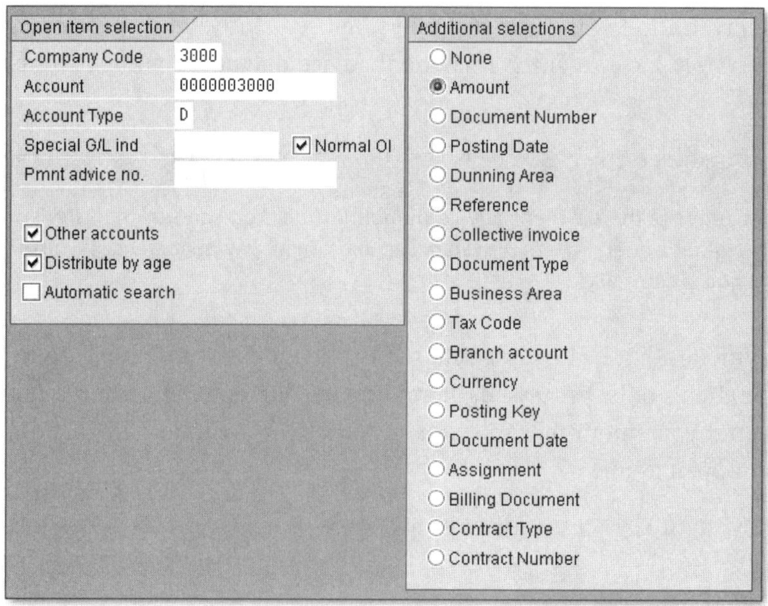

Figure 5.4 Additional Selections

Figure 5.4 shows you all of the available selection criteria for selecting open items. Of course, for each of these selections, you can enter a single value, multiple values, a range, or any combination thereof.

Lastly, let's talk about yet another way of selecting customer documents to apply incoming payment.

5.2.4 Selection Based on a Payment Advice

Payment advice notes are SAP documents that contain incoming payment details that can be used to assign and clear open items posted to a customer account.

There are several ways in which you can create payment advices, although electronic interfaces are one of the most common ways. For example, if you process incoming payments using the lockbox functionality or if you carry out electronic bank reconciliation in the SAP system, any unapplied or partially applied payments can be saved as a payment advice document. Alternately, you can also manually create payment advice documents. Manual creation of payment advices may be useful if, for example, you want to process a payment based on an offline (email/phone) conversation with your customers. Subsequently, while processing a payment, you simply have to enter a payment advice document number (refer to Figure 5.2).

Tip

You don't need to specify the payment advice number in full. You can use the asterisk "*" to search for a generic query. The SAP system searches for all payment advices whose key matches the query entered.

Because the payment advice already contains the customer or vendor account number and open items to be processed, there is no need to enter any other selection criteria. Even if you enter other selection criteria, they are ignored while displaying the list of open items.

Let's now see how to process list of open items.

5.3 Processing Open items

Figure 5.5 shows a screen that will be displayed after you enter criteria for selecting customer open items. If the figure appears crowded and complicated, that's because it's crowded and complicated. There are numerous controls and information fields on this screen that assist you in assigning open documents to an incoming payment.

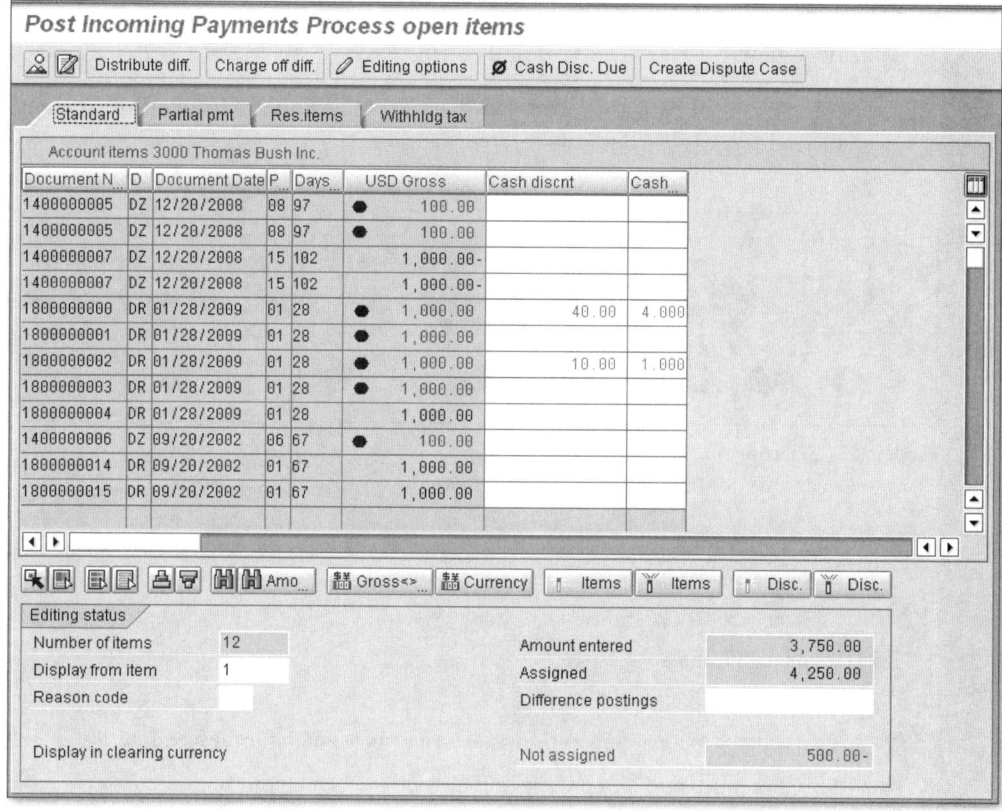

Figure 5.5 Process Open Items

Let's first look at the selection controls for selecting items.

5.3.1 Selection Controls

While processing an incoming payment, there is no difference between selecting invoices, credit memos, or other types of adjustment entries posted to a customer account. This helps you easily clear out an invoice, a credit memo, and an account adjustment entry in a single entry. Following are general guidelines:

- A double-click on the amount column acts as a toggle to assign/unassign an item to the incoming payment.
- A double-click on the discount columns act as a toggle to assign/unassign the discount amount to the invoice.

▸ A double-click on any other column takes you to the document display so that you can review or validate any details as necessary.

Figure 5.6 shows a part of the processing screen that contains selection options. Table 5.2 provides relevant details.

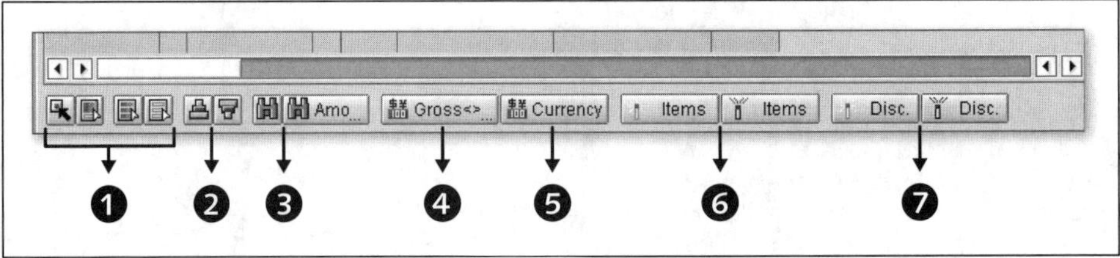

Figure 5.6 Selection Options

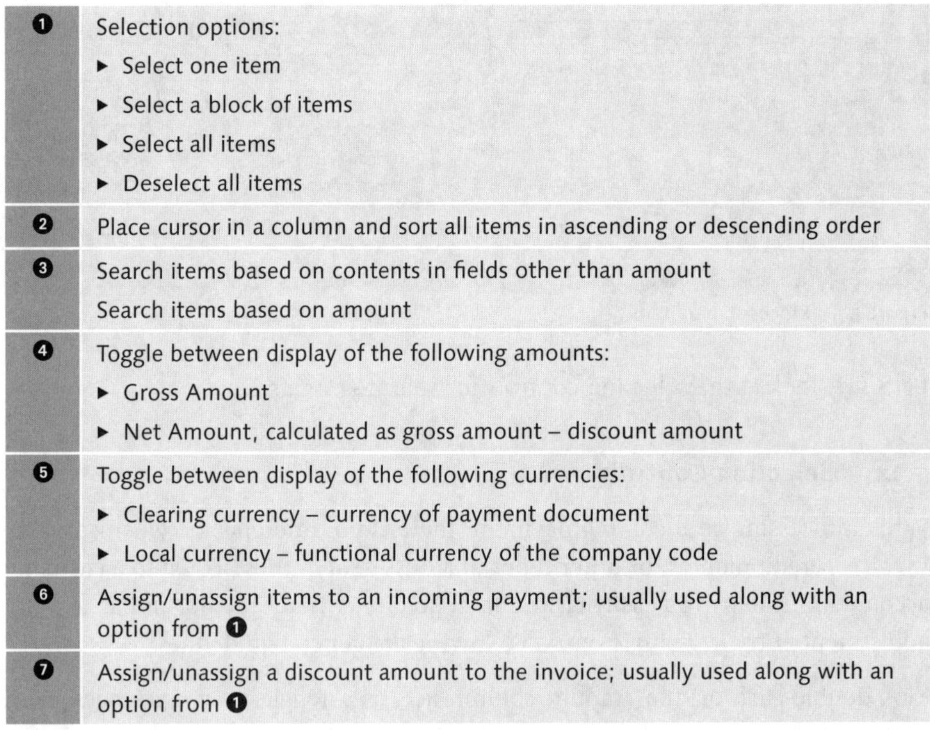

❶	Selection options: ▸ Select one item ▸ Select a block of items ▸ Select all items ▸ Deselect all items
❷	Place cursor in a column and sort all items in ascending or descending order
❸	Search items based on contents in fields other than amount Search items based on amount
❹	Toggle between display of the following amounts: ▸ Gross Amount ▸ Net Amount, calculated as gross amount – discount amount
❺	Toggle between display of the following currencies: ▸ Clearing currency – currency of payment document ▸ Local currency – functional currency of the company code
❻	Assign/unassign items to an incoming payment; usually used along with an option from ❶
❼	Assign/unassign a discount amount to the invoice; usually used along with an option from ❶

Table 5.2 Selection Options on the Item Processing Screen

While processing incoming payments, all selected items are displayed in a different color than items that aren't selected. To assist in this explanation, selected items in Figure 5.5 are highlighted with a black dot in the figure.

Let's discuss discount processing in more detail in the next section.

5.3.2 Discount Processing

Payment terms entered in the customer documents determine whether payment within a certain timeframe is eligible for any discount. For example, an invoice with a net payment term of 30 days may offer a 1.5% discount if payment is received within 10 days. The incoming payment transaction automatically calculates the eligible discount amount for each document based on its payment terms.

If a document is eligible for any discount, the corresponding discount amount and discount percentage are automatically displayed in corresponding columns on the screen. In Figure 5.5, the document 1800000000 is eligible for a $40 (4%) discount, and the document 1800000002 is eligible for a $10 (1%) discount. The discount amount is automatically posted to the GL account that is configured using SAP IMG • Financial Accounting • Accounts Receivable and Accounts Payable • Business Transactions • Incoming Payments • Incoming Payments Global Settings • Define Accounts for Cash Discount Granted • Cash Discount expenses Transaction SKT.

You can double-click on the discount columns to assign/unassign this discount; or you can change the discount amount as long as it's within the limits specified in the FI tolerance groups.

FI Tolerance Groups

Tolerance groups allow you to set document processing limits for your employees to ensure control and compliance with your corporate policy. Figure 5.7 shows an example of a tolerance group definition.

As shown in the figure, all employees associated with this tolerance group are eligible to process any documents or individual document item of up to $1 million, and they can offer maximum discounts up to 5% of the item. So in the example shown earlier, an employee at their discretion can give up to a $50 (5%) discount for documents 1800000000 to 1800000003; or up to a $5 discount for documents 1400000005.

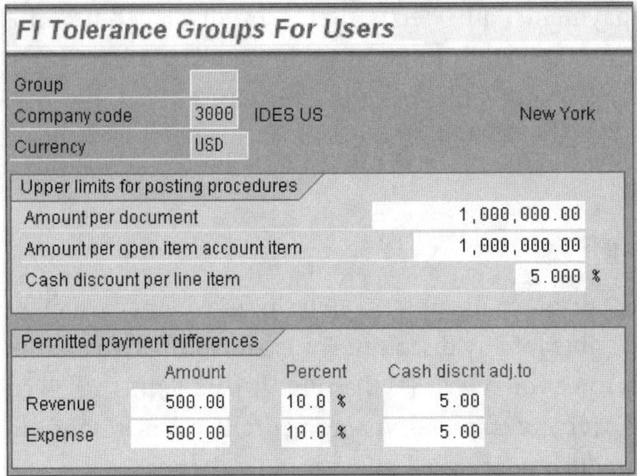

Figure 5.7 Tolerance Group Definition

Tip

You can assign different tolerance groups for your employees and customer accounts with different amount specifications. During transactional processing, such as processing an incoming payment, the lowest of the specifications assigned to the customer and to the employee is applicable.

Other fields in the tolerance group definition are relevant for payment differences, which we'll discuss later in this chapter.

In the next section, we discuss processing partial payments.

5.3.3 Partial Payments

You use the Partial Payments tab to process items for which you have received partial payments. Figure 5.8 shows the Partial Payment tab view of the same payment shown earlier in Figure 5.5.

You'll notice that instead of the gross amount, this screen displays the net amount (calculated as gross amount – discount amount) for each item. In the PAYMENT column, you enter the payment received against the item, and in the RCD column, you can enter a reason code to correspond to the difference in payment. Later in this chapter, we'll discuss the use of reason codes in processing payment differences.

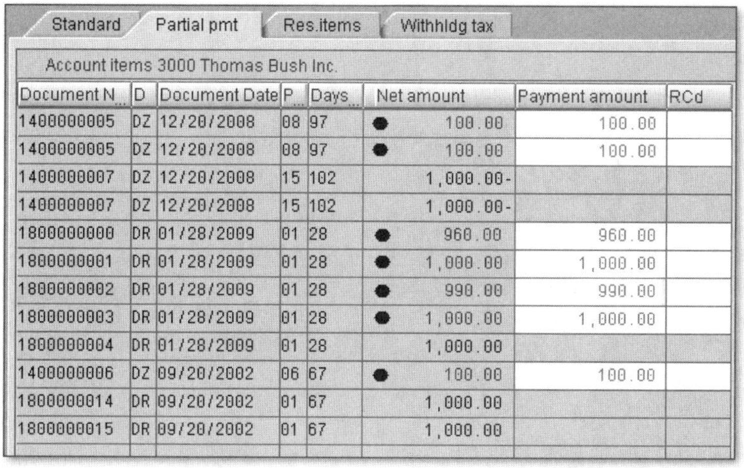

Document N...	D	Document Date	P...	Days...		Net amount	Payment amount	RCd
1400000005	DZ	12/20/2008	08	97	●	100.00	100.00	
1400000005	DZ	12/20/2008	08	97	●	100.00	100.00	
1400000007	DZ	12/20/2008	15	102		1,000.00-		
1400000007	DZ	12/20/2008	15	102		1,000.00-		
1800000000	DR	01/28/2009	01	28	●	960.00	960.00	
1800000001	DR	01/28/2009	01	28	●	1,000.00	1,000.00	
1800000002	DR	01/28/2009	01	28	●	990.00	990.00	
1800000003	DR	01/28/2009	01	28	●	1,000.00	1,000.00	
1800000004	DR	01/28/2009	01	28		1,000.00		
1400000006	DZ	09/20/2002	06	67	●	100.00	100.00	
1800000014	DR	09/20/2002	01	67		1,000.00		
1800000015	DR	09/20/2002	01	67		1,000.00		

Standard | Partial pmt | Res.items | Withhldg tax

Account items 3000 Thomas Bush Inc.

Figure 5.8 Partial Payments

Note

Posting a partial payment against a customer invoice doesn't clear the invoice. A partial payment of $1000 posted against an invoice of $2500 keeps both the documents as open items on the customer account. You clear the documents only after receiving the remaining $1500 from the customer.

On the other hand, in some instances, it may be easier to isolate a residual part of invoices. The next tab discusses processing residual items.

5.3.4 Residual Items

You use the Residual Items tab to generate the residual payment items from the original invoice documents. Figure 5.9 shows the Residual Items tab view of the same payment shown earlier in Figure 5.5.

This screen looks similar to the Partial Payments screen as it also shows the net amount (calculated as gross amount – discount amount) instead of the gross amount for each item. However, the difference is that on the residual items screen, you enter the amount for which payment isn't received in the RESIDUAL ITEMS column. In the RCD column, you enter the reason code that corresponds to the difference amount.

Standard | Partial pmt | Res.items | Withhldg tax

Account items 3000 Thomas Bush Inc.

Document N...	D	Document Date	P...	Days...	Net amount	Residual items	RCd
1400000005	DZ	12/20/2008	08	97	● 100.00		
1400000005	DZ	12/20/2008	08	97	● 100.00		
1400000007	DZ	12/20/2008	15	102	1,000.00-		
1400000007	DZ	12/20/2008	15	102	1,000.00-		
1800000000	DR	01/28/2009	01	28	● 960.00		
1800000001	DR	01/28/2009	01	28	● 1,000.00		
1800000002	DR	01/28/2009	01	28	● 990.00		
1800000003	DR	01/28/2009	01	28	● 1,000.00		
1800000004	DR	01/28/2009	01	28	1,000.00		
1400000006	DZ	09/20/2002	06	67	● 100.00		
1800000014	DR	09/20/2002	01	67	1,000.00		
1800000015	DR	09/20/2002	01	67	1,000.00		

Figure 5.9 Residual Items Screen

Note

Posting a residual item against a customer invoice clears the original invoice and creates a new document item for the residual amount. Thus if a payment of $1500 is posted against an invoice of $2500 on the residual item screen, the original invoice will be cleared from the customer account, and a new document item for $1000 will be posted to the customer account.

Whether to use the partial payments screen or the residual items screen depends on the reason for the difference in payment, as well your internal cash application business processes. For example, if a customer withholds part of a payment due to some dispute that may take a long time to resolve, you may choose to clear the original invoice and create a residual item for the difference in payment.

The Withholding Tax tab shows the tax withheld in a document item. However, we won't go into the details of customer withholding tax in this chapter. So let's focus on how to process the payment differences.

5.4 Payment Differences

In the previous section, we discussed how to enter incoming payments that don't exactly match with the invoice amounts. In this section, we'll look in detail at different ways in which you can process payment differences. For your easy reference, Figure 5.10 shows the lower portion of the item processing screen from Figure 5.5.

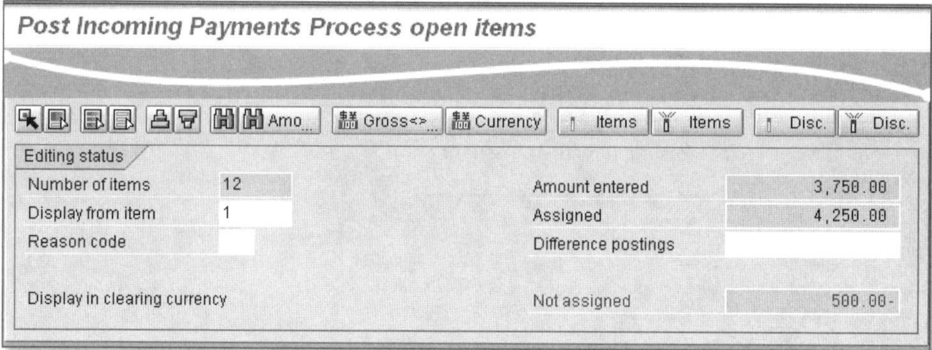

Figure 5.10 Process Differences

Following are the explanations for the amount fields displayed in the figure:

- The Amount Entered field shows the total amount entered on the first screen (bank amount + bank fees).
- The Assigned field shows the total of all items selected on the item processing screen (gross amount – discount – withholding tax).
- The Difference Postings field shows any amount identified and processed as the payment difference.
- The Not Assigned field shows the net total of the amount in fields Amount Entered, Assigned, and Difference Postings.

Let's first see how to post the difference back to customer account.

5.4.1 Post to a Customer Account

We discussed in Section 5.3.4, Residual Items, how you can specify residual items for each customer document so that it's created as an open item on the customer account. However, instead of creating individual document items for the difference amount in each invoice document, you can also post a single entry for the payment difference back to a customer account.

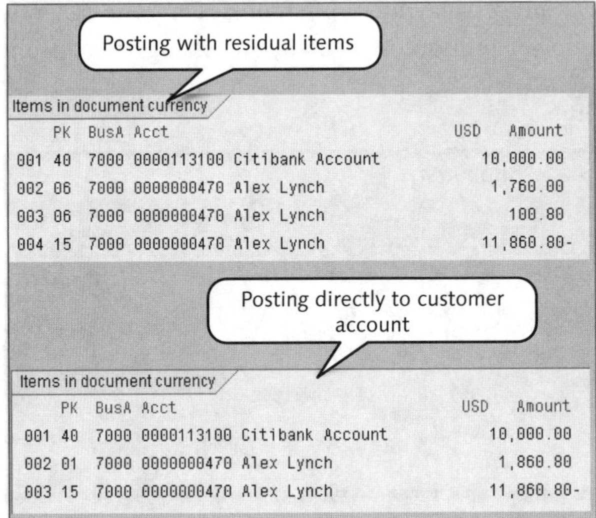

Figure 5.11 Post to Customer Account

Figure 5.11 shows the difference between these two approaches of posting entries back to the customer account. To post a single payment difference entry to a customer account, select the option CHARGE OFF from the item processing screen. On the next screen, you'll be presented with a standard accounting document interface where you can enter a posting key and an account. On the next screen, you can enter other document item details such as profit center or item text. By selecting the appropriate debit or credit posting key and selecting a customer account number, you can post the payment difference back to the customer account.

Tip

Because this process provides the generic interface to enter a posting key and an account number, you can post the payment difference to a different customer account such as to the head office or even to a vendor account.

Let's now see how to post payment difference back to GL accounts.

5.4.2 Post to a GL Account

If you want to post the payment difference to one GL account, then the process is similar to the one described in the previous section. You choose the CHARGE OFF option from the item processing screen, enter the appropriate debit or credit posting key, and enter a GL account. To complete the processing, you enter the amount and other supporting information on the next screen. If you want to post the payment difference to multiple GL accounts, you can repeat the process by entering one document item at a time. Alternatively, you can choose the option of GL fast entry.

We discussed the functionality of GL fast entry in Chapter 2. This functionality provides you with a simplified, customized layout where you can quickly enter the required debit and credit entries, along with supporting information. You access the fast entry screen by selecting the GOTO • G/L ITEMS FAST ENTRY menu option from the item processing screen.

However, if the payment difference amount isn't significant, you can automatically write it off by using the underpayment/overpayment functionality.

5.4.3 Underpayment/Overpayment

In Section 5.3.2, Discount Processing, we discussed tolerance groups that control the maximum document amounts and maximum discounts that employees can process. You also define and assign tolerance groups to customer accounts using SAP IMG • FINANCIAL ACCOUNTING • ACCOUNTS RECEIVABLE AND ACCOUNTS PAYABLE • BUSINESS TRANSACTIONS • INCOMING PAYMENTS • MANUAL INCOMING PAYMENTS • DEFINE TOLERANCES (CUSTOMERS).

Figure 5.12 shows the definition of a customer tolerance group for domestic customers. As you'll notice, you can specify separate tolerance limits for underpayments and for overpayments. You specify these limits as percentages and as absolute amounts in the local currency of the company code. These tolerance limits are combined with similar tolerance limits assigned to the employee processing an incoming payment; the lowest of all of the limits is used to automatically write off any underpayment or overpayment.

GL accounts for automatically posting underpayments and overpayments are defined under SAP IMG • FINANCIAL ACCOUNTING • ACCOUNTS RECEIVABLE AND ACCOUNTS PAYABLE • BUSINESS TRANSACTIONS • INCOMING PAYMENTS • INCOMING PAYMENTS GLOBAL SETTINGS • DEFINE ACCOUNTS FOR OVERPAYMENTS/UNDERPAYMENTS.

You may notice that you can maintain GL accounts for overpayments and underpayments by reason codes. Let's delve into reason code functionality in more detail.

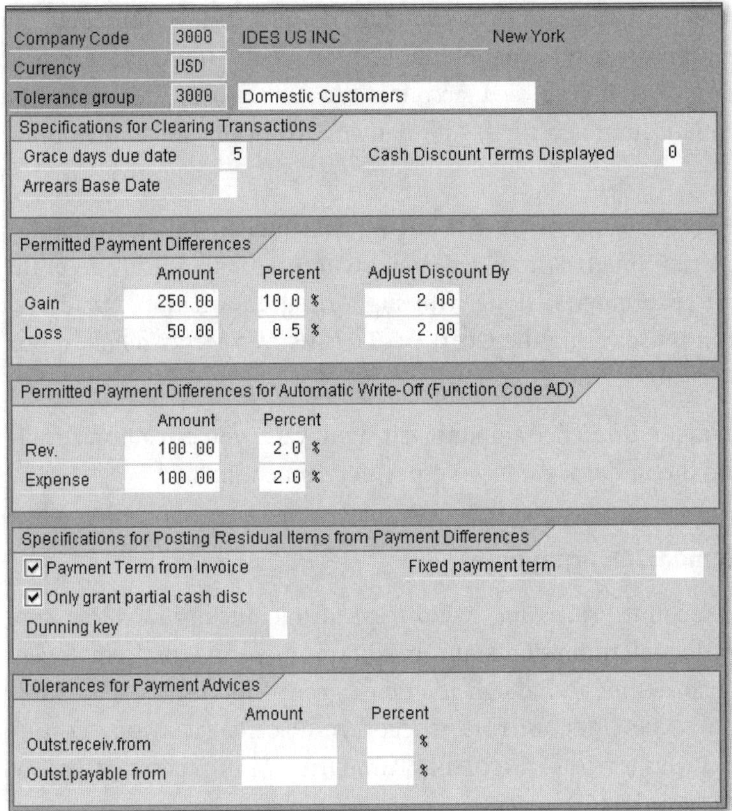

Figure 5.12 Customer Tolerance Group

5.5 Using Reason Codes

You'll find the reason codes configuration using SAP IMG • FINANCIAL ACCOUNTING • ACCOUNTS RECEIVABLE AND ACCOUNTS PAYABLE • BUSINESS TRANSACTIONS • INCOMING PAYMENTS • INCOMING PAYMENTS GLOBAL SETTINGS • OVERPAYMENT/UNDERPAYMENT. Reason codes provide a powerful, integrated functionality to classify and process payment differences.

5.5.1 Definition of Reason Codes

Figure 5.13 shows the configuration settings for reason codes that you can enter on partial payments, residual items, or process open item screens.

Classification of Payment Differences

Company Code 3000 IDES US INC New York

R..	Short text	Long text	CorrT	C	D	D	Ad...
DA	Different Payment $$	Different Paymant Amount					
DDG	Damaged goods	Damaged goods - disputed	SAP01		✔		
DG	Damaged goods	Damaged goods	SAP01				
FR	Freight	Freight charges	SAP01				
MD	Misc. deductions	Miscellaneous deductions	SAP01				
PD	Price variance	Price variance	SAP01				
PP	Partial payment	Partial payment	SAP01				
RT	Returns	Returns					
SP	Residual items	Residual item creation	SAP01	✔			
TP	Trade Promotion	Trade Promotion Deduction	SAP01				

Figure 5.13 Reason Code Definition

The CODE and DESCRIPTION fields in the configuration are self-explanatory. However, other fields require more explanation as given here in the order shown on the figure:

- CORR.T: This field refers to CORRESPONDENCE TYPE that we will discuss in Chapter 10. This field can be useful if you use specially designed notice or communication forms for certain types of payment differences such as trade promotion or damaged goods.
- C: By selecting this indicator, you specify that any payment difference with this reason is charged off to an underpayment/overpayment GL account. If this indicator isn't selected, the corresponding payment difference entry remains on the customer account.
- D: This indicator marks the payment difference item as a dispute item. You can display disputed items separately in the customer account display or in the credit management display.

Tip

In credit management, customer items marked as disputed items aren't included while calculating the total open receivables for a customer.

- D: If this indicator is selected, the reason code description isn't copied to the difference item created on the customer account. This option allows you to enter your own reason or description in the payment difference item.

- AD: If this indicator is selected for a reason code, then the program doesn't consider tolerance limits while processing corresponding payment difference items.

Let's see how you can use these reason codes to process payment differences.

5.5.2 Using Reason Codes

You can enter reason codes for individual documents on the partial payments screen (Section 5.3.3, Partial Payments) or on the residual items screen (Section 5.3.4, Residual Items). This option allows you to classify payment differences using reason codes at the most detailed level while processing an incoming payment.

Another option is to enter a single reason code for the total payment difference amount. For this type of allocation, you enter reason codes on the item processing screen (refer to Figure 5.10). This is the most summarized form of processing payment differences using a reason code.

However, you also have an option to take the total payment difference amount and allocate it to different reason codes without having to do it at the individual customer invoice level. To do this, choose the DISTRIBUTE DIFF option from the item processing screen.

Distribute difference

Allocation of remaining amount

Difference Amount

500.00- USD

Distribut.

Amount	RCd	Short text	Ref.key 1	Ref.key 2
200.00-	DG	Damaged goods	345X7232	
100.00-	RT	Returns		
150.00-	TP	Trade Promotion	121877	149880
50.00-	FR	Freight	X9812PCGF	

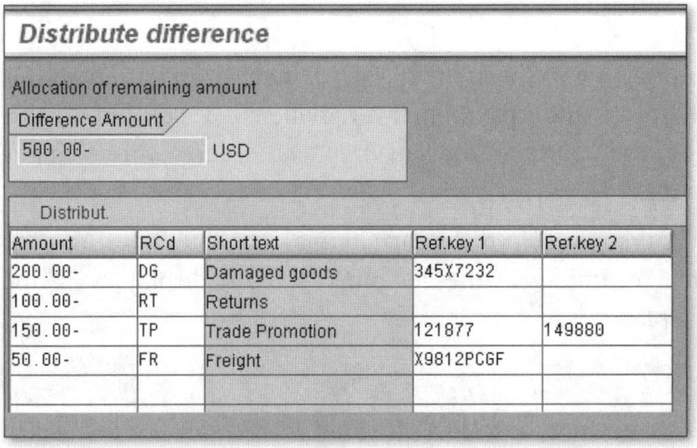

Figure 5.14 Distribute Differences

As Figure 5.14 shows, the DISTRIBUTE DIFFERENCE option allows you to enter multiple reason codes and the corresponding payment difference amount. Not only that, you can also enter additional, supporting information in two REFERENCE KEY fields. For example, you can use these reference fields to enter campaign numbers for the payment difference for trade promotions, or enter RMA numbers for the payment difference due to damaged goods.

Tip

If you use electronic interfaces to process incoming payments from your business partners, you may want to consider using the reason code conversion functionality. This functionality will help you convert reason codes specified by your business partners for any payment differences to corresponding reason codes used in your SAP system.

After you've completed selecting open items and processing any payment differences, you're ready to simulate and post the payment document.

5.6 Simulate and Post

An incoming payment transaction may generate automatic entries for residual items, discounts, underpayments or overpayments, automatic write-offs, and so on, so it's advisable to simulate a document before actually posting it to the SAP system.

Figure 5.15 shows document simulation for different entries we've discussed so far. As you can see, a document simulation provides you an opportunity to review automatic entries that are generated for discount amounts or reason code postings. It also provides you with an opportunity to validate that entries are posted to accurate GL accounts.

To simulate a document posting, select DOCUMENT • SIMULATE GENERAL LEDGER from any screen of an incoming payment processing transaction. However, you may want to review and validate numbers even before completing the entry of a document. This may be the case if an incoming payment includes large number of documents or adjustments to be processed.

For this purpose, you can use the Explain Difference pop-up window (Figure 5.16) for a quick review of the numbers entered at any point of time while processing an incoming payment. You access the Explain Difference option by selecting ENVIRONMENT • EXPLAIN DIFFERENCE from the open item processing screen.

Post Incoming Payments Display Overview

Document Date	04/01/2009	Type	DZ	Company Code	3000
Posting Date	04/01/2009	Period	4	Currency	USD
Document Number	INTERNAL	Fiscal Year	2009	Translatn Date	04/01/2009
Reference	CHK # 1000124122			Cross-CC no.	
Doc.Header Text				Trading part.BA	

Items in document currency

	PK	BusA	Acct		USD Amount	Tax amnt
001	40	9900	0000479000	Bank Charges	25.00	
002	40		0000113100	Citibank Account	3,725.00	
003	06		0000003000	Thomas Bush Inc.	200.00	
004	06		0000003000	Thomas Bush Inc.	50.00	
005	06		0000003000	Thomas Bush Inc.	100.00	
006	06		0000003000	Thomas Bush Inc.	150.00	
007	40		0000888000	Sales deductions wi	40.00	
008	40		0000888000	Sales deductions wi	10.00	
009	15		0000003000	Thomas Bush Inc.	4,300.00-	
010	40		0000230000	Foreign currency re	0.00	

D 4,300.00 C 4,300.00 0.00 * 10 Line items

Other line item

PstKy | Account | SGL Ind | TType | New co.code

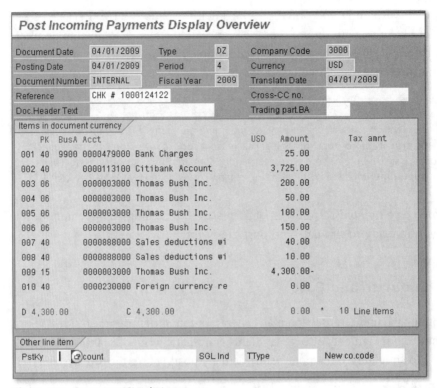

Figure 5.15 Document Simulation

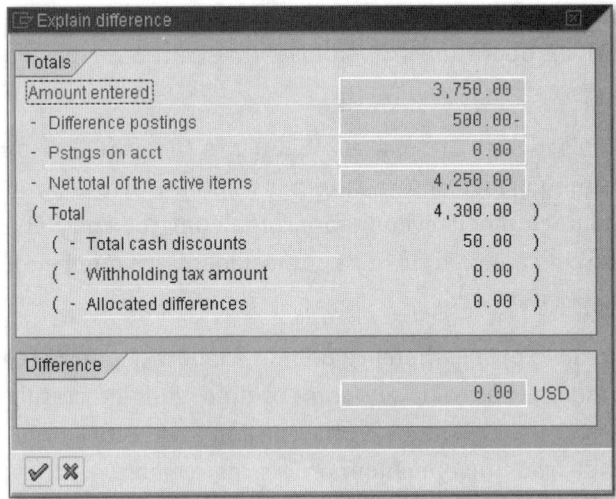

Figure 5.16 Explain Difference

Process incoming payment (Transaction F-28) is the main transaction for processing payments from customers, vendors, or any business partners. However, you may also want to be familiar with a few additional transactions and functionalities.

5.7 Additional Transactions

Transactions discussed in this section provide you with alternatives to process incoming payments. Let's first look at the Incoming Payments fast entry.

5.7.1 Incoming Payment Fast Entry

The process we discussed so far requires you to search for customer document numbers to apply payment against. However, sometimes, it may be easier and faster to process payments by directly entering the customer document numbers and corresponding payment amount. For this purpose, you can use the payment fast entry transaction.

On the first screen of the Incoming Payment Fast Entry transaction, you enter information that will remain constant for all of the payments you'll be processing in a session. Examples of this type of information are posting date, bank account, document date, company code, and so on. Subsequently, on the next screen, you have an option of entering customer information and document information.

As Figure 5.17 shows, this interface lets you enter document numbers and corresponding payment amounts manually. So when you select PROCESS OPEN ITEMS, these document items are already selected. Subsequently, you can process any remaining payment differences as we've discussed in previous sections. This process of entering payments can be considerably faster if your customer accounts have a large number of open items, and most of the payments are against two or three documents. You access payment fast entry using SAP MENU • FINANCIAL ACCOUNTING • ACCOUNTS RECEIVABLE • DOCUMENT ENTRY • PAYMENT FAST ENTRY (Transaction F-26).

Tip

You can select the SPECIFICATIONS option to change any constant parameters such as bank account or posting date while using the payment fast entry transactions. All subsequent payment documents will be posted with the revised parameters.

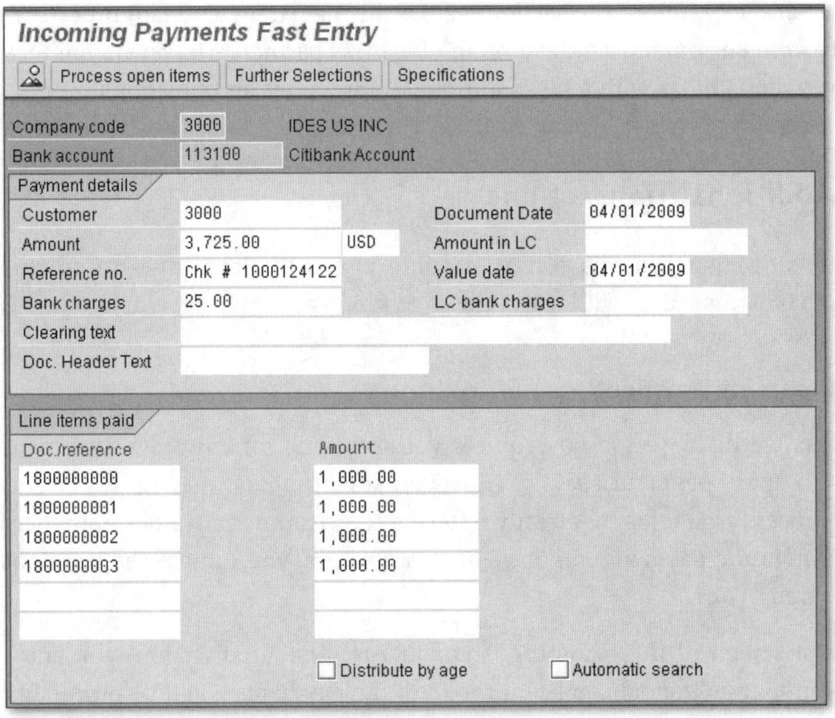

Incoming Payments Fast Entry

Process open items | Further Selections | Specifications

Company code	3000	IDES US INC
Bank account	113100	Citibank Account

Payment details

Customer	3000		Document Date	04/01/2009
Amount	3,725.00	USD	Amount in LC	
Reference no.	Chk # 1000124122		Value date	04/01/2009
Bank charges	25.00		LC bank charges	
Clearing text				
Doc. Header Text				

Line items paid

Doc./reference	Amount
1800000000	1,000.00
1800000001	1,000.00
1800000002	1,000.00
1800000003	1,000.00

☐ Distribute by age ☐ Automatic search

Figure 5.17 Incoming Payments Fast Entry

In the next section, let's look at processing incoming payments using payment advices.

5.7.2 Payment Advice Processing

We mentioned the use of payment advices for selecting open items in Section 5.2.4, Selection Based on a Payment Advice. More commonly, electronic bank interfaces automatically generate payment advice documents. However, this functionality can be useful to record incoming payment information in the SAP system when all details aren't available. This functionality also offers an option to decouple the payment entry process and the payment application process. So depending on your business processes, you may be able to use the payment advice processing functionality for improving operational efficiencies.

After entering data such as a company code, account type, account number, and bank details, you're presented with a line item screen (Figure 5.18) where you can enter additional details. In the upper part of the line item entry screen, you enter information such as PAYMENT AMOUNT, DEDUCTION AMOUNT, and DISCOUNT AMOUNT. In the lower part of the line item entry screen, in the ADDITIONAL DATA section, you have an option to enter different information such as document number, billing document number, and reference document number. This information can later be used to assist in selecting customer document items awhile applying payments.

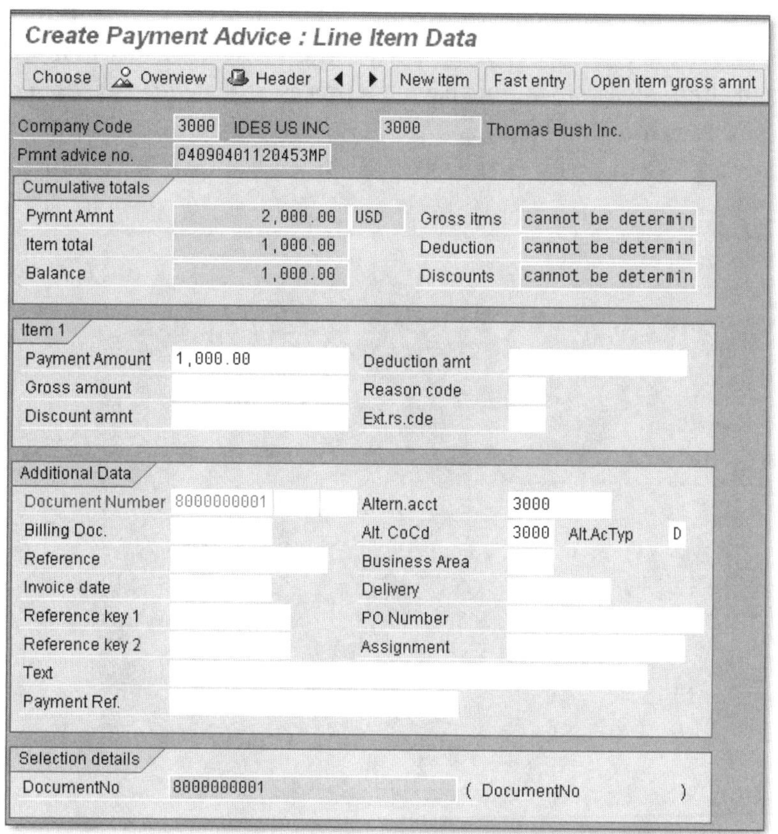

Figure 5.18 Create Payment Advice

You'll find payment advice transactions under SAP MENU • FINANCIAL ACCOUNTING • ACCOUNTS RECEIVABLE • DOCUMENT ENTRY • PAYMENT ADVICE menu path. There you'll find transactions to create, change, and display payment advice documents, payment advice reports, and transactions to carry out payment advice reorganizations. Payment advice reorganizations allow you to delete payment advices that are no longer relevant for processing.

Finally, let's look at another transaction that can be useful in processing incoming payments.

5.7.3 Transfer with Clearing

There may be times when payments are applied to incorrect customer accounts, or you want to match debits and credits posted to customer accounts without any additional incoming payment, or you want to make adjustments to payments that are already processed. You can use the transfer with clearing functionality in those situations or as an alternative to incoming payment processes that we've discussed so far. You access this transaction by using SAP MENU • FINANCIAL ACCOUNTING • ACCOUNTS RECEIVABLE • DOCUMENT ENTRY • OTHER • TRANSFER WITH CLEARING.

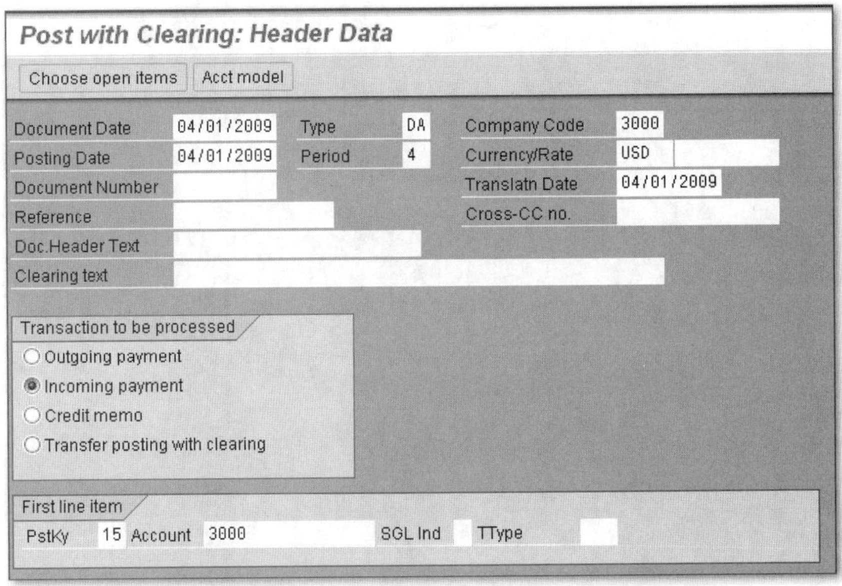

Figure 5.19 Transfer with Clearing

Figure 5.19 shows the first screen of the transfer with clearing transaction. Under TRANSACTION TO BE PROCESSED section, you can choose either the TRANSFER POSTING WITH CLEARING or the INCOMING PAYMENT option. After entering the appropriate posting key and customer account, you select CHOOSE OPEN ITEMS and the rest of the user interface is the same as discussed earlier.

In next section, we'll discuss reporting for incoming payments.

5.7.4 Reporting

To analyze payments applied and processed on customer accounts, you can use the customer line item analysis report in the SAP system.

Customer Line Item Analysis (FBL5N)

This is one of the most commonly used transactions to analyze entries posted to customer account. We discuss this transaction in Chapter 11.

You can set a line item layout of this transaction to include payment fields or other reference fields such as a reference document number, reference invoice number, reason code, reference key fields, and so on. In addition, any document journal or line item report that supports ALV (ABAP List Viewer) functionality can provide you with the required information.

If you use payment advice documents in the SAP system, then you'll find the payment advice overview transaction useful.

Payment Advice Overview

Transaction S_ALR_87012201 provides you with a payment advice overview (Figure 5.20). From the list, you can display payment advice details by double-clicking on a specific payment advice number. Using selection criteria on the first screen, you can generate the payment advice list by company code, customer, or employee.

Payment Advice Overview

CoCd	Account	A	Pmnt advice no.	Adv.header text	Pymnt Amnt	Cash disc.	Created	Created on
3000	*	D	010000002700001	No customer with MICR num	4,700.00	0.00	BLING	07/17/2009
3000	*	D	010000002700002	No customer with MICR num	2,500.00	0.00	BLING	07/17/2008
3000	*	D	010000002700003	No customer with MICR num	7,200.00	0.00	BLING	01/19/2009
3000	*	D	010000002700004	No customer with MICR num	4,000.00	0.00	BLING	05/11/2008
3000	*	D	010000002700005	No customer with MICR num	4,400.00	0.00	BLING	06/17/2009
3000	255	D	01010156451	Customer identified via i	6,600.00	0.00	TRAINY	05/12/2008
3000	3000	D	01303030232	Customer uniquely identif	2,000.00	0.00	BONGI	09/20/2009
3000	30099	D	062000000004		200.00	0.00	LYNN	01/15/2008
3000	30099	D	062000000005		436.72	0.00	LYNN	01/16/2009
3000	30099	D	06F110*00001		200.00	0.00	LYNN	01/15/2008

Figure 5.20 Payment Advice Overview

The next section provides a list of transactions relevant for processing incoming payments.

5.7.5 List of Transactions

Table 5.3 lists some of the transactions discussed in this chapter.

Transaction	Usage
F-28	Incoming payment
F-26	Incoming payment fast entry
F-30	Transfer posting with clearing
FBL5N	Customer line item display
FBE1/FBE2/FBE3	Create/change/display payment advice
S_ALR_87012201	Payment advice overview
S_ALR_87012205	Payment advice notes reorganization
OBXI	Define accounts for cash discounts granted
OBXL	Define accounts for overpayments/underpayments
OBXK	Define accounts for bank charges
OB09	Define accounts for exchange rate differences

Table 5.3 Incoming Payments Transactions

In the next section, we'll look at technical objects available for incoming payments functionality.

5.8 Technical Reference

This section lists the technical objects such as SAP Notes, authorization objects, and tables and structures relevant for using the incoming payments functionality. Considering the large number of technical objects available in the SAP system, this information should only be considered as a starting point for analysis.

5.8.1 SAP Notes

Table 5.4 is a list of SAP Notes relevant for incoming payments functionality.

SAP Note	Relevance
0000574517	Partial payment of down payment requests
0000093601	Cross company code clearing of payments
0000154398	"Automatic Search" in open item selection
0000025200	Allocate payment amounts while clearing multiple accounts
0000148533	Discount calculation for customer and vendor clearing
0000201700	Reason code automatic charge off in incoming payments
0000152454	Reference keys not transferred to residual items
0000213852	Analysis of down payment processing in FI
0000213567	Analysis of down payment processing in SD
0000137552	Discount amount in costing-based profitability analysis
0000110788	Manual clearing of branch office/head office
0001228601	Selection of display variant in open item processing
0000374922	Sorting of items after entry of selection criteria
0000547697	FAQ: Payment differences for selection with payment advice

Table 5.4 Incoming Payments – SAP Notes

In the next section, we'll look at authorization objects available for incoming payments transactions.

5.8.2 Authorization Objects

Table 5.5 lists some of the authorization objects to be considered for transactions discussed in this chapter.

Object	Description
F_BKPF_BED	Accounting Doc: Account Authorization for Customers
F_BKPF_BEK	Accounting Doc: Account Authorization for Vendors
F_BKPF_BES	Accounting Doc: Account Authorization for GL Accounts
F_BKPF_BLA	Accounting Doc: Authorization for Document Types
F_BKPF_BUK	Accounting Doc: Authorization for Company Codes

Table 5.5 Authorization Objects – Incoming Payments

Object	Description
F_BKPF_KOA	Accounting Doc: Authorization for Account Types
F_FAGL_LDR	General Ledger: Authorization for Ledger
F_SKA1_BUK	G/L Account: Authorization for Company Codes
F_AVIK_AVA	Payment Advice: Authorization for Advice Types
F_AVIK_BUK	Payment Advice: Authorization for Company Codes

Table 5.5 Authorization Objects – Incoming Payments (Cont.)

The next section provides a list of tables and structures.

5.8.3 Tables and Structures

Table 5.6 lists tables and structures relevant for processing incoming payments.

Table	Relevance
BKPF	Accounting document: header
BSEG	Accounting document: details
BSID	Secondary index for customer documents
BSAD	Secondary index for customer documents – cleared items
BSIK	Secondary index for vendor documents
BSAK	Secondary index for vendor documents – cleared items
DF05B	Input/output table for module SAPDF05X (F-28, F-26)
RF05A	Work fields for SAPMF05A (F-28, F-26)
AVIK	Payment advice header
AVIP	Payment advice item
AVIR	Payment advice subitem
T030	Standard accounts table (for account determination)

Table 5.6 Incoming Payments Tables and Structures

Now we'll look at objects and functionality available for enhancing and modifying incoming payments functionality.

5.9 Enhancements and Modifications

This section provides a list of available BTEs, enhancements, BAdIs, and BAPIs relevant for incoming payments processing. These are used to enhance and modify the standard functionality available in the SAP system.

5.9.1 Business Transaction Events (BTEs)

Using BTEs, you can attach additional function modules and custom logic to the standard SAP system. You may want to check whether BTEs available for accounting documents meet your requirements for enhancing incoming payments processes.

The next section discusses Business Add-Ins relevant for incoming payments functionality.

5.9.2 Business Add-Ins (BAdIs)

Business Add-In implementations are enhancements to the standard SAP system. Most BAdIs provided by the SAP system accommodate industry-specific or country-specific requirements. However, you can also use BAdI implementations to meet any unique requirements for your business. You may want to consider the following BAdIs for incoming payments functionality:

- FI_GET_INV_PYMT_AM
  - This BAdI can be used to determine payment amount for customer invoice documents.
  - This BAdI provides one method, GET_INV_PYMT_AMT, that is used to determine the payment amount for customer invoice documents.
- FI_PAYREF_BADI_010
  - Implementation of this BAdI influences the value in the payment reference field. Because payment reference is one of the values that influences matching the payment with the corresponding invoice, you can use this BAdI to influence automatic matching of incoming payments.
  - This BAdI provides one method, CREATE_KIDNO, for determination of the payment reference number.

The next section discusses available enhancement spots.

5.9.3 Enhancements

Using the following enhancements, you can modify the payment reference number field (KIDNO) while processing the customer billing document.

- SDVFX009: Billing document processing KIDNO (payment reference number)
  - This enhancement contains a function module, EXIT_SAPLV60A_001, that can be used to influence the value of the payment reference number.
  - This user exit falls under the Sales and Distribution area of the SAP system, so be sure to coordinate and validate any implementation with your corresponding SAP team member.

5.10 Summary

In this chapter, we discussed different features of processing incoming payments in the SAP system. As we discussed, at each step of payment processing, you have access to different options and functionalities to make payment processing more efficient.

In this chapter, we'll discuss the dunning functionality in the SAP system. The dunning process is used to send dunning notices or payment reminders to business partners who have fallen behind on payments. Most commonly, this process is used for customers, but the SAP system also supports dunning functionality for vendors that have a debit balance. Just like with all other functionality in the SAP system, this process can be made as simple or as complex as required by your business.

6 Dunning

Dunning in the SAP system provides comprehensive functionality to respond to business situations in which business partners have fallen behind on payments. You can customize the SAP system to represent dunning responsibilities, dunning groups, dunning levels, and dunning processes that match your business model and industry standards. You can calculate interest on open items, manage negotiated non-payment periods, prepare dunning notices, and send them by mail, email, or fax to business partners. You can also manage SAP system business situations where the collections group has followed up as much as possible, and any further collection efforts require involvement of the legal department or a collection agency.

In this chapter, we'll first review the dunning parameters in the SAP system, followed by configuring the dunning procedure. Then we'll review the process of the dunning run and associated functionality. Like other chapters, we'll end this chapter with technical references and information on available enhancements and modifications in the area of dunning processes.

6.1 Dunning Parameters

In this section, we'll review SAP concepts and parameters that are relevant to dunning functionality. These parameters help you configure a dunning process that meets your organizational as well as procedural business requirements. Technically, however, the configuration of all parameters except the dunning level (Section 6.1.2) is optional.

6.1.1 Dunning Area

The *dunning area* corresponds to an organizational unit within a company code that is responsible for carrying out dunning activities. For a customer account, you can set up different dunning parameters for different dunning areas.

Typically, dunning activities for a legal entity are carried out by a single department or organizational unit, in which case, you don't need to configure dunning areas in the SAP system. However, a company with a large customer base may have multiple organizational units responsible for carrying out dunning activities.

CoCd	Area	Text
1000	01	Domestic: Corporate Accounts
1000	02	Domestic: Government Agencies
1000	03	International: Europe
1000	04	International: Asia Pacific
1000	05	International: Rest of Americas

Figure 6.1 Dunning Areas

As shown in Figure 6.1, dunning areas may be structured based on product divisions, geographical regions, customer groups, or any combination of such business characteristics. This configuration activity is carried out using IMG • FINANCIAL ACCOUNTING • ACCOUNTS RECEIVABLE AND ACCOUNTS PAYABLE • BUSINESS TRANSACTIONS • DUNNING • BASIC SETTINGS FOR DUNNING • DEFINE DUNNING AREAS.

The next parameter signifies how much an item is in arrears.

6.1.2 Dunning Level

A *dunning level* designates one of the steps in a dunning process. A higher dunning level indicates a higher number of days an item is in arrears. For example, dunning level 1 may indicate an item that is in arrears for 15 days, and dunning level 2 may indicate an item that is in arrears for 30 days.

There is no separate configuration activity to define a dunning level. You define dunning levels when configuring the dunning procedure discussed in Section 6.2, Dunning Procedure.

6.1.3 Dunning Grouping Key

Typically, a dunning run generates one dunning notice per business partner. However, using a *dunning grouping key*, you can generate multiple dunning notices for a business partner based on different groups of dunned items. This may be useful, for example, to generate separate dunning notices for different customer contracts.

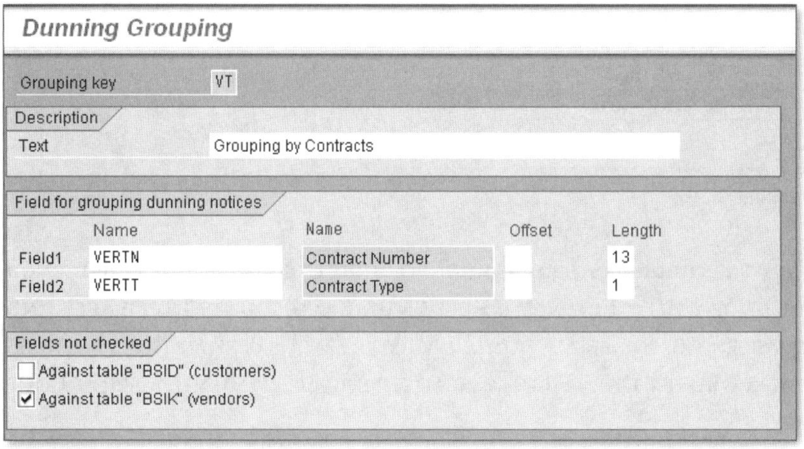

Figure 6.2 Dunning Grouping Key

Figure 6.2 shows the configuration of a dunning grouping key that can be used to group dunning items based on two fields, Contract Number and Contract Type. Fields Not Checked indicators in this configuration specify the type of accounts for which this check *won't* be carried out. Thus, the key shown in Figure 6.2 will carry out the grouping of dunning items for customers but not for vendors.

Assignment of a grouping key is carried out in a customer master. These grouping keys are configured using IMG • FINANCIAL ACCOUNTING • ACCOUNTS RECEIVABLE AND ACCOUNTS PAYABLE • BUSINESS TRANSACTIONS • DUNNING • DUNNING PROCEDURE • DEFINE DUNNING GROUPINGS.

The next dunning parameter we'll discuss is configuring dunning clerks.

6.1.4 Dunning Clerk

You can define your accounting business users as accounting clerks in the SAP system. Subsequently, contact information such as telephone number, fax number, or email can be printed on communications with business partners. Business partners, in turn, can use this information to question or dispute items on their account statements or dunning notices.

Accounting Clerks

CoCd	Clerk	Name of Accounting Clerk	Office user
1000	A1	Jeff Miller	JMILLER
1000	A2	Mich Saigal	MSAIGAL
1000	A3	Frank Gibbs	FGIBBS
1000	A4	Jack Patel	JPATEL
1000	A5	Wendy DeSoto	WDESOTO
1000	A6	Ibrahim Peerzada	IPEERZADA

Figure 6.3 Dunning Clerks

Figure 6.3 shows a sample configuration of accounting clerks. This configuration is carried out using IMG • FINANCIAL ACCOUNTING • ACCOUNTS RECEIVABLE AND ACCOUNTS PAYABLE • CUSTOMER ACCOUNTS • MASTER DATA • PREPARATIONS FOR CREATING CUSTOMER MASTER DATA • ENTER ACCOUNTING CLERK IDENTIFICATION CODE FOR CUSTOMERS.

After this configuration has been carried out, you can assign the Clerk ID as a dunning clerk in customer accounts. You can also print the contact information of the dunning clerk on dunning notices and other communications. The Office User field corresponds to the SAP logon user of that accounting clerk. This user ID can be used in the workflow process or to retrieve a user's contact information such as telephone number, fax number, and email address.

So far, we've discussed dunning parameters that are associated with customer master data. On the other hand, next parameter is assigned directly to an item being dunned.

6.1.5 Dunning Key

Dunning keys are assigned directly to the document item being dunned on the customer or vendor account. These keys are defined using IMG • FINANCIAL ACCOUNTING • ACCOUNTS RECEIVABLE AND ACCOUNTS PAYABLE • BUSINESS TRANSACTIONS • DUNNING • BASIC SETTINGS FOR DUNNING • DEFINE DUNNING KEYS.

Dunning Keys

Dunn.key	Max.level	Print sep	Text
1	1	☐	Triggers maximum dunning level 1
2	2	☐	Triggers maximum dunning level 2
3	3	☐	Triggers maximum dunning level 3
4	4	☐	Triggers maximum dunning level 4
5	5	☐	Triggers maximum dunning level 5
Z		☑	Payment has been made, separate item display

Figure 6.4 Dunning Key

As shown in Figure 6.4, a dunning key can be used to control two aspects of an item being dunned. If you've specified the Max Level for a dunning key, the dunning process limits the maximum dunning level assigned to the item being dunned. As you'll see in Section 6.2, Dunning Procedures, dunning levels control a large number of dunning parameters such as those for interest calculation, print controls, texts on dunning notice, and so on. By restricting the dunning level of an item, you can effectively influence values of all of these parameters for the item being dunned.

Another aspect controlled by the dunning key is whether the item being dunned should be printed separately on a dunning notice. This is done by selecting Print Sep indicator for the Dunn.Key. For example, you may want to print disputed items or specially negotiated items separately on a dunning notice.

The next parameter is also assigned directly to the document item being dunned.

6.1.6 Dunning Block

Document items with *dunning blocks* aren't included in a dunning run, even if all other dunning criteria, such as number of days in arrears and dunning amounts, are satisfied. For example, you may have received an email confirmation of customer payment, but the actual payment may not have yet been posted in the SAP system at the time of the dunning run.

Dunning Block Reasons

Lock	Text
	Freed for dunning
A	Manual block due to a telephone payment advice
B	Manual block due to complaints against vendor
R	Blocked by invoice verification

Figure 6.5 Dunning Blocks

Figure 6.5 shows an example of dunning blocks. A dunning block is directly assigned to the document item for which the dunning process should not be carried out. These codes can be defined using IMG • FINANCIAL ACCOUNTING • ACCOUNTS RECEIVABLE AND ACCOUNTS PAYABLE • BUSINESS TRANSACTIONS • DUNNING • BASIC SETTINGS FOR DUNNING • DEFINE DUNNING BLOCK REASONS.

Tip

You can use Transaction F8P2 to set the dunning block in customer line items that are already posted. You can choose customer line items based on selection criteria such as company codes, document numbers, customer accounts, posting dates, and document types.

In this section, we discussed the individual parameters that influence the dunning process. In the next section, we'll see the dunning procedure configuration that brings these parameters together.

6.2 Dunning Procedure

A *dunning procedure* is the most important dunning parameter associated with a customer account. It determines if, when, and how unpaid customer items are dunned. It controls the dunning frequency, number of dunning levels, minimum dunning amounts, dunning charges, and interest calculation, among other things.

Tip

Dunning procedure parameters are configured separately for each company code in which they are used. This design enables you to customize one dunning procedure to meet unique requirements of multiple company codes.

The setup of the dunning procedures is carried out using IMG • FINANCIAL ACCOUNTING • ACCOUNTS RECEIVABLE AND ACCOUNTS PAYABLE • BUSINESS TRANSACTIONS • DUNNING • DUNNING PROCEDURE • DEFINE DUNNING PROCEDURES. The following sections discuss each of the six screens involved in the dunning procedure setup.

6.2.1 Overview Screen

The Overview screen (Figure 6.6) is the first screen in a dunning procedure setup.

Maintain Dunning Procedure: Overview

Dunning levels | Charges | Minimum amounts | Dunning texts | Sp. G/L indicator

Dunn.Procedure 0002
Name Four-level dunning, every month

General data

Dunning Interval in Days	30	
No.of dunning levels	4	
Total due items from dunning level		
Min.days in arrears (acct)	6	
Line item grace periods	2	
Interest indicator	01	Standard itm int.cal
Public hol.cal.ID		

☑ Standard transaction dunning
☑ Dun special G/L transactions

Reference data

Ref.Dunning Procedure for Texts 0001 Four-level dunning, every two weeks

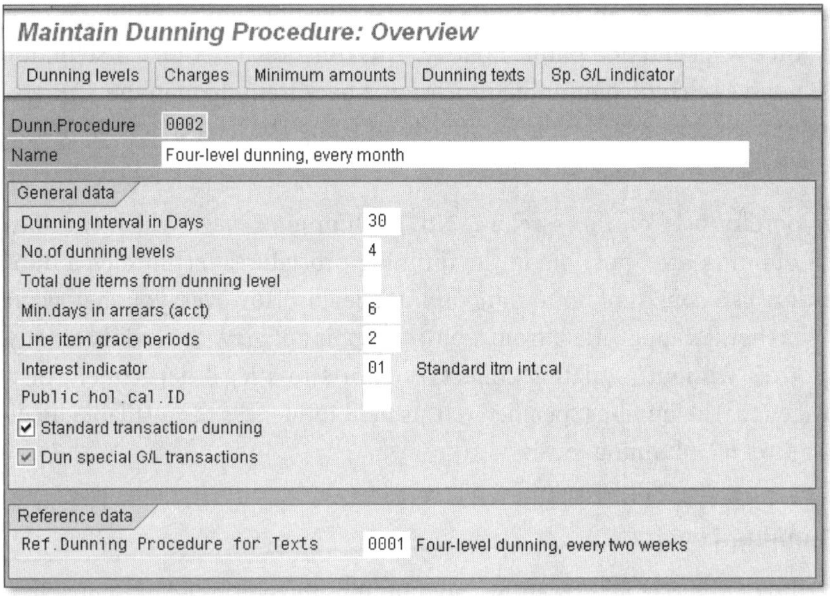

Figure 6.6 Dunning Procedure – Overview

The dunning frequency of a customer is determined by the field Dunning Interval in Days. A new dunning notice for a customer is generated only after the number of days specified in this field have elapsed, regardless of whether new items have become overdue during that time period.

By specifying grace days for an item in field Line item grace periods, you can avoid dunning items that have become overdue only recently. Whereas using the Min Days in Arrears (Acct) field, you can ensure that a dunning notice is generated only if at least one item on an account is in arrears for the specified number of days. In the example shown in Figure 6.6, a dunning notice won't include any item that is in arrears for two or fewer day, and it will be generated only after at least one item is in arrears for six or more days.

Tip

The grace number of days and minimum days in arrears are useful only for operational and procedural reasons. They don't have any influence on the calculation of days in arrears.

The field Public holiday calendar Id is used to specify a calendar indicating public holidays and weekends. If this calendar is maintained for a dunning procedure, then the dunning program ensures that a payment deadline on a dunning notice doesn't fall on a weekend or a public holiday. This functionality can be useful, for example, if you've scheduled dunning process as a background job in the SAP system. Configuration for the calendar is carried out using IMG • SAP NETWEAVER • GENERAL SETTINGS • MAINTAIN CALENDAR.

Another important field on this screen is No. of Dunning Levels, which specifies the highest dunning level possible in the dunning procedure. Technically, a dunning procedure can consist of up to nine dunning levels. However, you may want to review whether it's appropriate from a business point of view to send that many dunning notices without escalating collection efforts to a legal department or a collection agency. The number specified in this field influences the available fields on the next screen Ð dunning levels.

6.2.2 Dunning Levels

Figure 6.7 shows the second screen of the dunning procedure, where you carry out the setup for individual dunning levels. This screen displays number of dunning level columns corresponding to the number of dunning levels entered on the Overview screen. For each dunning level, you specify following parameters:

- Days in Arrears specifies the minimum number of days in arrears for an item to be assigned a corresponding dunning level. In the example shown in Figure

6.7, all items that are overdue for 2 to 15 days are assigned dunning level 1, and all items that are overdue for 16 to 29 days are assigned dunning level 2.

- If the Calculate Interest flag is selected, then the dunning process calculates interest on overdue items. Interest calculation is discussed in detail later in this chapter in Section 6.4, Transactions.

Maintain Dunning Procedure: Dunning levels

Charges | Minimum amounts | Dunning texts

Dunn.Procedure 0002

Name Four-level dunning, every month

Dunning level	1	2	3	4
Days in arrears/interest				
Days in arrears	2	16	30	44
Calculate interest?	☐	☐	☑	☑
Print parameters				
Always dun?	☐	☐	☐	☑
Print all items	☐	☐	☑	☑
Payment deadline			10	7

Legal dunning procedure

☐ Always dun in legal dunning proc.

Figure 6.7 Dunning Procedure – Dunning Levels

Additionally, for each dunning level, you can specify the following parameters that influence the standard system behavior of how dunning items are printed on a dunning notice.

- The standard behavior of the dunning process is that a dunning notice for a business partner isn't printed if there has been no change since the last dunning run. However, if the Always Dun? flag is selected, then a dunning notice is printed for that dunning level even if there has been no change since the last dunning run.
- If the Print All Items flag is selected, the dunning notice for that dunning level prints all items open on the customer account.

Tip

Typically, Always Dun and Print All Items flags are selected for the highest dunning level in a dunning procedure.

- By default, dunning notices are issued with the payment deadline date the same as the dunning date. However, the payment deadline can be set to a future date by maintaining the number of days in the Payment Deadline field.

On the next screen, you make amount specifications that determine the dunning level of a dunning item.

6.2.3 Minimum Amounts

The dunning program evaluates items being dunned and assigns dunning levels based on the minimum amounts (Figure 6.8) set up for a dunning procedure.

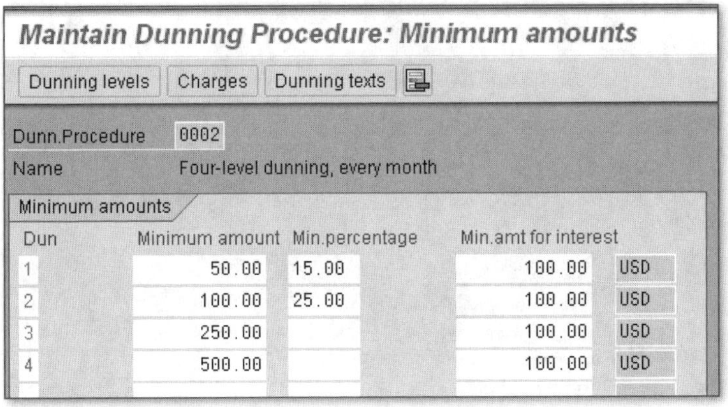

Maintain Dunning Procedure: Minimum amounts

Dunning levels | Charges | Dunning texts

Dunn.Procedure 0002

Name Four-level dunning, every month

Minimum amounts

Dun	Minimum amount	Min.percentage	Min.amt for interest	
1	50.00	15.00	100.00	USD
2	100.00	25.00	100.00	USD
3	250.00		100.00	USD
4	500.00		100.00	USD

Figure 6.8 Dunning Procedure – Minimum Amounts

Two specifications on this screen determine the dunning level assigned to a dunning item. Minimum Amount is self-explanatory; it specifies the minimum amount of the overdue item for it to be assigned a corresponding dunning level. On the other hand, Min Percentage specifies that the corresponding dunning level is assigned only if items being dunned have reached a specified percentage of the total open items. For example, if a customer account has an open receivable balance of hundreds of thousands of dollars, you may not want to assign that customer a higher dunning level for a $100 open item. If both minimum amount and minimum percentage are specified for a dunning level, both the criteria have to be met before that dunning level is assigned to a dunning item.

Tip

Minimum amounts for a dunning procedure are maintained separately for each currency. The dunning program validates and assigns the dunning level based on the amount calculations carried out in the dunning currency.

In addition to amount and percentage specifications, you can also specify on this setup screen the minimum amount for interest calculation for each dunning level. The functionality of the dunning interest calculation is discussed in Section 6.4.4, Interest Calculation.

In the next section, let's consider the calculation of dunning charges.

6.2.4 Dunning Charges

Depending on your business relationships and overdue amounts, you may want to charge your business partners interest on dunned items. You can add dunning charges to dunning notices based on the total amount being dunned. Figure 6.9 shows an example of dunning charges maintained for Dunning Procedure 0002. Dunning charges on a dunning procedure are maintained separately for each currency. The dunning program calculates the dunning charges based on the dunning currency of a dunning notice.

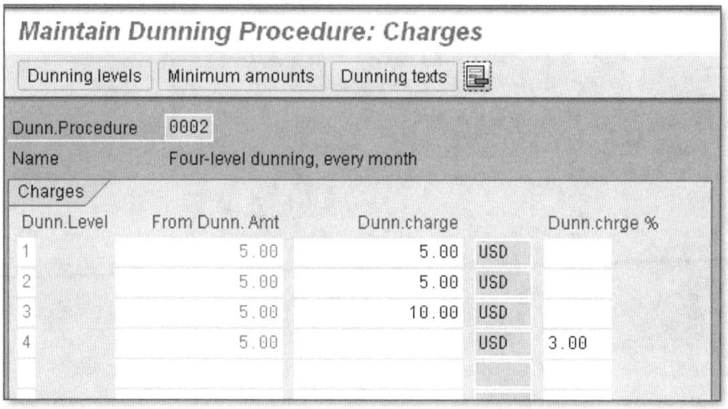

Maintain Dunning Procedure: Charges

Dunning levels | Minimum amounts | Dunning texts

Dunn.Procedure 0002

Name Four-level dunning, every month

Charges

Dunn.Level	From Dunn. Amt	Dunn.charge		Dunn.chrge %
1	5.00	5.00	USD	
2	5.00	5.00	USD	
3	5.00	10.00	USD	
4	5.00		USD	3.00

Figure 6.9 Dunning Procedure – Charges

For each dunning level, you specify either dunning charges as an absolute amount in the Dunn Charge field, or as a percentage in the Dunn Charge % field. This dunning charge is levied on the total dunning amount calculated using the amount specified in From Dunn Amount. So in the example shown in Figure 6.9, the dunning charge will be $5 for the first two dunning levels, $10 for the third dunning level, and 3% of the dunning amount for the fourth dunning level.

> **Note**
>
> Dunning charges and interest amounts are calculated by the dunning program and printed on dunning notices. However, additional development is required to post these values to Financial Accounting. Refer to Section 6.6.2, Enhancements, for more details.

So far, we haven't distinguished between standard transactions and special GL transactions. The next section discusses the dunning of special GL transactions.

6.2.5 Special GL Indicators

We've discussed special GL transactions in Chapter 2. You can specify which of the special GL transactions are included in a dunning run by using the setup screen shown in Figure 6.10.

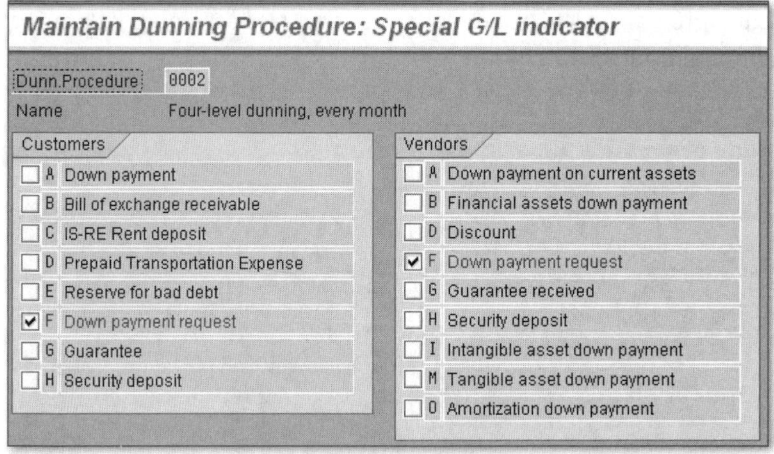

Figure 6.10 Dunning Procedure – Special GL Indicators

A dunning run includes all transactions of the special GL transaction types selected on this setup screen. The Dun Special GL Transactions flag on the Overview screen (Section 6.2.1, Overview Screen) is automatically selected to provide quick indication of whether one or more special GL indicators on this screen are selected.

The last screen in a dunning procedure setup influences the format and content of dunning notices and dunning texts.

6.2.6 Dunning Texts

Dunning notices with higher dunning levels typically include stronger dunning language, so it's imperative that you be able to define dunning texts separately for each dunning level.

Also, for the same dunning level, dunning texts may differ depending on whether the recipient is a customer or a vendor. Finally, dunning notices also have to cater to different requirements of company codes and dunning areas. Hence, in the SAP system, dunning texts (Figure 6.11) for a dunning procedure are defined for a combination of company code, account type (customer or vendor), dunning level, and dunning area. However, if several dunning procedures share the same dunning texts, then you can avoid additional data maintenance by specifying Reference Dunning Procedure for Texts on the Overview screen (refer to Figure 6.6).

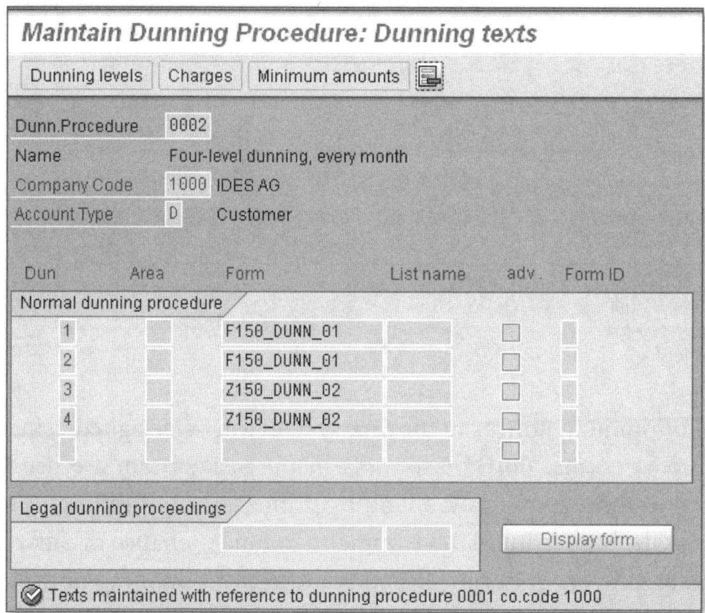

Figure 6.11 Dunning Procedure – Dunning Texts

In Figure 6.11, fields Form and Form ID assigned to each dunning level determine the format and content of corresponding dunning notices. The next section describes the definition of dunning forms.

6.2.7 Dunning Notice

Figure 6.12 shows a sample dunning notice printed from the SAP system.

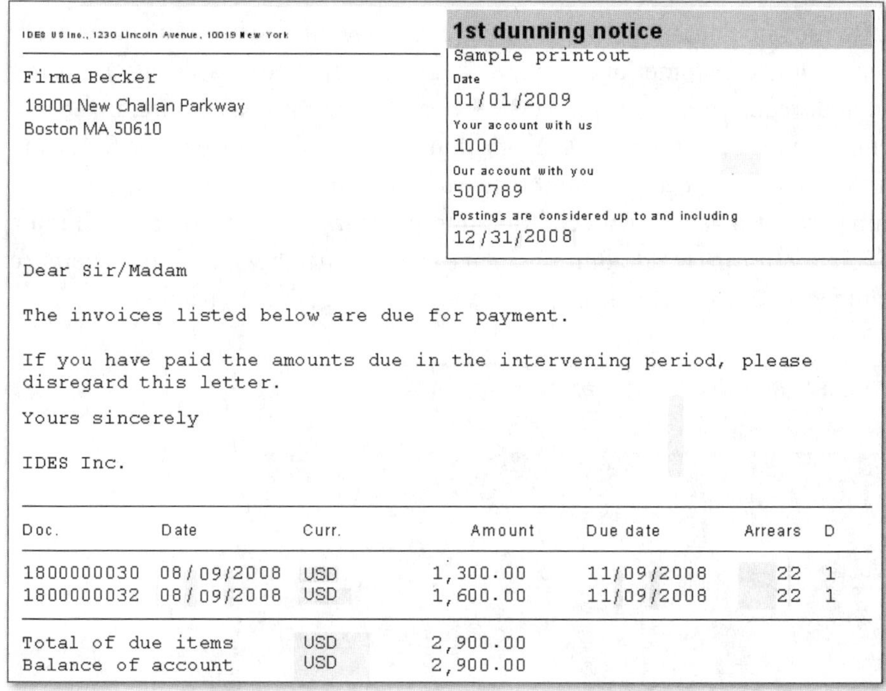

IDES US Inc., 1230 Lincoln Avenue, 10019 New York

Firma Becker
18000 New Challan Parkway
Boston MA 50610

1st dunning notice
Sample printout
Date
01/01/2009
Your account with us
1000
Our account with you
500789
Postings are considered up to and including
12/31/2008

Dear Sir/Madam

The invoices listed below are due for payment.

If you have paid the amounts due in the intervening period, please disregard this letter.

Yours sincerely

IDES Inc.

Doc.	Date	Curr.	Amount	Due date	Arrears	D
1800000030	08/09/2008	USD	1,300.00	11/09/2008	22	1
1800000032	08/09/2008	USD	1,600.00	11/09/2008	22	1
Total of due items		USD	2,900.00			
Balance of account		USD	2,900.00			

Figure 6.12 Dunning Notice

Dunning forms used for dunning notices in the SAP system can be designed using either SAPscript or Smart Forms. Both these tools in the SAP system are used for text management and form printing. We won't get into technical differences and nuances of these tools, but technical development and maintenance of Smart Forms do offer advantages over SAPscript. If you want to print dunning notices using Smart Forms, refer to Section 6.6.2, Enhancements, for details on the additional development required.

The definition of dunning notices and forms is carried out using configuration activity IMG • Financial Accounting • Accounts Receivable and Accounts Payable • Business Transactions • Dunning • Printout • Define Dunning Forms (with SAPscript) or Define Dunning Forms (with SAP SMART forms).

So far, we were focused on the important elements, concepts, and functionality of the dunning process. In the next section, we'll discuss the dunning run.

6.3 Dunning Run

You start the dunning run by selecting the menu path SAP MENU • Accounting • Financial Accounting • Accounts Receivable • Periodic Processing • Dunning or Transaction F150.

The definition of a dunning run consists of a combination of the run date and a unique identifier. Even though the unique identifier can be freely defined for each dunning run, it's advisable to follow consistent naming convention so that you can easily identify or search for dunning runs. A commonly used format of an identifier is a few characters designating the target group of a dunning run, followed by a sequential number. For example, identifier INTL01 can indicate the first dunning run for international customers on the run date. All dunning parameters for a dunning run are maintained on the Parameters tab.

6.3.1 Parameter Maintenance

Figure 6.13 shows the screen for maintaining dunning parameters. As discussed previously, Run On date and Identification uniquely identify a dunning run. Dunning Date is the date printed on dunning notices, and it's also used to calculate days in arrears for open items. Typically, Dunning Date is the same as the Run On date. However, these dates may be different if the dunning run is scheduled in advance or is backdated. Company Code, Customer Accounts, and Vendor Accounts provide additional selection criteria for the dunning run.

A very detailed log is generated during a dunning run for the customer and vendor accounts entered on the Additional Log tab. Because the detailed log includes information for every document evaluated for dunning, it should be enabled only for accounts or dunning runs for which such details are required and can be effectively analyzed.

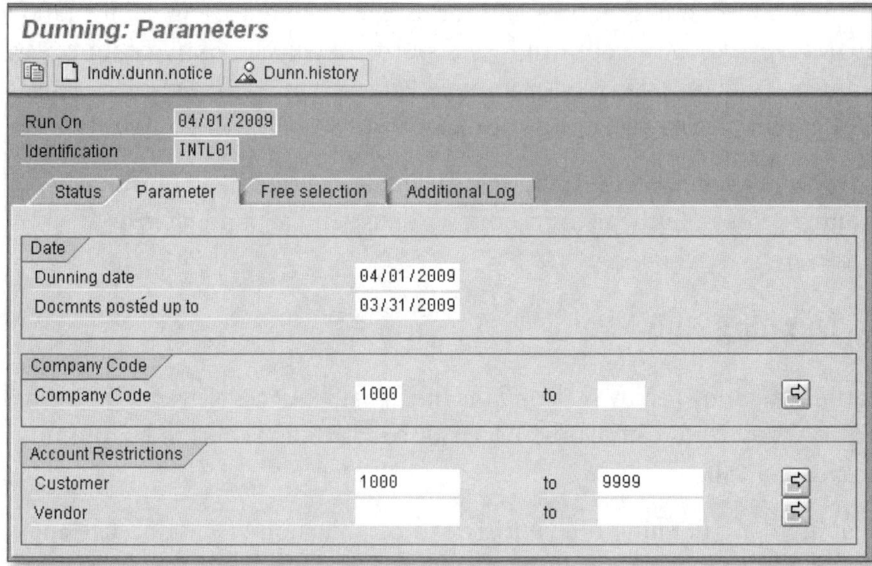

Figure 6.13 Dunning Run Parameters

You can use the Free Selection tab (Figure 6.14) to enter additional selections.

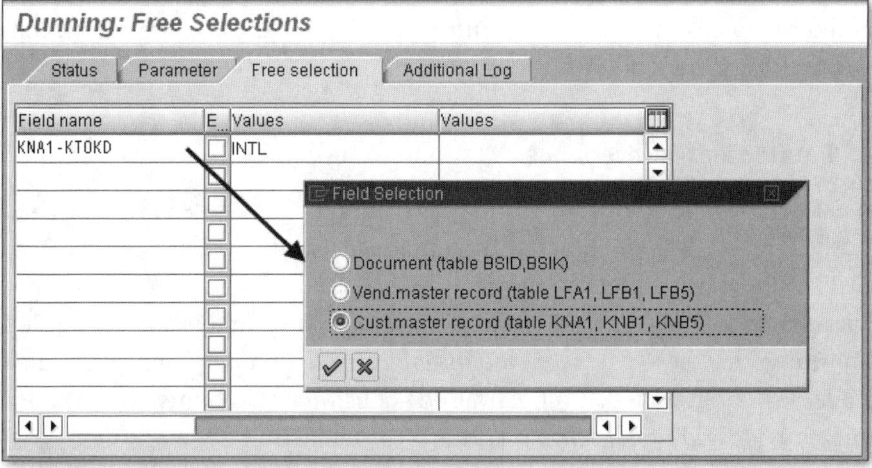

Figure 6.14 Dunning Run Free Selections

This can be useful if selections available on the Parameters tab aren't sufficient. On the Free Selection tab, you can use almost any field from financial documents, customer accounts, and vendor accounts as selection criteria. After dunning parameters are entered and saved, the next step is to create a dunning proposal.

6.3.2 Creating a Dunning Proposal

You prepare a dunning proposal by selecting the Schedule button on the dunning program. This option initiates the evaluation and processing of dunning items.

Evaluation of Dunning Items

Following are some of the points that explain evaluation of dunning items.

- Dunning is carried out on all overdue items selected based on dunning parameters and free selection criteria entered for a dunning run.
- Credit memos that aren't due or blocked result in payables to customer accounts regardless of individual due dates.
- The dunning program doesn't carry out dunning for items with a dunning block or items with an automatic payment method such as an automatic debit.
- Dunning notices aren't generated for an account if items don't exceed the minimum days in arrears, items are within the grace days, or if the overdue amount is less than minimum amount.
- Dunning notices aren't generated for an account if the dunning data hasn't changed since the last dunning run, and the Always Run indicator isn't selected in the dunning procedure.
- After an invoice is determined to be valid for inclusion in the current run, the next dunning level is calculated based on the dunning procedure parameters.
- Credit memos with invoice references receive the dunning level of the invoice and are cleared with dunning items starting with that dunning level.
- Credit memos without invoice references are cleared starting with the dunning items with the highest dunning level in the dunning run.

Clearing and printing of dunning notices are carried out in dunning currency.

Dunning Currency

If a dunning notice contains items of several currencies, the dunning currency is the same as the local currency. However, if the dunning notice contains items of only one currency, this is used as the dunning currency. Calculation of dunning charges is also carried out using this same logic.

It's important to note that the dunning program also checks blocked items to determine the dunning currency. This may lead to confusion if the blocked items are in different currencies because blocked items aren't printed on a dunning notice. Checking the dunning log or customer line items can clarify the determination of the dunning currency. The following options are available to you after the dunning proposal is generated.

- Using the Dunning List option, you can display all of the dunning items selected in the dunning proposal.
  - Program RFMAHN21 is used to display the dunning list that includes customer account information and document details.
- Using the Log option, you can display the dunning proposal log.
  - For customer and vendor accounts entered on the Additional Log tab, this option displays a very detailed log of items included in the dunning proposal.
- Using the Dunning History option, you can display the dunning history for customer or vendor accounts.
  - For all selected accounts, this option displays the dunning run date, identifier, dunning procedure, dunning level, and total dunned amount.
- Using the Delete option, you can delete the dunning selections.
  - If you want to change the dunning parameters after the dunning proposal has been generated, you have to first delete the dunning proposal.
- Using the Change option, you can change items selected in a dunning run.
  - Program RFMAHN21 is used to display the dunning list for potential changes. The next section describes this change option in more detail.

6.3.3 Changing a Dunning Proposal

By selecting the Change Master Data option from the dunning proposal change screen, you can influence the selection of dunning items included in the dunning proposal. It's also possible to change the texts maintained on the customer account master by selecting the Change Texts option. This can be useful, for example, if dunning texts maintained on the master account are printed on dunning notices.

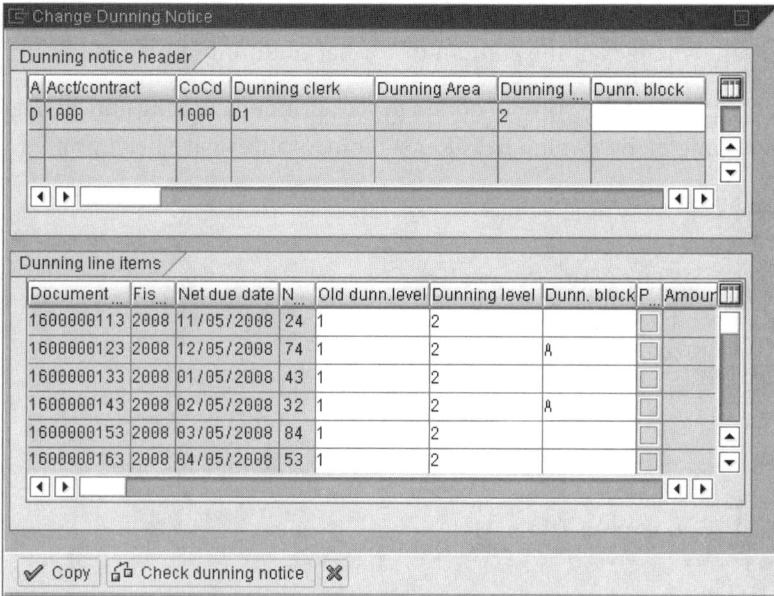

Figure 6.15 Change Dunning Notice

You can also exclude one or more items from the current dunning run by selecting the Change Dunning Notice option. As shown in Figure 6.15, you can place the dunning block on the customer account or on individual items selected in the dunning notice.

Tip

If you want to change a dunning notice in a way that changes dunning parameters such as dunning level and minimum amount; you should assign a dunning block to that customer, process the current dunning run without generating a dunning notice for that customer, and then make necessary changes to the dunning procedure configuration.

After the dunning proposal has been reviewed, you choose the Dunning Printout option when you're ready to print dunning notices.

6.3.4 Print Dunning Notices

You may first want to select the Sample Printout option to schedule the printing of sample dunning notices. This option enables you to carry out sample printing of dunning notices for selected customer or vendor accounts. This option can be useful to review any changes in the content or format of dunning notices.

Finally, you choose the Dunning Printout option to start printing dunning notices. Figure 6.16 shows a completed dunning run after dunning notices have been printed.

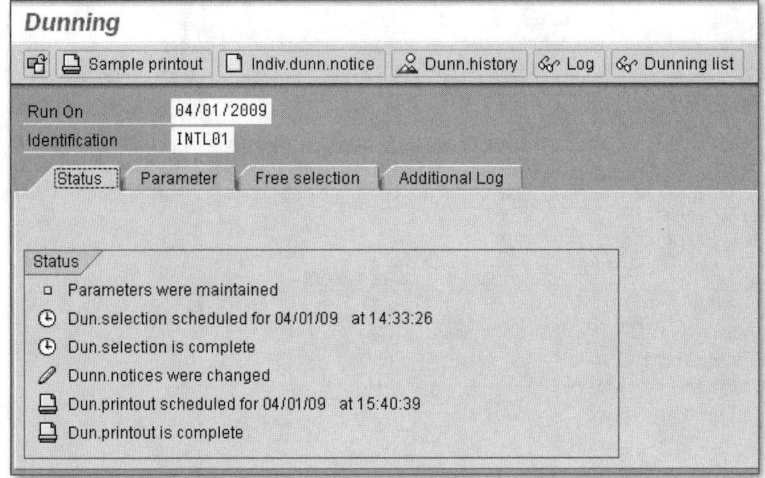

Figure 6.16 Dunning Run

By double-clicking on any status message shown in Figure 6.16, you can review detailed log information for that step.

So far, we've discussed the standard and most common flow of the dunning process. In the next section, we'll discuss additional functionality, variations of the dunning process, and other transactions.

6.4 Transactions

One of the most important transactions involved in the dunning process is the maintenance and review of the dunning data in the customer master.

6.4.1 Dunning Data in Customer Master (FD02)

Even though we'll make reference to the customer master, discussion in this section is equally applicable for dunning data maintained in vendor accounts.

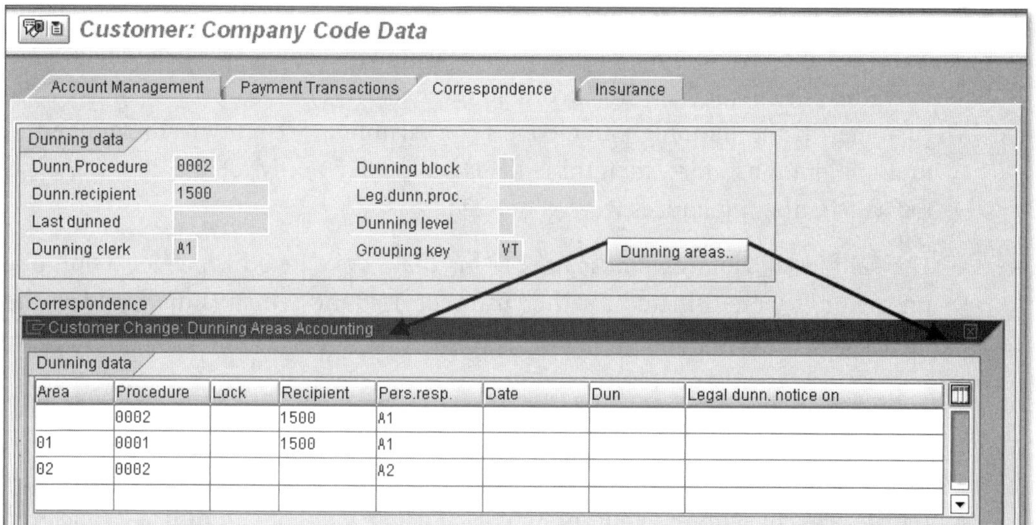

Figure 6.17 Dunning Data in the Customer Master

We've already discussed some of the dunning fields shown in the top part of Figure 6.17 such as Dunning Procedure (Section 6.2, Dunning Procedure), Dunning Clerk (Section 6.1.4, Dunning Clerk), Dunning Block (Section 6.1.6, Dunning Block), Grouping Key (Section 6.1.3, Dunning Grouping Key), and Dunning Area (Section 6.1.1, Dunning Area). Using Dunning Recipient, you can send dunning notices to a different business partner than the one who owes you receivables. At the least, the dunning procedure should be maintained in all customer accounts that are to be evaluated for dunning. Maintenance of other parameters is optional.

As shown in the bottom part of Figure 6.17, you can maintain separate dunning parameters for each dunning area that is responsible for dunning a customer account. However, you don't have to maintain these parameters separately if all the dunning areas in a company code share the same dunning parameters for a customer account.

Tip

When you dun a customer who is also a vendor, the dunning program automatically includes open items from both accounts and evaluates the net balance. However, only the dunning parameters maintained in the customer account are relevant for the dunning process.

After a dunning run is carried out, the Last Dunned field is updated with the date on which the last dunning notice for the customer account was generated. Similarly, the dunning level is updated with the highest dunning level reached by the customer. If the dunning parameters for a customer account are maintained in multiple dunning areas, then these fields are updated only for the dunning areas for which dunning notices were generated.

The field Legal Dunning Proc is used to maintain the date on which legal dunning proceedings were initiated for the customer account, which is discussed in the next section.

6.4.2 Legal Dunning

When an account reaches the last dunning level in a dunning procedure, you can transfer the collection to your internal legal department or a third-party collection agency to initiate legal dunning proceedings. The field Legal Dunning Proceedings (Figure 6.17) discussed in previous section is used to indicate the date on which legal dunning proceedings for a customer account are initiated.

Accounts, for which legal dunning proceedings have been initiated, aren't included in the normal dunning run. Instead, a separate dunning form is used to inform the legal department of any additional activities on the customer account. This form is maintained in the field Form for Legal Dunning Proceedings on the Dunning Texts tab (Section 6.2.6, Dunning Texts) of a dunning procedure. If you choose to use your standard dunning form also for accounts with legal dunning proceedings, you should ensure that the form is capable of printing the appropriate legal verbiage. Your SAP support personnel can help you with that change.

Unless there is any new activity, a new dunning notice isn't generated for accounts for which legal dunning proceedings have been initiated. If you want to ensure that a dunning notice is generated regardless of any new activity, you should select the field Always Dun in Legal Dunning Proc in the Dunning Levels tab (Section 6.2.2, Dunning Levels) of a dunning procedure.

Additionally, legal dunning proceeding runs differ from standard dunning runs in the following ways:

- A dunning run also displays documents with dunning blocks or documents with automated payment methods such as automatic bank debit.
- The dunning level on the master record doesn't change. Only the last dunning date is updated on the master record.

Another variation of the dunning process is the ability to print individual dunning notices.

6.4.3 Individual Dunning Notices

If you want to print a one-off dunning notice for a customer or a vendor, the individual dunning notice function can be useful. You access this functionality (Figure 6.18) by selecting the Indiv Dunning Notice option in the dunning run as discussed in Section 6.3, Dunning Run.

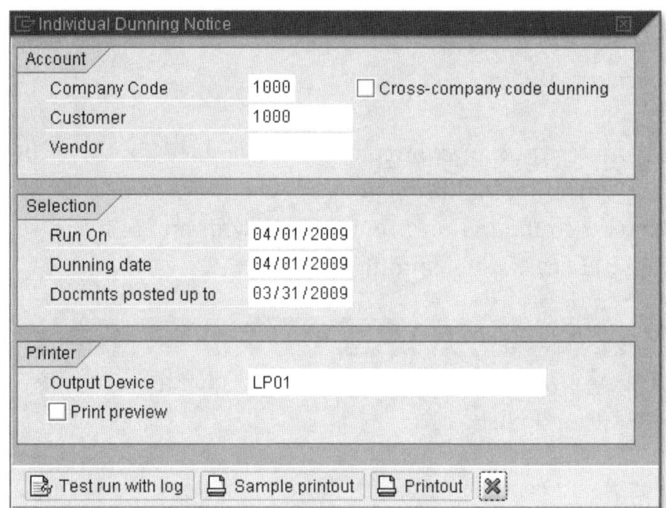

Figure 6.18 Individual Dunning Notices

As you can see, this is a quick way to specify all information relevant for a dunning notice — such as company code, account, and dates — and quickly print a dunning notice. If you select the Cross-Company Code Dunning flag, all items from all company codes are included in the dunning notice for an account.

In the next section, you'll see how interest and dunning charges are calculated and processed in a dunning procedure.

6.4.4 Interest Calculation

The Interest indicator is maintained in the Interest Indicator field on the Overview tab (Section 6.2.1, Overview Screen) of a dunning procedure. Configuration for these indicators is carried out using IMG • FINANCIAL ACCOUNTING • ACCOUNTS RECEIVABLE AND ACCOUNTS PAYABLE • BUSINESS TRANSACTIONS • DUNNING • DUNNING PROCEDURE • DEFINE INTEREST RATES.

'Interest Rates

Int ID	Crcy	Valid from	Debit %	Cred. %
01	DEM	01/01/2009	9.250	6.000
01	EUR	01/01/2009	9.250	6.000
01	FRF	01/01/2009	9.250	6.000
01	IQD	01/01/2009	9.250	6.000
01	JPY	01/01/2009	9.250	6.000
01	USD	01/01/2009	9.250	6.000

Figure 6.19 Dunning Interest Rates

As shown in Figure 6.19, interest rate in configuration are defined for a combination of interest indicator, currency, validity date, and whether a transaction is a debit or credit. This detailed configuration provides you with an ability to set interest rates that accurately reflect market conditions.

Tip

Interest calculation for dunning is *completely separate* from the month-end interest calculation program discussed in Chapter 10.

Dunning interest is calculated and can be printed on dunning notices. However, as mentioned in Section 6.2.4, Dunning Charges, additional development is required if you want these entries to automatically post to accounting.

The next section discusses dunning reports available in the SAP system.

6.4.5 Reporting

To analyze current and historical dunning of customer accounts, you can use customer line item analysis and dunning history reports in the SAP system.

Customer Line Item Analysis (FBL5N)

This is one of the most commonly used transactions to analyze entries posted to a customer account. We discussed this transaction in Chapter 11.

Customer Line Item Display

Stat	Type	Doc. Date	Net due date	DD	Σ	Amt in loc.cur.	LCurr	DocumentNo	Dunn. block	Dunn.level	Dunn.key	Dunn.area
	DR	08/15/2008	09/29/2008			1,000.00	USD	1800000028		1		
	DR	08/15/2008	09/29/2008			1,150.00	USD	1800000029		2		
	DR	08/15/2008	09/29/2008			1,300.00	USD	1800000030	A	2		
	DR	08/15/2008	09/29/2008			1,450.00	USD	1800000031	B	2		
	DR	08/15/2008	09/29/2008			1,600.00	USD	1800000032		2		
					▪	**6,500.00**	**USD**					
Account 1000					▪▪	**6,500.00**	**USD**					

Figure 6.20 Dunning: Customer Line Item Display

As shown in Figure 6.20, you can set a line item layout to include dunning fields such as Dunning Block, Dunning Level, Dunning Key, and Dunning Area. This report provides you with the current dunning status of open items. To analyze historical dunning data, you should use dunning history.

Dunning History (F150)

Dunning history can be accessed through the same transaction that you use for the dunning run (Section 6.3.2, Creating a Dunning Proposal).

FI Dunning - Dunning History

Display dunning notice | Choose

```
Comp.  Acct typ Account
Run Date    ID      Print Date Dun. date  Leg.dun.pr Procedure Sort field CPD   Area          Dun          Due items Crcy

1000    D        1000
01/01/2009  INTL02 04/09/2009 01/01/2009            0002                                       1          2,900.00  USD
01/01/2009  INTL03 04/11/2009 04/01/2009            0002                                       2          1,100.00  USD
End of the list
```

Figure 6.21 Dunning History

Dunning history can be displayed for a range of customer and vendor accounts across company codes. Dunning history (Figure 6.21) shows the corresponding dunning level, dunning block, dunning date, and dunning procedure used for all dunned items. The next section provides a list of dunning transactions.

6.4.6 List of Transactions

Table 6.1 lists some of the transactions discussed in this chapter.

Transaction	Usage
F150	Dunning
F8P2	Set dunning block in customer line items
FD02	Maintain dunning data in customer master
FK02	Maintain dunning data in vendor master
FBL5N	Customer line item display
FBL1N	Vendor line item display
OBL6	Generate list for dunning program configuration
OB42	Define dunning interest rates
FBMP	Define dunning procedures
SE71	Define dunning forms (SAPscript)
SMARTFORMS	Define dunning forms (Smart Forms)
OBMD	Maintain sort variants for dunning notice items
OBMK	Maintain sort variants for dunning notice header
SCAL	Maintain public holidays calendar

Table 6.1 Dunning Transactions

In the next section, we'll look at the technical objects available for the dunning functionality.

6.5 Technical Reference

This section lists technical objects such as SAP Notes, authorization objects, and tables and structures relevant for implementing dunning functionality. Considering the large number of technical objects available in the SAP system, this information should only be considered as a starting point for analysis.

6.5.1 SAP Notes

Table 6.2 lists the SAP Notes for implementing the dunning functionality.

SAP Note	Relevance
0000545290	FAQ: Dunning
0000543743	FAQ: Dunning
0000590421	Add additional fields to dunning list
0000957556	Dunning of credit memos without invoice reference
0000333506	Dunning items with negative arrears
0000369620	Dunning for direct debit customer
0000874603	Interest calculation – dunning program and interest program
0001022738	Sort dunning lines according to days in arrears
0000643215	Confirmation receipt for dunning notices sent by email
0000970870	Sending interest letters by fax or email
0001091687	Individual dunning notice functionality
0000006591	Resetting of dunning data after printing
0000018127	Dunning notice: dunning level lower than expected
0000825723	Dunning charges in local and foreign currencies

Table 6.2 Dunning Process – SAP Notes

In the next section, we'll look at authorization objects available for dunning processes and transactions.

6.5.2 Authorization Objects

Table 6.3 lists some of the authorization objects to be considered for transactions discussed in this chapter.

Object	Description
F_KNA1_BUK	Customer: Authorization for Company Codes
F_LFA1_BUK	Vendor: Authorization for Company Codes
F_MAHN_BUK	Automatic Dunning: Authorization for Company Codes
F_MAHN_KOA	Automatic Dunning: Authorization for Account Types
F_BKPF_BUK	Accounting Document: Authorization for Company Codes

Table 6.3 Authorization Objects – Dunning

Object	Description
F_BKPF_GSB	Accounting Document: Authorization for Business Areas
F_BKPF_KOA	Accounting Document: Authorization for Account Types

Table 6.3 Authorization Objects – Dunning (Cont.)

The next section provides a list of tables and structures.

6.5.3 Tables and Structures

Table 6.4 lists tables and structures relevant for dunning processes. Additionally, you should also be familiar with tables and structures used for financial documents.

Table	Relevance
MAHNS	Accounts blocked by dunning selection
MHNK	Dunning data (account entries)
MHND	Dunning data (document entries)
MHNKA	Version administration of dunning changes
MHNKO	Dunning data (account entries) version before the next change
MHNDO	Dunning data version before the next change
T040	Dunning keys
T040S	Blocking reasons for dunning notices
T047B	Dunning level control
T047C	Dunning charges
T047M	Dunning areas
T047R	Grouping rules for dunning notices
T047T	Dunning procedure names

Table 6.4 Dunning Tables and Structures

Now we'll look at objects and functionality available for enhancing and modifying dunning functionality.

6.6 Enhancements and Modifications

This section provides lists of available BTEs, enhancements, BAdIs, and BAPIs relevant for dunning processes. These are used to enhance and modify the standard functionality available in the SAP system.

6.6.1 Business Transaction Events (BTE)

Using BTEs, you can attach additional function modules and custom logic to the standard SAP system. Table 6.5 lists publish and subscribe (P/S) and process BTEs available for dunning functionality.

Type	BTE	Event/Process
P/S	00001705	Start of dunning notice printout
P/S	00001710	End of dunning notice printout
P/S	00001719	Additional activities before printing
P/S	00001720	Printing of dunning notice
P/S	00001730	Check dunning customizing (key text)
P/S	00001740	Check additional dunning customizing
P/S	00001750	Dunning parameter maintenance (key text)
P/S	00001751	Dunning parameter maintenance
P/S	00001760	Application code: Process dunning header
P/S	00001761	Application code: Process dunning items
P/S	00001764	Dunning: Alternative Check for Account Balance
Process	00001020	Processing after data selection but before printing
Process	00001030	Determine form for dunning notice
Process	00001040	Determine output device for printing dunning
Process	00001050	Read additional fields for dunning account entries
Process	00001051	Read additional fields for dunning customer items
Process	00001052	Read additional fields for dunning vendor items
Process	00001053	Set dunning grouping key for one-time accounts

Table 6.5 Dunning – Business Transaction Events

Type	BTE	Event/Process
Process	00001060	Influence whether an item is dunned
Process	00001061	Delete an item from dunning proposal
Process	00001070	Use alternative procedures for interest calculation
Process	00001071	Influence calculation of dunning charges

Table 6.5 Dunning – Business Transaction Events (Cont.)

The following examples show how BTEs can be used to influence the dunning process.

- **Event 00001060:** Influence whether an item is dunned
  - In the SAP system, customer accounts that are maintained with direct debit payments aren't dunned in the normal dunning run. Using this BTE, you can allow dunning of direct debit customers.
  - Refer to SAP note 0000369620 for more details on this implementation.
- **Event 00001071:** Influence calculation of dunning charges
  - By default, dunning charges are issued based on dunning currency, which may be different from local currency. Using this BTE, you can choose the currency in which dunning charges are issued.
  - Refer to SAP note 0000825723 for more details on this implementation.
- **Event 00001720:** Printing of dunning notice
  - By default, the dunning program prints dunning forms based on SAPscripts. With the help of this BTE, you can use Smart Forms for printing dunning notices.
  - You can use the F150_DUNN_SF Smart Form as a template or reference while designing your own Smart Forms for dunning forms.

The configuration menu path to implement these BTEs is IMG • Financial Accounting • Financial Accounting Global Settings • Tools • Customer Enhancements • Business Transaction Events. The next section discusses available enhancement spots.

6.6.2 Enhancements

Using the following enhancements, you can add customer routines to expand the available dunning functionality in the SAP system.

- **F150D001:** Customer exits in program for printing dunning notices
  - This enhancement contains function module `EXIT_SAPF150D_001`, which is used to send dunning notices by fax or email.

6.7 Summary

We started this chapter with a discussion of parameters that influence the dunning processes in the SAP system. Dunning procedures bring these parameters together and play a central role in a dunning run, in which open items of customer or vendor accounts are evaluated and dunning notices are printed. Variations of the dunning process cater to business requirements such as dunning head office or local office, dunning one-time accounts, calculation of interest on overdue receivables, calculating dunning charges, and so on.

This chapter focuses on the credit management functionality available in the SAP system. Requirements of credit management can vary considerably depending on industry norms and business partners. In this chapter, you'll learn how to set up and use credit management features to support complex business requirements.

7 Credit Management

The Credit Management component in the SAP system is used to maintain and evaluate the creditworthiness of business partners. This information helps in taking proactive as well as corrective actions to ensure that, at any time, financial exposure to a business partner is commensurate with the partner's ability to make payments. For businesses, it's prudent to monitor a customer's creditworthiness and open receivables closely through the entire order to cash process. This is especially the case for industries with long order to cash cycles, such as those in construction industries or make to order industries. So, while implementing credit management in the SAP system, you need the support and participation of the finance team as well as the sales team. Also, credit management configuration activities and transactions in the SAP system are part of the finance functionality as well as the sales functionality.

We'll start this chapter with an introduction to the credit management functionality and associated configuration activities. Next we'll look at different types of credit controls available to you, followed by how to process documents that are on credit block. At the end, we'll look at additional credit management functionalities. So let's begin with the credit management setup.

7.1 Credit Management Setup

In the Credit Management component, customer credits are maintained for one or more credit control areas.

7.1.1 Credit Control Area

The *credit control area* represents an organizational unit that is responsible for maintaining, evaluating, and monitoring credit limits of business partners. Let's look at the definition of credit control areas.

Define the Credit Control Area

You define the credit control area using SAP IMG • ENTERPRISE STRUCTURE • DEFINITION • FINANCIAL ACCOUNTING • DEFINE CREDIT CONTROL AREA. Figure 7.1 shows parameters associated with the credit control area. These parameters specify the update rule for credit monitoring and default values for new accounts.

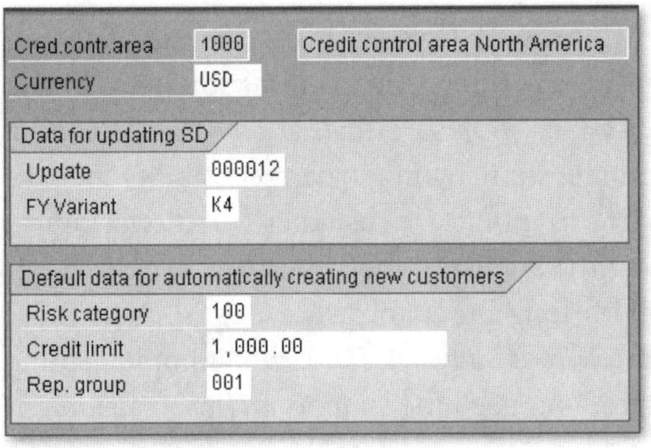

Cred.contr.area 1000 Credit control area North America
Currency USD

Data for updating SD
Update 000012
FY Variant K4

Default data for automatically creating new customers
Risk category 100
Credit limit 1,000.00
Rep. group 001

Figure 7.1 Credit Control Area – Parameters

An UPDATE rule determines whether credit exposure calculation takes into account values of open sales documents such as orders, deliveries and billing documents, and open financial documents. Table 7.1 lists possible values for Update rule that can be assigned to a credit control area.

Update Rule	Usage
<blank>	No update from sales documents, only FI documents
000012	Open orders + deliveries + billing documents + FI documents
000015	Open deliveries + billing documents + FI documents
000018	Open orders + billing documents + FI documents

Table 7.1 Credit Control Area – Update Rules

Secondly, default values such as RISK CATEGORY, CREDIT LIMIT and REP. GROUP ensure that any business transactions with new customers are subject to controlled credit management while their credit limits are being determined. The next section discusses these parameters in more detail, but before that, let's discuss the assignment of credit control areas to company codes.

Assign Credit Control Area

Credit control areas are assigned to company codes, which in turn determine the scope of the financial and sales transactions that are evaluated for credit monitoring. You may also assign credit control area to sales areas, which in turn are assigned to company codes. With the help of the enhancement routine mentioned in this chapter, it's also possible to use custom development to determine and assign a credit control area at the transactional level.

The optimum approach for defining credit control areas should be selected based on your credit management organizational structure. Centralized credit management processes can be served by a credit control area assigned to a company code, whereas if each sales organization manages credit exposure of its customers; you may use separate credit control areas for each sales area. To assign credit control area to a company code, you use SAP IMG • ENTERPRISE STRUCTURE • ASSIGNMENT • FINANCIAL ACCOUNTING • ASSIGN COMPANY CODE TO CREDIT CONTROL AREA.

If the OVERWRITE CC flag is set for the credit control area assignment to a company code (Figure 7.2), it's possible to overwrite the credit control area in transactions. Permitted credit control areas for a company code are maintained using SAP IMG• FINANCIAL ACCOUNTING • ACCOUNTS RECEIVABLE AND ACCOUNTS PAYABLE • CREDIT MANAGEMENT • CREDIT CONTROL ACCOUNT • ASSIGN PERMITTED CREDIT CONTROL AREAS TO COMPANY CODE.

Assign company code -> credit control area

Co...	Company Name	City	CCAr	Overwrite CC...
1000	IDES AG	Frankfurt	1000	☐
2000	IDES UK	London		☐
2100	IDES Portugal	Lisbon		☐
2200	IDES France	Paris	1000	☑
2201	IDES France affiliate	Paris		☐
2300	IDES España	Barcelona	1000	☑
2600	IDES IDES Italia	Milano		☐
2700	IDES Schweiz	Biel / Bienne	1000	☐
2800	China	China		☐
3000	IDES US INC	New York	3000	☑

Figure 7.2 Assign a Company Code to a Credit Control Area

In the next section, we'll discuss the organization of credit management data.

7.1.2 Organization of Credit Data

In this section, we'll discuss the preliminary settings and organization of customer data in credit management.

Preliminary Settings

Preliminary settings for credit management (Figure 7.3) are defined using SAP IMG• Financial Accounting • Accounts Receivable and Accounts Payable • Credit Management • Credit Control Account • Define Preliminary Settings for Credit Management.

Client-specific FI-AR-CR settings

Procedure parameters for credit check

☑ Read A/R Summary

☐ Read A/R summary from an external system

☑ Create A/R summary

Procedure parameters for DSO calculation

☑ All children

☐ Current balance

No. of months 3

Figure 7.3 Credit Management – Preliminary Settings

The first three parameters refer to *A/R summary*. A/R summary is a summarized version of accounts receivable (AR) data. Using A/R summary instead of current finance data can be useful if Sales and Finance are in distributed SAP systems, or there is a need to improve credit procedure performance. The READ A/R SUMMARY flag controls whether the credit procedure reads the A/R summary, the READ A/R SUMMARY FROM AN EXTERNAL SYSTEM flag indicates that the A/R summary is generated and read from an external system, and the CREATE A/R SUMMARY flag indicates you're allowed to generate the A/R summary in the current SAP system.

Tip

You can configure advanced credit management so that if A/R summary is older than a specific number of days and hours, the system sets the credit block "A/R Summary Obsolete" to indicate that the A/R summary needs to be regenerated. Though more common, regularly scheduled background jobs ensure that A/R Summary is always kept up-to-date.

The other three fields in Figure 7.3 control the calculation of the Days Sales Outstanding (DSO) in credit management transactions and reports.

- The ALL CHILDREN flag indicates that the DSO calculation is carried out for all customer accounts assigned to a credit account. The distinction between a credit account and a customer account is explained in Section 7.1.5, Credit Account.
- Using the NO OF MONTHS field, you can specify how many previous months are included in the calculation of the DSO. Common business practice is to calculate DSO using the last three months' of balance.
- CURRENT BALANCE specifies that the DSO calculation should be carried out using the current balance instead of the average balance. This flag is useful in countries where the DSO calculation is carried out using the current balance.

As you can imagine, values specified in this configuration activity have considerable impact on the credit management of customer data.

Organization of Customer Data

We discussed in Chapter 1, Customer Master Data, how one customer can be associated with multiple company codes in SAP. Similarly, a customer can also be associated with multiple credit control areas, which may be assigned to the same or different company codes. To create customer credit management data, you can use any customer master maintenance transactions discussed in Chapter 1, Section

7.5.1, Master Data Maintenance. Select the ENVIRONMENT • CREDIT MANAGEMENT menu path to access the credit management transaction.

As shown in Figure 7.4, the customer credit management transaction contains information on five tabs. For data maintenance, the CENTRAL DATA tab is used to maintain credit management data that is independent of credit control areas, and the STATUS tab is used to maintain credit management data for a specific credit control area.

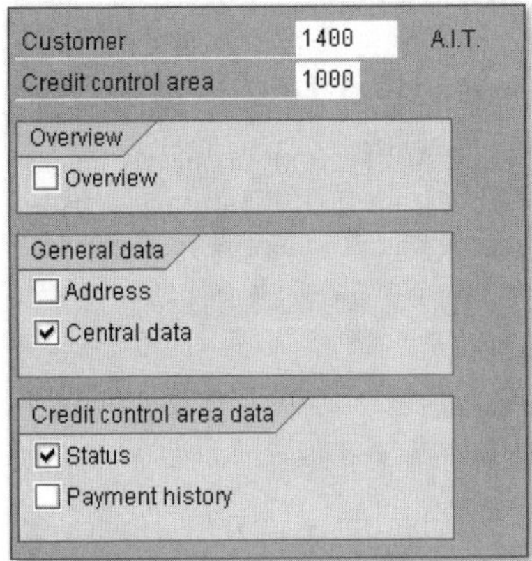

Figure 7.4 Credit Account – Initial Screen

Conceptually, we can group credit management data on these tabs into credit limits data, and other credit data such as internal and external data.

7.1.3 Maintenance of Credit Limits

Credit limits for a credit account are maintained on Central Data tab and the Status tab.

Central Data Tab

Figure 7.5 shows an example of the central credit management data for a credit account. Using the TOTAL AMOUNT field, you specify the total credit limit that a customer may receive across all credit control areas. For example, if customer credit is managed and monitored in multiple business units of your company, the value in this field specifies the upper limit for the combined total of all credit limits assigned in individual credit control areas. Using the INDIVIDUAL LIMIT field, you specify the upper limit for the credit limit assigned to a customer in any one credit control area.

As is evident, if your organization structure in the SAP system consists of only one credit control area, TOTAL AMOUNT and INDIVIDUAL LIMIT fields will contain the same values. The CURRENCY field specifies the currency in which credit limits are maintained, which is typically the same as the currency of the credit control area.

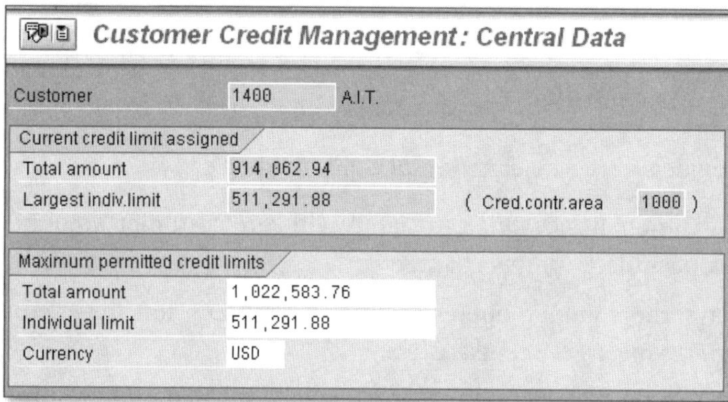

Figure 7.5 Credit Limits Data – Central Data Tab

While maintaining customer credit limits on this screen, you can use information in the other two fields as reference. TOTAL AMOUNT under the Current Credit Limit Assigned section shows you the total of credit limits granted to the customer across all credit control areas, whereas LARGEST INDIV. LIMIT shows you the largest credit limit assigned to the customer and the credit control area in which that credit limit is assigned. Information for a credit account that is specific to a credit control area is maintained on the Status tab.

Status Tab

Figure 7.6 shows the Credit Limit Data section of the Status tab of the customer's credit management data. The most important field on this data section is CREDIT LIMIT, which specifies the credit limit assigned to the customer account in the credit control area. All other value fields on this data tab are displayed for information purposes only.

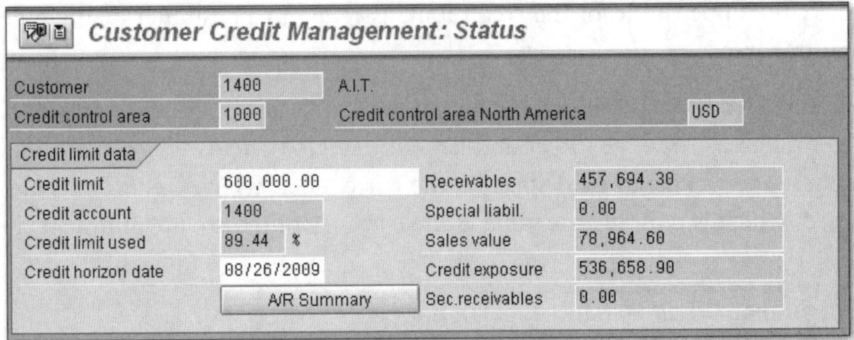

Figure 7.6 Credit Limits Data – Status Tab

The following list provides a brief explanation of other fields:

- CREDIT ACCOUNT is the credit account associated with the customer account. We'll discuss this concept later in this chapter.
- RECEIVABLES displays the total of open accounts receivables for the credit account, excluding any special GL transactions.
- SPECIAL LIABIL. displays the total of special GL transactions that are relevant for credit management.
- SALES VALUE displays the total of all sales documents taken into account for credit exposure calculation. The Update rule assigned to a credit control area (Section 7.1.1, Credit Control Area) determines the documents included in this calculation.
- CREDIT EXPOSURE displays the total credit exposure to the credit account. This value is the total of receivables, special liabilities, and sales value.
- CREDIT LIMIT USED shows credit exposure as a percentage of the credit limit assigned to the credit account.

In the next section, we'll look at other credit management data.

7.1.4 Other Credit Management Data

Figure 7.7 shows an example of the internal and external credit data for a credit account. This information is maintained on the Status tab.

Customer Credit Management: Status

Customer	1400	A.I.T.			
Credit control area	1000	Credit control area North America		USD	

Internal data

Risk category	001	Low risk		☐ Blocked
Credit rep.group	001	Credit Rep group 1		☐ Texts exist
Cust.cred.group	1100	Major domestic customers		Texts
Customer group			Last int.review	01/01/2008
Reference date	01/01/2008		Next int.review	01/01/2010

External data

Cred.info number	00-111-2223	Payment index		
Last ext.review	01/01/2008	Rating	Baa1	
Monitoring		Recmd.Cred.Lim.	680,000.00	USD

Figure 7.7 Credit Management – Other Data

Tip

By selecting the Blocked flag in the Internal Data section of the dialog box, you can block a customer for all credit management transactions such as order acceptance, deliveries, and goods issues.

Internal data refers to the credit data that is determined or assigned based on decisions that are internal to your organization, whereas external data refers to credit data obtained from external, governmental, or credit rating agencies. You need to maintain only those fields that you intend to use for reporting, analysis, or credit limit determination. You'll find related configuration activities under SAP IMG • FINANCIAL ACCOUNTING • ACCOUNTS RECEIVABLE AND ACCOUNTS PAYABLE • CREDIT MANAGEMENT, which we'll refer to in an abbreviated form as CREDIT MGMT FI IMG.

Let's focus on fields relevant for customer groupings such as a risk category.

Risk Category

RISK CATEGORY is used to group customers based on their credit risk, such as new customers, low risk, high risk, and so on. Risk categories are also used in the definition of credit checks in the advanced credit management functionality. You define risk categories using IMG • CREDIT CONTROL ACCOUNT • DEFINE RISK CATEGORIES.

As shown in Figure 7.8, each credit control area can have its own definition of risk categories. Other customer grouping fields relevant for credit management are the Cust. Cred. Group and the Customer Group.

Risk category	CCAr	Name
001	1000	Low risk
001	3000	Low risk
002	1000	High risk
002	3000	High risk
003	3000	High risk
100	1000	New customers
100	3000	New customers

Figure 7.8 Risk Categories

Customer Credit Group and Customer Group

The Cust. Cred. Group field enables you to group customers based on criteria relevant for credit management. As shown in Figure 7.9, you may group customers based on country, sales volume, or any similar criteria. You define these groups using IMG • Credit Control Account • Define groups.

Cred	CCAr	Group
1100	1000	Major domestic customers
1100	3000	Major domestic customers
1200	1000	Small/med. domestic customers
1200	3000	Small/med. domestic customers
1300	1000	Customers in Eastern Europe
1300	3000	Customers in South America
1400	1000	Customers in Austria
1400	3000	Customers in Eastern Europe

Figure 7.9 Customer Credit Groups

Customer credit groups are defined in the configuration and provide predefined values that can be assigned to credit accounts. On the other hand, the Customer Group field is a freely assignable field that can be used by credit managers to define their own groups for customers, such as those based on product lines or industries. Lastly, you may also assign to each credit account a credit representative group.

Credit Representative Group

The CREDIT REP. GROUP field lets you assign a group of credit representatives to a credit account. This information can then be used in the automatic credit release procedure discussed later in this chapter, or for other reporting and analytical processes. You define credit representative groups and assign credit representatives to it using IMG • CREDIT CONTROL ACCOUNT • DEFINE CREDIT REPRESENTATIVE GROUPS and DEFINE CREDIT REPRESENTATIVES.

Cred.rep.	CCAr.	Funct	ParC	Co	Pers.No.	Name	ID/number
001	1000	KB	1	☑	1051	Barbara Fischer	
001	1000	KB	2	☑	1052	Tom Mannheim	
001	1000	KM		☑	1440	Tom Bender	
001	3000	KB		☑	1051	Barbara Fischer	
002	1000	KB		☑	1051	Barbara Fischer	
002	1000	KM		☑	1440	Tom Bender	
002	3000	KB		☑	1051	Barbara Fischer	
002	3000	KM		☑	1440	Tom Bender	

Figure 7.10 Credit Representative Assignment

Figure 7.10 shows the assignment of credit representatives to credit representative groups. The credit representative assignment consists of the following information:

- Personnel number (Pers.No.) of an employee as defined in SAP Human Resources.
- Partner function (Funct) that indicates whether the employee performs the function of a credit representative (KB) or a credit manager (KM).
- Partner counter (ParC), which is a sequential number if multiple employees are assigned to the same function. This is useful because typically a credit representative group consists of more than one credit representative.
- Copy (Co) flag to ensure the credit representative number is copied into documents.

Another important aspect of internal credit data consists of different dates.

Dates for Internal Credit Data

Figure 7.7 shows three dates associated with internal credit data. You may use the REFERENCE DATE field to maintain the date on which information such as risk category, customer credit group, and credit representative group was determined. Similarly, LAST INTERNAL REVIEW DATE is used to maintain the date when the internal review of the credit account was carried out and the credit limit was determined. Based on your organizational processes, you may also maintain NEXT INTERNAL REVIEW DATE on the credit account.

From these three dates, only NEXT INTERNAL REVIEW DATE can be used in the definition of credit check rules. For example, a credit check rule can put a credit block on sales documents if an account is overdue for internal credit review.

In addition to credit data determined internally, many organizations gather credit-relevant data about their customers from external groups and agencies. The next section describes the maintenance of such external data for a credit account.

External Credit Data

The External Data section shown earlier in Figure 7.7 is used to maintain customer credit data obtained from external groups and rating agencies. The following is a list of some of the fields in this section and their possible usage:

- Credit Info Number is an external reference number such as a Dun & Bradstreet Number for a customer.
- Rating can be used to maintain customer credit rating by external agencies such as Moody's or S&P in the United States.
- Recmd. Cred. Lim. (recommended external credit limit) represents the credit limit suggested by an external agency.
- Last Ext. Review is the date on which the external credit data for the customer account was obtained. You can use this date to set up credit check rules so that a document is placed on hold if the external review of the customer account is past due.

So far, we've used the terms a customer account and a credit account interchangeably. However, in SAP Credit Management, a credit account is a separate entity in itself.

7.1.5 Credit Account

A *credit account* in the SAP system represents an account for which credit limits are assigned, evaluated, and monitored. Most commonly, a credit account for a customer is the same as the customer account. However, you may choose to assign the same credit account to multiple customer accounts if a group of business partners are monitored as a single entity for credit management. In Figure 7.6 shown earlier, you may have noticed the Credit Account field along with other credit limit fields. To assign different credit accounts to a customer, you have to select menu EDIT • CHANGE CREDIT ACCOUNT.

> **Tip**
>
> All values displayed on the Credit Limit Data tab (shown in Figure 7.6) refer to a credit account and not to the customer account. When you change the credit account assigned to a customer account, the total receivables are adjusted automatically. However, to update other values, you have to carry out credit data reorganization.

Now that we've discussed most of the parameters that influence the credit procedure, let's look at the setup for simple credit checks.

7.2 Simple Credit Check

Figure 7.11 shows the assignment of credit checks and credit groups to sales document types.

Sales Document Types - Credit Limit Check

SaTy	Description	Check credit	Credit group
Z001	std var order	D	04
Z1IN	Inquiry		
Z1OR	Standard Order	D	01
Z201	Std Order	D	01
Z300	CRM-Telesales	B	
Z4FD	Deliv.Free of Charge		
Z4OR	Standard Order	D	01
Z4QT	Quotation	A	
Z4SC	Service and Maint.	D	04
ZA05	Internet order	D	04

Figure 7.11 Simple Credit Check

You may configure these credit checks for sales documents using SAP IMG• SALES AND DISTRIBUTION • BASIC FUNCTIONS • CREDIT MANAGEMENT/RISK MANAGEMENT •

CREDIT MANAGEMENT • ASSIGN SALES DOCUMENTS AND DELIVERY DOCUMENTS. For a simple credit check, a document is validated to ensure that it won't make credit exposure with the business partner exceed the credit limit. This check is carried out using the credit limit specified in field CREDIT LIMIT shown earlier in Figure 7.6, for the CREDIT ACCOUNT and CREDIT CONTROL AREA associated with the sales document.

Table 7.2 lists the possible values for the credit check. For a simple credit check, only values A, B, and C are relevant.

Credit Check	Usage
<blank>	No credit limit check
A	Simple credit limit check with a warning message
B	Simple credit limit check with an error message
C	Simple credit limit check with a delivery block
D	Automatic credit control (discussed in the next section)

Table 7.2 Credit Limit Check for Sales Documents

However, if this simple credit check isn't sufficient to meet your business requirements, you can activate advanced credit management by assigning option D to the sales document. The next section discusses this option in more detail.

7.3 Advanced Credit Management

As Figure 7.12 shows, automatic credit control provides you with considerably advanced credit management functionality. You can configure automatic credit controls using SAP IMG • SALES AND DISTRIBUTION • BASIC FUNCTIONS • CREDIT MANAGEMENT/RISK MANAGEMENT • CREDIT MANAGEMENT • DEFINE AUTOMATIC CREDIT CONTROL or Transaction OVA8.

Tip
Automatic credit control rules are defined for a combination of Credit Control Area, Risk Category, and Credit Group. This helps you specify credit management rules independently for any combination of organizational areas, customer groups, and SAP document types.

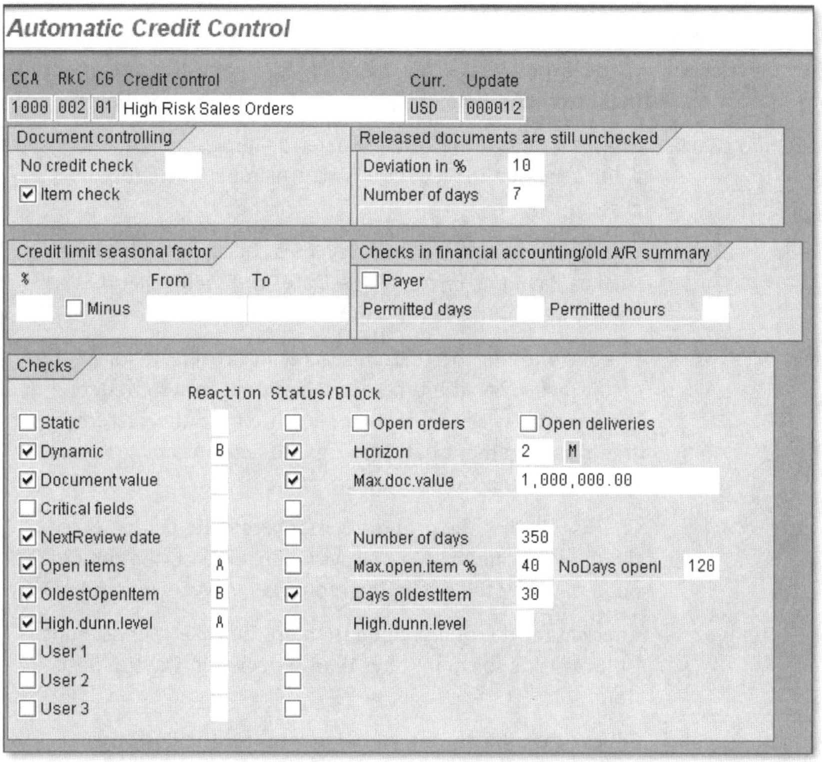

Figure 7.12 Automatic Credit Check

Let's discuss different fields of this transaction that control different aspects of credit management, starting with the types of credit checks.

7.3.1 Types of Credit Checks

Using automatic credit control, you can specify more than 10 types of credit checks on sales documents. For each type of credit check, you have to specify the necessary parameters as listed in Table 7.3.

Type of Credit Check	Purpose
Static credit check	Carries out a static credit check similar to a simple credit check. You choose whether credit exposure takes into account open orders and open deliveries.

Table 7.3 Credit Checks in Automatic Credit Control

Type of Credit Check	Purpose
Dynamic credit check	Credit exposure is calculated only for open sales documents that are in the timeframe specified in the Horizon field.
Document value check	Checks whether the value of sales document exceeds the value specified in MAX DOC VALUE (can be useful for new customers).
Critical fields check	Checks whether since the last credit check, any critical fields such as Payment Terms, Value Date, and Value Days have been changed in the sales document.
Next review date check	Checks whether the customer account is overdue for a credit review. At the time of evaluation, the system date is compared with the next review date from the customer credit management data, taking into account any grace days specified in the Number of Days field.
Open items check	Checks whether the proportion of overdue items that exceeds the days specified in No of Days Open, exceeds the total of open items by the percentage specified in Max Open Item %.
Oldest open item check	Checks that the oldest open item on the customer account isn't overdue for more days than specified in Days Oldest Item.
Highest dunning level check	Checks that the current dunning level for the customer account isn't higher than the dunning level specified in High Dunning Level.
User defined checks	Checks the credit limit based on user-defined criteria. Refer to SAP Includes `LVKMPFZ1`, `LVKMPFZ2`, and `LVKMPFZ3`.

Table 7.3 Credit Checks in Automatic Credit Control (Cont.)

If a sales document doesn't pass the credit check, you can choose whether the document is assigned a credit block. Additionally, by selecting the appropriate value in the Reaction field, you can choose whether a warning or an error is displayed to the user processing that transaction. You can also choose if the value by which the credit limit is exceeded is displayed along with the message. For example, if the user processing a transaction isn't authorized to know the credit limit of a customer, you can display an error or a warning message without the value by which the credit limit is exceeded.

Tip

For the credit check based on the highest dunning level, the SAP system first checks the dunning level from the customer account. If that dunning level is higher than the dunning level in the credit check based on the highest dunning level, the program then analyzes the open items to determine the latest dunning level after taking into account any recent payments that the customer may have made.

Now let's discuss other configuration parameters shown in Figure 7.12 that you can use for advanced credit management.

7.3.2 Document Control

If you want to avoid credit checks under certain circumstances, you can use parameters specified under the DOCUMENT CONTROLLING section. For example, if an external interface creates a large volume of sales documents in the SAP system, you can use this feature to ensure that credit checks are carried out only when necessary.

Field NO CREDIT CHECK specifies a technical routine that contains code to validate sales document and set values of the following two variables:

- BYPASS: Allows you to bypass individual credit checks.
- STATUS_RESET: Allows you to reset the status for individual credit checks.

These technical routines are defined using menu path SAP IMG • SALES AND DISTRIBUTION • SYSTEM MODIFICATIONS • ROUTINES • DEFINE REQUIREMENTS (Transaction VOFM) • REQUIREMENTS • CREDIT CHECKS.

In the next section, we'll discuss how to define credit tolerances.

7.3.3 Credit Tolerances

You have two parameters available to control system response when changes are made to a sales document that has already been checked for credit.

If any change to a sales document makes its value exceed the percentage specified in DEVIATION IN % from the original value, then another credit check is automatically carried out. If the change doesn't exceed the specified deviation percentage, but the document change is carried out after the days specified in the NUMBER OF DAYS field, then another credit check is also carried out automatically.

In the example shown in Figure 7.12, a new credit check will be carried out on an approved sales document if it is changed after 7 days from the original credit check or a change causes its value to deviate by more than 10%.

In the next section, we'll discuss the definition of seasonal factors.

7.3.4 Seasonal Factors

Using seasonal factor parameters, you can increase or decrease the credit limit of a customer for a specific time period. This can be useful, for example, if you want to increase the credit limits of retail outlets during the holiday season or reduce credit limits (and thus credit exposure) for a customer in a region during a period of political uncertainty.

As shown in Figure 7.12, you specify the seasonal factor as a PERCENTAGE by which the credit limit should be increased between FROM and TO dates. If the MINUS flag is selected, it indicates that the credit limit should be reduced by a specified percentage for the validity period.

At this point in this chapter, we have covered all of the important aspects for configuring the credit management functionality in the SAP system. Creating and modifying sales documents automatically triggers credit checks based on the credit management configuration. A sales document may receive one or more credit blocks depending on credit limits and the configuration of credit checks. You have to process and release all credit blocks of a sales document before you can carry out any subsequent activity such as deliveries or goods issues.

7.4 Processing Credit Blocks

The credit management menu of the SAP system contains different transactions such as all documents, sales documents, blocked documents, released documents, delivery documents, and so on. These separate transactions not only provide focused selection criteria to serve intended business requirements, but they also help in segregating transaction access based on appropriate authorizations. However, the underlying usage of these transactions is very similar, so it's easy to extrapolate your understanding of one transaction to other transactions.

For the purpose of this section, we'll discuss one of the most frequently used transactions that helps you process SD documents on credit blocks. This transaction is available under SAP Credit Management Menu • Exceptions • Blocked SD Documents (Transaction VKM1). First let's see the information available in display layout.

7.4.1 Types of Information Available

You have access to more than 100 information items that can be displayed for a blocked sales document. This includes information from customer accounts, sales documents, credit management, and other calculated values.

> **Tip**
>
> It's unlikely that you'll need access to all information items every time. A preferred approach is to create and save different layouts for different business purposes that only contain required, relevant information for that purpose.

The following list shows some of the information available in this transaction list:

- **From credit account**: Name, Address, Credit representative group, Credit control area, Risk category, Customer credit group, Customer group, Next review dates, Account blocked.
- **From sales document**: Sales document number, Sales document category, Sales organization, Distribution channel, Division, Purchase order number, Sold-to party, Sales office.
- **From credit management**: Credit value, Released value, Open orders, Open deliveries, Open billing documents, Total receivables.

Additionally, you get detailed information about all credit blocks on sales documents.

7.4.2 Credit Blocks Display

Figure 7.13 shows a blocked SD documents layout with different credit blocks.

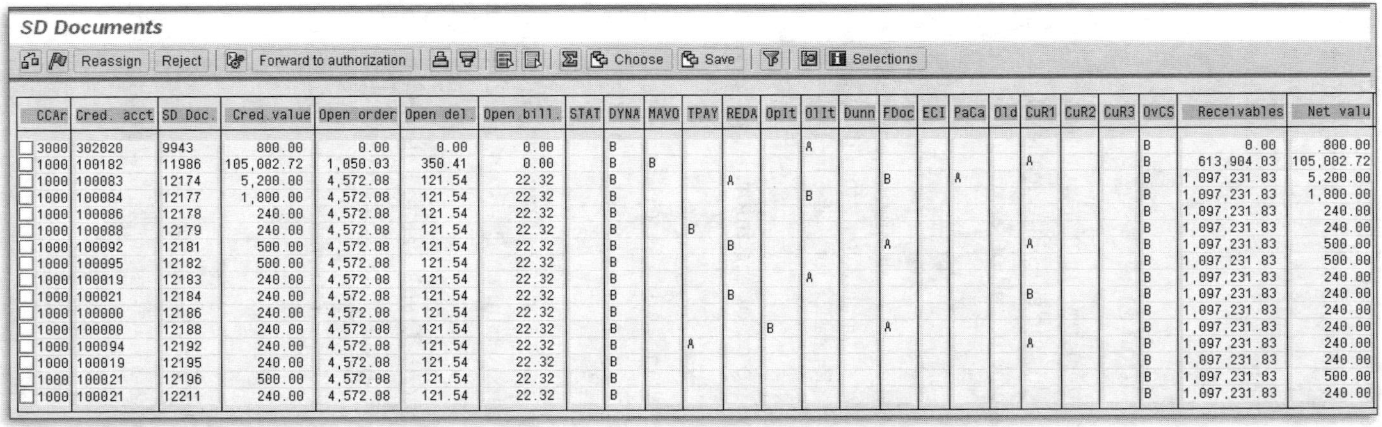

SD Documents

Reassign | Reject | Forward to authorization | Choose | Save | Selections

CCAr	Cred. acct	SD Doc.	Cred.value	Open order	Open del.	Open bill.	STAT	DYNA	MAVO	TPAY	REDA	OpIt	OlIt	Dunn	FDoc	ECI	PaCa	Old	CuR1	CuR2	CuR3	OvCS	Receivables	Net valu
3000	302020	9943	800.00	0.00	0.00	0.00		B					A									B	0.00	800.00
1000	100182	11986	105,002.72	1,050.03	350.41	0.00		B	B										A			B	613,904.03	105,002.72
1000	100083	12174	5,200.00	4,572.08	121.54	22.32		B			A				B		A					B	1,097,231.83	5,200.00
1000	100084	12177	1,800.00	4,572.08	121.54	22.32		B					B									B	1,097,231.83	1,800.00
1000	100086	12178	240.00	4,572.08	121.54	22.32		B														B	1,097,231.83	240.00
1000	100088	12179	240.00	4,572.08	121.54	22.32		B		B												B	1,097,231.83	240.00
1000	100092	12181	500.00	4,572.08	121.54	22.32		B			B				A				A			B	1,097,231.83	500.00
1000	100095	12182	500.00	4,572.08	121.54	22.32		B														B	1,097,231.83	500.00
1000	100019	12183	240.00	4,572.08	121.54	22.32		B					A									B	1,097,231.83	240.00
1000	100021	12184	240.00	4,572.08	121.54	22.32		B			B								B			B	1,097,231.83	240.00
1000	100000	12186	240.00	4,572.08	121.54	22.32		B														B	1,097,231.83	240.00
1000	100000	12188	240.00	4,572.08	121.54	22.32		B				B			A							B	1,097,231.83	240.00
1000	100094	12192	240.00	4,572.08	121.54	22.32		B		A									A			B	1,097,231.83	240.00
1000	100019	12195	240.00	4,572.08	121.54	22.32		B														B	1,097,231.83	240.00
1000	100021	12196	500.00	4,572.08	121.54	22.32		B														B	1,097,231.83	500.00
1000	100021	12211	240.00	4,572.08	121.54	22.32		B														B	1,097,231.83	240.00

Figure 7.13 Blocked SD documents

This transaction displays all of the credit checks that were triggered and the corresponding system response. The following list of columns shows the credit block status for credit checks defined in advanced credit management:

- **STAT**: Status of credit limit check.
- **DYNA**: Status of dynamic credit limit check.
- **MAVO**: Status of credit check against maximum document value.
- **TPAY**: Status of credit check against terms of payments.
- **REDA**: Status of credit check against customer review date.
- **OpIt**: Status of credit check against open items due.
- **OlIt**: Status of credit check against oldest open items.
- **Dunn**: Status of credit check against highest dunning level.
- **CuR1 to CuR3**: Status of credit check against user-defined checks.

If applicable, you can also refer to the following credit blocks in this transaction:

- **FDoc**: Status of credit check against financial document. Refer to SAP note 0000303409 for more details
- **ECI**: Status of credit check against export credit insurance. Refer to SAP note 0000141013 for more details
- **PaCa**: Status of credit check against payment card authorization. Refer to SAP note 0000792944 for more details
- **Old**: Credit check data is obsolete. This credit block is set if A/R summary is older than timeframe specified in automatic credit control (Section 7.1.2)

Finally, the following column displays overall credit check status for a sales document. This status is a combination of all other credit check statuses.

- **OvCS:** Overall credit status

Tip

Refer to SAP Note 110311 for information on how to enhance these transactions to display additional fields that aren't provided in the standard system.

After you've adjusted the layout to display the required information, you can carry out any of the following actions on sales documents.

7.4.3 Subsequent Actions

The following options are available for a document displayed in a sales documents list:

1. RELEASE: To release a sales document for subsequent activities. You may choose this option after validating necessary information.
2. REJECT: To reject a sales document. Subsequent activities on that sales document aren't possible until it's modified to pass the credit check. This may mean reducing the total order value or delaying order processing until the customer payment is received and their credit exposure is reduced.
3. REASSIGN: To specify a new sequence for sales documents. Using this option, you can sequence the documents for a credit account so that instead of one document with a high credit value, you can release several documents with low credit values.
4. RECHECK: To recheck and revalidate a sales document. This option helps in refreshing the list display after processing a batch of documents.
5. FORWARD: To forward a sales document to a different credit representative group. This may be necessary to handle any staffing situations or if a credit representative doesn't have enough authorization.
6. FORWARD TO AUTHORIZATION: To forward a sales document for payment card authorization. This option is used for sales documents that are blocked due to payment card authorization issues.
7. SEND: To send the list of blocked sales documents as an email attachment to other employee for reference, review, comments, or follow-up.
8. EXPORT: To export the list of blocked sales documents to a spreadsheet or word processing document.
9. ABC ANALYSIS: To display blocked sales documents in an ABC list (as described in the next section).

7.4.4 ABC Analysis

Figure 7.14 shows an example of ABC analysis based on credit value.

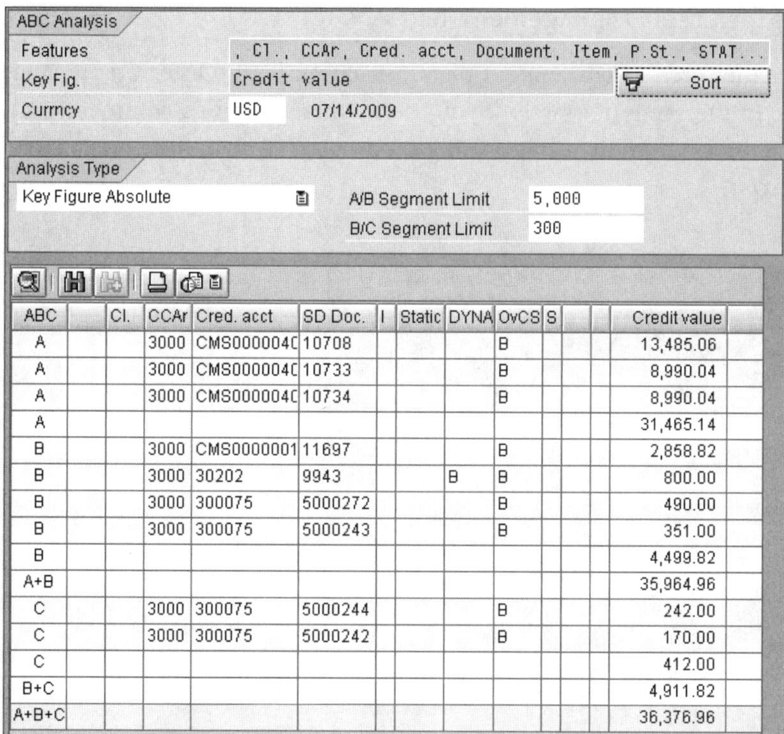

ABC Analysis

Features: , Cl., CCAr, Cred. acct, Document, Item, P.St., STAT...

Key Fig.: Credit value

Sort

Currncy: USD 07/14/2009

Analysis Type

Key Figure Absolute

A/B Segment Limit: 5,000

B/C Segment Limit: 300

ABC		Cl.	CCAr	Cred. acct	SD Doc.	I	Static	DYNA	OvCS	S			Credit value
A			3000	CMS0000040	10708				B				13,485.06
A			3000	CMS0000040	10733				B				8,990.04
A			3000	CMS0000040	10734				B				8,990.04
A													31,465.14
B			3000	CMS0000001	11697				B				2,858.82
B			3000	30202	9943			B	B				800.00
B			3000	300075	5000272				B				490.00
B			3000	300075	5000243				B				351.00
B													4,499.82
A+B													35,964.96
C			3000	300075	5000244				B				242.00
C			3000	300075	5000242				B				170.00
C													412.00
B+C													4,911.82
A+B+C													36,376.96

Figure 7.14 ABC Analysis of Blocked Sales Documents

Using this option, you can display blocked sales documents in the form of an ABC list based on absolute values or percentage values. The analysis can be carried out on any value such as total credit value, total receivables, or sales document value. This can be an extremely powerful tool in analyzing and determining sales documents that can be released for subsequent functions.

So far, we've discussed the standard flow of the credit management processes. In the next section, we'll discuss other transactions and functionalities of credit management.

7.5 Transactions

In this section, we'll look at other credit management transactions and functionalities. Let's first consider text maintenance for credit accounts.

7.5.1 Texts for Credit Management Texts (V.32)

We looked at other credit management data in Section 7.1.4, Other Credit Management Data. In the same transaction, you can maintain detailed comments and texts (Figure 7.15) for a credit account using menu paths EXTRAS • CENTRAL TEXTS or EXTRAS • TEXTS.

Maintain Text Determination Configuration: List

Text Object KNKK Credit management

Text IDs

ID	Meaning	Relevant text
0001	Internal information	☑
0002	External information	☑
0003	Actions	☑
0004	Collection Management	☐
0005	Trade References	☐
0006	Action Date	☐
0007	Customer Financial Statements	☐

Figure 7.15 Credit Management Texts

Comments maintained under TEXTS are specific to a credit control area, whereas comments maintained under CENTRAL TEXTS are visible across all credit control areas. These texts are freely definable using IMG • CREDIT CONTROL ACCOUNT • DEFINE TEXT IDS FOR CREDIT MANAGEMENT or Transaction OBT3. Another useful functionality is the ability to rebuild credit management data.

7.5.2 Rebuild Credit Management Data (F.28)

After you've carried out organizational changes in the SAP system, you have to rebuild the credit management data. Such organizational changes may include reassignment of credit control areas, customer groups, and risk categories, or any changes in the credit check parameters configuration. It's absolutely necessary after any such change that you carry out this process so that values and credit flags for active accounts and active documents are updated accurately.

As Figure 7.16 shows, you may run this process only for FI data, only for SD data, or for both types of data.

SD, FI: Recreation of Credit Data after Organizational Changes

Customer		to	
Credit control area		to	

Further sel. options
- ○ Only Recreate FI Data
- ○ Only Recreate SD Data
- ◉ Recreate FI and SD Data
- ☐ Create SD Change Documents
- ☑ Test run

Layout

Figure 7.16 Rebuild Credit Management Data

Which option you choose depends on the type of changes you've made. Also, if performance or volume isn't an issue, you may want to select the CREATE SD CHANGE DOCUMENTS flag so that there is a detailed audit trail in all active sales documents.

Tip

Some changes in credit management master data, such as changing the assignment of customer account to credit account, automatically trigger reorganization of credit data. SAP Note 0000030737 details the performance issues of the credit reorganization process.

To run this process, you use SAP MENU • ACCOUNTING • FINANCIAL ACCOUNTING • ACCOUNTS RECEIVABLE • CREDIT MANAGEMENT • TOOLS • RESET CREDIT LIMIT or Transaction F.28. The next section discusses the program used for updating credit information structures.

7.5.3 Reorganization of Credit Management Data

For the purpose of credit management, values of open orders, open deliveries, and open billing documents are maintained in information structures S066 and S067. Different transactions in the order to cash process update these information structures, so that they always contain the most up-to-date credit management details.

If values in these information structures are incorrectly updated, then you have to carry out reorganization of the credit management data. Program RVKRED77 is the correction report that is used to correct and update credit management entries to information structures S066 and S067. It's important to note that this transaction locks updates to other tables used in sales document processing. So it's advisable to run this transaction only when regular business operations in the SD and FI area aren't occurring. SAP Note 0000400311 provides more details on this transaction.

The next section discusses the creation and maintenance of A/R summary.

7.5.4 A/R Summary

We discussed previously that A/R summary is used if the SAP components of FI and SD are on different, distributed systems. Even if both SAP components are on same system, A/R summary can be used to improve the performance of credit management transactions. If creation of the A/R summary is enabled for the SAP system (refer to Figure 7.3); you can create it using SAP MENU • ACCOUNTING • FINANCIAL ACCOUNTING • ACCOUNTS RECEIVABLE • CREDIT MANAGEMENT • TOOLS • CREATE A/R SUMMARY or Transaction FCV1.

By choosing the appropriate creation parameter for payers, you can choose to create the A/R summary only for selected payers, for all payers, or for all payers excluding selected payers. The Permitted Age field simply indicates that the A/R summary should be created only if it's older than the timeframe specified in these fields. You'll find that if necessary, a transaction to delete the A/R summary also exists under the same menu path.

In the next section, we'll look at a functionality that allows postings to customer accounts without credit checks.

7.5.5 Posting Without Credit Check (AKOF)

In Section 7.1.4, Other Credit Management Data, we looked at a flag that blocks a credit account for all credit management transactions. However, at the other extreme, you may want to process sales transactions without any credit checks. You can set a flag for GL reconciliation accounts so that customers associated with that account aren't subject to credit checks. This functionality may be useful if your customers include federal or local governments.

You carry out this setting for reconciliation accounts using IMG • BUSINESS TRANSACTION: CREDIT MONITORING • DEFINE RECONCILIATION ACCOUNTS WITHOUT CREDIT MANAGEMENT UPDATE or Transaction AKOF.

Now let's look at reporting transactions.

7.5.6 Reporting

You can certainly use standard AR transactions to display customer account line items (FBL5N) and to display customer balances (FD10N). In previous sections, we also discussed other transactions that display lists of different sales documents that have different credit management blocks or status. Those transactions also serve as a good reporting and analysis tools. In addition, the SAP system provides several credit management reports such as the credit review list.

Credit Review (F.31)

Credit review provides a list of credit accounts across credit control areas with important credit management information (Figure 7.17).

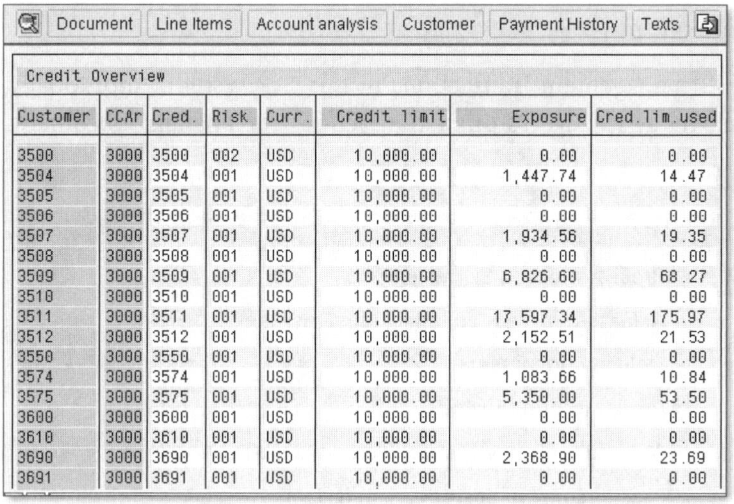

Document | Line Items | Account analysis | Customer | Payment History | Texts

Credit Overview

Customer	CCAr	Cred.	Risk	Curr.	Credit limit	Exposure	Cred.lim.used
3500	3000	3500	002	USD	10,000.00	0.00	0.00
3504	3000	3504	001	USD	10,000.00	1,447.74	14.47
3505	3000	3505	001	USD	10,000.00	0.00	0.00
3506	3000	3506	001	USD	10,000.00	0.00	0.00
3507	3000	3507	001	USD	10,000.00	1,934.56	19.35
3508	3000	3508	001	USD	10,000.00	0.00	0.00
3509	3000	3509	001	USD	10,000.00	6,826.60	68.27
3510	3000	3510	001	USD	10,000.00	0.00	0.00
3511	3000	3511	001	USD	10,000.00	17,597.34	175.97
3512	3000	3512	001	USD	10,000.00	2,152.51	21.53
3550	3000	3550	001	USD	10,000.00	0.00	0.00
3574	3000	3574	001	USD	10,000.00	1,083.66	10.84
3575	3000	3575	001	USD	10,000.00	5,350.00	53.50
3600	3000	3600	001	USD	10,000.00	0.00	0.00
3610	3000	3610	001	USD	10,000.00	0.00	0.00
3690	3000	3690	001	USD	10,000.00	2,368.90	23.69
3691	3000	3691	001	USD	10,000.00	0.00	0.00

Figure 7.17 Credit Overview List

The overview list shows risk category, credit limit, credit exposure, and percentage of credit limit used. From the overview screen, you can select any account and drill down to a document list, a line item list, the payment history, or the customer master data review. Another important report is the early warning list.

Early Warning List (FCV3)

Using the early warning list, you can proactively identify credit accounts that will have their sales documents go on credit blocks in the near future. You can carry out credit checks against oldest open items, overdue open items, maximum dunning level, next review date, age of A/R summary, and used credit limit.

There are two ways to run this program. You can either run the program without specifying any optional parameters, such as Maximum Number of Days for Oldest Open Item, in which case, the program generates the early warning list based on parameters specified in the configuration. Or, you can specify optional parameters while running this program, in which case, the program acts as a "what-if" simulation that shows what would happen if credit checks configuration was changed for that parameter.

The next section provides a consolidated list of important credit management transactions.

7.5.7 List of Transactions

Table 7.4 lists credit management transactions in the SAP system. Additionally, business users will frequently access other transactions for financial documents and sales documents.

Transaction	Usage
VKM1	Process blocked SD documents
VKM2 to VKM4	Released, forwarded, all SD documents
VKM5	Delivery documents
FD11	Credit account analysis
FD32, FD33	Maintain, display customer credit master data
F.34	Mass change of customer credit data
F.31	Customer credit account overview
F.32	Missing master data for credit accounts
FCV3	Early warning list
FDK43	Credit Mgmt: Master data list
S_ALR_87012215	Display changes to credit management
S_ALR_87012218	Credit master sheet
FCV1	Create accounts receivable summary

Table 7.4 Credit Management Transactions

Transaction	Usage
FCV2	Delete accounts receivable summary
F.28	Reset credit limit

Table 7.4 Credit Management Transactions (Cont.)

In the next section, we'll look at technical objects available for credit management functionality.

7.6 Technical Reference

This section lists technical objects such as SAP Notes, authorization objects, and tables and structures relevant for implementing credit management functionality. Considering the large number of technical objects available in the SAP system, this information should only be considered as a starting point.

7.6.1 SAP Notes

Table 7.5 is a list of SAP Notes for the credit management functionality.

SAP Note	Relevance
0000355242	Determination of credit control area
0000895630	Use of requirement for no credit check
0000374213	Credit check for highest dunning level
0000379007	Dynamic credit check of sales documents
0000018613	Credit management error analysis checklist
0000095627	Special GL transactions in DSO calculation
0001259643	Authorization checks in credit management
0000303409	Credit management and documentary payments
0000729370	Additional data for export credit insurance processing
0000110311	Enhance list display in credit management
0000052437	Credit check during make-to-order production

Table 7.5 Credit Management – SAP Notes

SAP Note	Relevance
0000396791	Credit release of orders with third-party items
0000366151	Translation of displayed fields into credit currency
0000377165	Update of credit values into SIS
0000860191	Performance of transactions VKM1, VKM2, and VKM4
0000555925	FAQ: Credit limit check in service order
0000400311	RVKRED77: Reorganization of credit data

Table 7.5 Credit Management – SAP Notes (Cont.)

In the next section, we'll look at authorization objects relevant for credit management processes and transactions.

7.6.2 Authorization Objects

Table 7.6 provides a list of authorization objects that should be considered for the purpose of credit management. These objects are in addition to the authorization objects required for carrying out finance transactions, sales transactions, and customer account maintenance.

Object	Description
F_KNKA_KKB	Credit Mgmt: Authorization for Credit Control Area
F_KNKA_MAN	Credit Mgmt: General Maintenance Authorization
F_KNKK_BED	Credit Mgmt: Account Authorization
F_KNKA_AEN	Credit Mgmt: Change Authorization for Certain Fields
V_KNKK_FRE	Customer Credit Limit: Edit SD Documents
V_VBUK_FRE	Credit Doc. Value Class: Processing of SD Documents
V_VBUK_FRE	Authorization According to Document Value Class
V_VNKK_FRE	Authorization According to Credit Limit

Table 7.6 Authorization Objects – Credit Management

The next section provides a list of tables and structures.

7.6.3 Tables and Structures

Table 7.7 lists tables and structures relevant for credit management processes. Additionally, you should also be familiar with tables and structures used for the customer master, financial documents, and sales documents.

Table	Relevance
KNKA	Customer master credit mgmt: Central data
KNKK	Customer master credit mgmt: Credit control area data
KNB4	Customer master payment history
KNC1	Customer master: Transaction figures
KNC3	Customer master: Special GL transaction figures
VBKRED	Work structure for release of credit limit
VBKREDET	Work structure for release of credit limit: details
KNKKF1	Credit Mgmt: FI Status data
KNKKF2	Credit Mgmt: Open items by days in arrears
S066	Credit Mgmt: Open orders
S067	Credit Mgmt: Open deliveries and billing documents

Table 7.7 Credit Management Tables and Structures

Now we'll look at objects and functionality available for enhancing and modifying the credit management functionality.

7.7 Enhancements and Modifications

This section provides a list of available BTEs, enhancements, BAdIs, and BAPIs relevant for credit management processes. These are used to enhance and modify the standard functionality available in the SAP system.

7.7.1 Business Transaction Events (BTE)

Using BTEs, you can attach additional function modules and custom logic to the standard SAP system. Table 7.8 lists publish and subscribe (P/S) and process BTEs available for the dunning functionality.

Type	BTE	Event/Process
P/S	00001510	Call up GUI for maintenance of user-defined fields
P/S	00001520	Save user-defined fields in credit management
P/S	00001530	Publish credit overview and master data sheet
P/S	00001540	Publish credit overview and master data sheet texts
P/S	00001550	Call up GUI for maintenance of key texts
P/S	00001560	Display user-defined fields in credit master sheet
P/S	00501005	Read credit-relevant data for a sales document
P/S	00501013	Display credit-relevant data for a sales document
Process	00001210	DSO Calculation 1 for report RFDKLI43
Process	00001213	DSO Calculation 2 for report RFDKLI43
Process	00001214	DSO Calculation 3 for report RFDKLI43
Process	00001220	Display DSO calculation details (Transaction FD32 → Overview → Extras → DSO calculation)
Process	00001230	Calculation of highest balance in the credit overview or credit master sheet reports
Process	00001240	Check credit information number

Table 7.8 Credit Management – Business Transaction Events

The following examples show how BTEs can be used to influence the credit management processes.

- **Events 00001510:** Call GUI for user-defined fields
  - Using this BTE, you can transfer key fields of the customer credit master data to an external component to update user-defined fields.
  - Subsequently, you can use BTE 00001520 to save these fields in the SAP system, and use BTE 00001560 to display these fields in the credit master sheet.
- **Event 00001240:** Check credit information number
  - This process is reached when credit information number is entered in the credit management master data.
  - You can use the `DUNS_NUMBER_CHECK` function module for this BTE and validate whether this number confirms to the D&B number rules.

The configuration menu path to implement these BTEs is IMG • Financial Accounting • Financial Accounting Global Settings • Tools • Customer Enhancements • Business Transaction Events.

The next section discusses available enhancement spots.

7.7.2 Enhancements

Using enhancements, you can add custom logic to carry out additional validations and custom business processing.

- FV45K001: User exit for credit control area determination
  - This enhancement contains function module EXIT_SAPFV45K_001 for implementing the custom logic for the credit control area determination.

7.8 Summary

We started this chapter with a discussion of parameters and concepts associated with credit management in the SAP system. You learned configuration of different parameters and processes to implement SAP Credit Management for different types of organizational structures, business partners, and prevalent business practices in industries. As we discussed, simple credit checks provide sufficient functionality for simple business scenarios. However, automatic credit control provides you with much more flexibility, albeit with added complexity, to monitor credit exposure to your business partners. At the end, we reviewed transactions available for processing sales documents on credit blocks and also discussed reports such as the credit overview and early warning reports that can help you proactively monitor credit exposure.

This chapter focuses on maintaining, processing, and reporting sales taxes in the SAP system. Tax regulations and calculations are considerably dependent on country-specific and industry-specific requirements. These functionalities are especially important for multinational companies to effectively and efficiently cater to varied requirements. The SAP system supports the unique tax requirements of different countries and different industries. However, these unique requirements are built upon a standard, consistent framework of configuration, calculation, and processing of sales taxes in business transactions. In this chapter, we'll look at the common tax framework used to provide common tax functionalities.

8 Tax Processing

Taxes are part of every business regardless of the industry and the country in which they operate. In smaller, nonmanufacturing, professional services companies, calculating taxes may be as simple as applying a flat rate to all customer invoices. Large manufacturing companies with multiple product lines, however, may even have a separate corporate sales tax planning department systematically analyzing sales and procurement business activities to find ways to legally reduce tax liability. Even if a company doesn't have to actually pay sales tax due to special circumstances related to its industry, location, or legal structure, it still has to maintain detailed records to meet reporting and compliance requirements.

Note

In SAP terminology, all taxes charged by the vendor are called input taxes, and all taxes levied on customers are called output taxes. This chapter refers to sales (output) taxes and purchase (input) taxes unless noted otherwise.

In this chapter, we'll first discuss concepts and configurations for tax calculation, followed by how to use tax calculation functionality in accounting documents and sales documents. Finally, we'll discuss tax exemption, tax reports, and other relevant functionality. For the most part, participation of business users involves using tax codes that are appropriate for business transactions, and generating and analyzing tax reports. However, to successfully complete these activities, you have to carry out elaborate configuration and master data maintenance. In this chapter we'll look at these activities in detail, starting with concepts and configuration.

8.1 Concepts and Configuration

The following is a high-level description of tax calculation in the SAP system.

1. A tax calculation procedure is associated with one or more countries in a system configuration. The tax calculation procedure consists of several line items. Each line item in a tax procedure corresponds to different types of taxes.
2. The account key assigned to each line item determines the GL accounts to which tax postings are made.
3. You configure multiple tax codes for a tax procedure. A tax code carries the definition of tax percentages for one or more tax line items.
4. All customers and products are assigned a taxability indicator classifying them into fully taxable, partially taxable, or tax-exempt.
5. When you process a customer invoice or similar transaction, applicable taxes are determined based on a combination of all of the preceding factors.

Let's look at each of these factors in detail, starting with the tax procedure.

8.1.1 Tax Procedure

In SAP, tax calculation procedures provide the framework to calculate sales and purchase taxes. You can assign only one tax calculation procedure to a country in SAP, which means that the procedure needs to provide a calculation framework for all types of taxes that are relevant for sales and purchase transactions in that country. The SAP system provides tax procedure templates for almost 50 countries that you can use as-is or modify as necessary. You carry out this configuration using SAP IMG • Financial Accounting • Financial Accounting Global Settings • Tax on Sales/Purchases • Basic Settings • Check Calculation Procedure • Define Procedures and Assign Country to a Calculation Procedure.

Figure 8.1 shows the configuration of a tax procedure called TAXUSJ. You may notice that this configuration is similar to the pricing procedure configuration discussed in Chapter 3.

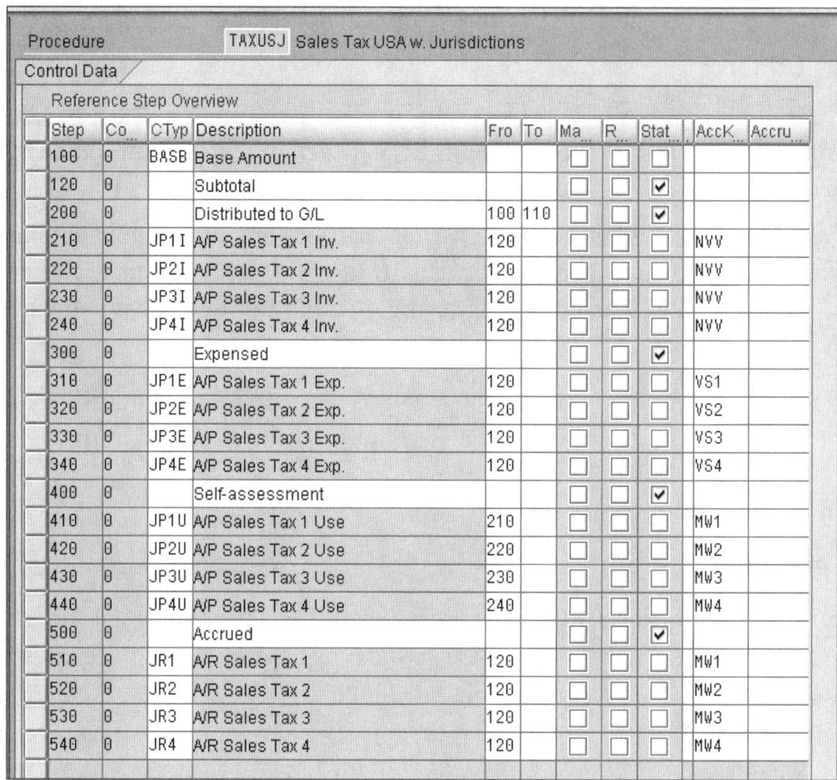

Procedure TAXUSJ Sales Tax USA w. Jurisdictions

Control Data

Reference Step Overview

Step	Co...	CTyp	Description	Fro	To	Ma...	R...	Stat...	AccK...	Accru...
100	0	BASB	Base Amount			☐	☐	☐		
120	0		Subtotal			☐	☐	☑		
200	0		Distributed to G/L	100	110	☐	☐	☑		
210	0	JP1I	A/P Sales Tax 1 Inv.	120		☐	☐	☐	NVV	
220	0	JP2I	A/P Sales Tax 2 Inv.	120		☐	☐	☐	NVV	
230	0	JP3I	A/P Sales Tax 3 Inv.	120		☐	☐	☐	NVV	
240	0	JP4I	A/P Sales Tax 4 Inv.	120		☐	☐	☐	NVV	
300	0		Expensed			☐	☐	☑		
310	0	JP1E	A/P Sales Tax 1 Exp.	120		☐	☐	☐	VS1	
320	0	JP2E	A/P Sales Tax 2 Exp.	120		☐	☐	☐	VS2	
330	0	JP3E	A/P Sales Tax 3 Exp.	120		☐	☐	☐	VS3	
340	0	JP4E	A/P Sales Tax 4 Exp.	120		☐	☐	☐	VS4	
400	0		Self-assessment			☐	☐	☑		
410	0	JP1U	A/P Sales Tax 1 Use	210		☐	☐	☐	MW1	
420	0	JP2U	A/P Sales Tax 2 Use	220		☐	☐	☐	MW2	
430	0	JP3U	A/P Sales Tax 3 Use	230		☐	☐	☐	MW3	
440	0	JP4U	A/P Sales Tax 4 Use	240		☐	☐	☐	MW4	
500	0		Accrued			☐	☐	☑		
510	0	JR1	A/R Sales Tax 1	120		☐	☐	☐	MW1	
520	0	JR2	A/R Sales Tax 2	120		☐	☐	☐	MW2	
530	0	JR3	A/R Sales Tax 3	120		☐	☐	☐	MW3	
540	0	JR4	A/R Sales Tax 4	120		☐	☐	☐	MW4	

Figure 8.1 Tax Procedure Configuration

Note

A tax jurisdiction code uniquely identifies a taxation authority that imposes the tax. It's especially relevant in countries that have a large number of taxation authorities such as the United States, with more than 67,000 tax jurisdictions. If tax jurisdiction codes are active in the SAP system, then all tax rates are maintained at the tax jurisdiction code level.

Note the following points from the preceding figure:

- The procedure definition consists of line items for the following types of taxes:
  - Purchase (A/P) tax posted to GL accounts
  - Purchase (A/P) tax expensed to line items

- Purchase (A/P) tax calculated as use tax or self-accrual tax
- Sales (A/R) tax

- Each type of tax consists of four line items, or four levels of tax calculations. In the United States, each level corresponds to tax levied by state, county, and city in a tax jurisdiction.
- The FROM and TO columns for each line item carry reference to the line items that provide a base value for the calculation. In the preceding figure, all line items except for those corresponding to the use tax refer to the base amount subtotal in line 120.

The three-character ACCOUNT KEY assigned to each line item determines the GL account to which tax postings will occur. Account keys are discussed in the next section.

8.1.2 Account Keys

You configure account keys for a tax procedure using SAP IMG • FINANCIAL ACCOUNTING • FINANCIAL ACCOUNTING GLOBAL SETTINGS • TAX ON SALES/PURCHASES • POSTING • DEFINE TAX ACCOUNTS (Transaction OB40).

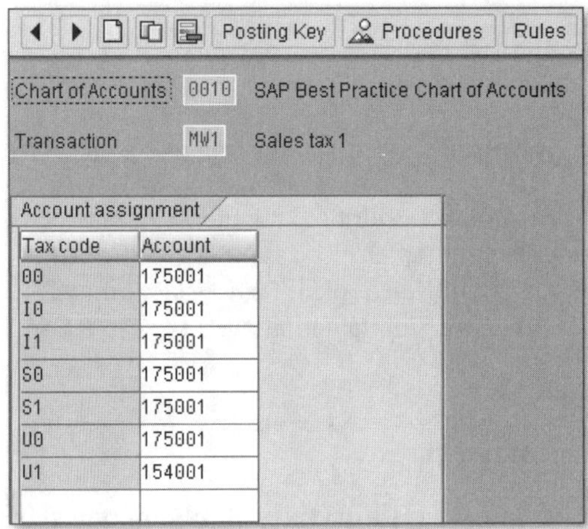

Figure 8.2 Tax Accounts

Figure 8.2 shows the configuration of a GL account assignment to a combination of account key MW1 and chart of accounts 0010. This type of assignment allows you to use the same tax calculation procedure for other company codes, even if they use different charts of accounts.

> **Tip**
>
> The Rules option helps you configure whether the GL account assignment for an account key is independent of tax codes. If the account assignment is independent of tax codes, all tax entries for an account key are posted to the same GL account regardless of the tax code in the business transaction.

Now let's see how to configure tax codes for tax procedures.

8.1.3 Tax Codes

Tax codes in the SAP system are used to specify tax percentage rates, tax calculations, and tax relevance of business transactions. While processing business transactions, the tax calculation procedure calculates the actual tax based on tax rates associated with tax codes and other control parameters. You configure account keys for tax procedures using SAP IMG • Financial Accounting • Financial Accounting Global Settings • Tax on Sales/Purchases • Calculation • Define Tax Codes for Sales and Purchases (Transaction FTXP).

Figure 8.3 shows an example configuration of tax code S1, with a pop-up showing GL accounts for active line items. Following are some of the points to consider while configuring tax codes:

- If you've enabled the tax jurisdiction code functionality, then you have to specify tax rates for each jurisdiction code separately. However, tax rates entered for a higher level jurisdiction code such as a state are automatically applied to lower level jurisdiction codes such as those for a county or a city.
- You have to define different tax codes for different tax rates. For example, you'll require separate tax codes for 7.5% sales tax and 5.5% sales tax.
- Tax rates are applicable from the Valid From date until different rates are entered with subsequent Valid From dates.

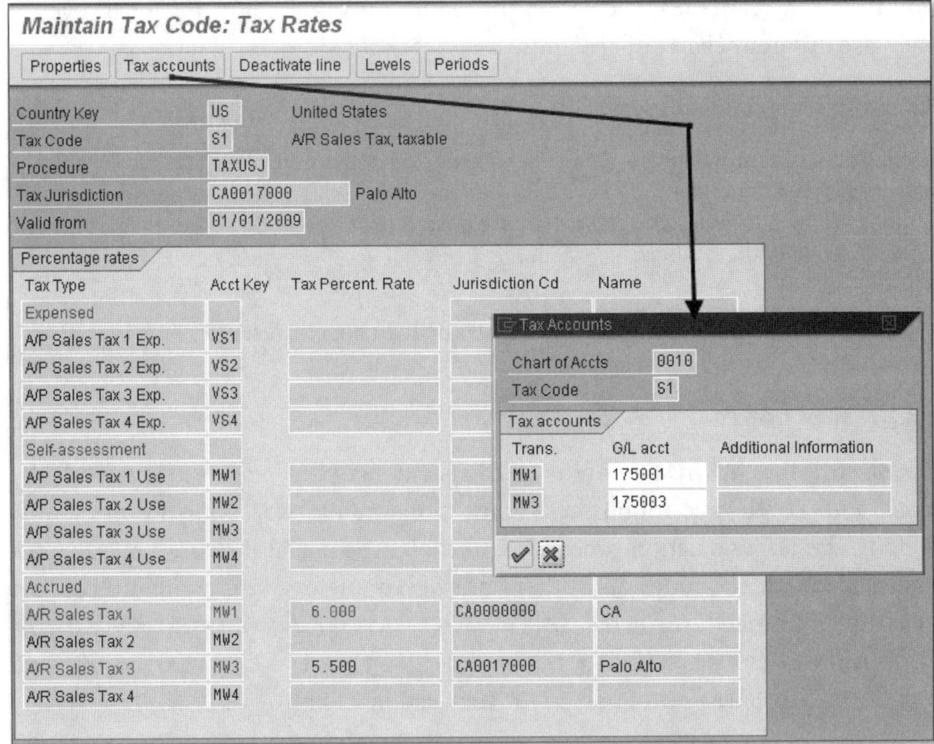

Figure 8.3 Tax Code Configuration

- It's advisable to use a consistent naming convention for tax codes to easily distinguish among tax codes for sales tax, purchase tax, use tax, and any other types of tax.
- By selecting the TAX ACCOUNTS option, you can view GL accounts for active items. In the preceding example, MW1 and MW3 are active items.

> **Note**
>
> If you change the GL account associated with a tax code from the tax code configuration menu shown in Figure 8.3, it will also change that in the main configuration shown in Figure 8.2.

Apart from these main options, the configuration screen provides you with the following additional options. The PERIODS option lets you view historical rates for a tax line item in the tax calculation procedure, whereas the LEVELS option toggles the display between tax jurisdiction information and levels information for each line item. The PROPERTIES option provides you with settings that are mostly relevant if you're configuring tax codes for European countries or for plants abroad; this functionality is discussed later in this chapter.

Another aspect that comes into play in tax determination is tax relevancy of customers and materials.

8.1.4 Tax Relevancy of Master Data

Tax relevancy of a sales transaction depends on tax relevancy of a customer as well as tax relevancy of a material. These tax relevancies, in turn, are dependent upon country-specific regulations.

Tip

These tax relevancy settings are relevant only for tax calculations for SD documents. As you'll see later in this chapter, tax calculations for documents that are directly posted in FI aren't impacted by these settings.

To define the tax relevancy of customers and materials, you use SAP IMG • SALES AND DISTRIBUTION • BASIC FUNCTIONS • TAXES • DEFINE TAX RELEVANCY OF MASTER RECORDS • CUSTOMER TAXES (Transaction OVK3) or MATERIAL TAXES (Transaction OVK4).

Change View "Material Taxes": Overview

Tax categ.	Name	Tax class.	Description
UTX1	State Sales Tax	0	Tax exempt
UTX1	State Sales Tax	1	Tax bracket 1
UTX1	State Sales Tax	2	Tax bracket 2
UTX1	State Sales Tax	3	Tax bracket 3
UTXJ	Tax Jurisdict.Code	0	Tax exempt
UTXJ	Tax Jurisdict.Code	1	Taxable
UTXJ	Tax Jurisdict.Code	9	Tax exempt

Figure 8.4 Material Tax Relevancy Indicators

Figure 8.4 shows the configuration of tax relevancy indicators for materials. The TAX CLASSIFICATION column is a freely definable code that you can use to classify materials based on their tax relevancy. The TAX CATEGORY column refers to the condition type used by sales pricing for tax calculation. You can refer to Chapter 3 for more details on sales pricing and condition types. These tax relevancy indicators have to be assigned to every customer and material.

Material Master – Tax Relevancy

Tax relevancy of a material is dependent on the country from which the delivery originates. For a company with plants in different countries, the same material may have different taxability depending on the plant from which it's delivered.

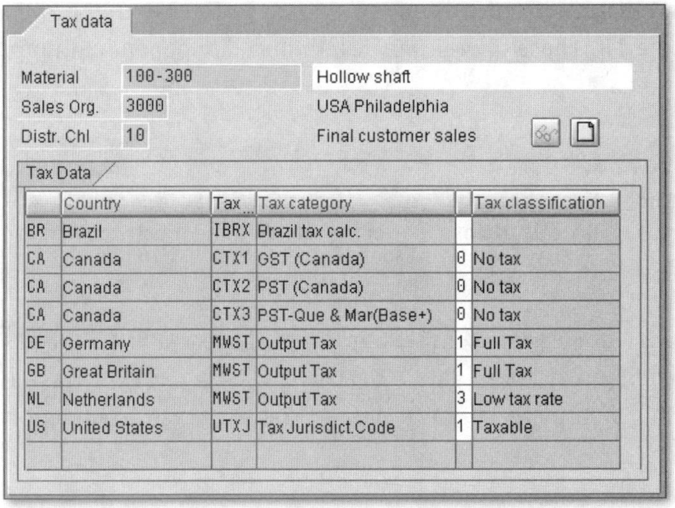

Tax data

Material 100-300 Hollow shaft
Sales Org. 3000 USA Philadelphia
Distr. Chl 10 Final customer sales

Tax Data

	Country	Tax...	Tax category		Tax classification
BR	Brazil	IBRX	Brazil tax calc.		
CA	Canada	CTX1	GST (Canada)	0	No tax
CA	Canada	CTX2	PST (Canada)	0	No tax
CA	Canada	CTX3	PST-Que & Mar(Base+)	0	No tax
DE	Germany	MWST	Output Tax	1	Full Tax
GB	Great Britain	MWST	Output Tax	1	Full Tax
NL	Netherlands	MWST	Output Tax	3	Low tax rate
US	United States	UTXJ	Tax Jurisdict.Code	1	Taxable

Figure 8.5 Material Master – Tax Data

Figure 8.5 shows the maintenance of material tax relevancy indicators for a sales organization and for all countries from which the material can be shipped. You maintain this data in Material Master (Transaction MM02) • Sales: sales org 1 tab • Tax data section. You maintain similar tax relevancy indicators in the customer master.

Customer Master – Tax Relevancy

Similar to a material, the tax relevancy of a customer also depends on the destination country for the delivery, so tax relevancy indicators for a customer are also maintained individually for each relevant country.

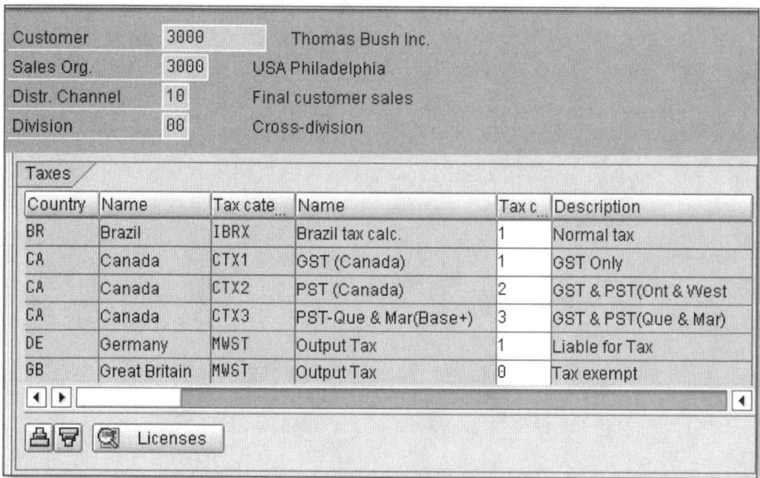

Figure 8.6 Customer Master – Tax Data

Figure 8.6 shows an example of maintaining tax relevancy indicators for a customer. You maintain these indicators in CUSTOMER MASTER (Transaction XD02) • SALES AREA DATA • BILLING DOCUMENTS TAB • TAXES section.

So far, we've discussed different attributes and configuration items relevant for tax calculations. In the next section, we'll discuss sales tax calculations in FI and SD documents.

8.2 Tax Calculations

The process of tax calculations is different for FI documents entered directly in AR component than it's for SD documents such as billing documents. Tax calculations in FI documents are relatively simple, whereas tax calculations in SD documents go through several extra steps.

8.2.1 Tax Calculations in FI Documents

FI documents refer to customer invoices, credit memos, and other documents entered directly in the AR component. We discussed these transactions in Chapter 2, Accounts Receivable Transactions. For the purpose of illustration, we'll discuss tax calculations in AR transactions using the Enjoy interface. Figure 8.7 shows the TAX tab of an Enjoy interface transaction.

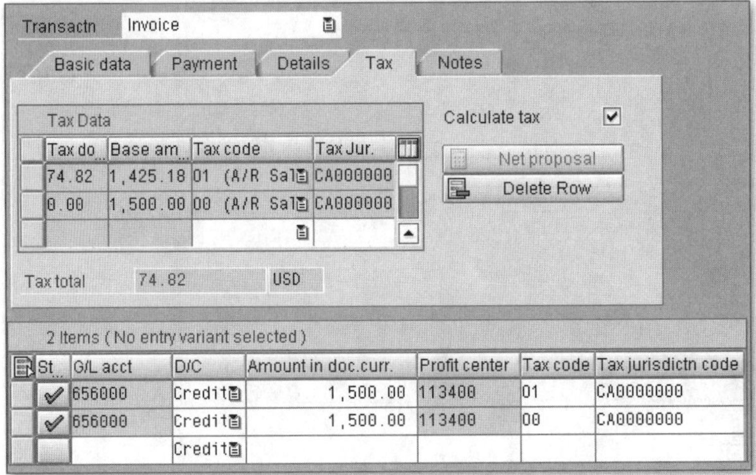

Figure 8.7 Tax Tab in the Enjoy Transaction

The following points are relevant for tax calculations in Enjoy transactions:

- You can either enter tax amount manually in the TAX AMOUNT field or let the system calculate it automatically by selecting the CALCULATE TAX indicator. You'll find both these fields on the BASIC DATA tab of the document header.
- The TAX CODE entered in the document header is automatically copied and applied to all document line item entries. Alternately, as shown in Figure 8.7, you can enter a different tax code for each document line item.
- By default, tax is calculated based on the full document amount. To enter a different amount as a base for tax calculation, change the values in the BASE AMOUNT field on the TAX tab
- By selecting the NET PROPOSAL button on the Tax tab, you can display the proposed tax amount.

Tip

This example illustrates tax information entry using the Enjoy interface. The process is similar if you choose to use the general interface for entering customer documents. In the general interface also, you can enter the tax code on each line item.

Based on tax codes entered in a document and corresponding percentages entered in the configuration, the transaction carries out the tax calculation for FI documents. If you choose to enter tax amount manually and if it's different from the amount calculated based on the system configuration, the system will issue a warning message. This is a fairly simple calculation process. However, tax calculations in SD transactions are more complex.

8.2.2 Tax Calculation in Sales Documents

Tax calculations in SD documents such as sales orders and billing documents are carried out by first taking into account the following factors:

- **Country of departure:** Country of the plant supplying the ordered products.
- **Destination country:** Country of the ship-to party specified on a sales order.
- **Tax relevance of a customer in the country of departure:** Typically, this is the tax relevance of the ship-to party in the country of departure.
- **Tax relevance of a product in the country of departure:** This refers to the tax relevance of the ordered products in the country of departure.

Tip

Section 8.6.1, SAP Notes, provides some references on special business scenarios. For example, if an order is processed in the sales organization of one country, and it's fulfilled from a plant based in a different country, you may want to use the country of the sales organization as the country of departure.

You maintain tax code determinations for all (yes, all!) relevant combinations of the preceding factors so that when a sales order is processed, relevant factors are taken into account to determine the appropriate tax code. However, granularity and applicability of sales tax may vary depending on whether it's a domestic shipment in the same country or a shipment to a different country. Even within the same country, tax calculations may vary by state, by province, or by region. Maintenance of tax code determination provides you with enough flexibility to maintain such combinations. You access tax code determination using SAP MENU • LOGISTICS • SALES AND DISTRIBUTION • MASTER DATA • CONDITIONS • SELECT USING CONDITION TYPE • CREATE (Transaction VK11).

Figure 8.8 shows the initial screen and the three subscreens for maintaining tax code determination conditions. As indicated by the COUNTRY field at the top of the screen, these conditions are relevant for shipments from a plant based in the United States.

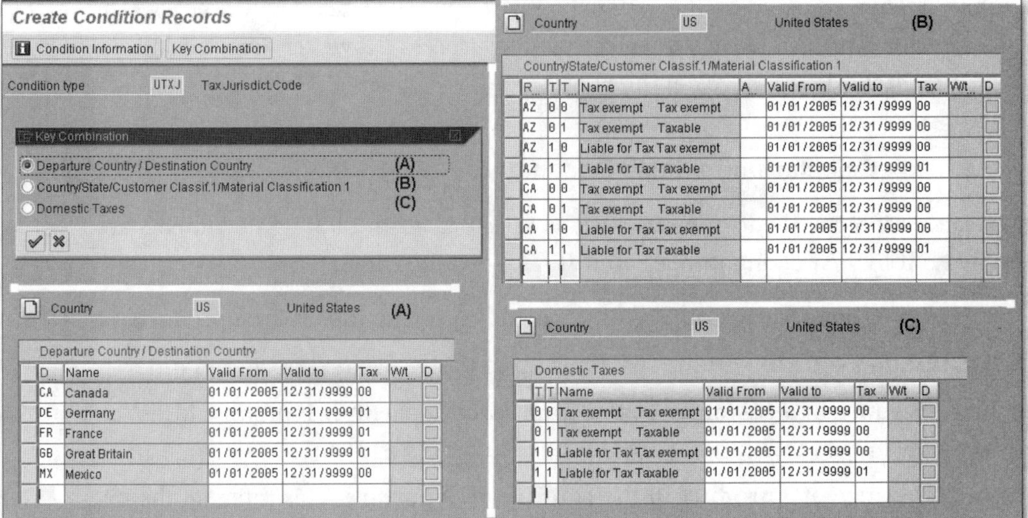

Figure 8.8 Tax Code Determination

- Screen (A) is relevant for international sales orders, in which the country of departure is different from the destination country.
- Screens (B) and (C) are relevant for domestic sales orders, in which the country of departure and destination country are same. Screen (B) is useful if you want to maintain tax code determinations by region.

These conditions are used to determine a tax code applicable for a sales transaction. The SD-FI interface in the SAP system uses this tax code to obtain the appropriate tax percentages (refer to Section 8.1.3, Tax Codes) and calculates applicable taxes on a sales order or in a billing document. The SD-FI interface also determines applicable tax GL accounts and generates necessary document line items in the FI document corresponding to the billing document.

In the next section, we'll discuss managing customer tax exemptions.

8.2.3 Tax Exemptions

In tax calculations, a fairly common business requirement is to manage tax exemption certificates for the customer. For example, foreign customers who pay taxes to tax authorities in their own countries may be exempt from taxes, or domestic customers who have received tax exemptions because of a special economic status granted to an industry or a geographical area may also be exempt from taxes. Typically, these exemption certificates are valid for a specific time period, after which a customer is expected to send in a new/renewal certificate.

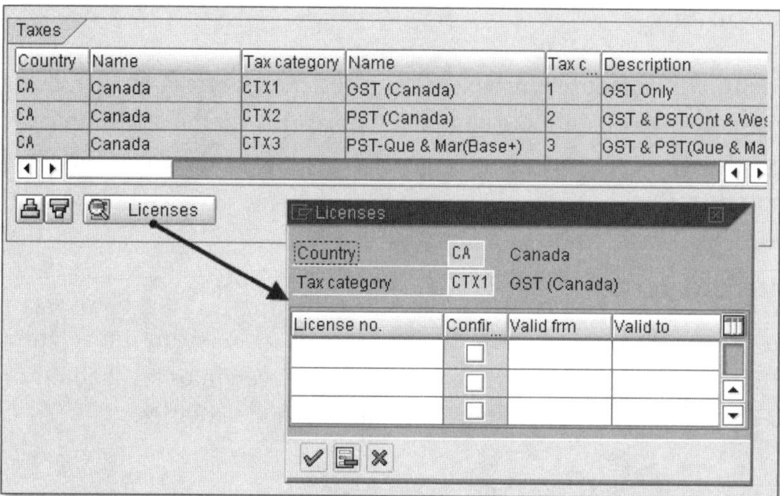

Figure 8.9 Customer Tax Exemptions

You maintain tax exemption certificates for a customer by selecting the LICENSES button (Figure 8.9) on the same master data screen where you maintain customer tax relevance indicators. You maintain exemption certificates or licenses for a combination of a COUNTRY and a TAX CONDITION. This is important because, as we discussed before, tax conditions represent different types of taxes. A customer may have received a tax exemption from federal taxes but not from local taxes, or vice versa. So it's necessary to maintain tax exemptions independently for each tax condition.

For each tax exemption certificate, you maintain the CERTIFICATE NUMBER and VALIDITY DATES fields. When a new certificate with new validity dates is received, you should maintain a separate entry in the customer master to preserve the data integrity and historical reference for previous tax exemption certificates.

Note

A customer tax exemption certificate is effective *only* if the CONFIRMED indicator is selected and the corresponding TAX CONDITION is configured to check for exemption certificates. Maintaining tax exemption certificates in the customer master doesn't have any effect if either of these requirements isn't fulfilled.

So far, we've seen configuration and calculation of taxes. Let's now focus on reporting customer taxes.

8.3 Tax Reporting

The SAP system supports comprehensive tax reporting ranging from quick reports that give an overview of tax liability to complex reports that can be used to file tax returns. In this section, we'll focus on three types of reports: line item reports, tax reports, and tax returns.

8.3.1 Line Item Reports

Line item reports provide you with a quick overview of tax-relevant information at the transactional level. We've discussed the line item screen in other chapters in this book such as dunning, AR transactions, and month-end activities.

Customer 3000

Tx	S...	Ty...	DocumentNo	Doc. Date	Σ	Amount in local cur.	LCurr
S0		DR	1800000003	01/28/2009		1,000.00	USD
S0		DR	1800000004	01/28/2009		1,000.00	USD
S0					▪	**2,000.00**	**USD**
S1		DR	1800000014	02/20/2009		1,000.00	USD
S1		DR	1800000013	02/20/2009		1,000.00	USD
S1					▪	**2,000.00**	**USD**
U1		DR	1800000002	01/28/2009		1,000.00	USD
U1					▪	**1,000.00**	**USD**

Figure 8.10 Customer Line Item Display

Figure 8.10 shows an example of the customer line item display summarized by TAX CODE. You can customize this output to display only relevant information for customer transactions by using the appropriate sort, filter, and layout management. Similarly, you can run the GL Account Line Items report for tax accounts to display tax details as posted into GL accounts. For the purpose of tax transactions, two relevant line item transactions are Customer Line Items (Transaction FBL5N) and GL Account Line Items (Transaction FBL3N).

In addition to these generic line item display reports, the SAP system also provides several tax reports.

8.3.2 Tax Reports

You'll find country-specific tax reports under the menu area SAP MENU • ACCOUNTING • FINANCIAL ACCOUNTING • GENERAL LEDGER • REPORTING • TAX REPORTS. Here you'll find some general tax reports under the GENERAL menu, and the rest of the tax reports grouped and organized by country. The sheer number of tax reports makes it impractical to discuss each one in this chapter. However, the following is an example of a U.S.-specific tax report.

Record of Use and Sales Taxes (USA)
Accounts Receivable

Jurisdiction AL0000000 Alabama
Tax code S0 A/R Sales Tax, exempt

Business partner	Account	LC tax base amount	LC tax amount	Tax Jur.	CTyp	Doc. Date	Reference
	400240	1,750.00-	0.00	AL0000000	JR3	02/15/2008	0090005758
	400240	1,750.00-	0.00	AL0000000	JR3	03/02/2008	0090005760
	400240	1,750.00	0.00	AL0000000	JR3	02/15/2008	0090005758
* Tax Code S0		1,750.00-	0.00	AL0000000			
*** State-level AL0000000		1,750.00-	0.00				

Jurisdiction AZ0000000 Arizona
Tax code S0 A/R Sales Tax, exempt

Business partner	Account	LC tax base amount	LC tax amount	Tax Jur.	CTyp	Doc. Date	Reference
	400372	29.25-	0.00	AZ0000000	JR3	04/22/2008	421085438
	400094	209.12-	0.00	AZ0000000	JR3	06/17/2008	0090007966
* Tax Code S0		238.37-	0.00	AZ0000000			
*** State-level AZ0000000		238.37-	0.00				

Figure 8.11 Tax Report

Figure 8.11 shows the output of a RECORD OF USE AND SALES TAX (USA) report. You can access this report with Transaction S_ALR_87012394. This report provides a reference for reporting sales and use tax in the United States. The documents are displayed per customer account and are totaled by tax code and, if applicable, by jurisdiction code. This report gives a total of the tax base amount and the tax amount, which can be useful while preparing tax returns.

8.3.3 Tax Returns

Considering the ever-changing nature of tax regulations and tax forms, most companies use tax-specific software and services to file tax returns. However, it's also possible to print or electronically file tax returns directly from SAP systems. You'll find configuration activities related to preparation of sales and purchase tax returns under SAP IMG • FINANCIAL ACCOUNTING • GENERAL LEDGER ACCOUNTING • PERIODIC PROCESSING • REPORT • SALES/PURCHASES TAX RETURNS. The following list describes some important configuration activities:

- **Define and assign sales/purchase groups:** Sales/purchase groups are relevant if you file a tax return that combines the tax details of multiple companies.
- **Define forms:** Define the SAP Forms corresponding to tax returns.
- **Define DME formats:** Define content and format of data files used for electronic filing of tax returns.

Other configuration activities provide functionalities to manage transactions and tax calculations in multiple currencies, to group multiple tax codes, and to group tax balances.

Tip

You may have to go through several test runs before you're approved for filing electronic tax returns. You'll also have to validate/modify tax forms or DME (distributed management environment) formats every year to ensure that they match the latest specifications and revisions released by the relevant tax authorities.

This program generates an advance tax return for tax on sales/purchases that consists of the following sections:

1. Output tax: Line items
2. Output tax: Totals list
3. Input tax: Line items
4. Input tax: Totals list
5. Tax difference: Line items
6. Balance per company code
7. Cross-company code balance

You can limit the scope of output results by choosing appropriate selection criteria. As you'll see later in this chapter, the SAP system also provides several BAdIs to customize printed or electronic returns generated using this program.

So far, we've covered the functionality of configuring, processing, and reporting taxes. Now we'll discuss other relevant functionalities, starting with the use of external tax software.

8.4 External Tax Software

Using external tax software considerably reduces the tax maintenance work within the SAP system. This is especially true in countries with a large number of tax jurisdictions, complex tax regulations, and a large number of frequent changes. The following SAP partners provide tax solutions that are certified to work with a broad range of SAP systems and system versions:

- Vertex (*www.vertexinc.com*)
- Taxware (*www.taxwaresystems.com*) – ADP Sales and Use Tax Solutions
- Sabrix (*www.sabrix.com*)

Understandably, using external software for tax calculation impacts all three aspects of tax calculations: configuration, processing, and reporting. Let's review each one in more detail.

8.4.1 Configuration

You'll find configuration tasks for activating external tax calculation software under SAP IMG • Financial Accounting • Financial Accounting Global Settings • Tax On Sales/Purchases • Basic Settings • External Tax Calculation.

The following are a few points about configuring external tax systems:

- The physical destination in the configuration activity specifies the connection and the directory that contains the commands to execute the tax software script.
- A typical installation gives you access to the following functions that interact with tax software:
  - `RFC_CALCULATE_TAXES_DOC` for tax calculation
  - `RFC_UPDATE_TAXES_DOC` for tax update
  - `RFC_FORCE_TAXES_DOC` for forced tax update
  - `RFC_DETERMINE_JURISDICTION` for determination of jurisdictions

- Tax jurisdiction codes are determined each time an address is entered or modified for a customer, a vendor, a plant, a company, or other relevant SAP master data. To determine an accurate tax jurisdiction code, the SAP system sends relevant address information to the tax calculation software.
- The software vendor is responsible for maintaining most up-to-date information for mapping an address to a jurisdiction code, including anomalies such as where addresses in the same ZIP code can correspond to different tax jurisdictions.
- You have to maintain other criteria, such as tax relevancy of customers and materials, in the tax software. Depending on the tax software, customer tax exemptions can be maintained either in the SAP system or in the tax software.

Tip

If you maintain customer tax exemption information in the tax software, then you have to maintain all customers as taxable in the SAP system.

- While maintaining tax codes, you don't enter tax percentages in the SAP system. Instead, you only enter 100% and – 100% in the configuration to indicate the type of tax, and the tax software takes care of determining accurate and most up-to-date tax percentages.

You should also validate the installation procedures of the tax software for any additional configuration requirements.

Now let's see how using tax software impacts tax calculation and processing in transactions.

8.4.2 Processing

If tax software is used to calculate sales and purchase taxes, taxes for SD documents are calculated as follows:

- The procedure that calculates prices, discounts, rebates, and other costs for SD (Sales and Distribution) or MM (Materials Management) documents invokes conditions for tax calculations.
- These conditions in turn invoke the tax interface system, which generates a communication structure filled with the necessary header and item details.

- This communication structure is passed to the external software, which calculates the appropriate tax and passes it back to the tax interface system.
- The tax interface system provides and applies calculated tax values to the SD document.

This process can accommodate tax calculations for up to six levels of jurisdictions such as national, state, county, and city. The tax calculation process for AR transactions directly posted in FI is similar to what is described in the preceding list. However, for FI documents, the tax procedure assigned to the country code invokes the tax interface to the tax software.

8.4.3 Reporting

An added advantage of using tax software for calculating and processing taxes is that these software products provide fairly advanced tax reporting capabilities. Apart from transactional reports required for management, analysis, and planning purposes, you can use custom report builders to build your own reports. Additionally, the software vendor takes care of ensuring that tax forms and tax returns in their software are up-to-date.

However, for the tax software to accurately report on taxes, it requires all tax data to be readily available. To meet this requirement, the SAP tax system interface updates tax data to an external audit file immediately when the accounting document is saved. This file is updated with tax information whenever a relevant accounting document is posted, such as during customer invoicing in SD, vendor invoicing in MM, or any manual invoice posting in FI.

Tip

The audit file will only be updated if the ACTIVATE EXTERNAL UPDATING indicator is set under the EXTERNAL TAX CALCULATION area in the configuration activities.

When the accounting document is posted, the external tax interface calculates the tax amounts to make sure that the tax information updated in the external audit file is the same as the tax information posted in the accounting document. If there are any discrepancies, the interface carries out a forced update of the tax data to the audit file. Tax data is also force updated to the audit file, if the document currency and functional currency of the company code are different. Periodically, you should run a report check update of the tax audit file. Figure 8.12 shows an example of such a report.

Report RFYTXDISPLAY can show the status for a list of documents as follows:

Status	Reference Document	Date and User	Text
Green	BKPF 1800000022 USXV2008	06/08/2008 DEBRUYNG	Updated to external system
Green	VBRK 90007687	08/04/2008 OEII	Forced to external system
	Possible reason for force: The document currency and the G/L currency differ		
Red	BKPF 1900000067 USXV2008	07/08/2008 DEBRUYNG	Error occurred in update
	Error message: doc: 1900000067; 1234 No more disk space		
Yellow	BKPF 1900000068 USXV2008	10/09/2008 DEBRUYNG	Scheduled in tRFC queue for update

Figure 8.12 Tax Audit File Report

Finally, the next section discusses other tax-relevant functionalities.

8.5 Other Functionalities

We discussed in Section 8.1.2, Account Keys, how you can assign GL accounts in a tax procedure. In the next section, we'll look at GL tax accounts.

8.5.1 GL Tax Accounts

Figure 8.13 shows tax-relevant fields on the CONTROL DATA tab of GL accounts maintenance (Transaction FS00).

The field TAX CATEGORY specifies whether a GL account is a tax-relevant account or a tax account. You can also use this field to specify the type of tax entries or tax codes that can be posted to this account. Figure 8.13 shows the values that are possible for the Tax Category field. If the POSTING WITHOUT TAX ALLOWED indicator is selected, then you can post entries to GL accounts without tax codes.

Tip

You can set up all GL accounts with TAX CATEGORY * (all tax types allowed) and the POSTING WITHOUT TAX ALLOWED indicator selected. However, you may want to consider potential control risks before carrying out such a setup.

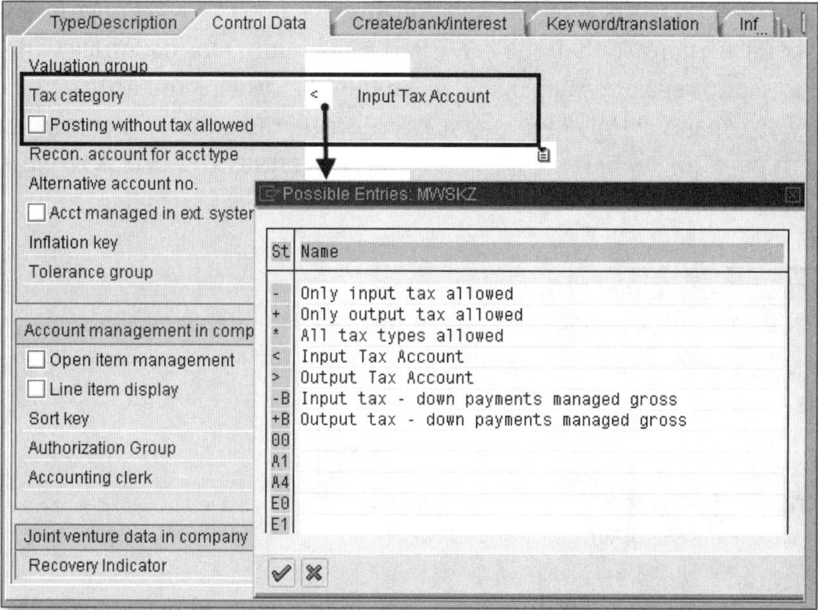

Figure 8.13 GL Account Tax Fields

In the next section, we'll discuss the plants abroad functionality.

8.5.2 Plants Abroad

As mentioned earlier in this chapter, one of the factors influencing taxability of business transactions is the country of departure. Typically, the country of departure is the country of the plant that carries out order fulfillment. Technical requirements of configuring a plant in the SAP system requires that it's linked with a company code, which typically forms the basis for preparing tax returns. This creates an interesting constellation for filing taxes; the company is in one country, whereas the plants and warehouses are located in a different country.

Warning

It isn't possible to activate the jurisdiction code functionality and plants abroad functionality for the same company code. However, you may have different company codes in the same SAP client that use one or the other functionality.

With the help of the PLANTS ABROAD functionality, it's possible to configure tax rules and tax calculations so that you can prepare tax returns for countries without having to set up separate company codes in the SAP system. You activate this functionality by using SAP IMG • FINANCIAL ACCOUNTING • FINANCIAL ACCOUNTING GLOBAL SETTINGS • TAX ON SALES/PURCHASES • BASIC SETTINGS • PLANTS ABROAD • ACTIVATE PLANTS ABROAD.

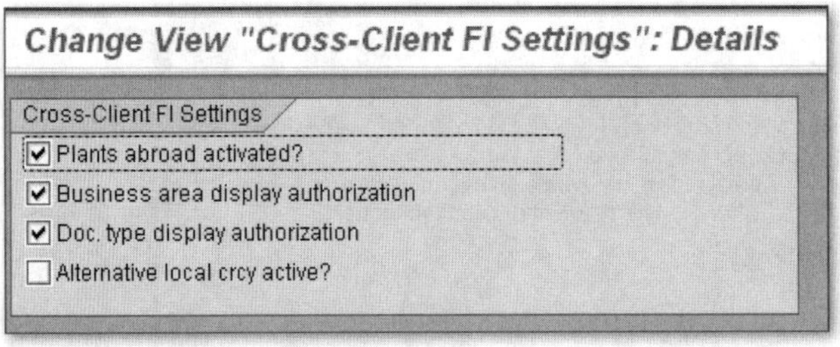

Figure 8.14 Activate the Plants Abroad Functionality

Figure 8.14 shows the configuration screen of this activity, where you set the flag to activate the plants abroad functionality. Note, however, that by activating this functionality, you have to carry out the following additional configuration maintenance:

- In the configuration of country codes (Transaction OY01), you maintain COUNTRY CURRENCY, which specifies the currency in which tax reporting is required.
- You maintain the reporting country in the tax code configuration (Section 8.1.3, Tax Codes). In this field, you specify a country other than the company code country, to which transactions with this tax code are reported.

As with the other chapters in this book, the following section provides SAP transactions for tax processing.

8.5.3 List of Transactions

Table 8.1 lists the tax-processing transactions in the SAP system, though as you may have noticed by now, tax-processing activities are usually part of other SAP transactions such as processing AR transactions or billing documents.

Transaction	Usage
XD02	Maintain customer tax data
MM02	Maintain material tax data
FS00	Maintain GL accounts tax data
VK11/VK12	Create/change tax code determination conditions
FBL3N	GL account line items
FBL5N	Customer account line items
S_ALR_87012357	Advance return for tax on sales/purchases
S_PL0_86000027	DME file for summarized advance tax return
S_ALR_87012365	Tax information (country)
OBBG	Assign tax procedure to a country
FTXP	Maintain tax codes
OVK1	Define tax relevancy indicators
OVK3	Maintain tax relevancy indicators for customers
OVK4	Maintain tax relevancy indicators for materials
OBETX	Define number range for external tax documents
OBCO	Define structure for jurisdiction codes
OBCN	Tax transaction keys
OB40	Assign GL accounts to transaction keys
OBCL	Assign tax codes for non-taxable transactions
OB69	Define tax base for company codes
OBCP	Define tax base for jurisdiction codes

Table 8.1 Tax Processing – Transactions

In the next section, we'll look at the technical objects available for tax-processing functionalities.

8.6 Technical Reference

This section lists technical objects such as SAP Notes, authorization objects, and tables and structures relevant for the tax-processing functionality. Considering the large number of technical objects available in the SAP system, this information should only be considered as a starting point.

8.6.1 SAP Notes

Tax calculation rules are highly complex and can vary widely from country to country. So apart from the following SAP Notes, you should also check the SAP Notes for country-specific tax functionality. Country-specific SAP Notes are under the XX-CSC-zz application area, where "zz" is the country code. SAP Notes for partner tax software can be found under the XX-PAR-TIF application area.

Table 8.2 lists some of the SAP Notes for the sales tax functionality.

SAP Note	Relevance
0001085758	New GL – Plants abroad stock transfer customizing
0000112609	How are tax codes transferred to sales conditions?
0000098532	Same exemption license number for more than one customer
0000441456	Shipments between US and Canada with jurisdiction codes
0000191932	Incorrect tax classification in the SD document
0000072040	Tax exemption licenses with condition technique
0000019195	Tax exemption check and tax indicator
0000382090	Tax interface: Format of account number
0000674649	What are the reasons for "Forced" updated?
0000392696	R/3 tax interface configuration guide
0000845219	Selecting financial reporting period in advance return for tax
0001085921	Document split (for possible impact on tax calculations)
0000869540	Posting direct tax to tax GL accounts
0000010560	Tax determination for plants abroad
0000019195	Tax exemption license check and tax indicator
0000063103	Tax procedure for plants abroad functionality
0000367175	No tax calculation function in FICO BAPIs
0000302998	Collecting pricing fields for tax user exit

Table 8.2 Tax Processing – SAP Notes

In the next section, we'll look at authorization objects relevant for tax-processing transactions and reports.

8.6.2 Authorization Objects

Processing taxes is intertwined with master data maintenance, transaction processing, reporting transactions, and configuration transactions. A user will be able to carry out tax-relevant processing if he has authorization to access the main transactions.

The next section provides a list of tables and structures.

8.6.3 Tables and Structures

Table 8.3 lists tables and structures relevant for tax processing. You should also be familiar with tables and structures used for FI documents and SD documents.

Table	Relevance
BKPF	Accounting document – header
BSEG	Accounting document – details
BSET	Tax data document segment
KNVI	Customer master tax indicators
KNVL	Customer tax exemption certificates
MG03STEUER	Control table for material tax indicators
SKB1	GL account company code data (for tax indicators)
T005	Country code parameters
TTXD	Structure of tax jurisdiction codes
TSTL	Tax determination rules for each country
TSKD	Tax relevancy indicators for customers
TSKM	Tax relevancy indicators for materials
T001W	Plant parameters
T007A	Tax keys
T007B	Tax processing in accounting
T030K	Tax account determination

Table 8.3 Tax Processing – Tables and Structures

Table	Relevance
T163KS	Assignment of tax indicators to account category
TTXP	Product codes for external tax interface
TTXJ	Check table for tax jurisdiction codes
TTXU	External tax interface: Audit file update information
TTXY	External tax interface: Tax information

Table 8.3 Tax Processing – Tables and Structures (Cont.)

Now we'll look at the objects and functionality available for enhancing and modifying the tax calculation functionality.

8.7 Enhancements and Modifications

This section provides a list of available BTEs, enhancements, BAdIs, and BAPIs relevant for the tax-processing functionality. These are used to enhance and modify the standard functionality available in the SAP system.

8.7.1 Business Transaction Events (BTE)

Using BTEs, you can attach additional function modules and custom logic to the standard SAP system. Table 8.4 lists publish and subscribe (P/S) and process BTEs available for the tax calculation functionality.

Type	BTE	Event/Process
P/S	00001910	Parked documents in preparing advance tax return
P/S	00002050	Tolerance check in taxes
P/S	00002051	Exchange rate used for translating tax base

Table 8.4 Tax Processing – Business Transaction Events

The following example shows how BTEs can be used in tax processing:

- **Event 00001910:** Parked document in advance tax return
  - This event is relevant for the inclusion of parked documents when preparing the advance return for tax on sales/purchases.

  - For example, you can use this BTE to include parked documents from external systems in the preparation of a tax return.

Additionally, you may want to check BTEs for billing documents and AR documents for their usage in influencing sales tax calculations and tax processing.

The next section discusses available enhancements for tax processing.

8.7.2 Enhancements

Using enhancements, you can add custom logic to carry out additional validations and custom business processing.

- FYTX0001: Control interface for external systems
  - This user exit enhancement is compatible with older versions of SAP R/3 systems. It should only be used if the implementation of FYTX0002 isn't possible due to the technical landscape of your SAP systems.
  - This enhancement contains a function module EXIT_SAPLV61A_001 that can be used to change values for tax fields in the COM_TAX structure.
- FYTX0002: Enhancements for tax interface
  - This enhancement helps you in influencing tax calculation and processing carried out by external tax software.
  - Compared to FYTX0001, this enhancement provides you with more input parameters that can be used in programming logic. It also provides you with more tax fields for which values can be changed.
  - This enhancement contains function module EXIT_SAPLFYTX_USER_001, and a system include CI_TAX_INPUT _USER that can be used to pass additional fields to an external tax system.
- SDVFX006: User exit tax line in transfer to accounting
  - This enhancement is part of a group of enhancements that can be used at the time of creating an accounting document from a billing document.
  - This enhancement contains function module EXIT_SAPLV60B_006 that can be used to change information in the tax line items.
- V54C0004: Shipment costs: determination of tax location
  - This enhancement can be used to change the location used for the tax calculation of shipment costs in the Transportation component.

- It contains a function module EXIT_SAPLV54C_004 that can be used to change the location (C_TXJCD) value based on user-specific criteria.

- V54D0001: Shipment costs: determination of tax countries
  - Similar to the previous enhancement, this one can be used to change the country value used for the tax calculation of shipment costs in the Transportation component.
  - It contains a function module EXIT_SAPLV54D_001 that can be used to change the tax country value based on user-specific criteria.

The next section provides information about available BAdIs.

8.7.3 Business Add-Ins (BAdIs)

The following BAdIs are available for tax processing:

- ADDR_TXJCD_CHECK
  - This BAdI is useful in the situations where the fields of a postal address aren't sufficient to determine the tax jurisdiction code for an address.
  - This BAdI contains a method SWITCH_ADDRESS_FIELDS that helps you override address fields that are transferred to the function module that determines the tax jurisdiction code from an address.
- TXJCD_EXTN
  - This BAdI implementation can be useful for scenarios where you want to change the tax jurisdiction code determined by an external tax system.
  - This BAdI contains a method TXJCD_CHANGE_ALLOWED that enables you to change the tax jurisdiction code as necessary.
  - SAP Notes 655674, 756696, and 1273003 provide more detail on the implementation and use of this BAdI.
- BADIs FI_TAX_BADI_010 - FI_TAX_BADI_016
  - These BAdIs provide you with different methods to enhance and influence the preparation of an advance return for tax on sales/purchases.
  - These BAdIs correspond to an advance return prepared using program RFUMSV00, Transaction S_ALR_87012357.

Warning

You should be extremely careful before using any BAdI that makes changes to tax data, as these changes aren't logged, and thus are untraceable. If you implement any such BAdI, you should also implement supplemental logic to support potential tax audit inquiries.

Table 8.5 provides a list of BAdIs, their intended purpose, and their available methods.

BAdI	Purpose/Methods
FI_TAX_BADI_010	Issue additional texts while preparing a tax return. Available methods: ▸ TOP_OF_PAGE ▸ END_OF_PAGE ▸ END_OF_LIST
FI_TAX_BADI_011	Change/influence document line item lists in a tax return. However, you can't change the currency or amount fields. Available methods: ▸ APPEND_TAX_ITEM ▸ SET_FLAGS
FI_TAX_BADI_012	Change/influence document tax line items retrieved from table BSET, before they are processed further. Available methods: ▸ SET_FLAG_USE_BADI_12 ▸ GET_BKPF_LATE
FI_TAX_BADI_013	Change/influence DME parameters when generating an advance tax return file (Tree type UMS1, Structure RFUMS_DPARAM). Available method: ▸ SET_DMEE_PARAMETER
FI_TAX_BADI_014	Change/influence field descriptions or column titles of the output lists in an advance tax return. An additional handle value helps you select one of the seven output lists. Available method: ▸ MODIFY_FIELDCAT
FI_TAX_BADI_015	Change/influence tax items before they are output in a tax return. Available methods: ▸ END_OF_SELECTION ▸ SET_FLAG_USE_BADI_15

Table 8.5 Tax Processing – BAdIs

BAdI	Purpose/Methods
FI_TAX_BADI_016	Change/influence tax items before they are output in a tax return. Available methods: ▸ END_OF_SELECTION ▸ SET_FLAG_USE_BADI_16

Table 8.5 Tax Processing – BAdIs (Cont.)

The next section discusses BAPIs for the functionalities discussed in this chapter.

8.7.4 BAPI

Refer to BAPIs for accounting and billing documents because tax calculations and processing are integral parts of processing accounting and billing documents.

Depending on the usage and design of a BAPI, either you have to do tax calculations in the SAP system prior to making a BAPI call, or you have to pass all relevant tax parameters so that the BAPI logic can calculate taxes.

8.8 Summary

As noted earlier, the focus of this chapter was on sales taxes and on the common tax framework in the SAP system. The tax concepts and tax configuration discussed in the beginning of this chapter are applicable for any country and in any industry. The configuration of tax procedures, tax account keys, and tax codes is generic enough and, at the same time, flexible enough to manage any unique requirements. Maintenance of tax relevant indicators and values in the customer master, material master, and GL account master is extremely important. These values influence tax calculations in SD documents.

The SAP system provides a large number of reports to meet the specific requirements of different countries. Additionally, the versatility of the tax returns program helps you configure it to meet requirements of manual or electronic tax filing. In the end, we discussed functionalities such as using external tax software.

This chapter focuses on different types of revenue recognition techniques available in the SAP system. This chapter is useful if your business requires that, from the accounting point of view, timing and methodology of the revenue recognition processes are separate from the customer billing process. If in your business all revenues are realized at the time of customer invoicing, you don't necessarily need the functionalities discussed in this chapter.

9 Revenue Recognition

In the revenue recognition process, sales revenues are recognized in a fiscal period from the accounting point of view. In the standard – and also the simplest – form of revenue recognition process, revenues are recognized at the same time as customer invoicing. On the other hand, there are revenue recognition methods that are governed by considerably more complex accounting principles and processes. These revenue recognition methods specify if, when, and what portion of sales revenue can be recognized for different types of business scenarios. For example, if a customer pre-pays for a service contract, customer invoicing may occur in one month, but revenues have to be recognized over the entire life of the service contract.

Which revenue recognition method is applicable depends on factors such as country-specific and industry-specific accounting standards, as well as types of goods and services being delivered. It's fairly common for a business to use different types of revenue recognition methods for different types of revenue streams such as product sales, service contracts, consulting, and so on. Let's first look at the standard revenue recognition process.

Tip

Use of any revenue recognition functionality, other than standard revenue recognition, may be subject to special release restrictions in the SAP system. SAP Note 0000820417 describes the process and provides references for obtaining the special release from SAP. However, even without such a special release, you can configure the SAP system to automatically post to deferred revenue accounts at the time of invoicing, and then carry out revenue recognition using manual postings.

9.1 Standard Revenue Recognition

In the standard revenue recognition process, customer revenues are recognized at the time of customer invoicing. When customer invoices are processed in the SAP system, the corresponding revenues are directly posted to sales revenue accounts in the income statement. The process of determining revenue accounts is controlled by the SAP system configuration, and it can be as simple or as complex as required by your business.

Note

For more complex business requirements and corresponding technical discussion, you can refer to my other book *SAP Account Determination* (SAP PRESS, 2006).

Here we'll discuss a common business requirement to separate revenues based on customer types, product types, and sales business units. To group customers and products for the purpose of revenue account determination, the SAP system uses account assignment groups.

9.1.1 Account Assignment Groups

Account assignment groups (AAGs) enable you to group different types of customers and products for the purpose of revenue account determination. As shown in Figure 9.1, you can set up a Customer AAG such as direct, distributors, resellers, OEM, and so on. Similarly, you can set up a Material AAG such as products, maintenance, service, consulting, training, and so on.

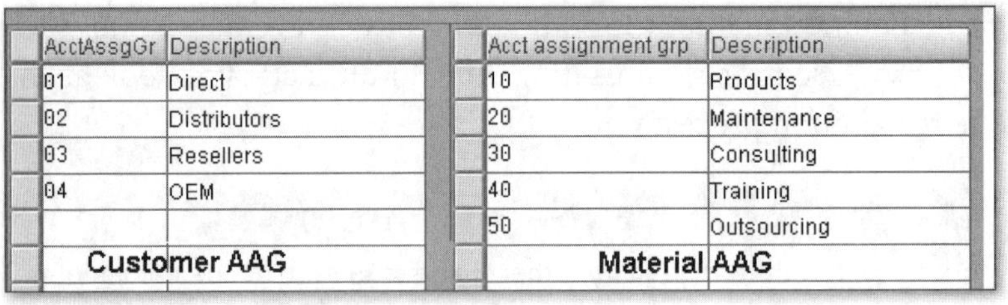

AcctAssgGr	Description
01	Direct
02	Distributors
03	Resellers
04	OEM

Customer AAG

Acct assignment grp	Description
10	Products
20	Maintenance
30	Consulting
40	Training
50	Outsourcing

Material AAG

Figure 9.1 Account Assignment Groups

Account assignment groups are configured using SAP IMG • SALES AND DISTRIBUTION • BASIC FUNCTIONS • ACCOUNT ASSIGNMENT/COSTING • REVENUE ACCOUNT DETERMINATION • CHECK MASTER DATA RELEVANT FOR ACCOUNT ASSIGNMENT.

You can use standard master data maintenance transactions such as XD01 and XD02 to assign AAGs to customers. The field is available on SALES DATA • BILLING DOCUMENTS. Similarly, you can use master data maintenance transactions such as MM01 and MM02 to assign AAGs to materials. The field is available on the SALES: SALES ORG 2 tab in the master data transaction.

These AAGs can be combined with the sales organization for the account determination process.

9.1.2 GL Account Determination

We discussed in Chapter 1, Customer Master Data, how the sales organization in the SAP system can be used to identify the sales business unit. On the other hand, in configuration activities related to sales pricing (discussed in Chapter 3, you assign unique identifiers called account keys to different amounts such as revenues, taxes, discounts, and so on. In most SAP implementations, account key ERL in sales pricing corresponds to revenues.

By combining AAGs and sales organizations with account keys for revenues, you can assign revenue accounts for different revenue streams that meet your business requirements. Figure 9.2 shows such an example of GL account assignment, using AAG values shown in Figure 9.1.

Cust.Grp/MaterialGrp/AcctKey

App	CndTy.	ChAc	SOrg.	AAG	AAG	ActKy	G/L Account	Provision acc.
V	KOFK	0010	1000	10	01	ERL	400010	
V	KOFK	0010	1000	10	02	ERL	400020	
V	KOFK	0010	1000	10	03	ERL	400030	
V	KOFK	0010	1000	10	04	ERL	400040	
V	KOFK	0010	1000	20	01	ERL	400100	145001
V	KOFK	0010	1000	20	02	ERL	400100	145002
V	KOFK	0010	1000	20	03	ERL	400100	145003
V	KOFK	0010	1000	20	04	ERL	400100	145004

Figure 9.2 GL Account Determination

In Figure 9.2, the CHAC field refers to the chart of accounts assigned to the company code; the SORG field refers to the sales organization; the two AAG fields refer to the customer account assignment group and material account assignment group, respectively; and the ACTKY field refers to the account key configured in the sales pricing.

Obviously, the important fields in this configuration activity are G/L Account, which specifies the revenue account, and Provision Account, which specifies any applicable deferred revenue account. At the time of posting accounting entries for the customer invoice, the SAP system checks whether the provision account is configured for the combination of criteria being evaluated. Revenues are posted to a provision account, if one is configured; otherwise, revenues are directly posted to the revenue account for immediate revenue recognition. In this example, the following is true:

- All product revenues (AAG = 10) are posted to different revenue accounts that are determined based on customer groups (AAG = 01 to 04).
- Maintenance revenues are posted to different deferred revenue accounts based on customer groups (AAG = 01 to 04).
- Regardless of the customer group, the recognized maintenance revenue is posted to the same GL account (400100).
  - In standard revenue recognition, accounting entries from deferred revenue to recognized revenue have to be posted manually.

The example just discussed evaluates only the sales organization, customer account assignment group, and material account assignment group to determine revenue accounts. However, if required, you can configure the SAP system so that you can use other evaluation criteria such as product divisions, order types, and product reason codes. You'll find these configuration activities under SAP IMG • Sales And Distribution • Basic Functions • Account Assignment/Costing • Revenue Recognition • Maintain Account Determination • Assign G/L Accounts For Revenues And Deferred Revenues.

If you intend to carry out manual postings to recognize revenues from deferred revenue accounts to recognized revenue accounts, information presented in the rest of this chapter may not be relevant for you. However, if you're planning to explore advanced revenue recognition functionality in the SAP system, then read on. Considering the interrelation and complexity of different concepts related to revenue recognition processes, you should read the rest of the chapter sequentially.

In the next section, we'll discuss revenue recognition parameters that influence the advanced revenue recognition processes.

9.2 Revenue Recognition Parameters

Parameters that influence the revenue recognition process are configured for the item category definition in the SAP Sales and Distribution (SD) component, so it will be helpful to first get an overview of SD item categories.

9.2.1 SD Item Categories

A sales order or a contract in the SAP system consists of one or more items. An item category assigned to each item specifies several parameters that influence pricing, invoicing, revenue recognition, and several other business processes. Figure 9.3 shows some of the available item categories in the SAP system, along with the detail configuration screen of one of the most commonly used item categories: TAN (standard item).

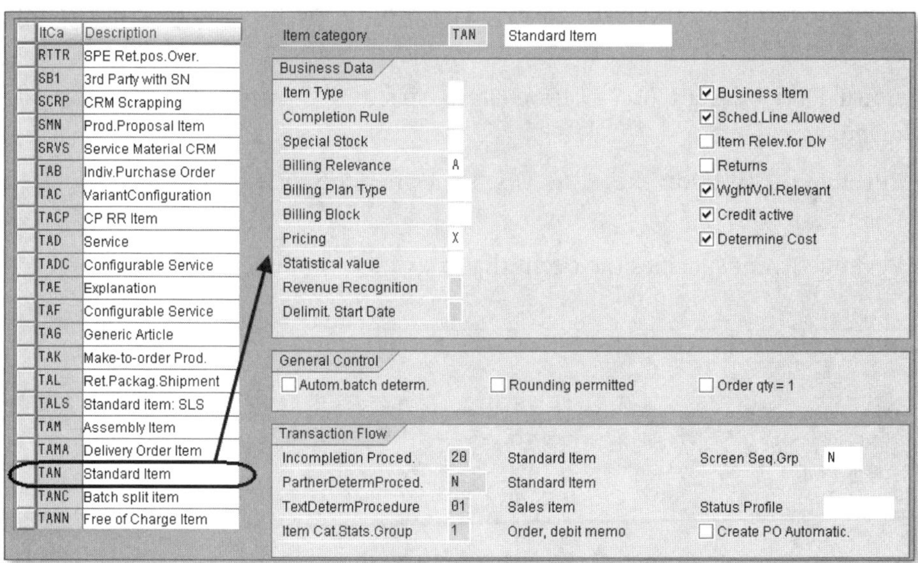

Figure 9.3 SD Item Categories

The configuration shown in Figure 9.3 is carried out using SAP IMG • Sales And Distribution • Sales • Sales Documents • Sales Document Item • Define Item Categories. During an SAP project, this configuration is carried out by the SD team in consultation with other teams. For the purpose of the revenue recognition processes, the only relevant parameters are Billing Relevance and Billing Plan Type.

The BILLING PLAN TYPE field can represent periodic billing or milestone billing. You'll find a detailed discussion of billing plans in Chapter 4. The BILLING RELEVANCE field specifies the basis for billing a sales document item, to which the ITEM CATEGORY field is assigned. The following list shows some of the billing relevance indicators available in the SAP system.

- **<blank>:** Not relevant for billing.
- **A:** Billing is based on outbound delivery.
- **B:** Billing is based on the sales document (e.g., cash sales).
- **D:** Pro forma billing.
- **I:** Billing occurs based on the billing plan.

In addition, the following four parameters (Figure 9.4) assigned to an item category influence revenue recognition processes:

- Revenue recognition category (Rev. Recognition) specifies the type of revenue recognition.
- Accrual period start (Acc. Period Start) specifies the start date for accruing revenues.
- Revenue distribution (Revenue Dist.) specifies the distribution of recognized revenues.
- Revenue Event specifies the event that triggers revenue recognition.

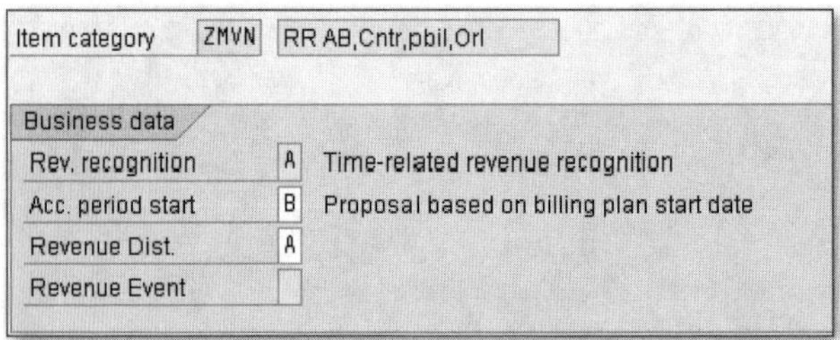

Figure 9.4 Revenue Recognition Parameters

These parameters are configured using SAP IMG • SALES AND DISTRIBUTION • BASIC FUNCTIONS • ACCOUNT ASSIGNMENT/COSTING • REVENUE RECOGNITION • SET REVENUE RECOGNITION FOR ITEM CATEGORIES. Before we discuss different types of revenue recognition processes in detail, following is a brief review of each of these parameters, starting with the Rev. Recognition parameter.

Tip

In standard delivery, the maintenance of parameters shown in Figure 9.4 is disabled in the SAP system. You can enable this parameter maintenance with the help of SAP Note 000000768561. However, it's highly recommended by SAP to request and obtain special release (described at the beginning of this chapter) before enabling and using this functionality.

9.2.2 Revenue Recognition

The Rev. Recognition parameter associated with an ITEM CATEGORY specifies the type of revenue recognition process carried out for sales revenues posted with that ITEM CATEGORY. Table 9.1 lists the available values for this field and their usage.

Item Category	Usage
blank	Standard revenue recognition
A	Time-related revenue recognition
B	Service-related revenue recognition
D	Billing-related, time-related revenue recognition
F	Credit/debit memos with reference to predecessor

Table 9.1 Revenue Recognition Category

Using time-related revenue recognition, you can recognize sales revenues over a specific timeframe based on a sales document (A) or in billing (D). Typically, these categories are used for revenue recognition of service contracts and maintenance contracts. Using service-related revenue recognition (B), you can recognize revenues based on a specific business event that confirms completion of service. Later in this chapter, we'll discuss these processes in more detail.

9.2.3 Accrual Period Start

The Acc. Period Start parameter is relevant only for time-related revenue recognition (Rev. Recognition = A or D). Because in a time-related revenue recognition process, revenues are distributed over a specific period of time, this parameter influences the accurate determination of the revenue accrual start date. Table 9.2 lists the available values for this parameter and their usage.

Accrual Period Start Date	Usage
Blank	Not relevant
A	Proposal based on contract start date
B	Proposal based on billing plan start date

Table 9.2 Revenue Recognition: Accrual Period Start Dates

The billing plan for value "B" can be a periodic billing plan or a milestone billing plan. We'll discuss this parameter later in this chapter in the time-related revenue recognition process.

9.2.4 Revenue Distribution

The Revenue Dist. parameter is also relevant only for time-related revenue recognition (Rev. Recognition = A or D). This parameter controls *how* revenues are distributed across different periods in time-related revenue recognition.

There are four possible values for this parameter (Table 9.3) depending on how the revenue recognition process handles any corrections and whether revenues are recognized linearly or based on a billing plan.

Revenue Distribution	Usage
Blank	Total value linear, correction value undistributed
A	Total value linear, correction value linearly distributed
B	Total value per billing plan, correction value undistributed
C	Total value per billing plan, correction value linearly distributed

Table 9.3 Revenue Distribution for Revenue Recognition

This parameter is also discussed in more detail later in this chapter along with time-related revenue recognition. Finally, let's talk about Revenue Event.

9.2.5 Revenue Event

This parameter is relevant for service-related revenue recognition (Rev. Recognition = B). It specifies the business event or activity that acts as a trigger for the revenue recognition process. Table 9.4 lists the available values for this parameter and their usage.

Revenue Event	Usage
Blank	Not event related
A	Incoming invoice
B	Acceptance date
X	Customer-specific event X
Y	Customer-specific event Y
Z	Customer-specific event Z

Table 9.4 Revenue Event for Service-Related Revenue Recognition

This parameter is discussed in more detail later in this chapter along with service-related revenue recognition. Now that we've discussed the four main parameters that influence revenue recognition processes, the following sections discuss those processes in detail.

9.3 Time-Related Revenue Recognition

Time-related revenue recognition (Rev. Recognition "A" or "D") can be used without any billing plan, with a periodic billing plan, or with a milestone billing plan. If you aren't familiar with the functionality of billing plans in the SAP system, you may want to read Chapter 4 before continuing further. This type of revenue recognition recognizes revenue over a specific period of time.

Time-related revenue recognition requires the calculation and determination of different values such as Accrual Start Date, Accrual End Date, Accrual Term, Total Number of Accrual Entries, Accrual Amount, and so on. Some of these calculations remain the same regardless of the business scenario. For example:

- Accrual Term is always calculated as the timeframe between Accrual Start Date and Accrual End Date.
- Total Number of Accrual Entries is identical to the Total Number of Posting Periods in Accrual Term. The SAP system determines the total number of posting

periods based on the fiscal year associated with the company code in which the revenues are posted.

- Accrual Amount for each period is calculated using the following formula.

Calculation of Monthly Accrual Amount

Accrual Amount = Total Accrual Value x

(Duration of Posting Period/Duration of Accrual Period)

However, calculations of other values are influenced by the specific business scenario, contract information, and billing plan information. Let's look at these scenarios in more detail.

9.3.1 Time-Related Revenue Recognition Without a Billing Plan

Without any billing plan, calculations for time-related revenue recognition are carried out using contract data:

- Accrual Start Date is proposed based on the contract start date. The value of the Accrual Period Start parameter should be set as "A."
- Accrual End Date is calculated based on the contract end date.
- Total Accrual Value is the same as the net value of the contract item.
- The value of the Revenue Distribution parameter should only be set as <blank> or "A." This means that revenue recognition is linear, and the recognized revenue for each month is the same as the monthly accrual amount.
- Depending on the value of the REVENUE DISTRIBUTION parameter, any revenue corrections are either recognized immediately in the current or next open posting period if the value is <blank> or distributed over remaining open periods of the accrual term if the value is "A."

9.3.2 Time-Related Revenue Recognition with a Periodic Billing Plan

If the periodic billing plan is associated with a contract or sales order item, information from the billing plan is used to determine the required values:

- Accrual Start Date is proposed as the earlier of the start date of the billing plan and the start date of the first settlement period. The value of the ACCRUAL PERIOD START parameter should be set as "B."

- Calculation of the Accrual End Date value is bit more involved in this case:
  - If the billing plan horizon is specified, the Accrual End Date is calculated as the end date of the last settlement period.
  - If the billing plan horizon isn't specified but the Contract End Date is available, the Accrual End Date is calculated as the Contract End Date.
  - If the billing plan horizon isn't specified and the Contract End Date is also not available, the Accrual End Date is calculated as the end date of the last settlement period.
- Total Accrual Value is calculated as the total value of all existing settlement periods.
- Amount Recognized per Month is calculated based on the billing plan. This requires the value of the Revenue Dist. parameter to be set as "B" or "C."
- If the REVENUE DIST. parameter value is "B," any revenue corrections are recognized immediately either in the current or next open posting period. If the value of the parameter is "C," any revenue corrections are distributed over the remaining open periods of the Accrual Term.

9.3.3 Time-Related Revenue Recognition with a Milestone Billing Plan

In this case, time-related revenue recognition uses information from a milestone billing plan:

- Accrual Start Date is proposed as the billing date of the first milestone.
- Accrual End Date is calculated as the Contract End date, if it's available. If the Contract End Date isn't available, then the Accrual End Date is calculated as the last milestone date.
- Total Accrual Value is calculated as the item net value if the Contract End Date is available. If the Contract End Date isn't available, then the Total Accrual Value is calculated as the total value of all existing milestones.
- Amount Recognized per Month is calculated based on the billing plan. This requires the value of the REVENUE DIST. parameter to be set as "B" or "C."
- If the REVENUE DIST. parameter value is "B," any revenue corrections are recognized immediately either in the current or next open posting period. If the

value of the parameter is "C," any revenue corrections are distributed over the remaining open periods of the Accrual Term.

In the next section, we'll discuss service-related revenue recognition.

9.4 Service-Related Revenue Recognition

Service-related revenue recognition (Rev. Recognition "B") is useful when revenue recognition is carried out based on a specific event. For the service-related revenue recognition process, the Accrual Term is irrelevant because it depends on a specific event to occur.

The value for the Revenue Event parameter determines the type of service-related revenue recognition process. Implementation of service-related revenue recognition can be very involved, and space constraints limit the level of detail that can be provided in this chapter. The following sections only provide an overview of the business process flow and a reference to the SAP note that contains detailed implementation steps.

The next section provides an overview of service-related revenue recognition by incoming invoice.

9.4.1 Service-Related Revenue Recognition by Incoming Invoice

This type of revenue recognition is relevant for third-party business transactions where goods or services requested by a customer are directly delivered to that customer by a vendor. For such a business scenario, an invoice received from the vendor is used as the base for the revenue recognition process. For this type of revenue recognition process, the Revenue Event parameter is set to "A."

Tip

Refer to SAP Note 0001000830 for more details on the implementation of service-related revenue recognition by incoming invoice.

The process flow for this type of revenue-recognition is relatively simple. After receiving the purchase order from your company, the vendor delivers goods or services directly to your customer. After your customer confirms receipt of the goods or completion of services, your vendor sends an invoice that triggers the revenue recognition process. Revenue recognition is carried out based on the quantities invoiced in the incoming invoice.

If there is a considerable time delay between receiving the confirmation from your customer and receiving the invoice from your vendor, you can initiate the revenue recognition process prior to receiving the vendor invoice. Refer to Section about manual processing of revenue recognition documents later in this chapter.

The next section provides an overview of service-related revenue recognition by proof of delivery.

9.4.2 Service-Related Revenue Recognition by Proof of Delivery

This type of revenue recognition is relevant for sales transactions that are relevant for the proof of delivery (POD) process. These are the sales transactions where the POD Relevant indicator is enabled in the sales order shipping data, in the item category of delivery, or in the ship-to customer master data. For this process, POD confirmation from the customer is used as the base for the revenue recognition process. In the configuration, this type of revenue recognition process requires the Revenue Event parameter to be set to "A."

Tip

Refer to SAP Note 0001025066 for more details on the implementation of service-related revenue recognition by proof of delivery. SAP Note 0001000830 referenced earlier is a prerequisite for this implementation.

For POD-relevant sales transactions that are subject to service-related revenue recognition, revenue lines are automatically allocated a posting block. This block prevents revenue lines from being posted until the POD confirmation occurs.

When customer confirmation of goods receipt is processed in the SAP system, the posting block is automatically removed from the revenue lines. This process also supports situations where the customer only confirms receipt of partial delivery. Revenue recognition is posted only for quantities confirmed in the POD process.

In the next section, you'll get an overview of service-related revenue recognition by customer acceptance date.

9.4.3 Service-Related Revenue Recognition by Customer Acceptance Date

This type of revenue recognition is for sales transactions that are relevant for billing, regardless of their relevance to delivery of goods or services. For these transactions, entry of the acceptance date in sales documents is used as the base for the revenue recognition process. For this type of revenue recognition process, the value of the REVENUE EVENT parameter is set to "B."

> **Tip**
>
> Refer to SAP Note 0001120297 for more details on the implementation of service-related revenue recognition by customer acceptance date.

In these types of sales transactions, revenue entries are created by the system when the sales document is processed. However, these revenue entries are automatically allocated a posting block so that they can't be posted to accounting. When the acceptance date is entered in the sales document, the posting block is removed from the revenue entries. The Acceptance Date field (VEDA-VABNDAT) is displayed on the Contract Data tab in the sales document.

This process supports any subsequent changes to the acceptance date, price, or other field values that can potentially impact revenue recognition. For example, if a sales document item is rejected using a reason for rejection, then regardless of the Acceptance Date value, the SAP system generates adjustment entries that remove updated revenues.

If the standard revenue events discussed so far aren't sufficient to meet your business requirements, you can use customer-specific events that are discussed in the next section.

9.4.4 Service-Related Revenue Recognition by Customer-Specific Event

You can use up to three different events to act as a base for this type of service-related revenue recognition. The definition and identification of this event is entirely dependent on your business processes. The SAP system only provides the framework so that you can customize service-related revenue recognition for your specific requirements. For this type of revenue recognition process, the value of the REVENUE EVENT parameter should be set as "X," "Y," or "Z."

Tip

Refer to SAP Note 0001125456 for more details on implementing service-related revenue recognition by customer-specific event.

One of the biggest differences in this type of revenue recognition as compared to other types is that you have to implement this functionality with the help of Business Add-Ins. This approach makes implementing this type of revenue recognition considerably more complex from a technical point of view.

However, your business requirements may require this type of implementation. For example, let's say your business requires revenue recognition to be carried out only after user the Status field on the Status tab of a sales order is changed to "Released." Because none of the other service-related revenue recognition processes support this requirement, you'll have to use BAdIs to implement revenue recognition based on customer-specific events.

Additional complexity arises due to the fact that the event that triggers this revenue recognition process may not be a standard SD document. For example, your requirement may consist of revenue recognition only after payment for an invoice is received. Because this payment document isn't a standard SD document, you have to also implement a BAdI to display customer-specific event documents.

These are just some of the factors to be considered while implementing service-related revenue recognition based on customer-specific events.

In the next section, we'll discuss commonly used revenue recognition transactions.

9.5 Transactions

One of the most important aspects of revenue recognition is its timing with respect to the customer invoicing process, so let's discuss that first.

9.5.1 Timing of Revenue Recognition

Depending on the statutory and business requirements, revenues may have to be recognized for a sales transaction before or after customer invoicing takes place. This timing difference means these processes may run in different posting periods or even different fiscal years. To ensure accurate processing and posting of revenues, the SAP system uses two GL accounts: deferred revenue account and unbilled receivables account.

We discussed in Section 9.1.2, GL Account Determination, how a deferred revenue account is used in the standard revenue recognition process. The SAP system uses the same definition of deferred revenue recognition accounts for advanced revenue recognition processes. If the advanced revenue recognition methods aren't used, then you simply have to post revenue recognition entries manually.

On the other hand, the unbilled receivables account is used only with advanced revenue recognition processes. This GL account is used to post revenues that are recognized but not yet invoiced to a customer. This account is maintained in configuration under SAP IMG • Sales And Distribution • Basic Functions • Account Assignment/Costing • Revenue Recognition • Maintain Account Determination • Assign Account For Unbilled Receivables.

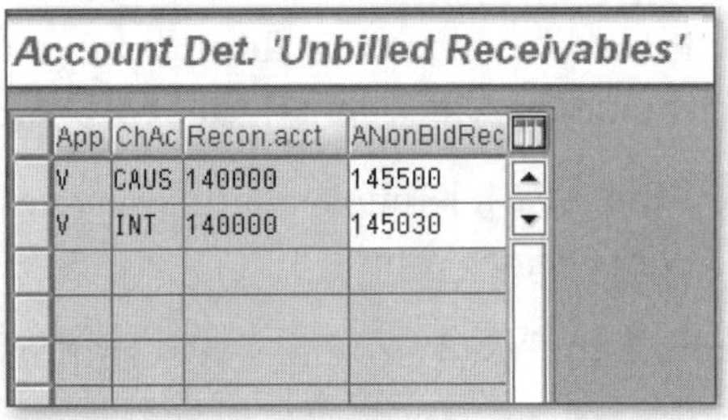

Account Det. 'Unbilled Receivables'

App	ChAc	Recon.acct	ANonBldRec
V	CAUS	140000	145500
V	INT	140000	145030

Figure 9.5 Revenue Recognition – Unbilled Receivables Account

As Figure 9.5 shows, unbilled receivables accounts are configured separately for each customer reconciliation account. This functionality can be useful, for example, if you use different reconciliation accounts for different groups of customers such as domestic trade partners and foreign trade partners. In such situations, you can configure different unbilled revenue accounts so that you can monitor the unbilled revenues for each group of customers separately.

During the customer billing process, first any balance in the unbilled receivables account is adjusted, before any accounting entries are made to the deferred revenue account. Table 9.5 provides an overview of how these accounts are used in different revenue recognition processes.

	Billing Process	Revenue Recognition Process
Standard revenue recognition without deferred revenue account	Dr Receivables ▸ Cr Revenues	Not Applicable
Standard revenue recognition with deferred revenue account	Dr Receivables ▸ Cr Deferred Revenue	(Manual Process) Dr Deferred Revenue ▸ Cr Revenues
Revenue recognition before customer billing	Dr Receivables ▸ Cr Unbilled Receivables	Dr Unbilled Receivables ▸ Cr Revenues
Customer billing before revenue recognition	Dr Receivables ▸ Cr Deferred Revenues	Dr Deferred Revenues ▸ Cr Revenues

Table 9.5 Accounting Entries in Revenue Recognition

For credit memos, the process is somewhat different. When credit memos are created with reference to a sales order, the process first checks whether a balance exists on the deferred revenue account. If not, then a posting is made to the unbilled receivables account. When credit memos are created without any reference, the process posts directly to the unbilled receivables account.

Now it's time to explore commonly used revenue recognition transactions, starting with the one used to process the revenue recognition list.

9.5.2 Processing Revenue List (VF44)

Process revenue list is one of the most important revenue recognition transactions, which you can use to create a collective run for processing multiple revenue recognition documents. It's used to post new revenue recognition entries as well as to make adjustment entries to already recognized revenues.

You access this transaction using SAP MENU • LOGISTICS • SALES AND DISTRIBUTION • BILLING • REVENUE RECOGNITION • EDIT REVENUE LIST. Figure 9.6 shows the selection parameter screen of the revenue process list. Most selection fields on the screen such as COMPANY CODE, SALES DOCUMENT TYPE, SALES DOCUMENT NUMBER, and SOLD-TO PARTY are self-explanatory, so we'll only focus on the other fields that require some explanation.

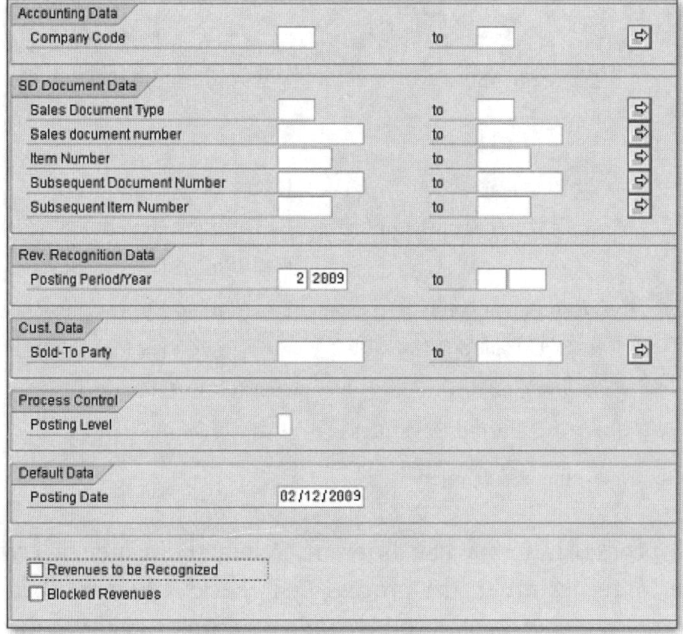

Figure 9.6 Revenue Recognition Process – Selection Parameters

Posting Date and Posting Periods

POSTING DATE specifies the date on which revenue recognition entries are posted to FI, and POSTING PERIOD/YEAR specifies the range of posting periods for which revenue recognition documents are evaluated in the processing run. At least the lower limit (from) of the posting period/year has to be specified for this transaction to evaluate and process any revenue recognition entries.

Posting Level

The POSTING LEVEL indicator is used to control the granularity and detail at which accounting documents are posted. The choice of posting level depends entirely on your revenue monitoring and reconciliation requirements. For routine maintenance contracts, you may want to post revenues at a summarized level, whereas for special consulting contracts, you may want to post revenues at a more granular level. Table 9.6 lists the available values for this field.

Posting Level	Creation of Revenue Recognition Accounting Documents
Blank	One document for each sales document.
1	One document for the entire collective processing run; if first document contains more than 999 lines, additional documents are created with the *same* collective processing number.
2	One document for every sales document item.
3	One document for every sales document item, per posting period. This can be useful, for example, if you carry out a single processing run for multiple posting periods.
4	One document for the entire collective processing run; if first document contains more than 999 line items, additional documents are created with a *new* collective processing number.

Table 9.6 Posting Level for a Revenue Recognition Run

Notice the difference in values 1 and 4, especially in how the collective processing number is assigned to additional accounting documents if the first document contains more than 999 lines. This difference is important because the collective processing number is used across revenue recognition functions ranging from reporting and analysis of error logs to cancellation and reconciliation.

List Item Selections

REVENUES TO BE RECOGNIZED and BLOCKED REVENUES let you choose revenue recognition items to be displayed for further processing. For example, if you intend to process only blocked revenue recognition items, selecting BLOCKED REVENUES will limit the scope of output list.

Figure 9.7 shows a sample of an output list for selections shown in Figure 9.6. After the list is displayed, you can carry out any of the following actions:

- Block revenue items from being processed by using SET BLOCKING ID. This option can be useful if you're waiting for external confirmation or approval before recognizing revenue for that sales document.

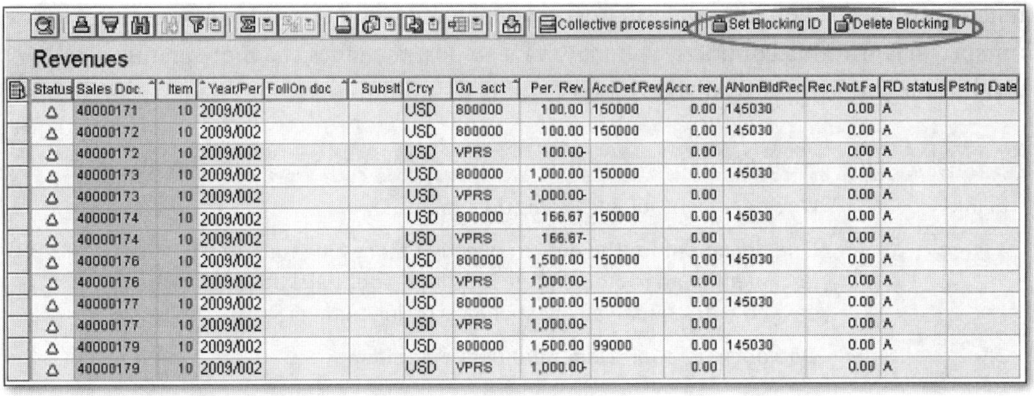

Collective processing | Set Blocking ID | Delete Blocking ID

Revenues

Status	Sales Doc.	Item	Year/Per	FollOn doc	Subst	Crcy	G/L acct	Per. Rev.	AccDef.Rev	Accr. rev.	ANonBldRec	Rec.Not.Fa	RD status	Pstng Date
△	40000171	10	2009/002			USD	800000	100.00	150000	0.00	145030	0.00	A	
△	40000172	10	2009/002			USD	800000	100.00	150000	0.00	145030	0.00	A	
△	40000172	10	2009/002			USD	VPRS	100.00-		0.00		0.00	A	
△	40000173	10	2009/002			USD	800000	1,000.00	150000	0.00	145030	0.00	A	
△	40000173	10	2009/002			USD	VPRS	1,000.00-		0.00		0.00	A	
△	40000174	10	2009/002			USD	800000	166.67	150000	0.00	145030	0.00	A	
△	40000174	10	2009/002			USD	VPRS	166.67-		0.00		0.00	A	
△	40000176	10	2009/002			USD	800000	1,500.00	150000	0.00	145030	0.00	A	
△	40000176	10	2009/002			USD	VPRS	1,000.00-		0.00		0.00	A	
△	40000177	10	2009/002			USD	800000	1,000.00	150000	0.00	145030	0.00	A	
△	40000177	10	2009/002			USD	VPRS	1,000.00-		0.00		0.00	A	
△	40000179	10	2009/002			USD	800000	1,500.00	99000	0.00	145030	0.00	A	
△	40000179	10	2009/002			USD	VPRS	1,000.00-		0.00		0.00	A	

Figure 9.7 Revenue Recognition Processing List

- Open blocked revenue items for processing with DELETE BLOCKING ID. This option can be useful if you want to unblock revenue recognition lines after receiving POD confirmations from a customer.
- Process multiple, unblocked, revenue items and post accounting entries by using COLLECTIVE PROCESSING.
- Display accounting documents corresponding to already processed revenue recognition items.

Because the output list is displayed as an ALV (ABAP List Viewer) list, you can use ALV features such as layout management, sort, subtotal, and filter for processing revenue recognition items. However, there may be instances when it's necessary to cancel revenues that are already recognized.

9.5.3 Revenue Cancellations (VF46)

To cancel revenues, you need to use transaction SAP MENU • LOGISTICS • SALES AND DISTRIBUTION • BILLING • REVENUE RECOGNITION • MAINTAIN CANCELLATION LIST. Figure 9.8 shows the selection screen.

Selection parameters for the revenue cancellation list are similar to the parameters available for processing the revenue recognition list, except that COLLECTIVE RUN NUMBER is also available as a selection parameter. Using this parameter, you can cancel revenues for all sales documents processed in one revenue recognition run.

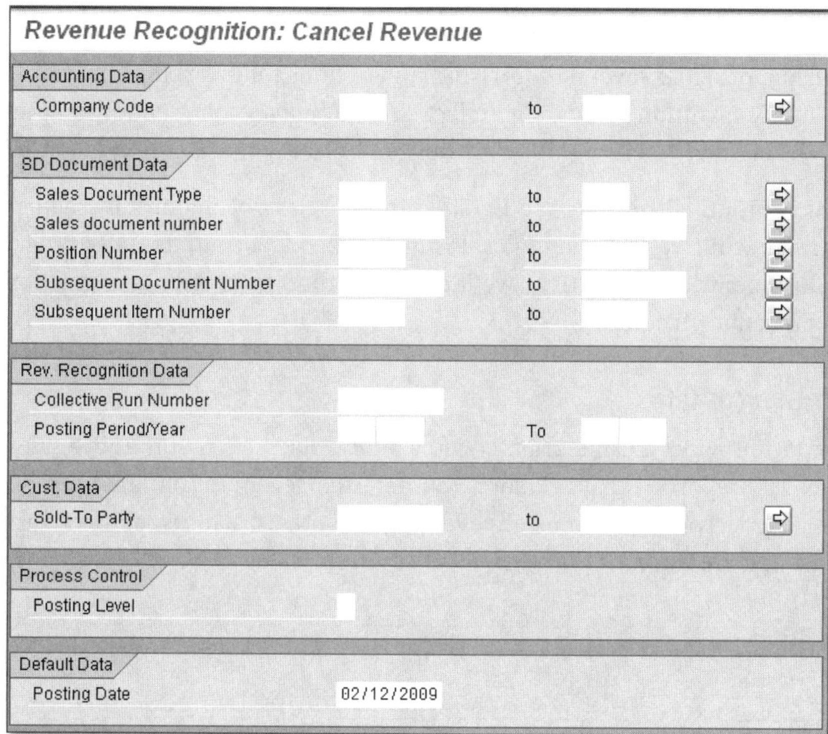

Figure 9.8 Revenue Cancellations

There are a few points to note about this cancellation process:

- Processing of the revenue cancellation list is similar to the processing of a revenue recognition list.
- This cancellation process isn't cancellation in the traditional sense, in that it *doesn't* automatically post reversal entries in FI.
- Instead, this process adjusts existing revenue recognition control items and creates additional control items for revenue cancellations.
- These additional control lines for revenue cancellations should be processed using the revenue recognition process described in Section 9.5.2, Processing Revenue List (VF44).

The next section provides information on reporting and monitoring transactions for the revenue recognition functionality.

9.5.4 Reporting and Monitoring

The SAP system provides several reports and transactions for analyzing and monitoring revenue recognition processing. In fact, SAP strongly recommends monitoring and analyzing revenue recognition entries periodically, at least once a month.

Revenue recognition entries are also updated in the sales document flow, which you can display while viewing any sales document such as a contract, sales order, or billing document. In this section, we'll discuss additional reports available for monitoring revenue recognition.

Revenue Report (VF45)

Revenue report provides a value-oriented view of revenue recognition from a sales perspective. The report displays (Figure 9.9) deferred revenues, unbilled receivables, invoiced receivables, recognized revenues, and other balances for sales document items that are relevant for revenue recognition.

Accounting | ›Display Revenues and Bill.Docs

Control Lines

Sales Doc.	Item	Crcy	Total val.	AccDef.Rev	Accr. rev.	ANonBldRec	Rec.Not.Fa	Recog.Rev.	Unrec.Rev.	Inv. Rev.	RD status	Rev. recog
40000171	10	EUR	600.00	150000	0.00	145030	100.00	100.00	500.00	0.00	A	A
40000172	10	EUR	0.00	150000	0.00	145030	100.00	100.00	100.00-	0.00	A	A
40000173	10	EUR	6,000.00	150000	0.00	145030	2,000.00	2,000.00	4,000.00	0.00	A	A
40000174	10	EUR	1,000.00	150000	0.00	145030	333.34	333.34	666.66	0.00	A	A
40000175	10	EUR	6,000.00	150000	0.00	145030	0.00	0.00	6,000.00	0.00	A	B
40000176	10	EUR	9,000.00	150000	0.00	145030	0.00	0.00	9,000.00	0.00	A	A
40000177	10	EUR	6,000.00	150000	0.00	145030	0.00	0.00	6,000.00	0.00	A	A
40000178	10	EUR	9,000.00	99000	0.00	145030	5,225.81	5,225.81	3,774.19	0.00	A	A
40000179	10	EUR	9,000.00	99000	0.00	145030	1,500.00	1,500.00	7,500.00	0.00	A	A

Figure 9.9 Revenue Recognition: Revenue Report

Using different options, you can branch out to display sales documents, accounting documents, and subsequent sales documents from the output list. Another report available for monitoring revenue recognition entries is the comparison report.

Revenue Comparison Report (VF48)

Revenue comparison report compares accrual account balances in accounting and in sales. It determines the accounting balance based on all entries posted to an accrual account, and it determines the sales balance for that accrual account based on entries in the revenue recognition tables. Figure 9.10 shows a sample output of revenue comparison report.

Balances Account 990000

Currency USD
- Balance from Revenue Recognitions___ 7,553.76
- Balance from Billing Documents_______ 10,103.48
- Balance from Other Postings__________ 0.00

Total Balance 537.38-

Document	Item	Crcy	Billed Revenues	Recognized Revenues	Total Accrual Value	Balance
40000105	10	USD	100.00-	100.00	600.00	0.00
40000105		USD	100.00-	100.00	600.00	0.00
40000114	10	USD	74,193.55-	0.00	110,000.00	74,193.55-
40000114		USD	74,193.55-	0.00	110,000.00	74,193.55-
40000139	10	USD	2,000.00-	2,000.00	500.00-	0.00
40000139		USD	2,000.00-	2,000.00	500.00-	0.00
40000142	10	USD	36,000.00-	36,000.00	47,000.00	0.00
40000142		USD	36,000.00-	36,000.00	47,000.00	0.00
40000144	10	USD	39,032.26-	39,032.26	60,000.00	0.00
40000144		USD	39,032.26-	39,032.26	60,000.00	0.00

Figure 9.10 Revenue Comparison Report

The bottom part of the report shows different balances for sales transactions that are relevant for revenue recognition. This information is displayed from the revenue recognition tables. One of the validations of these numbers is that the total of the "balance" column in the bottom part should match with the total balance displayed in the top part of the report.

The top part of the report shows the revenue recognition balance calculated from the revenue lines table (A), balance from billing documents from the reference line table (B), balance in FI from postings that aren't from sales documents (C), and the total balance based on all FI postings (D). One of the validations of these numbers is that the value of (A – B – C) should match with the value of D.

If these validations fail, then there can be data inconsistencies, and you may have to run adjustment and correction transactions.

9.5.5 Adjustments and Corrections

If you notice any discrepancies or errors in revenue recognition entries, then you'll have to use one of the adjustments and corrections transactions provided in the SAP system.

Revenue Recognition Inconsistency Check (VF47)

This is one of the most important and versatile correction transactions for revenue recognition functionality. As the partial selection screen of this transaction shows in Figure 9.11, this transaction provides a large number of selection options to identify and correct data inconsistencies.

Check Type

Only Check Current Documts	☐		
Check Reference Lines	☐	Docs From:	Incl. FI: ☐ Compr. ☐
Check Control Line Status	☑		
Check Total Amount	☐		
Read Revenue Lines inSD	☐		
Read Revenue Lines inFI	☐	incl. Collective Run No:	☐
		Incl. FI Index	☐ Pckt size

Displ.type

Messages: Document Level	☐
Only Docs with Error Messages	☐

Change Type

Change Control Lines	☐	Also for Currency Change SD/FI:	☐
Delete Control Lines	☐		
Create Reference Lines	☐		
Create Revenue Lines	☐	Posting Period:	

☑ Test Run Without Update

Figure 9.11 Revenue Recognition Inconsistency Check

Due to space constraints, we won't be able to discuss all of the available options of this transaction. However, following are some of the important points to note about this transaction:

- If Only Check Current Documents is selected, then only those revenue recognition lines are checked that have not been completed yet.
- If Check Reference Lines is selected, the program reconciles entries in the sales document flow with the entries in the revenue recognition tables.
- If Check Control Line Status is selected, the program validates control lines in the revenue recognition table with the sales document fields such as billing plan, billing block, and reason for rejection.
- If Change Control Lines or Delete Control Lines is selected, the program overwrites or deletes control lines from the revenue recognition tables.

- This transaction can identify the following types of revenue recognition errors:
  - Account determination errors
  - Inconsistencies between data in revenue recognition tables
  - Incorrect values and balances based on SD and FI data
  - Status problems in revenue recognition control lines
  - Currency problems
  - Database lock problems
  - Assignment problems

The next section describes the asynchronous update of revenue recognition entries.

Document Updates (VF42)

When information items, such as pricing, billing plan, settlement period, billing block, and amounts, in a sales document are changed, the corresponding entries in the revenue recognition tables should also be updated. By default, these entries aren't updated synchronously at the time when these changes are made. These entries are either updated automatically at the time of processing the revenue recognition list (Section 9.5.2, Processing Revenue List [VF44]), or they can be updated asynchronously using the SD document update transaction shown in Figure 9.12.

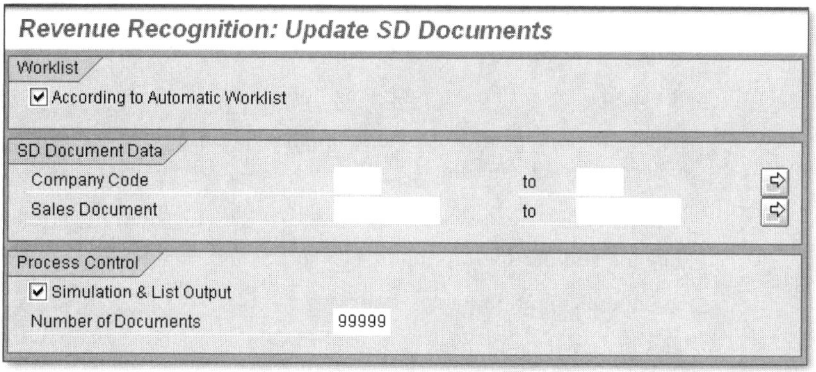

Revenue Recognition: Update SD Documents

Worklist

[x] According to Automatic Worklist

SD Document Data

Company Code ___ to ___

Sales Document ___ to ___

Process Control

[x] Simulation & List Output

Number of Documents 99999

Figure 9.12 Revenue Recognition – Update the SD Document

In this program, if the According to Automatic Worklist flag is selected, then it evaluates only those sales transactions for which revenue recognition control lines already exist. If the flag isn't selected, then all sales transactions based on the selection options are evaluated for any updates.

If this program hasn't been run, then any updates to revenue recognition control lines are carried out during the revenue processing list transaction (VF44). So to improve the performance of the revenue processing list, you may want to run this transaction periodically as a background job. The following section provides a single reference point for revenue recognition transactions.

9.5.6 List of Transactions

Table 9.7 lists all transactions discussed in this chapter.

Transaction	Usage
OVK5	Maintain material account assignment group
OVK8	Maintain customer account assignment group
VKOA	Maintain GL account determination
VOV7	Maintain sales document item categories
OVEP	Maintain revenue recognition parameters for item categories
VF44	Process revenue recognition list
VF46	Process revenue cancellation list
VA43	Display document flow for a contract
VA03	Display document flow for a sales order
VF03	Display document flow for a billing document
FB03	Display document flow using document relationship browser for an accounting document
VF45	Revenue report
VF48	Revenue comparison report
VF47	Revenue recognition inconsistency check
VF42	Sales document updates

Table 9.7 Revenue Recognition Transactions

Now, we'll discuss a few implementation considerations.

9.5.7 Implementation Considerations

Following are some important points that need to be considered regarding the revenue recognition functionality:

- When GL accounts are changed in revenue recognition customizing, it doesn't have any impact on sales documents for which the revenue recognition process has already started.
- Even though the revenue recognition functionality in the SAP system is fairly comprehensive, several aspects such as those listed next aren't supported or are only partially supported:
  - Revenue recognition doesn't support the New GL functionality to calculate and post different amounts in different ledgers.
  - Revenue recognition doesn't support a shortened fiscal year or processing down payments, intercompany billing, or sales taxes.
  - Revenue recognition doesn't support a statistical update to the Sales Information System (SIS).
  - Data migration from legacy systems for active revenue recognition documents, if possible, involves considerable technical complexity.
  - Retroactive activation of revenue recognition isn't supported.

If any of these aspects are important for your revenue recognition processes, you may have to implement workarounds to support your business requirements. In the next section, we'll delve into the technical details.

9.6 Technical Reference

This section provides a technical reference for the revenue recognition functionality. Considering the large number of technical objects available in the SAP system, this information should only be considered as a starting point for analysis.

9.6.1 SAP Notes

With the large number of SAP Notes available for any particular topic in the SAP system, it's impossible and somewhat counter-productive to list all available notes. The list of SAP Notes in Table 9.8 should be considered only a sample list.

SAP Note	Relevance
0000768561	Activate revenue recognition functionality
0000820417	Implementation guide for revenue recognition
0000678260	Functional constraints of revenue recognition functionality
0000769080	Report for checking whether revenue recognition is active
0001120297	Revenue recognition by acceptance date
0001125456	Revenue recognition by customer-specific event
0001000830	Revenue recognition by incoming invoice
0001025066	Revenue recognition by POD
0000777996	Account settings for revenue recognition process
0000532876	FAQ: Revenue recognition process
0000832338	Analysis tools for revenue recognition
0001131589	Filling the reference number in revenue recognition
0000940789	Activation of document summarization in revenue recognition
0000896404	User exits for the revenue recognition relevancy
0000789700	Analysis report for customizing in revenue recognition
0001256525	Important revenue recognition notes up to 09/2008
0000801065	Manual completion of sales documents (V_MACO)
0000781192	Update sales documents manually
0000891585	FASB 52: Transferring exchange rate date to FI

Table 9.8 Revenue Recognition – SAP Notes

Tip

There are an unusually large number of SAP Notes for the revenue recognition functionality. SAP periodically releases a collective note titled "Important Revenue Recognition Notes up to [a date]." Always look for the latest note to keep the revenue recognition functionality in your SAP system up to date.

In the next section, we'll look at authorization objects relevant for the revenue recognition functionality.

9.6.2 Authorizations

Revenue recognition functions primarily access information from sales and financial documents, so users should have access to relevant authorizations in those areas. Table 9.9 provides a sample list of authorization objects to be considered for transactions discussed in this chapter.

Object	Description
V_VBRR_BUK	Revenue Recognition: Authority Checks
F_BKPF_BUK	Accounting Document: Authorization for Company Codes
F_BKPF_KOA	Accounting Document: Authorization for Account Types
F_FAGL_LDR	General Ledger: Authorization for Ledger
F_SKA1_BUK	G/L Account: Authorization for Company Codes
V_KONH_VKO	Condition: Authorization for Sales Organizations
V_KONH_VKS	Condition: Authorization for Condition Types
V_VBAK_AAT	Sales Document: Authorization for Sales Document Types
V_VBAK_VKO	Sales Document: Authorization for Sales Areas
V_VBRK_FKA	Billing: Authorization for Billing Types
V_VBRK_VKO	Billing: Authorization for Sales Organizations
V_VBSK_STO	Billing: Authorization for Cancellation Collective Runs

Table 9.9 Authorization Objects – Revenue Recognition

The next section lists tables and structures in the SAP system.

9.6.3 Tables and Structures

Table 9.10 lists tables and structures relevant for revenue recognition processes. Additionally, you should also be familiar with tables and structures used for FI documents and SD documents.

Table	Relevance
VBFA	Document flow table
VBREVAC	Revenue recognition: Compression of FI revenue postings
VBREVC	Revenue recognition: Worklist of changed sales documents
VBREVE	Revenue recognition: Revenue lines
VBREVK	Revenue recognition: Control lines
VBREVR	Revenue recognition: Reference document lines

Table 9.10 Revenue Recognition Tables and Structures

Subsequent sections list the available enhancements and modifications.

9.7 Enhancements and Modifications

This section provides a list of the available BTEs, enhancements, BAdIs, and BAPIs that are relevant for revenue recognition processes.

9.7.1 Business Transaction Events (BTE)

Using BTEs, you can attach additional function modules and custom logic to the standard SAP system. Table 9.11 lists publish and subscribe (P/S) and process BTEs available for the revenue recognition functionality.

Type	BTE	Event/Process
P/S	00503101	Revenue realization: Copy conditions
P/S	00503102	Revenue realization: Start/end of selection period
P/S	00503103	Revenue realization: Determine selection period
P/S	00503104	Revenue realization: Billing <-> FI document
P/S	00503105	Revenue realization: Forecast revenue lines
P/S	00503106	Revenue realization: Revenue amount adjustment
P/S	00503107	Revenue realization: Det. acct non-billed receiv.
P/S	00503108	Revenue realization: Display variants

Table 9.11 Revenue Recognition BTE

Type	BTE	Event/Process
P/S	00503109	Revenue realization: Enter split criterion
P/S	00503110	Revenue realization: Change accounting data
P/S	00503111	Revenue realization: Change document date/type
P/S	00503113	Revenue realization: Status change
P/S	00503114	Revenue realization: Addnl value/quantity fields
P/S	00503115	Revenue realization: Set exchange rate date
P/S	00503116	Revenue realization: Influence summarization
Process	00503101	Deactivate module: `SD_REV_REC_SALES`
Process	00503102	Deactivate module: `SD_REV_REC_EVENT`
Process	00503103	Deactivate module: `SD_REV_REC_BILLING`
Process	00503121	SD-SLS: Get account assignment from CRM
Process	00503122	SD-SLS: Get account assignment from IAOM
Process	00503140	SD-SRV: Get account assignment from IAOM

Table 9.11 Revenue Recognition BTE (Cont.)

Following are examples of BTE implementations for revenue recognition processes.

- **Event 503111:** This event is implemented to influence the posting date and document type used in revenue recognition.
  - In the standard SAP system document type, "RV" with internal number assignment is used for revenue recognition. Using this BTE, you can influence the document type used for revenue recognition.
- **Event 503115:** This event is implemented to influence the exchange rate used in revenue recognition.
  - Its implementation ensures compliance with the statutory requirement that the same exchange rate is used over the entire accrual period for revenue recognition transactions involving multiple currencies.
  - It also ensures a zero balance in the deferred revenue and unbilled receivables accounts at the end of the accrual period.
  - SAP Notes 0000891585 and 0000680937 provide more information.

- **Event 503116:** This event is implemented to influence the summarization of revenue recongition entries on the balance sheet accounts.
  - In the standard SAP system, revenue recognition entries are posted to balance sheet accounts with reference to document items of the corresponding sales documents. This can create a very large volume of entries in balance sheet accounts.
  - Using this BTE, you can post summarized revenue recognition entries to balance sheet accounts.
  - SAP Notes 0000940784 and 0000036353 provide more information on implementation of this logic.

The configuration menu path to implement these BTEs is SAP IMG • SALES AND DISTRIBUTION • SYSTEM MODIFICATIONS • BUSINESS TRANSACTION EVENTS.

The next section discusses available BAdIs.

9.7.2 Business Add-Ins (BAdIs)

As discussed in Section 9.4.4, Service-Related Revenue Recognition by Customer-Specific Event, BAdI implementation is necessary if you intend to use service-related revenue recognition by customer-specific events. The following BAdIs are available for this implementation:

- `BADI_SD_REV_REC_PODEV`
  - This BAdI is used to implement customer-specific events for service-related revenue recognition.
  - This BAdI provides one method that is used to maintain customer-specific events.
- `BADI_SD_REV_REC_PODEV_DISP`
  - Implementation of this BAdI enables revenue recognition Transactions VF43 and VF44 to display customer specific event documents.
  - This BAdI provides one method that is used to display customer-specific event documents.

9.8 Summary

In this chapter, we focused on the revenue recognition functionality available in the SAP system. Using standard revenue recognition, you can post revenues at the time of customer invoicing to accurate revenue accounts or deferred revenue accounts. Subsequently, you can post realized revenues manually, or you can obtain special release from SAP to enable advanced revenue recognition functionality. Considering the technical complexities involved in enabling and maintaining revenue recognition functionality, it's highly recommended to carry out this process thorough the evaluation of business requirements and their correlation with the available SAP functionality.

In the next chapter, we'll focus on month-end processing tasks in accounts receivable.

This chapter focuses on periodic processing activities in the Accounts Receivable component. Most of the periodic processing activities occur during month-end closing. Apart from these common month-end activities, you'll also find in this chapter details about year-end activities. Additionally, we'll discuss the functionality to print common customer documents and account statements. Depending on the volume of such printing requirements, these activities could be part of month-end processing or even weekly processing.

10 Periodic Processing

In this chapter, we'll look at the available periodic processing functionalities such as month-end processing and year-end processing activities. One classification of these processes can be whether they are mandatory or optional, whereas another classification of these processes can be a business requirement or a technical requirement. For example, closing a month for posting is a mandatory business requirement as well as a mandatory technical requirement of the SAP system, whereas interest calculation or balance confirmation processes are technically optional. You use and implement those only if they are relevant for your business.

In this chapter, you'll find processes listed under month-end processing and year-end processing sections. Even though some of these processes are tied to specific periodicity, you can use other processes at any time. For example, the month-end closing has to be carried out monthly, and the balance carry forward has to be carried out annually. However, depending on frequency and volume of documents and statements, you can choose to carry out correspondence printing as an ad hoc activity, monthly activity, or weekly activity.

Let's start with the month-end processing activities first.

10.1 Month-End Processing

Depending on the industry and the size of an organization, month-end closing can be a simple checklist maintained on a spreadsheet, or it may require finely orchestrated and synchronized coordination between different departments and different locations. In this chapter, we'll focus only on month-end activities from the AR perspective. However, several transactions and functionalities discussed in this chapter are also applicable in other areas of financial accounting such as AP or general ledger accounting.

Note

Many transactions and programs discussed in other chapters in this book are also extremely relevant for month-end closing. For example, the dunning process (Chapter 6, Dunning), recurring entries and internal clearing transactions (Chapter 2, Accounts Receivable Transactions), release blocked billing documents (Chapter 3), and incoming payment reconciliation (Chapter 5) are all important parts of month end activities.

Let's first start with outgoing payments.

10.1.1 Outgoing Payments

A customer account may receive credit for any number of reasons such as product returns, rebates or discounts, reimbursements, retroactive settlements, or dispute resolutions. Most commonly, payments received from customers are adjusted for such credits to reduce processing and reconciliation of additional documents and payments. We discussed the functionality of adjusting credit document at the time of cash application in Chapter 5.

However, you may have to issue payments to customers in certain business situations. For example, consider scenarios when a customer closes an account with a utility company, or a customer doesn't want to adjust a credit amount due to procedural or legal reasons.

Tip

In most companies, the AP group is responsible for issuing all payments, including payments to customers. The outgoing payments functionality is introduced here mainly to cover all areas of this topic.

To enter a payment document for a customer, select SAP MENU • ACCOUNTING • FINANCIAL ACCOUNTING • ACCOUNTS RECEIVABLE • DOCUMENT ENTRY • OTHER • OUTGOING PAYMENTS (Transaction F-31).

Figure 10.1 shows the first screen for entering outgoing payments. As you can see, the first screen for entering outgoing payments for a customer is similar to the screen for processing incoming payments from customers discussed in Chapter 5, Incoming Payments. In the highlighted area, the ACCOUNT TYPE value of "D" indicates that this payment is for the customer account entered in the ACCOUNT field. The rest of the process for selection of open documents and processing any payment differences is also similar to the processing of incoming payments. Subsequently, AP personnel can issue a check against this document.

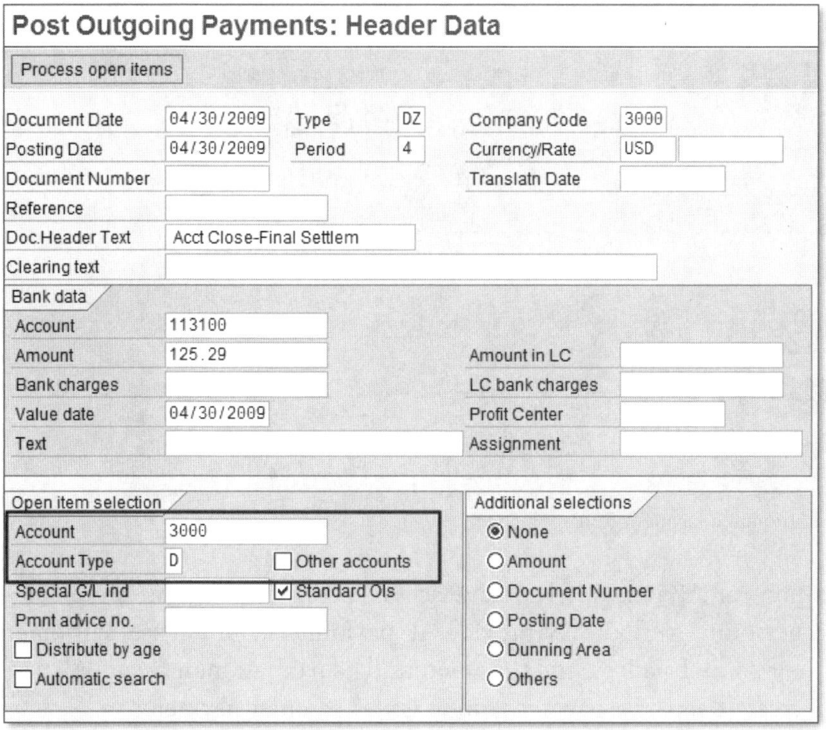

Post Outgoing Payments: Header Data

Process open items

Document Date	04/30/2009	Type	DZ	Company Code	3000
Posting Date	04/30/2009	Period	4	Currency/Rate	USD
Document Number				Translatn Date	
Reference					
Doc.Header Text	Acct Close-Final Settlem				
Clearing text					

Bank data

Account	113100		
Amount	125.29	Amount in LC	
Bank charges		LC bank charges	
Value date	04/30/2009	Profit Center	
Text		Assignment	

Open item selection

Account	3000	
Account Type	D	☐ Other accounts
Special G/L ind		☑ Standard OIs
Pmnt advice no.		

☐ Distribute by age
☐ Automatic search

Additional selections

◉ None
○ Amount
○ Document Number
○ Posting Date
○ Dunning Area
○ Others

Figure 10.1 Post Outgoing Payments

Another option is to use the automatic payment program for processing outgoing payments for customers.

Automatic Payment Program

You access automatic payment program through SAP MENU • ACCOUNTING • FINANCIAL ACCOUNTING • ACCOUNTS PAYABLE • PERIODIC PROCESSING • PAYMENTS (Transaction F110). This is the main program used by the AP group for processing outgoing payments to vendors. However, as Figure 10.2 shows, the versatility of this program allows you to use it for issuing payments to customer accounts as well.

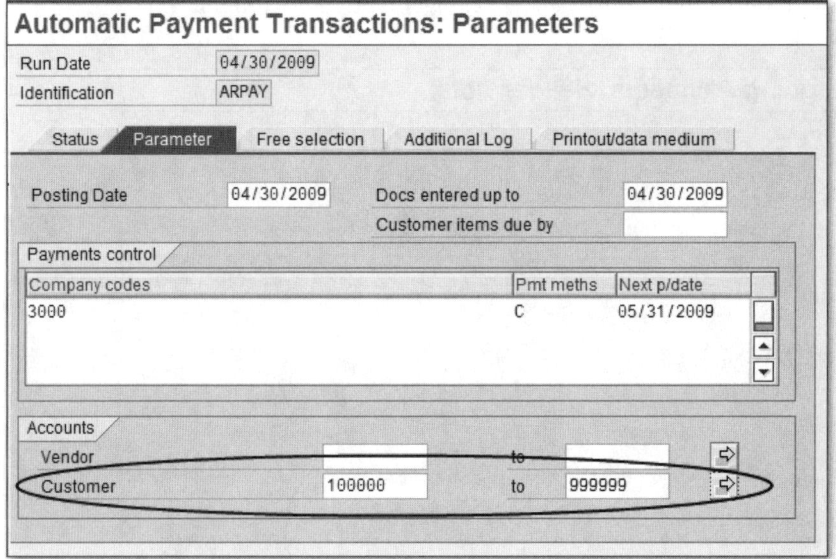

Figure 10.2 Automatic Payment Run

It's uncommon for AP personnel to have access to this transaction. More commonly, AR personnel periodically provide AP personnel with a list of customer accounts, their credit balances, and the amount to be paid. At month-end, AP personnel will create a separate payment run to issue customer payments.

In the next section, we'll discuss automatic clearing program.

10.1.2 Automatic Clearing

An automatic clearing program is available for GL accounts, customer accounts, and vendor accounts. It uses a preconfigured criterion to group together open items per account. If the net balance of a group of items is zero or falls within specified tolerances, the program assigns clearing document number(s) to all items and marks them as cleared. This process can be used to clear as many open items on customer accounts as possible. In turn, this improves the efficiency of other processes such as cash application, account reconciliation, and customer statement generation.

Let's see how to configure and process clearing rules and transactions.

Automatic Clearing Rules

You'll find this configuration activity under ACCOUNTS RECEIVABLE IMG • BUSINESS TRANSACTIONS • OPEN ITEM CLEARING • PREPARE AUTOMATIC CLEARING. Figure 10.3 shows the configuration activity to specify automatic clearing rules.

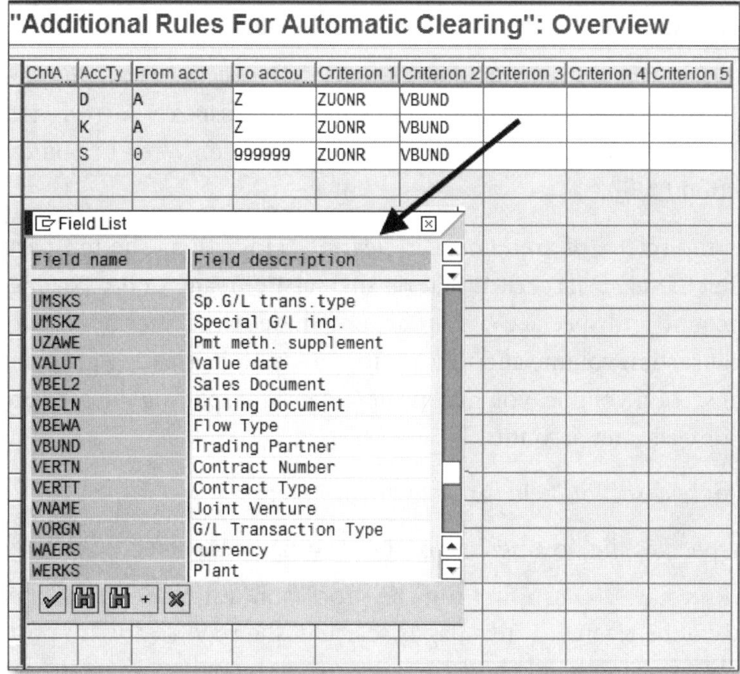

Figure 10.3 Automatic Clearing Rules

The following points are noteworthy while configuring these rules.

- If CHART OF ACCOUNTS is not specified, the rules are valid across all charts of accounts, and thus for all company codes.
- It's possible to specify different clearing rules for different customer accounts by using a range of FROM ACCOUNT and TO ACCOUNT values.

- You can specify up to five CRITERIA to be used for grouping documents, where each criterion refers to a document field. In the preceding example, documents are grouped based on ZUONR (Assignment) and VBUND (trading partner).

Tip

The configuration activity provides you with a choice of more than 300 fields that can be used as a document grouping criterion! However, considering the procedural measures such as training and support activities, it's advisable to structure clearing rules around as few fields as possible.

Let's now look at the automatic clearing process details.

Automatic Clearing Process

You'll find automatic clearing transaction under SAP MENU • ACCOUNTING • FINANCIAL ACCOUNTING • ACCOUNTS RECEIVABLE • PERIODIC PROCESSING • AUTOMATIC CLEARING • WITHOUT CLEARING CURRENCY (Transaction F.13) or WITH CLEARING CURRENCY (Transaction F13E).

Figure 10.4 shows the screen of an automatic clearing transaction. The top part of the screen carries GENERAL SELECTION criteria such as Company Code, Posting Date, Customer Account, and Special G/L Transaction. These selection criteria have direct impact on transaction volume and thus performance of the clearing process. For a very large transaction volume, you may want to consider splitting the process by company code or customer accounts.

The POSTING PARAMETERS section fields are explained here:

- CLEARING DATE specifies the posting date of the clearing documents.
- Using the TEST RUN flag, you can first run the process in test mode to see the documents that will be cleared. If this flag is selected, the process doesn't post any documents but carries out all checks.
- INCLUDE TOLERANCES is a very important indicator for this process.
  - If it's selected, the clearing process takes into account tolerance specifications assigned to customer accounts and to the employees.
  - If it isn't selected, the clearing process doesn't take into account any tolerances. So debits and credits have to match each other exactly.

Automatic Clearing

General selections

Company code	3000	to		⇨
Fiscal year	2009	to		⇨
Assignment		to		⇨
Document number		to		⇨
Posting date		to		⇨

☑ Select customers

☐ Special G/L transactions

Special G/L Indicator-Custom		to		⇨
Customer accounts	3000	to		⇨

Posting parameters

Clearing date 05/02/2009 Period 5

☐ Include tolerances

☑ Test run

Minimum number of line items

Output control

☑ Documents that can be cleared

☑ Documents that cannot be clrd

☑ Error Messages

Figure 10.4 Automatic Clearing

Note

Refer to Chapter 5, Incoming Payments, for more details on configuration and the use of tolerance groups.

Using Output Controls, you can print the following lists:

- Documents that can be cleared
- Documents that can't be cleared
- An error log, which is more useful when printed with the Documents That Can't Be Cleared list

This program can be useful in scenarios where customer accounts contain large numbers of debit and credit transactions with a common attribute, such as a contract number or an agreement number. Additionally, this program can be useful at new system implementations where the transaction history from other legacy systems is transferred into SAP. For example, you can transfer invoice, payment, and adjustment documents into the SAP system with a common reference number. Subsequently, you can use the clearing program to clear the documents based on that reference number.

The process discussed so far assumes that documents being grouped and cleared are posted in the same currency. If you want to run the clearing process on documents posted in different currencies, you should use the other transaction mentioned at the beginning of this section: Automatic Clearing with Clearing Currency (Transaction F13E). In this transaction, you specify the clearing currency that is used to group and clear the documents. The process automatically posts any applicable exchange loss/gain entries in the clearing documents.

Before we move on to the next topic, let's discuss how you can use the sort key assigned to the customer master data to improve the effectiveness of a clearing process.

Sort Key

In Chapter 1, Customer Master Data, we briefly discussed the SORT KEY field. This field is maintained in the customer master data in COMPANY CODE DATA VIEW • ACCOUNT MANAGEMENT TAB • ACCOUNTING INFORMATION section.

A sort key determines the value updated into the allocation field of accounting documents. As we discussed at the beginning of this section, you can use an allocation field in the definition of automatic clearing rules.

Tip

A sort key can be configured to copy whole or parts of other field values into the allocation field. So, you can have the same clearing rule based on the allocation field assigned to all customer accounts but differentiate the criteria used for document clearing by using carefully designed sort keys.

Another common month-end activity is accrual processing.

10.1.3 Accrual Processing

You'll find several different ways to process month-end accruals in the SAP system. Depending on the volume and the complexity of accrual entries, you can decide to use any or all of the following options for processing accruals:

- Use the condition technique in sales and billing documents to post accruals. Accounting entries for these types of accruals are posted during the billing process.
- Use AR transactions to post accrual documents with a unique criteria, such as a different document type. Subsequently, use an individual reversal or mass reversal program to reverse the accruals.
- Use one recurring entry to post accruals at regular intervals such as monthly or quarterly; and use another recurring entry to post accrual reversals at the same frequency.
- Use an accrual/deferral transaction to post accrual documents with a future reversal date. Subsequently, use an accrual reversal program to reverse all applicable accruals
- Configure and use the accrual engine to process accruals. Implementation and use of the accrual engine requires considerably more effort compared to the previous options.

We discussed the first option in the previous list of using the condition technique in Chapter 3. We discussed the following two options in Chapter 2, Accounts Receivable Transactions. In this section, we'll focus on the remaining two options, starting with the accrual/deferral transactions.

Entry of Accrual Documents

The accrual processing transactions are part of the General Ledger component in the SAP system. For entering accrual documents, you access SAP MENU • ACCOUNTING • FINANCIAL ACCOUNTING • GENERAL LEDGER • PERIODIC PROCESSING • CLOSING • VALUATE • ENTER ACCRUAL/DEFERRAL DOCUMENT (Transaction FBS1).

Figure 10.5 shows the first screen of an accrual deferral document entry. As you may notice, the entry interface is almost the same as an AR document entry using the general interface. We discussed this interface in Chapter 2, Accounts Receivable Transactions. The top part of the screen consists of the document header where you enter fields such as DOCUMENT DATE, POSTING DATE, COMPANY CODE, CURRENCY, and other REFERENCE information.

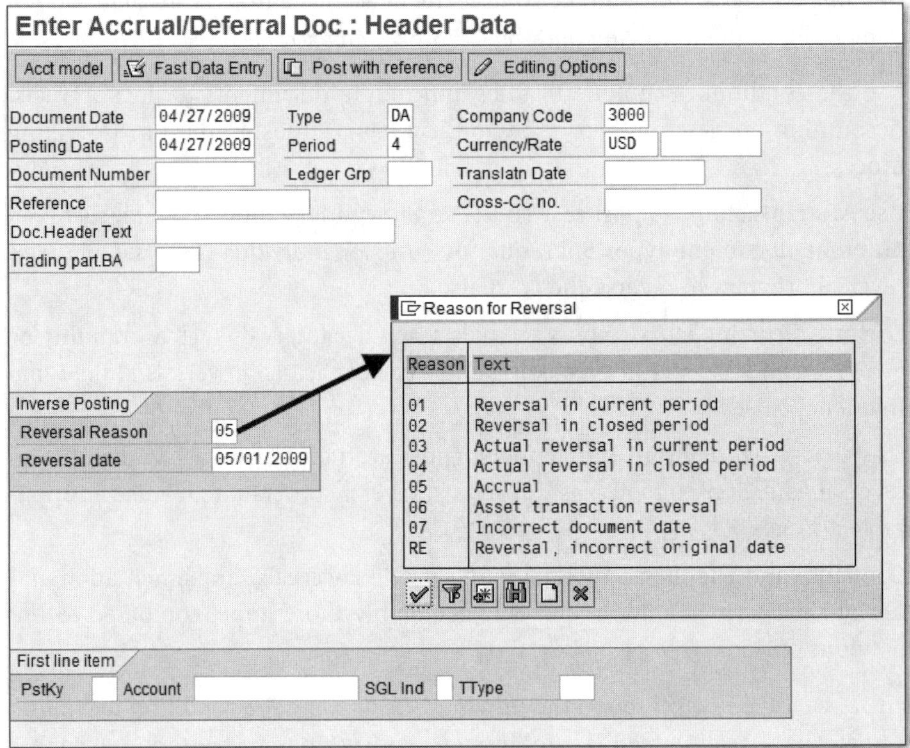

Figure 10.5 Enter Accrual/Deferral Documents

The middle part of the screen contains information relevant for accrual reversal. In this section, you specify REVERSAL REASON and the REVERSAL DATE for reversal document posting. You can set up different reason codes for different types of accruals because reason codes are freely configurable codes. You configure these codes using SAP IMG • FINANCIAL ACCOUNTING • ACCOUNTS RECEIVABLE AND ACCOUNTS PAYABLE • BUSINESS TRANSACTIONS • ADJUSTMENT POSTINGS/REVERSAL • DEFINE REASONS FOR REVERSAL.

On the bottom portion of the screen, you enter the POSTING KEY and an ACCOUNT for the first accrual document line item. Entering the remaining information and other document line items is similar to the entry of AR documents using the general interface.

Using this transaction, you can enter accrual entries at any time during the month while specifying the exact date in the future when the entry should be reversed. This functionality can be useful for accrual reversals that don't follow a set pattern or that are far out in the future. As part of month-end processing, you can run the accrual reversal program to make reverse postings.

Reversal of Accrual Documents

The accrual reversal program is used to post reversals of the documents posted using the accrual/deferral entry discussed in the previous section. You access the reversal program using SAP MENU • ACCOUNTING • FINANCIAL ACCOUNTING • GENERAL LEDGER • PERIODIC PROCESSING • CLOSING • VALUATE • REVERSE ACCRUAL/ DEFERRAL DOCUMENT (Transaction F.81).

Figure 10.6 shows the screen of the accrual reversal transaction.

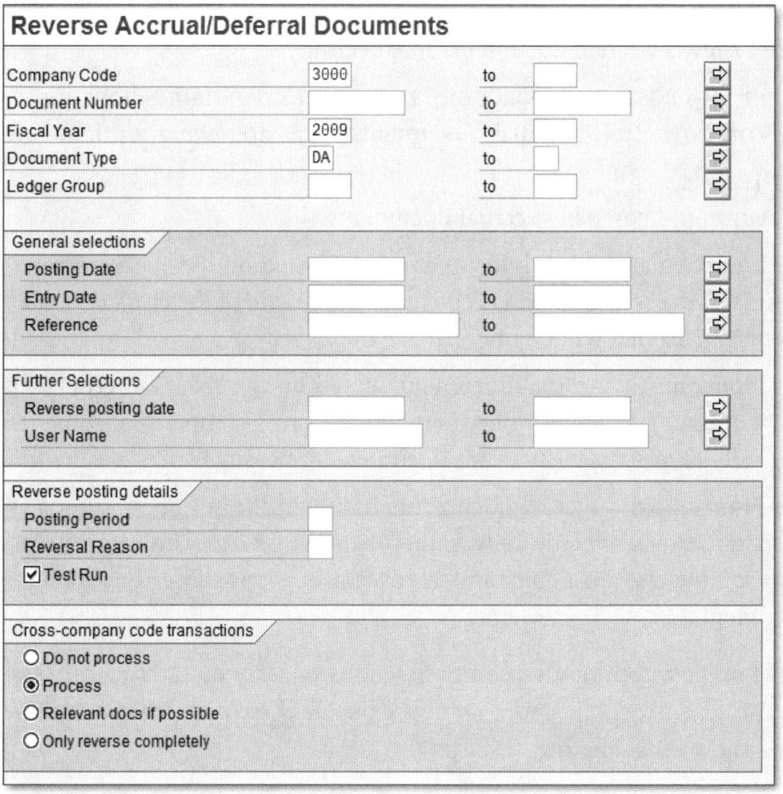

Reverse Accrual/Deferral Documents

Company Code	3000	to	
Document Number		to	
Fiscal Year	2009	to	
Document Type	DA	to	
Ledger Group		to	

General selections

Posting Date		to	
Entry Date		to	
Reference		to	

Further Selections

Reverse posting date		to	
User Name		to	

Reverse posting details

Posting Period

Reversal Reason

☑ Test Run

Cross-company code transactions

○ Do not process

◉ Process

○ Relevant docs if possible

○ Only reverse completely

Figure 10.6 Reverse Accrual Postings

The following are the relevant points for this transaction:

- You can choose accrual documents that are to be reversed based on several criteria such as COMPANY CODE, DOCUMENT TYPE, POSTING DATE, REFERENCE, and USER NAME.

> **Tip**
>
> The POSTING DATE field on this screen is a selection criteria that refers to the posting date entered in the original accrual document and not to the posting date on which accrual reversals will be posted. The posting date on accrual reversal documents is the REVERSE POSTING DATE.

- You can even select accrual documents based on a REVERSAL DATE, although it's usually sufficient and more efficient to select accrual documents based on the POSTING PERIOD and REVERSAL REASON.
- The TEST RUN option enables you to review all accrual reversals before posting them. Based on the results of a test run, you can adjust selection criteria to select more or fewer accrual documents for reversal.
- The indicator for CROSS-COMPANY CODE TRANSACTIONS determines how to process cross-company code accrual documents. The following options are available:
  - Don't reverse intercompany accrual documents.
  - Reverse intercompany accrual documents only based on the specified selection criteria. If the selection criteria includes only some of the cross-company documents, an accrual will be only partially reversed.
  - Reverse intercompany accrual documents based on the selection criteria. If the selection criteria includes only some of the cross-company documents, automatically reverse other relevant documents if possible.
  - Reverse intercompany accrual documents based on the selection criteria. If the selection criteria include only some of the cross-company documents, carry out complete reversal. If complete reversal is not possible, don't reverse any documents.

This is one of the most commonly used transactions to carry out accrual processing. However, for considerably more complex business requirements, you may consider using the accrual engine.

Accrual Engine

The Accrual Engine provides an automated and efficient means of processing complex accruals, such as a large number of active customer contracts involving different types of revenue and cost components that you have to accrue over different timeframes.

The SAP Accrual Engine can be set up to suit your requirements for accrual types, accrual components, accounting principles under which you carry out accruals, and other relevant parameters. You configure relevant settings under the configuration area SAP IMG • FINANCIAL ACCOUNTING • FINANCIAL ACCOUNTING GLOBAL SETTINGS • ACCRUAL ENGINE. We won't go into the details of all configuration activities required to set up an Accrual Engine. However, the following is a list of the main activities:

- Define ACCRUAL TYPES for possible accrual components that correspond to different types of costs and revenues such as maintenance contract revenue or marketing cost sharing.
- Configure ACCRUAL OBJECTS and ACCRUAL OBJECT CATEGORIES. For example, a maintenance contract is a type of ACCRUAL OBJECT for ACCRUAL OBJECT CATEGORY "contracts."
- Define the ACCRUAL METHOD and corresponding function modules. Accrual methods determine the calculation of accrual values.
- Configure other related settings for accrual processing, such as assignment of document type, GL accounts, and number range.

After all configuration activities are completed, you create and maintain accrual objects. Figure 10.7 shows an example of a one-year customer contract consisting of one revenue component and one expense component.

This example consists of a contract for which the revenue component is $5,000 per month and the cost component is $500 per month. After this accrual object is created, the Accrual Engine can accurately calculate and post summarized accrual entries each month. To create accrual objects, you select SAP MENU • ACCOUNTING • FINANCIAL ACCOUNTING • GENERAL LEDGER • PERIODIC PROCESSING • MANUAL ACCRUALS • CREATE ACCRUAL OBJECTS (Transaction ACACTREE01).

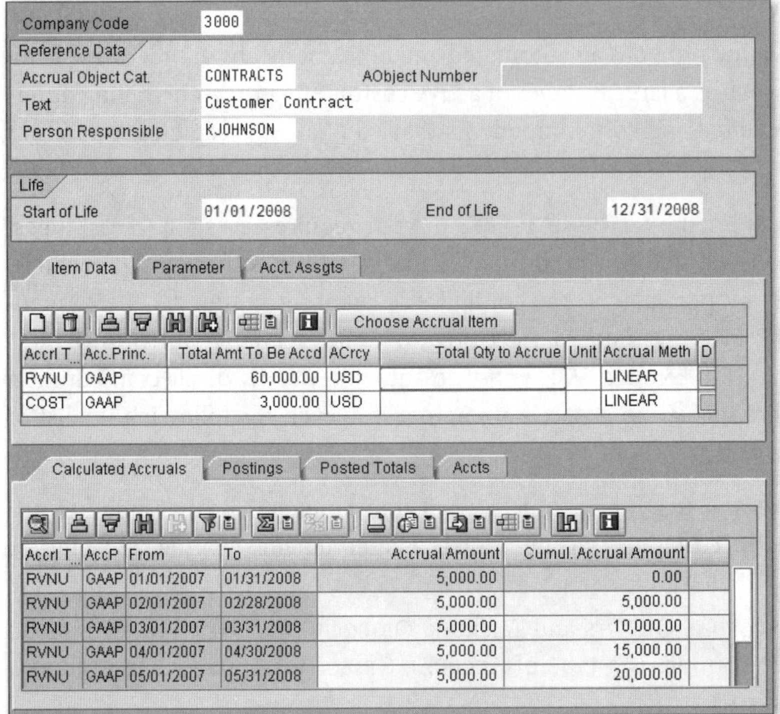

Figure 10.7 Create Accrual Object

As is evident from Figure 10.7, the Accrual Engine provides visibility into different components of an accrual. Not only that, if the original contract undergoes any change (e.g., early termination, addition of new services), you can update corresponding accrual objects, and the Accrual Engine will automatically carry out necessary corrections during the subsequent accrual run.

Tip

The Accrual Engine can be particularly important in AR for the accruals based on customer service contracts. Obviously, the main purpose of making the accrual process more efficient is defeated if you have to manually create each contract as an accrual object. So the SAP system provides a template program, ACAC_DATA_TRANSFER_EXAMPLE, that can be used to transfer accrual data from other application components.

Considering the extra effort required in implementing and supporting the Accrual Engine functionality, it's an advisable approach only if the business requirements involve a very large volume of complex accruals.

Let's now look at another month-end activity of revaluation of foreign currency receivables.

10.1.4 Foreign Currency Revaluation

Currency revaluation is an important month-end closing activity to translate foreign currency balances and open items into the functional currency of a company code. This ensures that all of the underlying data used for preparing financial statements is in the same currency. It's unlikely that the AR group will carry out currency revaluation in isolation. More commonly, revaluation of AR will be synchronized and even carried out by GL accounting group. It's included in this chapter to provide an understanding of how this process uses AR data.

The transaction to start foreign currency revaluation is under SAP MENU • ACCOUNTING • FINANCIAL ACCOUNTING • GENERAL LEDGER • PERIODIC PROCESSING • CLOSING • VALUATE • FOREIGN CURRENCY VALUATION. Transaction F.05 is for the classic general ledger, whereas FAGL_FC_VAL is for the new general ledger.

Figure 10.8 shows part of the currency revaluation transaction where you specify customer related parameters. You must select the VALUATE CUSTOMER OPEN ITEMS indicator to ensure that receivables in foreign currency are included in the currency revaluation. For a very large volume of open items, you can further limit the selection for a revaluation run based on criteria such as customers, reconciliation accounts, and currencies.

The following steps describe the process of revaluation of customer open items. The example is for customer invoices, but the process is similar for any type of customer document:

1. All customer invoices create postings on customer accounts, customer reconciliation accounts, and revenue accounts.
2. The currency revaluation process posts adjustment entries for all open invoices in a foreign currency, based on the then applicable exchange rate. These adjustment entries post any change in exchange rate valuation to
   - A balance sheet adjustment account, to adjust the reconciliation account
   - An exchange rate differences account, to adjust the revenue account

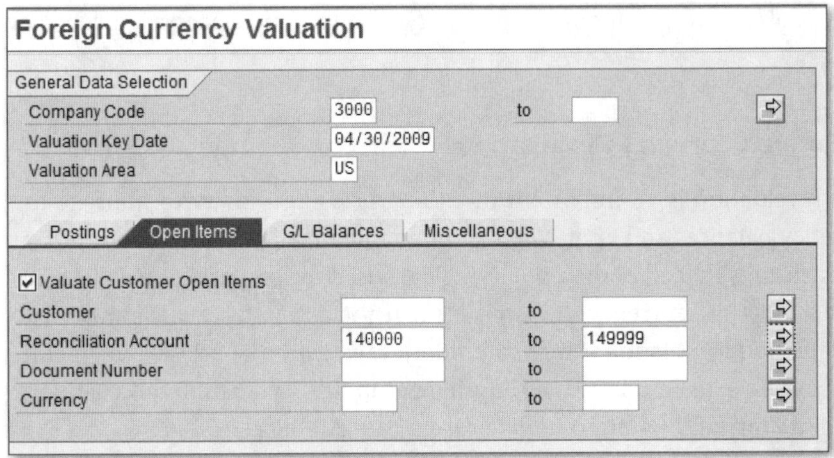

Figure 10.8 Foreign Currency Revaluation

3. It's common to run the currency revaluation process so that it will post a reversal of these adjustment entries on the first day of the next posting period. This approach ensures that these adjustment entries, which essentially correspond to unrealized gains or losses for open items, are reversed, and the items are in the same state as before.
   - Alternatively, you can choose not to reverse these adjustment entries. In which case, all open items maintain revaluated loss/gain amounts.
4. What happens when invoices are cleared by incoming customer payments, depends on whether adjustment entries from the revaluation run were reversed.
   - If the entries were reversed, then full exchange gain/loss is posted to the realized gain/loss accounts.
   - If the entries were not reversed, then only the net exchange gain/loss is posted to realized gain/loss accounts. This net value takes into account any gain/loss posted during previous revaluation runs.

The configuration for currency revaluation accounts is carried out using SAP IMG • Financial Accounting • General Ledger Accounting • Periodic Processing • Valuate • Foreign Currency Valuation • Prepare Automatic Postings For Foreign Currency Valuation (Transaction OBA1) • Exchange Rate Diff: Open Items/GL Acct (KDF).

Chart of Accounts	CAUS	Chart of accounts - United States
G/L Account	140000	
Currency		
Currency type		

Exchange rate difference realized

Loss	230000
Gain	280000

Valuation

Val.loss 1	230100
Val.gain 1	280100
Bal.sheet adj.1	140099

Figure 10.9 GL Accounts for Currency Revaluation

Figure 10.9 shows an example configuration screen for these GL accounts. You can specify currency revaluation accounts for a combination of CHART OF ACCOUNTS, RECONCILIATION ACCOUNT, CURRENCY, and CURRENCY TYPE.

Tip

You can use the Currency field to separate valuation differences arising out of high-inflation currencies from the differences arising out of other currencies.

For each combination, you configure the following GL accounts:

- Relevant for the currency revaluation process:
  - VAL. LOSS1 to which any unrealized losses are posted
  - VAL. GAIN1 to which any unrealized gains are posted
  - BAL. SHEET ADJ.1 to which the offsetting entries for the preceding two accounts are posted
- Relevant when open items are cleared:
  - REALIZED LOSS to which realized losses are posted
  - REALIZED GAIN to which realized gains are posted

You can use the same GL account to post gains and losses. However, you should at least use separate GL accounts to post realized gains/losses, unrealized gains/losses, and balance sheet adjustments.

In the following section, we'll discuss the month-end activity to open or close posting periods.

10.1.5 Open/Close Posting Periods

In the SAP system, opening and closing posting periods is controlled by a posting period variant assigned to each company code. A posting period variant provides you with an added level of abstraction to control period opening/closing process. You configure and assign the posting period variant in the configuration area SAP IMG • FINANCIAL ACCOUNTING • FINANCIAL ACCOUNTING GLOBAL SETTINGS • LEDGERS • FISCAL YEAR AND POSTING PERIODS • POSTING PERIODS.

Posting Periods: Specify Time Intervals

Var.	A	From acct	To account	From per.1	Year	To period	Year	From per.2	Year	To period	Year	AuGr
3000	+			1	2007	12	2009	13	2009	16	2009	
3000	A		ZZZZZZZZZZ	1	2007	12	2009	13	2009	16	2009	
3000	D		ZZZZZZZZZZ	1	2008	12	2009	13	2009	16	2009	
3000	K		ZZZZZZZZZZ	1	2008	12	2009	13	2009	16	2009	
3000	S		ZZZZZZZZZZ	1	2008	12	2009	13	2009	16	2009	

Figure 10.10 Open and Close Posting Periods

Figure 10.10 shows the transaction used to open and close posting periods. You access this transaction using SAP MENU • ACCOUNTING • FINANCIAL ACCOUNTING • GENERAL LEDGER • ENVIRONMENT • CURRENT SETTINGS • OPEN AND CLOSE POSTING PERIODS. Following are the relevant points to consider about this process:

- You can open and close posting periods across multiple companies by assigning the same POSTING PERIOD VARIANT to each company code.
- The ACCOUNT TYPE field lets you open and close posting periods for different activities such as GL, AR, AP, or asset accounting.
  - Account type "D" specifies open/close periods for AR.
  - Account type "+" is a required entry, and it specifies open/close periods for all other types of accounts for which a separate entry isn't maintained.
- The ACCOUNT range specifies the accounts for which period open/close specification is applicable.

  - The accounts always refer to the GL accounts. So for account type "D," the account range specifies reconciliation account numbers, not customer account numbers.

- You specify two ranges of posting periods — PERIOD 1 AND PERIOD 2 —that can independently control the open periods. Any posting period that isn't included in either of these period ranges is closed for any new postings.
- AUTHORIZATION GROUP allows you to limit users to post to only periods specified in the PERIOD 1 range.

Tip

Using authorization group, you can restrict open periods specified in period 1 for general posting, while using period 2 to keep additional periods open only to a selected group of users for year-end closing or audit purpose.

In the next section, we'll discuss the interest calculation process. Even though not commonly used in all of the companies, this month-end activity is complex enough to warrant a separate section.

10.2 Interest Calculation

The interest calculation functionality enables you to calculate interest or penalties for overdue payments. This functionality can be especially useful in the banking and financial industries, where charging interest or penalties on receivable balances is a common practice. Even though we'll focus only on interest receivable calculations, the process described in this section is also applicable for interest payable calculations. The SAP system supports the following two types of interest calculations:

- Interest calculations on items — all items or only arrears
- Interest calculations on net balances

Regardless of the type of interest calculation, the configuration and use of interest calculation consists of the following activities:

1. **Configure interest indicators**
   Configure parameters for item selection or period determination, calculation process, subsequent processing, output control, and interest posting.

2. **Configure interest rates and interest terms**
   Configure interest rate calculations based on criteria such as balance and reference interest rates.
3. **Configure interest posting and printing**
   Configure parameters for interest posting and printing interest forms.
4. **Maintain interest indicators**
   Maintain interest indicators and other information in customer master data.
5. **Process interest calculation**
   Run the transactions to carry out interest calculation, posting, and printing.

Let's look at some of these activities in more detail.

10.2.1 Interest Indicators

The interest indicator in the SAP system is a key that determines interest calculation parameters. You configure interest indicators in the configuration area SAP IMG • FINANCIAL ACCOUNTING • ACCOUNTS RECEIVABLE AND ACCOUNTS PAYABLE • BUSINESS TRANSACTIONS • INTEREST CALCULATION • INTEREST CALCULATION GLOBAL SETTINGS.

> **Note**
>
> Every interest indicator is assigned an interest calculation type that specifies whether the interest indicator is for interest calculation on account items or on account balances.

In this configuration area, you configure interest indicators for arrears, for account items, and for account balances. The difference between interest indicators for arrears and for items is that interest indicators for items don't consider items that are already cleared.

Figure 10.11 shows an example of interest indicator configuration for account items. Following are the details of relevant parameters:

- Using ITEM SELECTION parameters, you can specify whether any already cleared items are selected for interest calculation. By selecting ONLY ITEMS CLEARED WITH PAYMENT, you can exclude account items cleared with internal account adjustments.

Change View "Prepare Item Interest Calculation": Details

Interest ind. P1

Item Selection

- [x] Open Items
- ( ) All Cleared Items
- (•) Only Items Cleared with Payment
- ( ) No Cleared Items

Interest Determination

- [ ] Always Calculate Int. from Net Dte

Ref. Date 1

Calendar type G

Transfer days 2

Tolerance days 1

Factory Calendar ID

- [ ] Calculate interest on items paid before due date
- [x] Only calculate interest on debit items

Interest Postprocessing

Amount limit

- [ ] No interest payment

Output Control

- [x] Print Form

Number range 21

Posting

- [x] Post interest

Posting Conditions

Terms of Payment

Tax Code 00

- [ ] Posting with Invoice Ref.

Transfer Content

Transfer Content

Figure 10.11 Interest Indicator Configuration

- During an interest run, interest for an item is calculated from the last interest run date, unless you have selected Always Calculate Interest from Net Date indicator.
- Using Transfer Days, you can specify the time it takes to process incoming payments, thereby avoiding interest calculation for the days when payment was received but was not yet processed. Similarly, by using Tolerance Days, you can specify the grace period before interest calculation begins.

- If selected, the Calculate Interest on Items Paid Before Due Dates indicator calculates credit interest for items paid prior to their due dates.
- If selected, Only Calculate Interest on Debit Items doesn't calculate the interest on credit items.
- Using postprocessing parameters, you can specify that interest settlement should be generated only if it's greater than the specified Amount, or should not be generated if it results in an interest payment.
- If the Print Form indicator is selected, the interest calculation process prints forms for interest settlements.
- Calculated interest is posted to the customer account only if the Post Interest indicator is selected. You may not want to select this indicator if the interest run is carried out only for information and analysis purposes.
- Other posting parameters let you specify the payment term, tax code, and invoice reference details for interest settlement posting.

For interest calculation based on account balances, the postprocessing, output control, and posting parameters are similar to what we have already discussed. However, instead of item selection, you specify the following parameters:

- Settlement Day specifies the settlement day of interest calculation.
- Interest is posted to a customer account per the frequency specified in Interest Calculation Frequency.

Tip

If standard functionality isn't sufficient, you can configure an interest indicator that uses the custom function module for interest calculation. Subroutine INTEREST_RATES_EX provides a sample interface for this purpose.

The next step in the process is configuring the interest terms.

10.2.2 Interest Terms

You configure interest rates and interest terms in the configuration area SAP IMG • Financial Accounting • Accounts Receivable And Accounts Payable • Business Transactions • Interest Calculation • Interest Calculation.

Time-Dependent Interest Terms

Int.calc.indicator	IM
Currency Key	USD
Eff. from	01/01/1990
Sequential number	1
Term	Debit interest: balance interest calc.
Interest rates	
Ref. interest rate	
Premium	10.000000
Amount from	50,000.00

Figure 10.12 Interest Terms Calculation

Figure 10.12 shows an example of how the SAP system uses this configuration to determine an interest rate for each interest indicator. Let's look at each of these fields:

- Currency: Using the currency key, you can assign different interest rates for different currencies to the same interest indicator.
- Effective From: Specifies the date from which the definition is valid.
- Sequential Number: This number is relevant if for staggered or scaled interest rates. This number, along with the Amount From field, specifies different amount scales to which you can assign different interest rates.
- Reference Interest Rate: This is the key under which the reference interest rate is defined. This field is relevant only for the configuration of time-dependent interest rates.
- Premium: This field, in combination with the reference interest rate, determines the resulting interest rate.
  - If the reference interest rate key is specified, the resulting interest rate is calculated by adding or subtracting the value specified in this field to the reference interest rate.
  - If the reference interest rate key isn't specified, the resulting interest rate is the same as the value specified in this field.

The following section discusses the assignment of GL accounts and print forms to the interest calculation process.

10.2.3 Posting and Printing

You configure GL account assignment for interest calculation in the configuration area SAP IMG • Financial Accounting • Accounts Receivable And Accounts Payable • Business Transactions • Interest Calculation • Interest Posting.

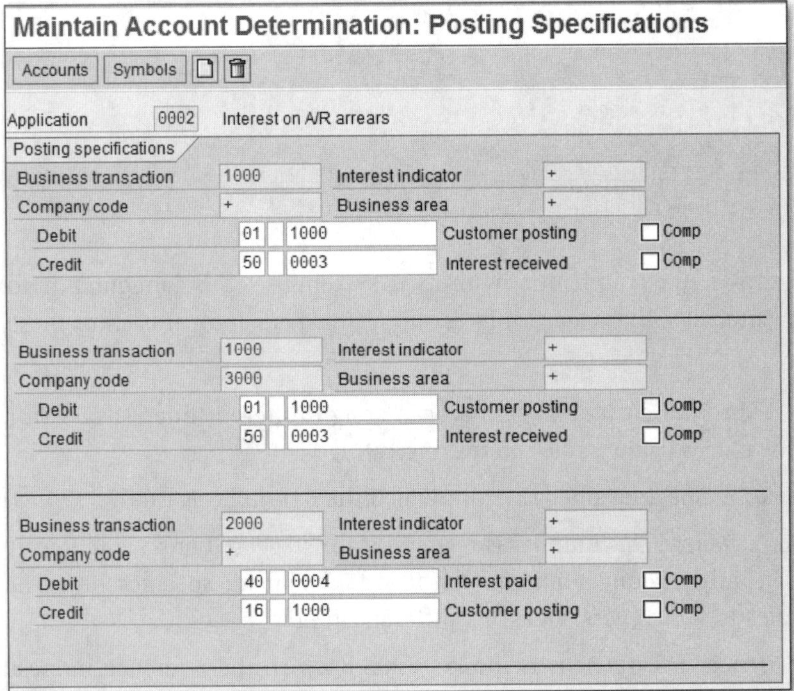

Figure 10.13 Interest GL Accounts

As shown in the configuration screen (Figure 10.13) of the GL account assignment, you can specify a posting key and a GL account for the following combination of criteria:

1. Application specifies the type of interest calculation. Different configuration activities refer to different applications.
   - **0002:** Interest on AR arrears.
   - **0005:** AR balance interest calculation.
   - **0009:** Interest on AP arrears.
   - **0006:** AP balance interest calculation.

2. Business Transaction specifies the interest processing activity.
   - **1000:** Interest earned.
   - **2000:** Interest paid.
3. Interest Indicator.
4. Company Code.
5. Business Area.
6. Debit or Credit transaction.

If the same GL account is used for the same purpose across company codes, interest indicators, and business areas, you don't have to make a configuration entry for every combination. As the figure shows, you can use "+" to make a generic entry that is applicable for all combinations.

Tip

The values such as "1000" and "0001" in Figure 10.13 don't represent actual GL accounts. They represent account symbols, to which you assign GL accounts in a separate configuration activity.

If you want to print interest forms, you can assign custom forms to a combination of an interest indicator and a company code. This configuration is carried out in the configuration area SAP IMG • Financial Accounting • Accounts Receivable And Accounts Payable • Business Transactions • Interest Calculation • Print.

Let's now see how to process interest calculation.

10.2.4 Interest Processing

Interest processing transactions carry out interest calculation based on the interest indicator and other relevant data maintained in the customer master. In Chapter 1, Customer Master Data, we discussed the customer master in detail. You maintain the interest calculation data in the customer master using Create/Change Customer Master • Company Code Data View • Account Management tab • Interest Calculation section.

You'll find the transaction to process interest calculation under the menu area SAP MENU • ACCOUNTING • FINANCIAL ACCOUNTING • ACCOUNTS RECEIVABLE • PERIODIC PROCESSING • INTEREST CALCULATION. This menu area contains several transactions for item interest calculation, arrears interest calculation, and balance interest calculation. The following list provides an overview of the available controls in these interest-processing transactions:

- Selection Controls
  - The primary selection criteria in any interest calculation program are customer accounts, company codes, interest indicators, and the interest calculation date or the interest calculation period.
  - You can use dynamic selections to specify additional selection criteria, which can result in scope reduction and improved performance.
- Posting Controls
  - In this section, you specify whether to post interest calculation documents.
  - You also specify field values such as Posting Date, Document Date, Cost Center, Plant, Dunning Block, and so on for interest settlement documents.
  - Using the Test Run option, you can simulate interest calculation processing before actually posting the documents.
- Output Controls
  - In this section, you specify the type and name of the printed interest forms.
  - You select whether to print a separate line for each document item and interest rate.
  - You choose whether to print an interest rate table at the end of the item list.

Each interest calculation transaction contains numerous other options that influence different aspects of interest processing and interest posting. Space constraint prevents us from going into detail about every option in every transaction. However, you can display detailed information about an interest processing transaction by selecting HELP • APPLICATION HELP from the main transaction screen.

In the next section, we'll look at another equally detailed topic of highly versatile functionality of correspondence.

10.3 Correspondence

Correspondence functionality in the SAP system enables you to print documents and statements from Financial Accounting components. Payment notifications, document printouts, account statements, and standard letters are all examples of correspondence. All configuration activities for correspondence functionality are under the configuration area SAP IMG • FINANCIAL ACCOUNTING • FINANCIAL ACCOUNTING GLOBAL SETTINGS • CORRESPONDENCE. In the SAP system, Correspondence Type is used to differentiate between different types of documents and statements.

10.3.1 Correspondence Types

Correspondence types define the contents and the structure of the correspondence documents and statements. Table 10.1 provides a list of several predefined correspondence types available in the SAP system.

Correspondence Type	Usage
SAP01	Payment notice with line items
SAP02	Payment notice without line items
SAP06	Account statement
SAP08	Open item list
SAP09	Internal document
SAP10	Individual correspondence
SAP11	Customer credit memo (from Finance)
SAP13	Customer statement
SAP19	Customer invoice (from Finance)

Table 10.1 Correspondence Types

The predefined correspondence types can be used as is, or you can create new correspondence types to meet specific business requirements.

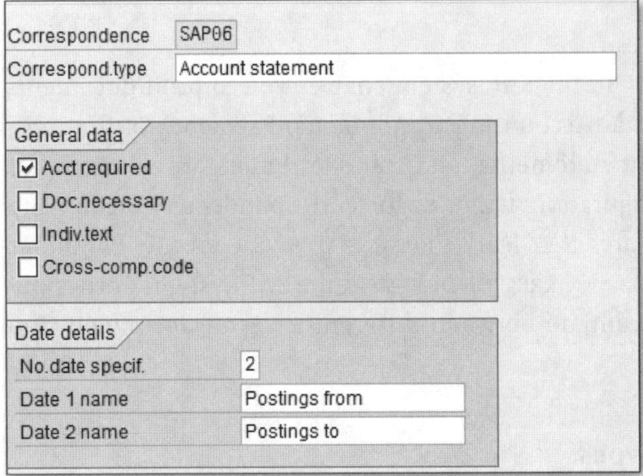

Figure 10.14 Correspondence Type Configuration

Figure 10.14 shows the configuration screen for a correspondence type. Let's look at each option in detail.

- ACCT. REQUIRED: This flag indicates that the correspondence type requires an account as one of its parameters.
  - For example, this flag should be set for account statements but not for customer invoices or credit memos.
  - Depending on the correspondence type, the account can be a GL account, a customer account, or a vendor account.
- DOC. NECESSARY: This flag indicates that the correspondence type requires a document number as one of its parameters.
  - For example, this flag should be set for customer invoices or credit memos but should not be set for account statements.
- INDIV.TEXT: This flag indicates that the language of the correspondence text is accepted as one of the parameters.
  - This option allows you to use the same correspondence type to print letters, documents, and statements in different languages.
- CROSS-COMP. CODE: This flag indicates that the correspondence type can be used for documents and statements containing cross-company code transactions.

- DATE DETAILS: In this section, you specify the number of dates required in the correspondence type parameters. Possible values are
  - **0:** For correspondence types such as customer documents
  - **1:** For correspondence types such as open item lists as of a key date
  - **2:** Or correspondence types such as customer statements for a date range

These parameters provide considerable flexibility to allow configuration of almost any type of letter, document, or statement. After you've configured the required correspondence types, the next step is to assign SAP report programs and program variants to each correspondence type. This assignment can be made for one specific company code or generic for all company codes.

In the SAP system, the only correspondence types available for a company code are the generic correspondence types and the correspondence types specifically assigned to that company code. You can review this assignment using SAP IMG • FINANCIAL ACCOUNTING • FINANCIAL ACCOUNTING GLOBAL SETTINGS • CORRESPONDENCE • ASSIGN PROGRAMS FOR CORRESPONDENCE TYPES.

Tip

You can assign one company code to act as a correspondence company code for other company codes. So if Company Code 3000 is assigned to Company Code 1000, all correspondence types and parameters created for Company Code 3000 are available to Company Code 1000 as well.

In the next section, we'll discuss how to configure and request these correspondence types.

10.3.2 Requesting Correspondence Types

The SAP system provides four call-up points where users can choose to request one or more correspondence types. You carry out this configuration in the activity SAP IMG • FINANCIAL ACCOUNTING • FINANCIAL ACCOUNTING GLOBAL SETTINGS • CORRESPONDENCE • DETERMINE CALL-UP FUNCTIONS. Figure 10.15 shows this configuration screen.

As is evident from Figure 10.15, you can make call-up point specifications generic for all company codes or specific for a company code.

Call Options of Correspondence Types

CoCd	Corr.	Correspondence type	DocEnt	Pmnt	DocD...	AccDsp
	SAP01	Payment notice with line items	☐	☑	☐	☐
	SAP02	Payment notice without line items	☐	☑	☐	☐
	SAP03	Payment notice to sales department	☐	☑	☐	☐
	SAP04	Payment notice to accounting departme	☐	☑	☐	☐
	SAP05	Payment notice to legal department	☐	☑	☐	☐
	SAP06	Account statement	☑	☑	☑	☑
	SAP08	Open item list	☑	☑	☑	☑
	SAP09	Internal document	☑	☐	☑	☑
	SAP10	Individual correspondence	☑	☑	☑	☑
	SAP11	Customer credit memo	☑	☐	☑	☑
	SAP12	Failed payments	☑	☑	☐	☐
	SAP13	Customer statement (single statement)	☑	☑	☑	☑
	SAP14	Open item list with pmnt advice (single)	☑	☑	☑	☑
	SAP15	Open item list (association)	☑	☑	☑	☑
	SAP16	Open item list with pmnt advice (assoc.	☑	☑	☑	☑

Figure 10.15 Call Options of Correspondence Types

Thus, you have an additional option to control the availability of correspondence types by company code. The following list describes the availability of a correspondence type based on the indicator selected in this configuration activity:

- Document Entry
  - The correspondence type is available in invoice and credit memo entry transactions such as FB70, FB75, F-22, and F-27.
- Payment Posting
  - The correspondence type is available in payment posting transactions such as F-28 and F-26.
- Document Display
  - The correspondence type is available in document display and document change transactions such as FB03 and FB02.
- Account Display
  - The correspondence type is available in account display transactions such as FBL3N.

In all of the relevant transactions, you use the menu ENVIRONMENT • CORRESPONDENCE to access available correspondence types as shown in Figure 10.16.

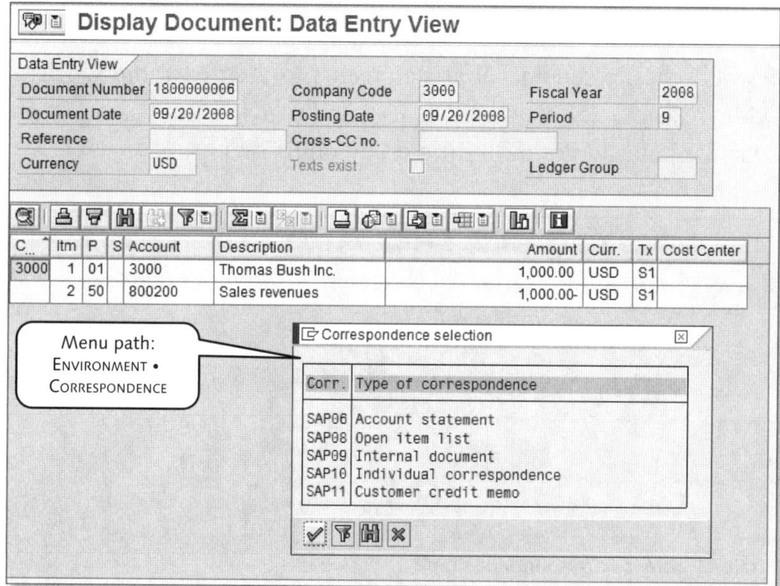

Figure 10.16 Select Correspondence Type

You submit a correspondence request by first selecting a correspondence type from the list and subsequently entering any necessary parameters. The SAP system assigns it a correspondence request number that you can use later to print or process the correspondence. You access correspondence print transactions under the menu path SAP MENU • ACCOUNTING • FINANCIAL ACCOUNTING • ACCOUNTS RECEIVABLE • PERIODIC PROCESSING • PRINT CORRESPONDENCE • AS PER REQUESTS (Transaction F.61).

Tip

You can print a correspondence letter or statement immediately after generating a correspondence request. However, depending on the type and the volume of correspondence printing, it may be more efficient to generate correspondence requests throughout the day on as-needed basis. Then you can schedule an end-of-the-day print job to take care of printing and sending correspondence.

In the next section, we'll discuss how to use correspondence types to print customer statements.

10.3.3 Customer Statements

Many companies periodically send account statements to their customers. These statements provide visibility to overdue balances and provide the customer an opportunity to dispute any charges or point out any omissions.

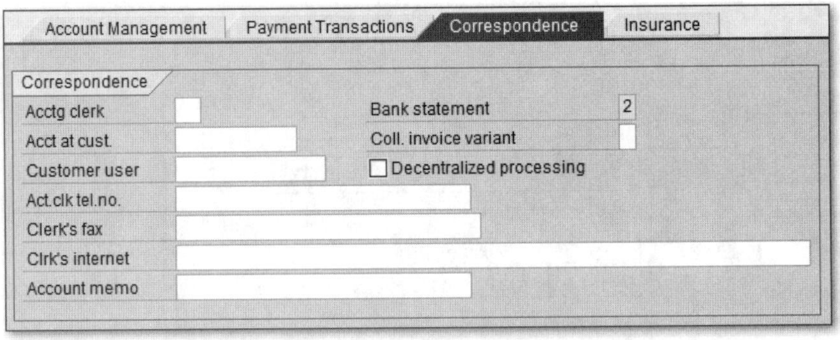

Figure 10.17 Maintain Customer Correspondence Data

You can use the ad-hoc process described in the previous section to print occasional, infrequent customer statements. However, for regular, high-volume customer statement printing, the customer statement functionality is more useful. To use this functionality, you should maintain the appropriate data in the customer master as shown in Figure 10.17. This data is maintained in COMPANY CODE DATA VIEW • CORRESPONDENCE TAB • CORRESPONDENCE DATA section.

In particular, the value in the BANK STATEMENT field indicates the frequency of the customer account statement such as weekly, monthly, or yearly. It's important to note that this field is simply a selection criterion that can be used during the customer statement run. It doesn't enforce any date validations. Other fields on this tab contain contact details of your company personnel that are responsible for managing this customer account. In turn, you can print this contact information on customer statements or any other customer correspondence.

Warning

It may be tempting to update each customer account with an exact employee name and detailed contact information. However, you may want to consider the possibility of future or frequent changes and their impact on data maintenance.

To print customer statements, you select SAP MENU • ACCOUNTING • FINANCIAL ACCOUNTING • ACCOUNTS RECEIVABLE • PERIODIC PROCESSING • PRINT CORRESPONDENCE • PERIODIC ACCOUNT STATEMENTS (Transaction F.27).

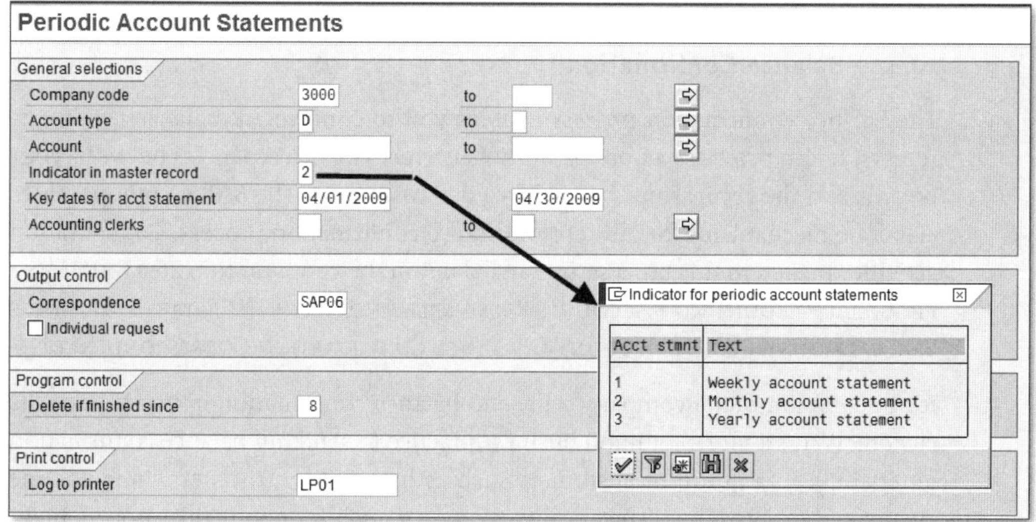

Figure 10.18 Customer Statements

Figure 10.18 shows the transaction screen for processing customer statements. The MASTER DATA INDICATOR, along with other selection criteria, helps you select customers for which customer statements are printed. The figure shows the use of CORRESPONDENCE SAP06, which is a predelivered correspondence type for customer statements. However, you can also use any custom-configured correspondence type in its place.

In addition to the customer statements functionality, the SAP system provides dedicated programs and functionality for another correspondence type: the balance confirmation process. Balance confirmations are typically sent out only once a year, so let's discuss it in the next section on year-end processing.

10.4 Year-End Processing

The total number of technical and business activities required at the time of year-end processing is typically very large. However, these activities are performed in different SAP components such as Accounts Payable, Asset Accounting, Inventory Management, Payroll, Investment Management, and, of course, GL. Because this book is focused only on AR, we'll focus on the two activities of balance confirmation process and balance carry forward process.

10.4.1 Balance Confirmation

The balance confirmation process enables you to confirm AR balances with customers. It also provides an opportunity to correct any discrepancies between your records and the records maintained by your customers. The SAP system provides elaborate mechanisms for all steps of balance confirmation process. Configuration activities related to this process are carried out in the configuration area SAP IMG • Financial Accounting • Accounts Receivable And Accounts Payable • Business Transactions • Closing • Count • Balance Confirmation Correspondence.

It's uncommon that a company will send balance confirmation letters to all of its customers. It's a more common business practice to send out balance confirmation letters only to a group of customers such as high-value customers, high-volume customers, or customers specifically asking for such letters. If this process highlights any pattern in discrepancies, then you can expand the balance confirmation process to an all-encompassing process. Let's start with the transaction used to print balance confirmation letters.

The transaction used to generate balance confirmation letters and statements is available under SAP Menu • Accounting • Financial Accounting • Accounts Receivable • Periodic Processing • Print Correspondence • Balance Confirmations • Print Letters (Transaction F.17). Parameters available on the main screen of this transaction can be grouped into selections and output controls. Let's look at each one in more detail.

Balance Confirmation Letters — Selections

Figure 10.19 shows the partial screen of the balance confirmation transaction. This transaction is used to print balance confirmation letters or statements to customers.

The part of the screen visible in Figure 10.19 contains selection criteria that can be used to print balance confirmation letters. Following are the field details:

- Company Code, Customer, and Total Balance are self-explanatory selection criteria.

Customer Balance Confirmation

Customer		to	
General selections			
Company code	3000	to	
Reconciliation key date	04/30/2009		
Further selections			
☑ Individual customers			
☑ Head offices and branches			
☑ One-time customers			
Accounts without postings			
Only accounts posted to since			
Total balance		to	
Every nth customer selected			
Sample size			

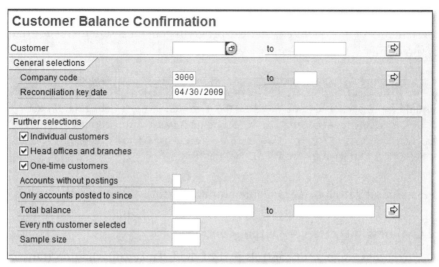

Figure 10.19 Balance Confirmation Selections

- RECONCILIATION KEY DATE specifies the date as of which account balances have to be reconciled.
- The customer selection indicators enable you to select customers based on whether they are Individual Customers, One-Time Customers, or customers with Head Office and Branches
- The ACCOUNTS WITHOUT POSTINGS indicator value has the following influence:
  - 1: Select only the accounts that have not posted to since the year specified in ONLY ACCOUNTS POSTED TO SINCE field.
  - 2: Select only the accounts that have been posted to since the year specified in ONLY ACCOUNTS POSTED TO SINCE field
  - No value selects all accounts

Occasionally, it may be helpful or sufficient to carry out a "token" balance confirmation process for a far fewer customer accounts without having to specify individual customer account numbers. This type of balance confirmation process may be done to simply satisfy requirements such as a management review, an internal audit, or an external audit. The following two selection criteria can be used in such scenarios:

- As the name implies, EVERY NTH CUSTOMER SELECTED will print balance confirmations only for every nth customer.

- Using Sample Size, you can specify the maximum number of balance confirmation statements to be generated, and the program generates statements for that many, randomly selected customer accounts.

Tip

You can add more section criteria fields to this transaction using configuration activity SAP IMG • FINANCIAL ACCOUNTING • ACCOUNTS RECEIVABLE AND ACCOUNTS PAYABLE • BUSINESS TRANSACTIONS • CLOSING • COUNT • BALANCE CONFIRMATION CORRESPONDENCE • SPECIFY SELECTION CRITERIA FOR BALANCE CONFIRMATION.

In the next section, let's look at available output controls.

Balance Confirmation Letters — Output Controls

Figure 10.20 shows the output controls part of the balance confirmation transaction. Parameters in this section have influence on the output controls and print controls. Let's look at each parameter in detail.

- FORM SET determines the form used for balance confirmation printing.
- SORT VAR FOR CORRESPONDENCE determines the sort order of correspondence output letters and statements, whereas LINE ITEM SORTING determines the sorting of items within a correspondence.

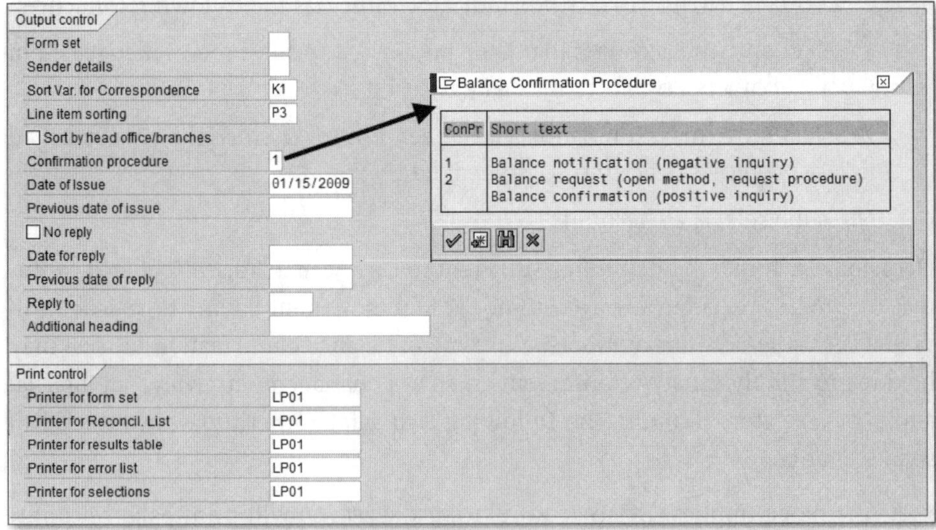

Figure 10.20 Balance Confirmation Output Controls

- Confirmation Procedure determines the purpose and subsequent steps of the balance confirmation process.
  - If this field value is blank, you ask the customer for a confirmation response regardless of whether the balance matches.
  - If this field values is 1, you inform the customer to respond only if there's mismatch in the reported balances.
  - If this field value is 2, you inquire and request your customers to send the balance of your account, according to the customer's accounting department.
- The Date of Issue and Date of Reply fields provide the "as of" and "reply by" dates in the customer correspondence.
- The date fields Previous Date of Issue and Previous Date of Reply are relevant when you send out reminder letters or statements to request balance confirmation responses again.

Tip

You may want to take into account your mailroom operations while setting up the value for Sort Var for Correspondence. For example, it may be helpful to sort the outgoing letters and statements by ZIP code.

In the Print Controls screen section, you specify the printer for the following lists:

- Printer for Form Set to print correspondence letters and statements
- Printer for Reconcil. List to print balance reconciliation lists
- Printer for Results Table to print report results
- Printer for Error List to print error logs
- Printer for Selections to print selection criteria

Lastly, let's discuss the balance carry forward process that is carried out as part of year-end processing.

10.4.2 Balance Carry Forward

This year-end process carries forward customer account balances to the new fiscal year. You access this transaction using SAP Menu • Accounting • Financial

ACCOUNTING • ACCOUNTS RECEIVABLE • PERIODIC PROCESSING • CLOSING • CARRY FORWARD • BALANCE CARRY FORWARD (Transaction F.07).

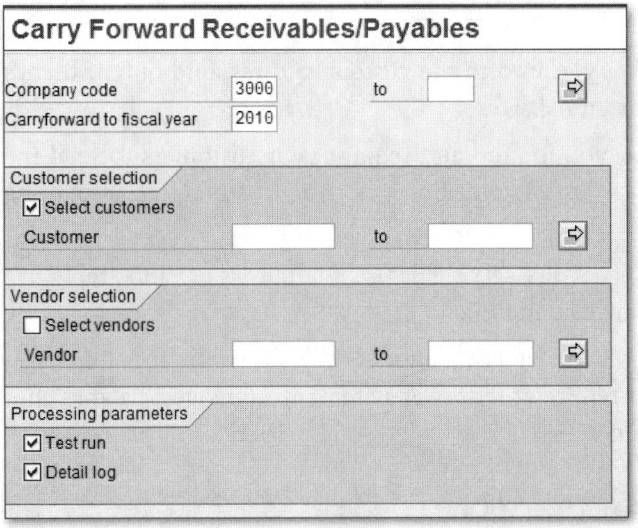

Figure 10.21 Balance Carry Forward

Figure 10.21 shows the transaction screen to run this process. Following are the important points to keep in mind about this transaction:

- It's highly recommended that you run this program at the beginning of the new fiscal year and not at the end of previous fiscal year.
- Any posting to a customer account into the new fiscal year automatically carries forward customer balances to the new fiscal year, regardless of whether this program is run.
- After this program is run, any posting to any of the previous fiscal years will automatically carry forward balances to the subsequent fiscal year.
- This program can be run as often as desired or as necessary.
- The TEST RUN flag allows you to validate balance carry forward entries without actually posting them.
- The DETAIL LOG flag generates a detailed listing of every account and its carried forward balance.

As the preceding list shows, the SAP system makes sure to keep customer balances updated across fiscal years. However, if you notice any discrepancies in customer account balances across fiscal years, you may want to run this transaction again before investigating other causes.

In the next section, we'll delve into transactions and technical details.

10.5 Technical Reference

This section will provide technical references for the transactions discussed in this chapter. Considering the large number of technical objects available in the SAP system, this information should only be considered as a starting point for analysis. To begin with, the following section provides a quick reference for the transactions discussed in this chapter.

10.5.1 List of Transactions

Table 10.2 lists transactions relevant for the topics discussed in this chapter.

Transaction	Usage
F-31	Customer outgoing payment
F-18	Customer outgoing payment + form print
F110	Automatic payment run
F.13	Automatic clearing without specifying clearing currency
F13E	Automatic clearing with clearing currency specified
FBS1	Enter accrual/deferral document
F.81	Reversal of accrual documents
ACACTREE01/02	Create/change accrual objects
ACACACT	Start periodic accrual run
ACACPSITEMS	Display total values in Accrual Engine
ACACPSDOCITEMS	Display line items in Accrual Engine
F.05	Foreign currency valuation – classic
FAGL_FC_VAL	Foreign currency valuation – New GL
S_ALR_87003642	Open/close posting periods
FINT	Item interest calculation

Table 10.2 Periodic Processing – Transactions

Transaction	Usage
FINTSHOW	Interest run display
F.26	Balance interest calculation
F.2A	Arrears interest calculation without open items
F.2B	Arrears interest calculation with open items
F.2C	Arrears interest calculation without postings
F.61	Print correspondence –per requests
F.63	Delete correspondence requests
F.62	Print internal documents without correspondence requirements
F.27	Customer statements
F.17	Print balance confirmation letters
F.07	Year-end balance carry forward

Table 10.2 Periodic Processing – Transactions (Cont.)

The next section provides a list of some of the SAP Notes.

10.5.2 SAP Notes

With the large number of SAP Notes available for any particular topic in the SAP system, it's impossible and somewhat counter-productive to list all available notes. The list of SAP Notes in Table 10.3 should be considered only a sample list.

SAP Note	Relevance
0001038853	FAQ: Clearing program doesn't clear any items
0000874603	Interest calculation in dunning program and interest program
0000956981	Sending interest letters by fax or email
0000970870	Sending interest letters by fax or email
0000736223	Using BAdIs in interest calculation
0000988859	Variable sender address when sending emails
0000389706	Company code clearing of customer accounts

Table 10.3 Periodic Processing – SAP Notes

SAP Note	Relevance
0000809831	Activation of the Accrual Engine
0000766338	Balance valuation: Additional characteristics
0000948535	Additional fields for postings made by GL closing programs
0000078329	Open and close posting periods: Maintain current settings
0000145468	Missing check for closed posting periods in billing documents
0000549119	Correspondence: FAQ
0000643215	Correspondence: Confirmation of receipt with sent email
0001360070	Email functions for correspondence
0000988859	Variable sender address when sending emails
0000402917	Balance carry forward not correct (very detailed note)

Table 10.3 Periodic Processing – SAP Notes (Cont.)

In the next section, we'll look at authorization objects relevant for the transactions discussed in this chapter.

10.5.3 Authorizations

Table 10.4 provides a sample list of authorization objects to be considered for transactions discussed in this chapter.

Object	Description
F_REGU_BUK	Automatic Payment: Activity Authorization for Company Codes
F_BKPF_BUK	Accounting Document: Authorization for Company Codes
F_BKPF_KOA	Accounting Document: Authorization for Account Types
F_KNA1_BED	Customer: Account Authorization
F_KNA1_BUK	Customer: Authorization for Company Codes
F_ACE_DST	Accrual Engine: Accrual Objects
F_ACE_PST	Accrual Engine: Accrual Postings
ACAC_OBJECTS	Manual Accruals: Accrual Objects

Table 10.4 Periodic Processing – Authorization Objects

Apart from the authorization objects mentioned previously, users will also require other standard authorization objects for accounting documents and customer transactions. The next section lists tables and structures in the SAP system.

10.5.4 Tables and Structures

Table 10.5 lists tables and structures relevant for the transactions discussed in this chapter.

Table	Relevance
KNA1	Customer master: General data
KNB1	Customer master: Company code data
BKPF	Accounting document: Header
BSEG	Accounting document: Details
BSID	Secondary index for customer documents
BSAD	Secondary index for customer documents: cleared items
ACEDSASSGMT	Standard account assignments for accrual O
ACEDSOH	Accrual subobject header data
ACEDSOI	Item data for accrual subobject
ACEDSOI_ ACCOUNTS	Accounts for accrual postings per accrual
ACEDSOP	Accrual subobject parameters
ACEOBJ	Accrual objects
ACEPSOH	Accrual subobject: header data in posting
ACEPSOI	Accrual item: values in posting component
ACEPSOIT	Line items for accrual item in Accrual Engine
ACEPSPPLOG	Logical periodic accrual run
ACEPSPPSEL	Select options periodic posting run
T001B	Permitted posting periods

Table 10.5 Periodic Processing – Tables and Structures

In addition to this list, some of the transactions discussed in this chapter such as interest calculation, correspondence, and account statements make use of data contained in configuration tables. Subsequent sections list the available enhancements and modifications.

10.6 Enhancements and Modifications

This section provides a list of available BTEs, enhancements, BAdIs, and BAPIs that are relevant for periodic processes.

10.6.1 Business Transaction Events (BTE)

Using BTEs, you can attach additional function modules and custom logic to the standard SAP system. Table 10.6 lists publish and subscribe (P/S) and process BTEs available for the periodic processing functionality.

Type	BTE	Event/Process
P/S	00001040	Reverse clearing following a standard posting
P/S	00001041	Reverse clearing with reversal of clearing document
P/S	00004110	Item interest calculation: Get due date
P/S	00004190	Item and balance interest calculation: Posting
Process	00001070	Interest determination in dunning
Process	00004152	Items and balance interest calculation: Formula
Process	00002310	Correspondence: Get output device
Process	00002410	Balance confirmation: Determine output device

Table 10.6 Periodic Processing – BTE List

The following is an example of BTE implementation for the interest calculation process.

- **Event 00004152:** This event is implemented to influence the interest calculation formula.
  - In the standard SAP system, a fixed formula is used to calculate interest based on the total amount, interest indicator, and other relevant parameters.
  - Using this BTE, you can configure your own formula for interest calculation. All relevant configuration parameters are available for the interest calculation.

The next section discusses available enhancements for the functionalities discussed in this chapter.

10.6.2 Enhancements

Using enhancements, you can add custom logic to carry out additional validations and custom business processing. The following list provides some of the enhancements for the functionalities discussed in this chapter:

- ACCR0001: Accruals/Deferrals: User Exits for Master Data
  - This enhancement helps you in validating master data while processing accrual and deferral documents.
  - This enhancement contains function module EXIT_SAPMACCR01_001, which can be used to validate basic accrual data.
- RFKORIEX: Automatic correspondence
  - This enhancement lets you determine how the letters for all correspondence types are output.
  - This enhancement contains function module EXIT_RFKORIEX_001, which can be used to determine the correspondence output method such as printer, fax, or email.

The next section discusses the available BAdIs.

10.6.3 Business Add-Ins (BAdIs)

The following BAdIs are available for the functionalities discussed in this chapter:

- ACE_UI_NAVIGATION
  - This BAdI is useful for implementing navigation to the original object from the accruals object number. It contains a method called NAVIGATE.
  - This BAdI can be configured to point to the object that corresponds to the accrual object. For example, the original object can be in an external application such as stock option grants, commission agreements, or maintenance contracts.

- `ACEPS_ACCDET_STRUC`
  - This BAdI implementation is used to fill the structure for the account determination in Accrual Engine.
  - This BAdI contains a method called `ACCDET_STRUCT_FILL` that enables you to influence account determination in accrual processing.
- `FAGL_PERIOD_CHECK`
  - This BAdI enables you to extend existing checks of open posting periods.
  - This BAdI contains a method called `PERIOD_CHECK` for implementing any additional period checks and validations.
- `FI_INT_SAP01 and FI_INT_CUS01`
  - These BAdIs provide enable you to enhance standard or custom interest calculation functionality in the SAP system.
  - These BAdIs contain several methods that can be used to influence the selection of items (INT_SEL_MOD), modify the list of selected items (INT_ADD_ITEMS), create an interest posting (INT_POST), change print options (INT_PRINT_OPTIONS), implement non-linear formulae (INT_FORMULA), and others.
  - SAP Note 956981 explains how to use this BAdI to send interest letters by fax or email.

10.7 Summary

In this chapter, we focused on commonly used period-end processes such as accrual processing, currency revaluation, and period-end closing. You can calculate interest on a net customer balance or on individual document items in arrears. We also looked at the fairly comprehensive correspondence functionality that can be used to print commonly used letters and documents. The SAP system provides enhanced functionality for correspondence types used for printing customer statements. Year-end processing requires a few additional activities such as balance carry forward and, if applicable, balance confirmation processing.

In the next chapter, we'll focus on AR reporting capabilities.

This chapter focuses on AR reporting transactions. Every chapter in this book includes a specific reference to reporting transactions for relevant functionalities. So the focus in this chapter is on some standard AR reports and reporting tools available in the SAP system. In particular, we'll discuss reporting tools such as evaluations, drill-down reporting, and SAP queries, and how they can be used for generating AR reports.

11 Accounts Receivable Reporting

Throughout this book, you may have already seen many reporting transactions that meet your operational, management, and analysis requirements. The intent of this chapter isn't to repeat information about those reports, so the information in this chapter should be read in conjunction with the information presented in other chapters. Another point to consider while reading this chapter is that today most SAP implementations use SAP NetWeaver BW (business intelligence) for generating reports from the SAP system. The AR reporting capabilities discussed in this chapter don't compare with the powerful and flexible reporting capabilities of the SAP NetWeaver BW system.

However, information presented in this chapter introduces you to the standard AR reports available in the SAP system and also introduces you to the reporting tools that can be used for generating AR reports. We'll begin with the customer line item display.

11.1 Line Item Display

The customer line item display is one of the most versatile AR transactions with the capabilities to meet diverse demands of different user groups. We have discussed the use of this report briefly in the previous chapters of this book such as for dunning, incoming payments, and taxes. In this section, we'll evaluate different functionalities of this report in more detail. You access this report using

SAP MENU • ACCOUNTING • FINANCIAL ACCOUNTING • ACCOUNTS RECEIVABLE • ACCOUNT • DISPLAY/CHANGE LINE ITEMS (Transaction FBL5N).

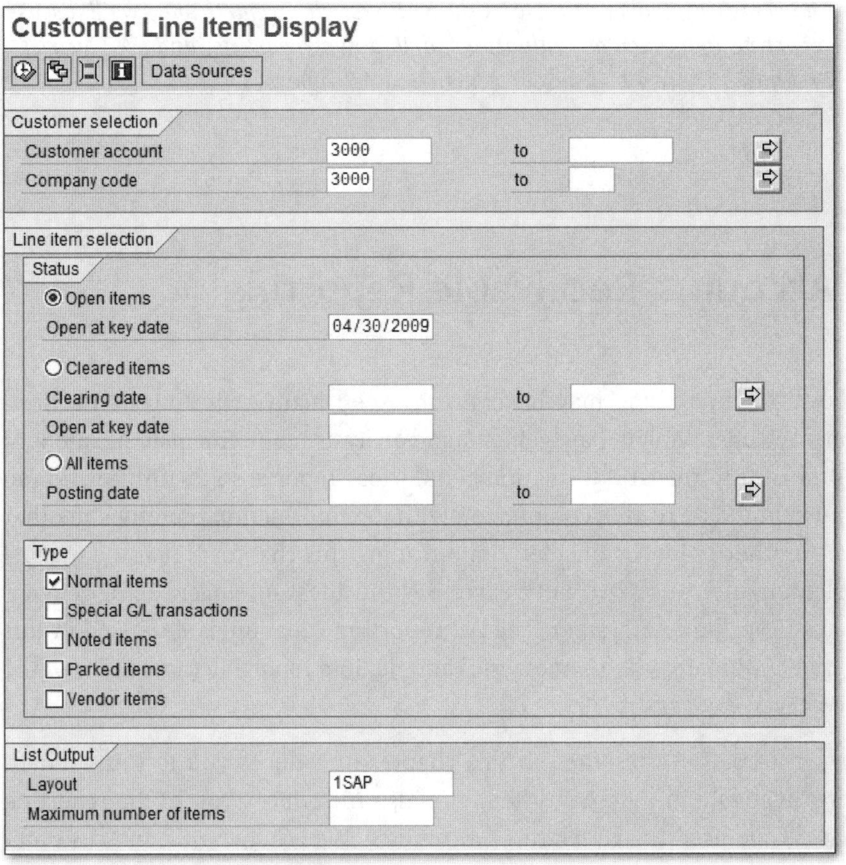

Figure 11.1 Line Item Display — Selections

Figure 11.1 shows the initial screen of this transaction. Apart from the standard selection criteria such as customer accounts and company codes, this transaction provides fairly advanced selection capabilities. Table 11.1 lists different selection scenarios.

To perform this action...	Follow these steps...
Select based on additional criteria such as country, accounting clerk, or document type	Choose Edit • Dynamic Selections to access additional selection fields.
View a list of open items as of a key date	Select Open Items, and enter the key date in the corresponding Open at Key Date.
View a list of items cleared between a date range	Select Cleared Items, and enter the date range in Clearing Date.
View a list of items open as of a key date regardless of when they were cleared	Select Cleared Items, and enter the key date in the corresponding Open at Key Date.
View a list of items that were open as of a key date and cleared between a date range	Select Cleared Items, enter the key date in the corresponding Open at Key Date, and enter the date range in Clearing Date.
View a list of items posted between a date range, regardless of whether they are open or cleared	Select All Items, and enter the date range in Posting Date.
View a list of all items posted to an account	Select All Items, and don't enter the date range in Posting Date.
Select AP items posted to vendor accounts for customers that are also set up as vendors	Select the Vendor Items indicator under Type.
Select specific types of documents such as normal items, special GL transactions, or noted items	Select the appropriate document types under the Type section.

Table 11.1 Line Item Selection Scenarios

As different scenarios in the preceding table indicate, by selecting the appropriate selection values, you can use this transaction to generate numerous types of AR reports. In addition, the following two functionalities make this report even more powerful:

- Selection variants, which enable you to save predetermined selection criteria
- List layout, which enables you to save the formatting of the list output

> **Note**
>
> The selection variants functionality can be used with all reporting transactions. However, the list layout functionality isn't available in all reporting transactions. The list layout functionality is available only in report transactions that support the ALV (ABAP List Viewer) interface.

Let's discuss both these options in more detail, starting with selection variants.

11.1.1 Selection Variants

Selection variants provide enable you to save predefined selection criteria. Several features of variants make them invaluable in efficient and controlled deployment of reports to a wide user base. Following are some of the examples:

- The variants can be set up so that they can be modified only by their creator. So a manager can create a task-specific variant and release it to a large group of employees without having to worry that it may be accidentally modified.
- The just described feature combined with protected fields can ensure that users can access only the authorized data. Of course, a properly implemented authorization concept can achieve the same purpose. However, variants provide an easy and quick alternative for relatively simple situations.
- Variants allow you to hide unwanted or unused fields from selection screens. This functionality can be used to simplify screens of commonly run reports by hiding unused fields.

You can save variant for a transaction by selecting the SAVE icon or by using the menu path GOTO • VARIANTS • SAVE AS VARIANTS.

Figure 11.2 shows a selection variant screen for a customer line item display report. This variant can be used to display document line items for domestic customers that are identified based on a reconciliation account.

> **Tip**
>
> You should follow consistent naming convention for selection variants. This is especially important for frequently and widely used transactions such as customer line item displays.

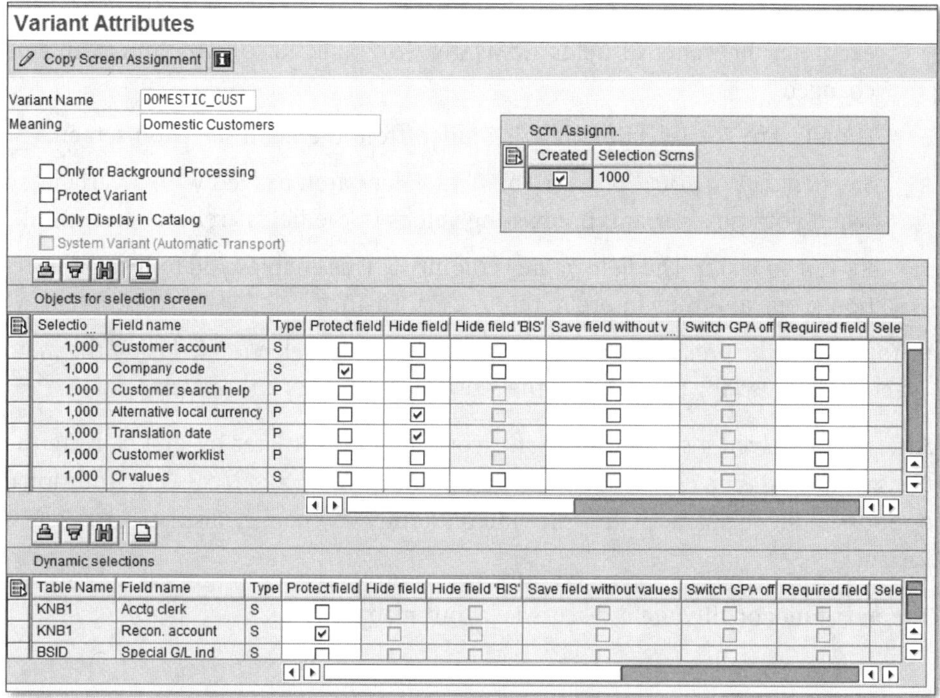

Figure 11.2 Line Item Variants

Some points to keep in mind about the variant maintenance screens include the following:

- IF THE ONLY FOR BACKGROUND PROCESSING indicator is selected, the variant can be used only in background jobs.
- If the PROTECT VARIANT indicator is selected, the variant can be changed only by the person who created it or last changed it.
- The ONLY DISPLAY IN CATALOG indicator provides further privacy and security by suppressing this variant in the standard lookup help. If this indicator is selected, no one will even be aware of the existence of this variant unless they have access to the variant catalog display.
- The main part of the variant maintenance is the section where you can set attributes of individual selection screen fields. Following are some important attributes that you can set for selection fields:

- PROTECT FIELD: Value of the selection field can't be changed. In the preceding example, the value of fields COMPANY CODE and RECON ACCOUNT can't be changed
- HIDE FIELD: The selection field is hidden from the main selection screen.
- SAVE FIELD WITHOUT VALUES: The field values aren't saved with a variant, so when you use a variant, preexisting values in the fields aren't overwritten.
- REQUIRED FIELD: The field value is required. This enables you to restrict selection scope and thus improve report performance.

- You can set the preceding attributes not only for the selection fields on the main screen but also for the fields in the ADDITIONAL SELECTION section.

After you've saved a selection variant, you can access it later by first starting the transaction and then choosing the menu option GOTO • VARIANTS • GET. Additional options under the same menu provide an ability to change, display, or delete a variant.

The next functionality we'll discuss is layout management.

11.1.2 Layout Management

Layout management is a powerful functionality that helps you generate report outputs for specific requirements with predefined format, sort, and filter criteria. Figure 11.3 shows an example of a line item layout for customer line item display list output.

Note that layout management is available only in transactions that support the ALV type of list output. As shown in Figure 11.3, the availability of ALV output options is shown by the colored cube icons in the toolbar of the result output screen. To modify the currently displayed layout, you should select SETTINGS • LAYOUT • CURRENT.

The layout management pop-up consists of following tabs:

- Displayed Columns
  - On this tab, you select the columns to display and their display sequence.
  - The columns available for display are shown in the list on the right side. The list of columns is different for different reporting transactions.

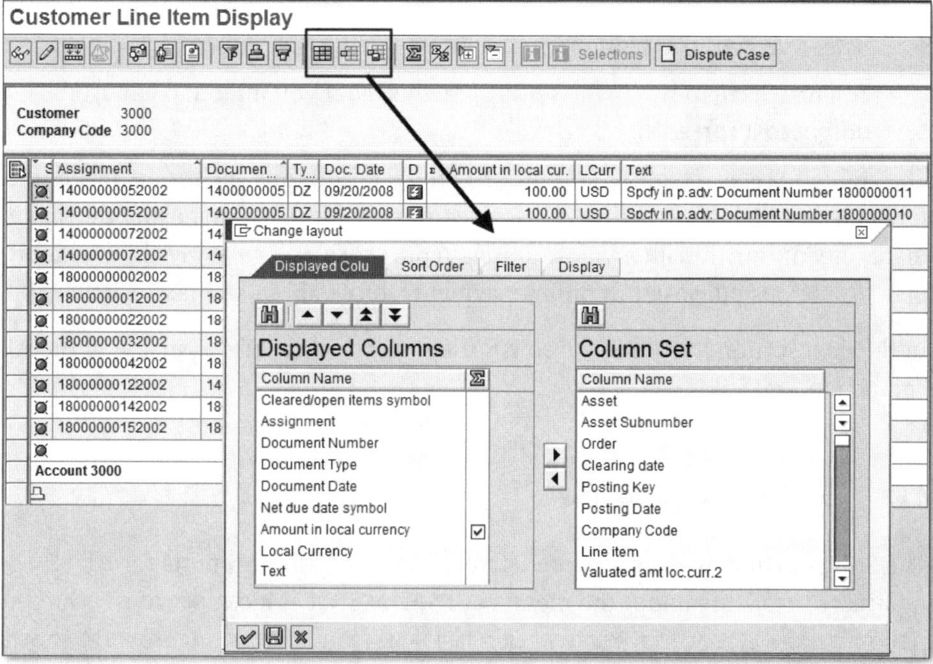

Figure 11.3 Line Item Layout

Tip

By selecting SETTINGS • SPECIAL FIELDS, you can make some additional fields available in the layout display (refer to SAP Note 984305 for more details).

- Sort Order
  - On this tab, you specify the sort columns and their sort criteria.
  - You can also specify whether any of the sort columns should display amount subtotals.
- Filter
  - On this tab, you specify the filter criteria for the selection columns.
  - You can specify filter conditions on columns even if they aren't displayed on the report output list.
- Display
  - On this tab, you specify output formatting such as the display of gridlines, column headings, and row patterns.

- You can also specify whether the report output should automatically print the date, title, and page numbers.
- You may have to tweak the settings on this tab if you intend to export the list output to a spreadsheet.

The ability to select columns and to sort, filter, and subtotal the results makes this functionality highly versatile. As discussed in previous chapters, using the layout management functionality, you can use a report such as a customer line item display for various purposes: dunning, payments, receivables, and tax review.

In the next section, we'll review some of the standard reports available in the AR component.

11.2 Standard Reports

The SAP system delivers some predefined, commonly used reports for AR. These reports are available under the menu path SAP MENU • ACCOUNTING • FINANCIAL ACCOUNTING • ACCOUNTS RECEIVABLE • INFORMATION SYSTEM. Figure 11.4 shows more than 20 standard AR reports in the SAP system.

As shown in this figure, standard AR reports are grouped into the following sections:

- Customer Balances: These reports provide customer balance information such as monthly totals, annual totals, and debit, credit, or net balances.
- Customer Items: These reports provide different views of customer items, such as due date analysis and receivable aging report.
- Master Data: These reports are based on customer master data. The examples of these reports include customer listing, customer address list, and customer changes.

Note

Many of these standard reports don't support the ALV form of list output. For such reports, the only options to control the format and content of report output are the options available on the selection screen.

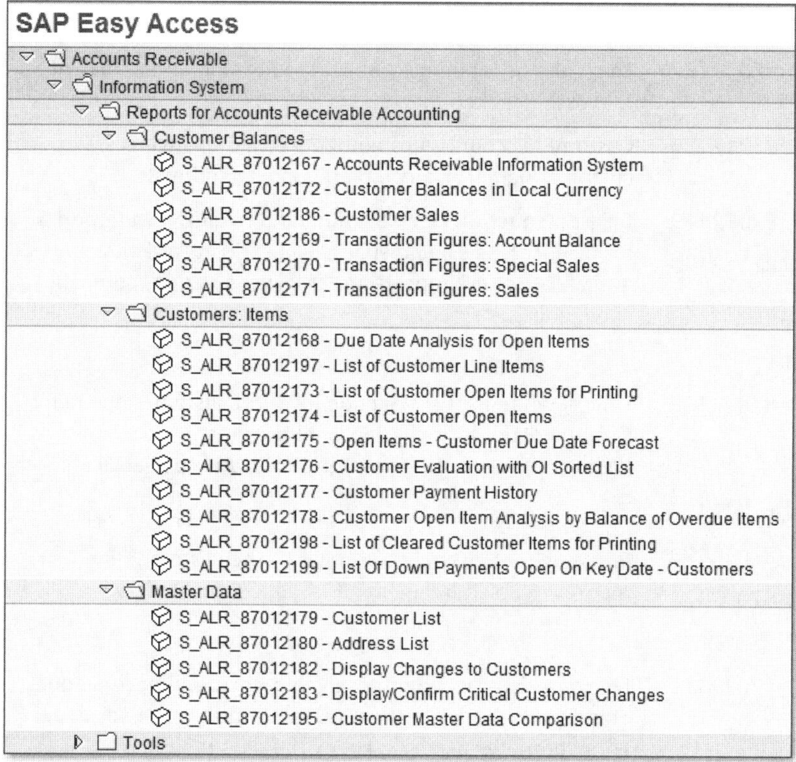

Figure 11.4 Standard AR Reports

It's impractical to describe each report in detail, so the next section provides a quick reference for standard AR reports.

11.2.1 Standard AR Reports

Table 11.2 provides a brief description of the type of information available in standard AR reports.

	This report ...	Provides this information...
Customer Balances		
1	S_ALR_87012167	Customer evaluations based on different criteria. Refer to Section 11.4, AR Evaluations, for more details on customer evaluations.

Table 11.2 Standard AR Reports

	This report ...	Provides this information...
2	S_ALR_87012172	Trial balance (opening, debits, credits, and ending balance) for customer accounts.
3	S_ALR_87012186	Customer account sales numbers based on invoices, customer name, and complete mailing address.
4	S_ALR_87012169	Drill-down reports (see Section 11.3, Drill-Down Reports) for balances, sales, and special sales. Characteristics available in these reports are fiscal year, period, company code, and customer.
5	S_ALR_87012170	
6	S_ALR_87012171	
Customer Items		
7	S_ALR_87012168	Drill-down report (see Section 11.3) for customer due items. Characteristics for this report are document type, company code, country, posting key, customer, and special GL.
8	S_ALR_87012197	Print customer item lists, similar to the customer line item report discussed in Section 11.1, Line Item Display.
9	S_ALR_87012173	
10	S_ALR_87012174	
11	S_ALR_87012198	
12	S_ALR_87012175	Due date forecast when receivable items will become due. This report is only for the receivables that aren't yet due. For overdue receivables, check the next report.
13	S_ALR_87012176	AR aging report. This report is discussed in more detail in Section 11.2.3, AR Aging Report.
14	S_ALR_87012177	Monthly payment history of customers showing timeliness of their payments.
15	S_ALR_87012178	Very similar to AR aging report. However, this report provides analysis as to whether a customer makes full use of payment terms or avails of maximum possible cash discount.
16	S_ALR_87012199	List of open down payments as of a key date. Customer down payments are discussed in Chapter 4.
Master Data		
17	S_ALR_87012179	Customer master data list. You can selectively print data from general and company code data views of a customer master.

Table 11.2 Standard AR Reports (Cont.)

	This report ...	Provides this information...
18	S_ALR_87012180	Customer address list. This report output can be used for mail merge or similar purposes.
19	S_ALR_87012182	Changes made to all customer master data. You can restrict output for one or more data views.
20	S_ALR_87012183	List of customers for which critical field values have been changed. You can use this list to review, accept, or refuse the changes.
21	S_ALR_87012195	Checks for customer accounts that are created in sales but not in AR, or vice versa.

Table 11.2 Standard AR Reports (Cont.)

From the reports listed in the preceding table, the drill-down reports and customer evaluations are discussed later in this chapter. For now, we'll focus on some of the standard reports starting with the customer master list.

11.2.2 Customer Master List

A customer master list (S_ALR_87012179) provides a quick way to generate a report of selected customer master data based on user-defined selection criteria. Figure 11.5 shows the selection screen of the customer master list.

You may recall from Chapter 1, Customer Master Data, that customer master data is divided into different data views, and each data view is divided into different data tabs. The selection options for this report enable you to selectively choose specific data sections from the general data view and company code data view of a customer master.

The field Account Sorting provides several options for sorting the report output. By effective using this field, you can generate customer lists by countries, by account groups, and by search terms. In addition to the typical uses of such customer lists, these options help you identify duplicate customer accounts or customer accounts with which you have business relationships across multiple companies and multiple countries. You may want to keep in mind, however, that this report doesn't support ALV output format.

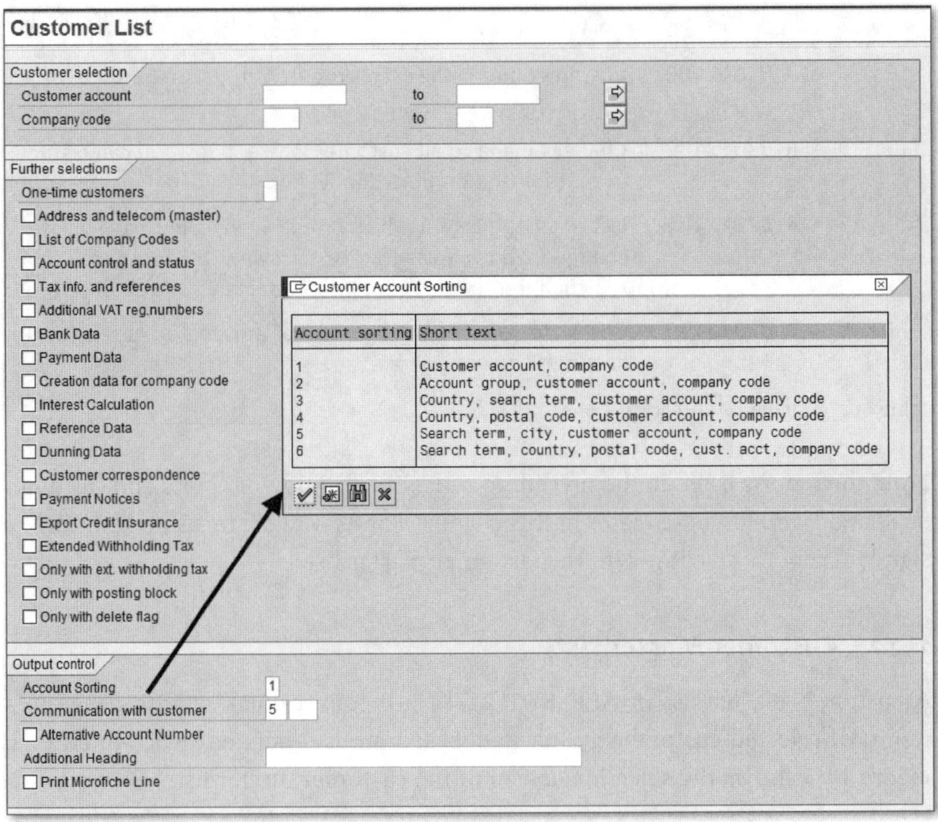

Figure 11.5 Customer List

Let's now look at the AR aging report.

11.2.3 AR Aging Report

The AR aging report is one of the most frequently requested and used reports. The standard SAP report for AR aging (S_ALR_87012176) provides a comprehensive and an extremely flexible solution to meet varied requirements of companies operating in different industries.

Figure 11.6 shows a selection variant of the AR aging transaction. This variant shows the most important and relevant selection fields of the AR aging report.

Customer Evaluation with OI Sorted List

Customer selection

Customer account		to	
Company code	3000	to	

Reporting Time Frame

Fiscal Year	2009	to	

Line item selection

Open items at key date	05/01/2009

Further selections

Balance		to	
Master Record Recon. Account		to	
Posting Date		to	
Document Date		to	
Net Due Date		to	

Output control

OI list sorting (1,2)	1
Summarization level (0-5)	1
OI list summarization (0-2)	0

- [x] Net due date sorted list
- [x] Discount due date sorted list
- [x] Incoming payments sorted list
- [ ] List sorted by doc. dates — [ ] Doc. Date
- [x] Days overdue sorted list

Due Date Sorted List	30 60 90
Rounding factor/decimal places	0 / 0

- [ ] Assign Items

Figure 11.6 AR Aging Report

Let's discuss the significance of these fields in more detail:

- CUSTOMER ACCOUNT, COMPANY CODE, FISCAL YEAR, and the fields in the FURTHER SELECTIONS section provide the selection criteria to restrict the scope of the AR aging report.
- OPEN ITEMS AT KEY DATE is the date as of which the AR aging report is generated.
- DUE DATE SORTED LIST allows you to specify AR aging time periods. You can specify up to 5 time periods, though more commonly used time periods are 30, 60, and 90 days.

- Table 11.3 shows the dates that you can use as the basis for calculating AR aging time periods. The numbers in the parentheses show the value of SORTED LIST TYPE field in result output.

To use the following date as the basis for AR aging time periods ...	... Do the following
Posting date (6)	Select the DAYS OVERDUE SORTED LIST INDICATOR.
Document date (5)	Select the LIST SORTED BY DOC DATES and DOC DATE indicators.
Incoming payment date (4)	Select the INCOMING PAYMENTS SORTED LIST INDICATOR.
Net payment due date (1)	Select the NET DUE DATE SORTED LIST INDICATOR.
Cash discount 1 due date (2, 3)	Select the DISCOUNT DUE DATE SORTED LIST INDICATOR.

Table 11.3 AR Aging Date Options

Tip
It's possible to generate a report that shows AR aging by all types of dates at the same time. However, the results can be confusing and difficult to interpret. A more meaningful approach is to generate the report based on only one of the dates that suitably satisfies the business requirements.

- The indicators SUMMARIZATION LEVEL, OI LIST SORTING, and OI LIST SUMMARIZATION control the details displayed in the report output. However, these indicators don't have any impact on the ALV form of the report output.

Figure 11.7 shows the sample output of the AR aging report in ALV format. Notice that for the same receivable data for the same customers, AR aging numbers are different for output list type 5 (document date) and 6 (posting date).

Standard AR reports discussed so far in this chapter are helpful in getting information from the AR component. However, the AR group typically also requires information from the Sales component. The next section discusses standard SD reports.

Open Item Sorting on Key Date 04/30/2009 in Local Currency

CoCd	Customer	Crcy		Total balance in LC	To 0	From 1 To 30	From 31 To 60	From 61 To 90	From 91
3000	3508	USD	5	156.76-		156.76-			
3000	3511	USD		8,798.67		977.63	977.63	6,843.41	
3000	3512	USD		10,696.24-		1,119.24-	8,457.76-	1,119.24-	
3000	3690	USD		7,208.38-		2,407.50	2,407.50	6,427.18-	5,596.20-
3000	4250	USD		51.36-		17.12-	17.12-	17.12-	
3000	4252	USD		19,260.00-		1,284.00-	1,284.00-	16,692.00-	
3000	4253	USD		5,993.32-		672.15-	3,416.78	6,169.95-	2,568.00-
3000	4254	USD		2,996.74-		336.08-	1,708.38	1,159.04-	3,210.00-
3000	4257	USD		6,978.83		225.75	6,527.33	225.75	
		USD		**30,585.30-**		**25.53**	**5,278.74**	**24,515.37-**	**11,374.20-**
3000	3508	USD	6	156.76-		156.76-			
3000	3511	USD		8,798.67		977.63	977.63	977.63	5,865.78
3000	3512	USD		10,696.24-		1,119.24-	8,457.76-	1,119.24-	
3000	3690	USD		7,208.38-		2,407.50	2,407.50	1,407.50	13,430.88-
3000	4250	USD		51.36-		17.12-	17.12-	17.12-	
3000	4252	USD		19,260.00-		1,284.00-	1,284.00-	1,284.00-	15,408.00-
3000	4253	USD		5,993.32-		672.15-	3,416.78	6,169.95-	2,568.00-
3000	4254	USD		2,996.74-		336.08-	1,708.38	1,159.04-	3,210.00-
3000	4257	USD		6,978.83		225.75	6,527.33	225.75	
		USD		**30,585.30-**		**25.53**	**5,278.74**	**7,138.47-**	**28,751.10-**

Figure 11.7 AR Aging Output

11.2.4 Standard SD Reports

The SAP SD (Sales and Distribution) component consists of several subcomponents such as master data, sales, sales support, shipping, and billing. Each of these subcomponents contains a menu option called INFORMATION SYSTEM that contains reporting transactions for the corresponding functionality. Figure 11.8 shows the menu paths for each of these information systems.

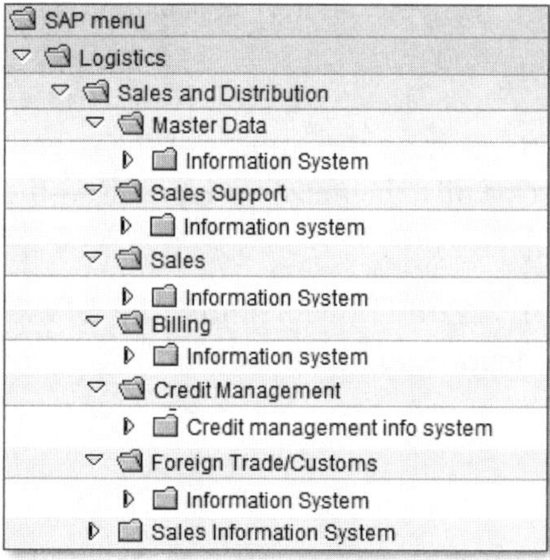

Figure 11.8 Standard SD Reports Menu

Each information system menu provides an extensive list of operational and analysis reports. Table 11.4 provides a list of some useful reports and transactions.

Transaction	Use
VC/2	A comprehensive report for information such as partners and contact persons, pricing, credit exposure, and recent orders
VA45	List of customer contracts
VA05	List of customer sales orders
SDO1	List of customer sales orders within a time period
V.02	List of incomplete sales orders
V.15	List of backorders (orders that are still due for shipping)
VF05	List of customer billing documents and document details
VFX3	List of blocked billing documents
VF25	List of invoice lists
VB98	List of customer rebate agreements

Table 11.4 Standard SD Reports

From the transactions listed in Table 11.4, we won't be discussing sales and contract reports in this book. However, you'll find information related to billing reports in Chapters 3 and 4.

Note

You may notice the menu item SALES INFORMATION SYSTEM (SIS) at the bottom of Figure 11.8. However, all reports under this menu item require extensive configuration and testing before they can generate useful output.

This detour to standard SD reports was necessary from the context of the overall discussion in this section. However, the rest of this chapter only focuses on the reporting capabilities of the AR component.

In Table 11.2, we identified some of the reports as drill-down reports. The following section explores the drill-down report functionality in more detail.

11.3 Drill-Down Reports

Drill-down reports are the reports created using the SAP system's drill-down reporting tool. Drill-down reports provide functionalities for interactive data analysis based on a predefined set of characteristics. Figure 11.9 shows an example of the customer balances report (S_ALR_87012169).

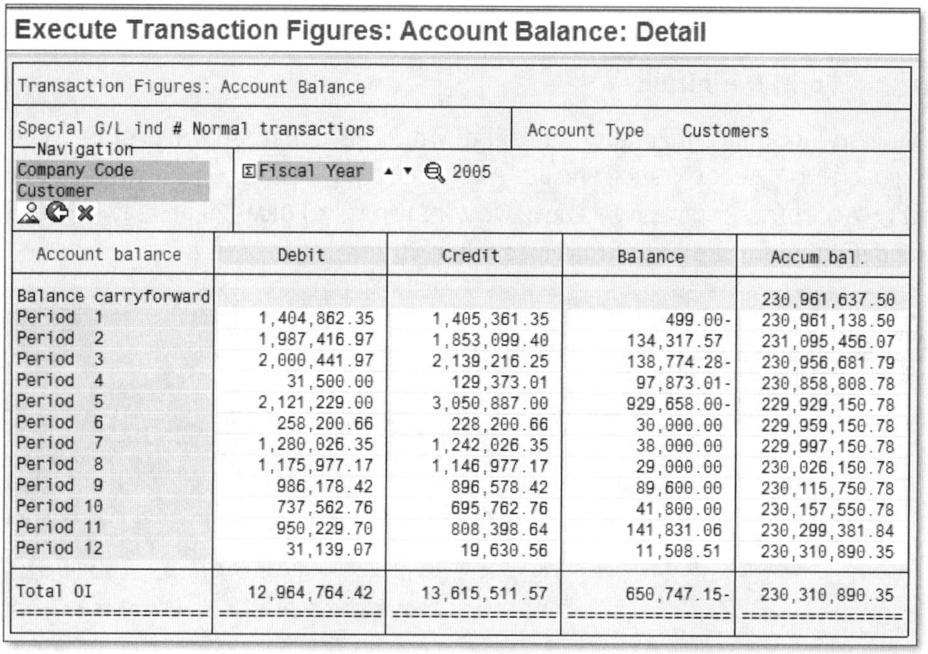

Execute Transaction Figures: Account Balance: Detail

Transaction Figures: Account Balance

Special G/L ind # Normal transactions — Account Type: Customers

Navigation: Company Code, Customer — Fiscal Year 2005

Account balance	Debit	Credit	Balance	Accum.bal.
Balance carryforward				230,961,637.50
Period 1	1,404,862.35	1,405,361.35	499.00-	230,961,138.50
Period 2	1,987,416.97	1,853,099.40	134,317.57	231,095,456.07
Period 3	2,000,441.97	2,139,216.25	138,774.28-	230,956,681.79
Period 4	31,500.00	129,373.01	97,873.01-	230,858,808.78
Period 5	2,121,229.00	3,050,887.00	929,658.00-	229,929,150.78
Period 6	258,200.66	228,200.66	30,000.00	229,959,150.78
Period 7	1,280,026.35	1,242,026.35	38,000.00	229,997,150.78
Period 8	1,175,977.17	1,146,977.17	29,000.00	230,026,150.78
Period 9	986,178.42	896,578.42	89,600.00	230,115,750.78
Period 10	737,562.76	695,762.76	41,800.00	230,157,550.78
Period 11	950,229.70	808,398.64	141,831.06	230,299,381.84
Period 12	31,139.07	19,630.56	11,508.51	230,310,890.35
Total OI	12,964,764.42	13,615,511.57	650,747.15-	230,310,890.35

Figure 11.9 Drill-Down Report Output

A drill-down report consists of two components:

- A form definition that specifies rows and columns for report output
- A report definition that specifies characteristics available for report output

One of the advantages of having these separate components is that the same form definition can be used with multiple report definitions. Thus, you can create different report definitions to meet different business requirements, while keeping a consistent reporting output format.

> **Tip**
>
> The drill-down reporting tool isn't unique to AR. Several other SAP modules such as General Ledger, Accounts Receivable, and Profitability Analysis also use the drill-down reporting tool for generating reports.

In the following sections, we'll discuss the definition of forms and reports in detail.

11.3.1 Form Definition

You carry out the configuration of drill-down forms under SAP IMG • FINANCIAL ACCOUNTING • ACCOUNTS RECEIVABLE AND ACCOUNTS PAYABLE • INFORMATION SYSTEM • ACCOUNTS RECEIVABLE • DRILL-DOWN REPORTS • FORM. Figure 11.10 shows the definition for the account balance report form.

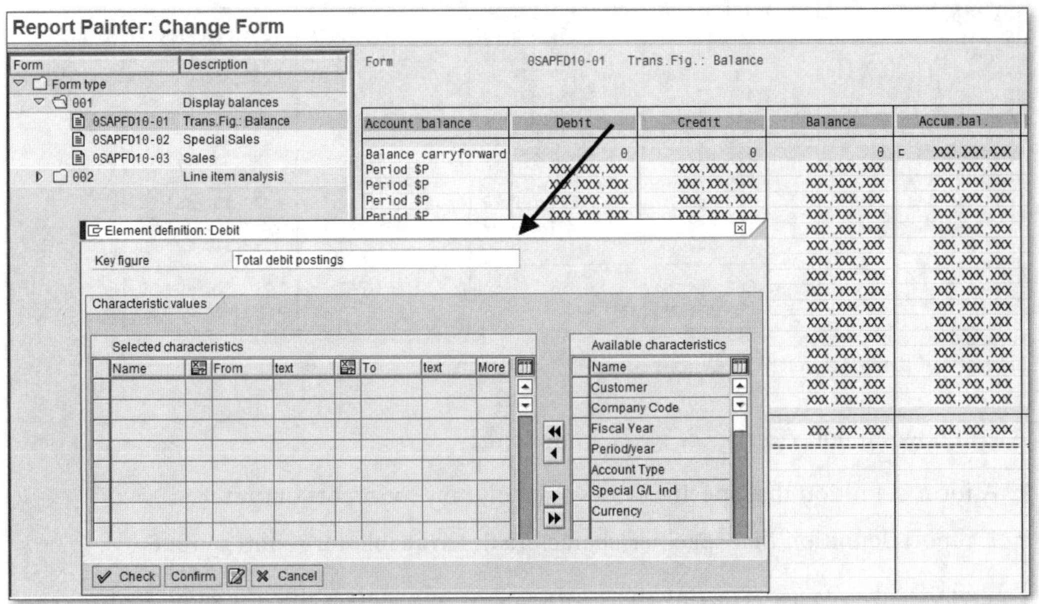

Figure 11.10 Drill-Down Report Form

A column or a row in a form definition represents either a key figure (a value) or a characteristic (a criterion). Keep the following points in mind while configuring the drill-down report form:

- You can define only the following types of AR drill-down report forms:
  - Account balances
  - Line item analysis
- Account balance reports help you analyze customer account balances.
  - Key figures available for these reports include Total debit postings, total credit postings, period balance, and accumulated balance.
  - Characteristics available for these reports include fiscal year, posting period, account type, company code, customer, and currency.
- Line item reports help you analyze customer documents.
  - The document amount in local currency is the only key figure available for these types of reports.
  - Characteristics available for these reports include accounting clerk, planning group, document type, dunning level, and other characteristics available for account balance reports.

Let's see the use of this form in a report definition.

11.3.2 Report Definition

You carry out the configuration of drill-down forms under SAP IMG • FINANCIAL ACCOUNTING • ACCOUNTS RECEIVABLE AND ACCOUNTS PAYABLE • INFORMATION SYSTEM • ACCOUNTS RECEIVABLE • DRILL-DOWN REPORTS • REPORT. Figure 11.11 shows the definition for the account balance report.

As the figure shows, the main screen of the report definition involves linking it to a form and choosing the characteristics available in the report output. One of the main flexibilities of the drill-down reporting tool is the variety of output format that it can generate. The Output Type tab provides the following options for report output:

- Graphical output that can display graphs, drill-down lists, and interactive user interface for data analysis.
- Classic drill-down report that can display print-friendly report output. This format is more appropriate for large volumes of data.

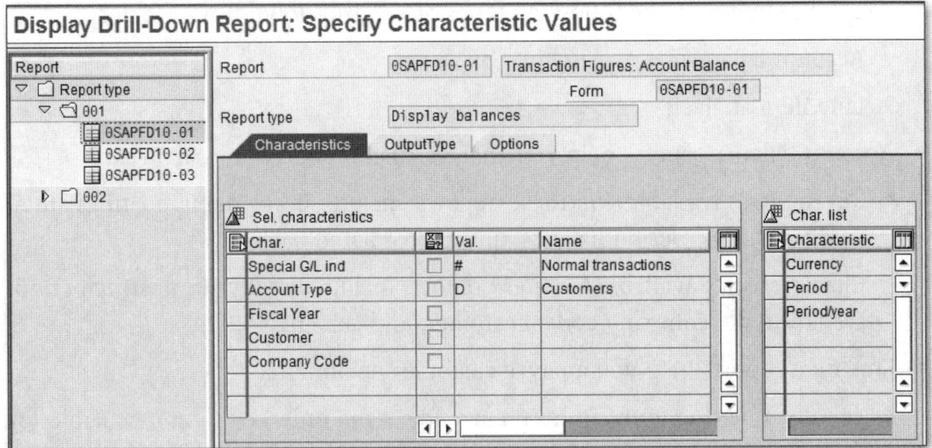

Figure 11.11 Drill-Down Report Definition

- ALV output that displays report results in ALV format. As we discussed previously in this chapter, ALV format provides a spreadsheet-like functionality to analyze data.
- Spreadsheet format that lets you take the report output directly to a spreadsheet program.

In addition to the standard list reports, drill-down reports also enable you to generate additional analysis reports such as ranked lists and ABC analysis. You can access these additional features under the EDIT menu of the report output.

Let's now look at the other AR reporting tool: evaluations.

11.4 AR Evaluations

AR evaluations enable you to analyze AR data based on predefined characteristics. You can access all active AR evaluations with the Report S_ALR_87012167 mentioned in Table 11.2. Figure 11.12 shows an output of one such evaluation.

> **Note**
>
> The main difference between evaluations and drill-down reports is that you can create new drill-down reports, but you can't create new types of evaluations. Another difference between the two is that drill-down reports always fetch real-time data, whereas evaluations are generated based on the latest date of data refresh.

Due date analysis

Company code IDES US INC Values in: USD

Country	Due	Not due	Total OI's
United States	28,749,944.76	0.00	28,749,944.76
Germany	516,012.50	0.00	516,012.50
France	405,000.00	0.00	405,000.00
Great Britain	371,000.00	0.00	371,000.00
Switzerland	168,500.00	0.00	168,500.00
Canada	42,666.67	0.00	42,666.67
Utd.Arab.Emir.	70.00	0.00	70.00
Total	30,253,193.93	0.00	30,253,193.93

Figure 11.12 Evaluation Output

Table 11.5 lists the evaluations available for the AR information system.

Evaluation Type	Description	Program (Create)
01	Due date analysis	RFDRRE01
02	Payment history	RFDRRE02
03	Currency analysis	RFDRRE03
04	Overdue items analysis	RFDRRE04
05	DSO analysis	RFDRRE05
06	Payment terms offered/taken	RFDRRE06

Table 11.5 Evaluation Types

One of the most powerful features of evaluations reporting is that you can generate these evaluations grouped by any criteria, such as a company code, country, credit control area, dunning level, accounting clerk, and others.

The process of activating and using AR evaluations involves the following steps:

1. Create a variant for the evaluation program mentioned in Table 11.5.
   - In this step, you create a variant for an evaluation program specifying the characteristic for grouping. For example, to generate Due Date Analysis by Accounting Clerk, you create a variant for Program RFDRRE01 with Accounting Clerk as the grouping criteria (Transaction SE38).

2. Select and activate AR evaluations that are relevant for your business.
   - In this step, you select or deselect AR evaluations using SAP MENU • ACCOUNTING • FINANCIAL ACCOUNTING • ACCOUNTS RECEIVABLE • INFORMATION SYSTEM • TOOLS • CONFIGURE • SELECT EVALUATIONS (Transaction OBAJ).
3. Schedule a periodic job to refresh the evaluation data.
   - In this step, you schedule the daily or weekly job to refresh evaluation data. You schedule this job using SAP MENU • ACCOUNTING • FINANCIAL ACCOUNTING • ACCOUNTS RECEIVABLE • INFORMATION SYSTEM • TOOLS • CONFIGURE • CREATE EVALUATIONS (Transaction F.29).

These evaluations are useful for generating summary analytics based on different criteria. However, another advantage of using evaluations is that double-clicking on any summary number takes you directly to the customer line item report for further analysis. Figure 11.13 shows a typical user interface to access AR evaluations. This is the first screen displayed when you access customer evaluations Transaction S_ALR_87012167.

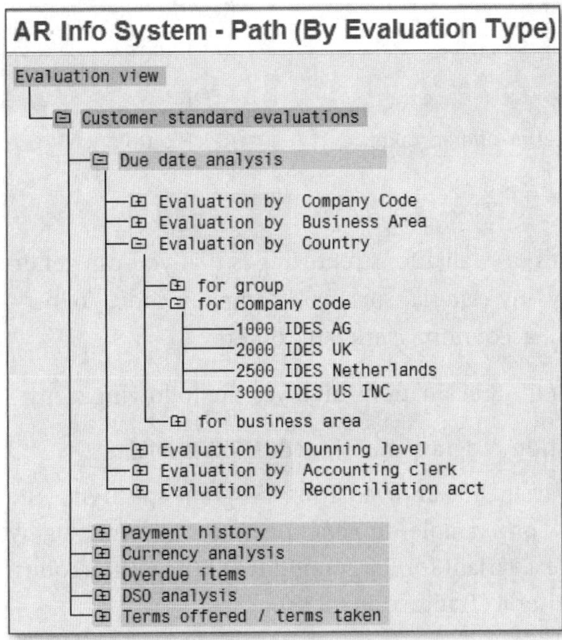

Figure 11.13 AR Evaluations

In the next section, we'll discuss SAP queries and how they can be used for AR reporting.

11.5 SAP Queries

SAP queries provide you with an advanced tool for creating necessary reports. This tool provides an almost direct access to database tables containing live data, so you'll need to interact with your SAP support team for the initial setup.

Tip

SAP queries provide a quick and easy way to generate spreadsheet-like output results. The output formatting capabilities are limited, however, so if you require reports with complex formatting, you may want to evaluate other options to generate a report.

The following components are important in the implementation of SAP queries:

1. User group
2. InfoSet
3. Query

Let's look at these concepts in more detail.

11.5.1 User Groups

A user group enables you to group users based on their authorization and their requirements to access data. You have to consider different factors when assigning users to user groups. However, two primary factors you have to balance are the following:

- The user's need to access business data
- The user's authorization to access business data

One of the ways you can handle this requirement is by creating user groups simply based on these two criteria. Subsequently, you can assign users to these user groups regardless of their organizational position or their department in your company. Because the same user can be assigned to multiple user groups, you can still provide a user access to queries as necessary.

You create user groups for SAP queries using SAP MENU • ACCOUNTING • FINANCIAL ACCOUNTING • ACCOUNTS RECEIVABLE • INFORMATION SYSTEM • TOOLS • QUERY FOR AR (TRANSACTION FQUD) • ENVIRONMENT • USER GROUPS.

Warning

All SAP query definitions are associated with a user group. So it's technically possible to have different versions of the same query in different user groups. However, you should ensure that it doesn't cause any data reconciliation issues.

After creating a user group, the next step is to associate user IDs and InfoSets to the user group.

11.5.2 InfoSets

An InfoSet specifies the structure of a dataset used for creating queries. It helps you select a dataset based on database tables that you'll use for reporting in queries. Not only that, it also allows you to create additional, calculated data values that you can use in query reports. For example, in an InfoSet based on AR data, you can use additional columns to fetch and report data from sales documents or billing documents. Figure 11.14 shows the definition of an InfoSet.

This relatively complex figure shows a definition of an InfoSet based on a predefined logical database in the SAP system. The definition screen can be divided into two areas for the purpose of explanation. The tree structure on the left represents different database tables and fields available in those tables. Any additional calculated fields are also shown in the left window. The right side window shows the FIELD GROUPS to which you assign fields that are part of the InfoSet. The FIELD GROUPS don't have any technical significance. They enable you to logically group InfoSet fields. In Figure 11.14, the Dunning Data fields are grouped into field group BA.

Note

It's advisable to create InfoSets so that they can be used to meet as many stakeholder requirements as possible without adversely impacting query performance. If you're concerned about user access, you can easily control it with the help of user groups.

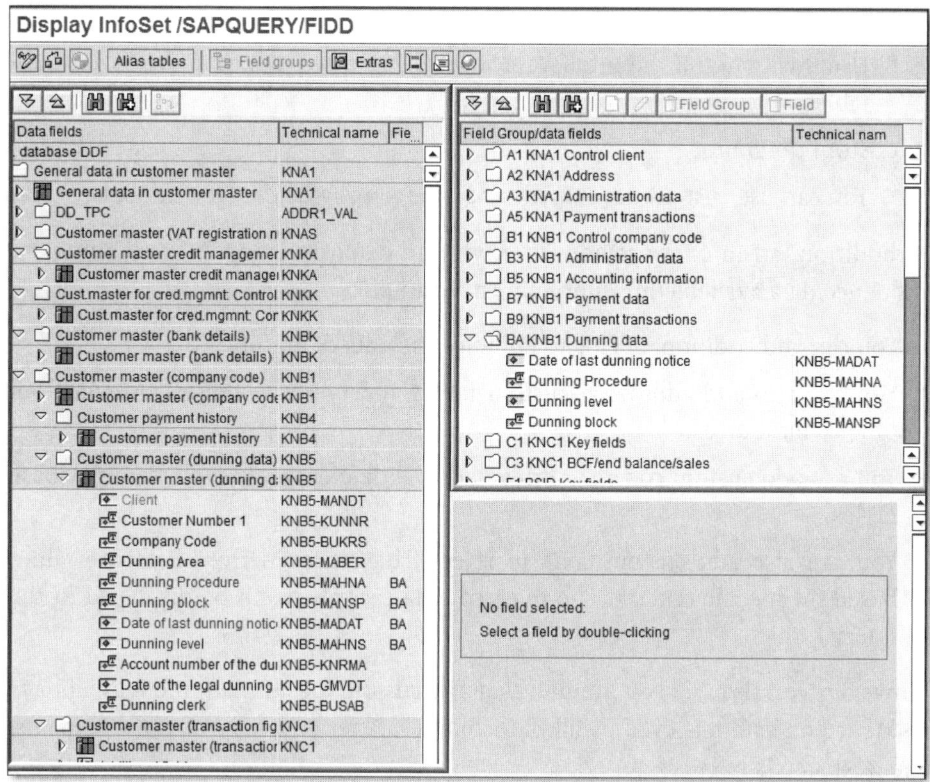

Figure 11.14 InfoSet Definition

You create InfoSets for SAP queries using SAP MENU • ACCOUNTING • FINANCIAL ACCOUNTING • ACCOUNTS RECEIVABLE • INFORMATION SYSTEM • TOOLS • QUERY FOR AR (TRANSACTION FQUD) • ENVIRONMENT • INFOSETS.

The data source for an InfoSet can be any of the following:

- A logical database
  - Logical databases represent predelivered, application-specific sets of database tables, table indexes, and an optimized data retrieval program.
  - If possible, this should be the first choice for creating an InfoSet.
- Direct read from the database table
  - Use this option if the InfoSet retrieves data from only one database table.
  - It's possible to add additional tables to the InfoSet definition even if you've defined it with this option.

- Table join
  - Use this option if the InfoSet retrieves data from a join of multiple database tables.
- Custom program
  - You can use custom-developed programs to provide data for InfoSets.

In addition, an InfoSet provides you with an extensive range of capabilities to influence data available for querying. For example:

- You can add additional fields to enhance the data of an InfoSet.
- You can also add additional custom tables and populate themwith data from other data sources.
- You can add custom code to retrieve and validate data retrieved from database tables.
- You can also add custom code to reject data retrieved from database tables based on specific criteria. The rejected data records won't be displayed in the query results.

However, you should keep in mind that any custom logic for an InfoSet will have influence on data retrieved by all of its queries. After you've created the InfoSets, the next step is to create SAP queries.

11.5.3 Queries

SAP queries provide a quick and easy way to obtain reporting data. Because the SAP query definition is based on an InfoSet, it can output only the data that an InfoSet definition can provide. You create SAP queries using SAP MENU • ACCOUNTING • FINANCIAL ACCOUNTING • ACCOUNTS RECEIVABLE • INFORMATION SYSTEM • TOOLS • QUERY FOR AR (TRANSACTION FQUD).

Figure 11.15 shows the definition of a customer address list query based on the InfoSet discussed in the previous section.

The query definition screen is divided into two areas. The window on the left shows the available fields for query definition, whereas the window on the right shows a sample output so that you can visualize the sequence and display of the query output. As mentioned before, the definition of a query is a simple process. Any field from an InfoSet can be selected as a selection field or a list field.

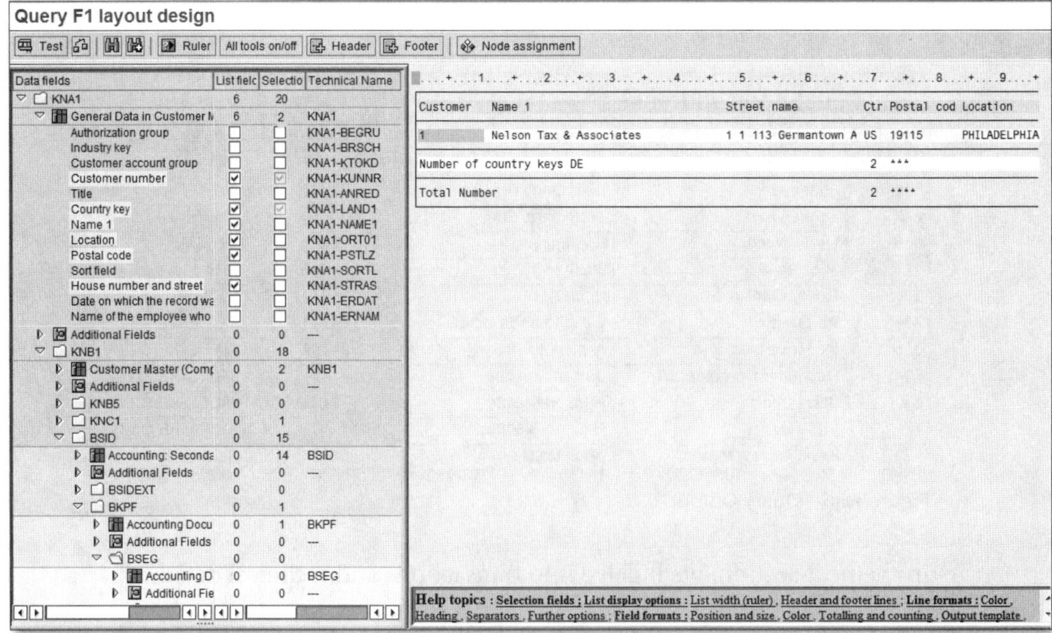

Figure 11.15 Query Definition

- If the SELECTION FIELD indicator is selected in the query definition, the corresponding field is available as one of the selection criteria when users execute the query.
  - Based on the selections made in the preceding example, the customer number and country from the customer general data will be available as selection criteria.
- If the LIST FIELD indicator is selected in the query definition, the corresponding field is output in the query results.
  - The sequence of the field in the query output depends on the sequence in which you select the field in the query definition.

Tip

The typical implementation approach for SAP queries is that after understanding the business requirements, the SAP support team sets up query InfoSets containing the necessary and relevant data. Subsequently, selected business users are made responsible for creating queries based on these InfoSets and maintaining them for the wider group of business user groups.

Figure 11.16 shows the output of the query defined in this section.

List of customer addresses

Customer	Name 1	Street name	Ctry	Postal code	Location
282	Tracy Herbert	West Lionshead Circle	US	81658	VAIL
540	Agnes Iams	Dell Range Blvd		82009	CHEYENNE
472	Agnes Varda	Dell Range Blvd			CHEYENNE
505	David Lynch	Marshall St		82831	ARVADA
271	Jack Norman	South and East		84043	LEHI
270	Robert Rankin	North Main		84074	TOOELE
268	Pat Davis	West South Temple		84101	SALT LAKE CITY
525	Ian Robertson	Ashton Street		84106	SALT LAKE CITY
524	Rodriguez Gonzales	Oakland Avenue			SALT LAKE CITY
539	Steve Garib	Hudson Avenue			SALT LAKE CITY
471	Steve Martin	Hudson Avenue			SALT LAKE CITY
273	Kevin Andrew Mundy	North Main		84631	FILLMORE

Figure 11.16 Query Output

In the next section, we'll delve into transactions and technical details.

11.6 Technical Reference

This section provides technical references for the functionalities discussed in this chapter. Considering the large number of technical objects available in the SAP system, this information should only be considered as a starting point for analysis. We already looked at the list of transactions in different sections of this chapter. So let's skip the customary section on the list of transactions, and look at the list of some of the SAP Notes.

11.6.1 SAP Notes

With the large number of SAP Notes available for any particular topic in the SAP system, it's impossible and somewhat counter-productive to list all of the available notes. The list of SAP Notes in Table 11.6 should be considered only a sample list.

SAP Note	Relevance
0000443158	DSO calculation evaluation for multiple credit control areas
0000165087	Authorization check in drill-down reports
0000431926	FAQ: Termination of drill-down reports
0000155752	Authorization check in mass printing of drill-down reports
0000388703	Option to run drill-down reports in background
0000972651	Line item display: Authorization check for transaction call
0000152335	Display of a purchase order in line item display
0000569939	Line items: Sort according to absolute amount
0000112312	Line item: Display offsetting account information
0000984305	Line item: Definition of special fields
0000550764	SAP query: FAQ
0000451216	SAP query: Test tool to analyze results of table joins
0000393160	SAP query: Access queries using a job, transaction, or report
0000769338	Single line output for overdue items analysis report
0001003807	Authorization for customer master list report
0000210706	SAP query: Get parked documents with logical database
0000048296	Implementing table joins in SAP query
0000525809	SAP query: Adjusting InfoSets with the Data Dictionary
0000024578	User authorizations in SAP query

Table 11.6 AR Reporting – SAP Notes

In the next section, we'll look at authorization objects relevant for the transactions discussed in this chapter.

11.6.2 Authorizations

Table 11.7 provides a sample list of authorization objects to be considered for the functionalities discussed in this chapter.

Object	Description
F_T060_ACT	Info System: Account Type/Activity for Evaluation View
F_IT_ALV	Line Item Display: Change and Save Layout
K_KA_RPT	CO: Interactive Drill-Down Reporting — Reports
F_BKPF_BED	Accounting Doc: Account Authorization for Customers
F_BKPF_BLA	Accounting Doc: Authorization for Document Types
F_BKPF_BUK	Accounting Doc: Authorization for Company Codes
F_BKPF_BUP	Accounting Doc: Authorization for Posting Periods
F_BKPF_KOA	Accounting Doc: Authorization for Account Types
F_KNA1_APP	Customer: Application Authorization
F_KNA1_BED	Customer: Account Authorization
F_KNA1_BUK	Customer: Authorization for Company Codes
F_KNA1_GEN	Customer: Central Data
S_QUERY	SAP Query Authorization

Table 11.7 AR Reporting – Authorization Objects

Apart from the authorization objects mentioned here, users will also require other standard authorization objects for accounting documents and customer transactions.

The next section is about tables and structures.

11.6.3 Tables and Structures

The customary list of tables and structures isn't relevant for this chapter because the report data resides in different tables for different functionalities.

You should check the tables and structures list in the chapters corresponding to the report output. In particular, you'll find that the list of tables and structures for AR transactions (Chapter 2, Accounts Receivable Transactions) provides data for most of the reports discussed in this chapter.

Subsequent sections of this chapter discuss enhancements and modifications for the functionalities discussed in this chapter.

11.7 Enhancements and Modifications

This section provides a list of available BTEs, enhancements, BAdIs, and BAPIs that are relevant for AR reporting transactions.

11.7.1 Business Transaction Events (BTE)

Using BTEs, you can attach additional function modules and custom logic to the standard SAP system. Table 11.8 lists publish and subscribe (P/S) and process BTEs available for the AR reporting functionality.

Type	BTE	Event/Process
P/S	00001610	Line item display: GUI call-up
P/S	00001620	Line item display: Key texts
P/S	00001630	Line item display: Prior to first list
P/S	00001640	Line item display: Additional header lines
P/S	00001650	Line item display: Add to data per line

Table 11.8 AR Reporting – BTE List

The following is an example of a BTE implementation for a line item display:

- Event 00001650: Display offsetting account in line item display.
  - In the standard SAP system, the line item display doesn't include information about the offsetting account in a document.
  - You can double-click on a line item to display the document, but the business requirement is to display the offsetting account in the line item display along with other information.
  - Using this BTE, you can supplement standard logic with additional code that fetches offsetting account information for each line item.
  - SAP Note 0000112312 provides more details on how to implement the business requirement using this BTE.

The next section discusses available enhancements for the functionalities discussed in this chapter.

11.7.2 Enhancements

Using enhancements, you can add custom logic to carry out additional validations and custom business processing. The following list provides some of the enhancements for the functionalities discussed in this chapter:

- `RFEPOS00`: Check selection conditions in the line item display.
  - This enhancement helps you in checking and, if necessary, enforcing selection conditions in a line item display. This could be done for performance improvement or maybe even for access authorization.
  - This enhancement contains the function module `EXIT_RFEPOS00_001`, which can be used to validate selection criteria entered by a user.
- `RFDRRANZ`: User exit for customer evaluations
  - This enhancement lets you provide display text for customer evaluations based on user-defined grouping characteristics.
  - This enhancement contains function module `EXIT_RFDRRANZ_001`, which can be used to fetch text information. The enhancement documentation provides more details on how to implement this functionality.

Let's now summarize the functionalities discussed in this chapter.

11.8 Summary

In this chapter, we started with the line item display transaction, which is one of the most versatile AR transactions. Judicious use of variants and layouts with the line item display transaction can generate numerous customer reports. Standard AR and standard SD reports available in the SAP system provide several commonly used reports such as the AR aging report, customer list, customer balance report, and so on. Reporting tools for drill-down reporting and evaluations enable you to analyze receivable data by different criteria. Lastly, the SAP query functionality provides access to database tables so that you can develop your own view of a dataset and create SAP queries based on datasets.

This chapter provides an overview of the SAP Financial Supply Chain Management (FSCM) components. In particular, we'll focus on the functionalities of FSCM components that are directly related to Accounts Receivable functionalities, that is, Credit Management, Collections Management, and Dispute Management. Also, unlike other chapters in this book, this chapter provides only limited configuration information. Instead, this chapter is focused on a high-level overview of features and functionalities of FSCM components.

12 Financial Supply Chain Management Overview

The objective of this chapter is to provide an introduction to the exciting, advanced functionalities available in the SAP Financial Supply Chain Management (FSCM) product offerings. If your interest is piqued by what you read here, then SAP PRESS has many books that provide more details on the FSCM components. SAP FSCM suite includes the following components.

- Credit Management
- Collections Management
- Dispute Management
- Cash and Liquidity Management
- Biller Direct, In-house Banking, and Electronic Banking
- Treasury and Risk Management

Tip

Before deciding to implement FSCM components, it's important to compare your business requirements with the functionalities available in the SAP ERP system. For example, the SAP ERP system provides robust credit management functionality that may be more than sufficient for many companies. On the other hand, the SAP ERP system provides very limited functionalities for efficient collections management and dispute management.

Our primary focus in this chapter will be on three components: Credit Management, Collections Management, and Dispute Management. As you'll see in this chapter, these three FSCM components are integrated very closely to Accounts Receivable (AR) processes. In particular, you'll find that Collections Management and Dispute Management components are very closely linked with the customer open item management transaction. Let's start with Credit Management.

12.1 Credit Management

The Credit Management functionality in the FSCM component is fairly advanced compared to the credit management functionality discussed in Chapter 7, Credit Management. In this section, we'll look at three important aspects: organizational structure, credit scoring, and credit exposure check.

12.1.1 Organizational Structure

From an organization's point of view, managing credit consists of formulating an effective credit management policy, which determines the areas of responsibility for credit management, the criteria on which credit limits of customers are determined, and the scenarios in which any further business with customers is considered at risk. In SAP, credit segments are used by companies to differentiate credit managing, monitoring, and reporting based on criteria such as divisions, business segments, or any other criteria relevant for business.

Credit-relevant information for business partners (business partners in SAP FSCM Credit Management correspond to customers defined in SAP ERP) is managed in their credit profiles. Figure 12.1 shows an example of a credit profile for a business partner. Let's look at some of the important fields and functionalities of a business partner credit profile. Credit Group enables you to group your business partners for reporting purposes, such as domestic/foreign customers, small/medium/large customers, and so on.

Using credit ratings, you can ascertain the creditworthiness of a business partner. You can establish your own methods to determine the credit ratings of your business partners; however, most large companies choose to obtain credit ratings of their business partners from external information providers such as financial institutions or government agencies and then integrate that information in SAP Credit Management.

Scoring

Rules	Rule for Existing Business Custome	Score for Business Customers
Score	9	Valid To 31/12/2010
Risk Class	Medium Default Risk	Calculated Very High Default Ri
Check Rule	03 Default - All Checks Active (Stat. (	Default - All Checks Active (Stat. Credit Limit)
Credit Group	2 Small/Medium Custo	

External Credit Information

Rating Procedu...	Rating	Trend	Valid From	Valid To	Rated on	Text
D&B Risk	2	Positive	01/01/2007	12/31/2010	02/13/2009	This rating has been fluctuating
Moody's	Baa3	Constant	03/01/2007	04/30/2010	02/28/2009	Validate this with Mr. Smith
FICA	537	Negative	06/01/2007	08/31/2010	06/13/2009	

Figure 12.1 Business Partner Credit Profile

Because different rating agencies typically use different rating notations, SAP provides you with the functionality to assign ranks to each of these ratings. Using ranking, you can map external ratings from different providers into a common, consistent measure to use in Credit Management. To use an example from Figure 12.1, you can assign the internal ranking of 002 (and interpret it as Good Credit) to credit ratings received from Moody's (Baa3), FICA (537), and D&B (2).

For internal controls, you can block a business partner in Credit Management for things such as fraud, insolvency, bad payment history, and so on, and you can also record whether a business partner has filed for bankruptcy or if foreclosure proceedings have been initiated. Using all of this information in addition to a black list and a white list (also called a negative list and a premium list, respectively) of business partners, you can influence the calculation and results of credit scores and credit limits. Let's look at these calculations in more detail.

12.1.2 Credit Scoring

Continuing to refer to Figure 12.1, Credit Management uses freely definable and customizable formulae in the credit rule to determine the internal credit score for a business partner. Using this credit score, it automatically determines the risk class that represents the grouping of business partners from the perspective of credit risk, such as low risk, medium risk, high risk, and so on. Finally, using other formulae (also freely definable and customizable) associated with the credit rule, the system calculates and proposes a credit limit in each credit segment for a business partner. Of course, you can override credit scores and credit limits proposed by the system.

This completely flexible design provides what you need to define credit rules that can automatically calculate credit limits for a large number of business partners and can be as complex or as simple as required to meet the specific requirements of your industry and your company. In the credit rule formulae, you can use several different criteria from the business partner credit profile and other calculated values. For example, these formulae can be based on parameters such as industry sector, nationality, occupation, sex, street, postal code, region, foreclosure, bankruptcy, country, affidavit, risk class, credit score (to calculate credit limit), credit segment, and so on.

Tip

Here are some examples of credit rule formulae that you can configure in FSCM Credit Management:

- If Business Partner in "white list" → Score = 100
- If Credit Segment = "GREEN_TECH" → Limit = $10,000.00
- If Credit Segment = "DEFENCE_DEPT" → Limit = $100,000,000,000.00
- If D&B Rating is between 0 and 10 → Limit = 21000 – (Score * 8.5)

All of these formulae are defined in a credit rule with a validity period (six months, a year, etc.) that enables you to easily ascertain if the credit score and credit limit are still valid or whether they need to be recalculated. Using the mass change functionality, you can efficiently calculate and update credit rules, credit scores, credit limits, and checking rules (discussed later) for large numbers of business partners.

Because you can manually override a credit score, credit limit, and other automatically calculated parameters, you can also use the SAP Business Workflow functionality to automatically trigger a notification to a credit analyst if sensitive credit-related data is changed for a business partner.

12.1.3 Credit Exposure Check

After the Credit Management functionality in FSCM is activated, a credit check is carried out in real time in SAP SD and AR by using checking rules.

Checking Rules

The credit profile of every business partner includes a checking rule used to calculate its credit exposure. These checking rules are freely definable and consist of a sequential execution of one or more of the following types of checks:

- Credit check based on credit insurance, collateral, and other information
- Credit check based on maximum document value to ensure that order or delivery values can't exceed certain value (e.g., for new customers)
- Dynamic credit check that only evaluates credit exposure within a specific timeframe (credit horizon)
- Credit check based on maximum dunning level reached (refer to Chapter 6, Dunning, for more details on dunning process)
- Credit check based on the maximum age of oldest open item
- Credit check based on the payment behavior index calculated using DSO (Day Sales Outstanding)

If the available checking rules and credit limit calculations aren't sufficient for your credit management processes, you can create your own routines to influence credit limit check calculations.

SAP enables you to carry out credit checks at the time of creation (or modification) of a sales order, goods delivery, or goods issue. Determining the most appropriate option for you depends on your business and your industry. Typical timeframes among order creation, delivery creation, and (if applicable) goods issue also influence this decision. For example, the timeframes for building an airplane or a ship span years; for make-to-order manufacturers, it can be months; and for e-commerce companies, it can be a few days or instantaneous. Credit limits are checked in real time and are updated in Credit Management to calculate credit exposure.

Credit Exposure

For every credit segment, you can choose whether credit exposure calculations should be calculated based on open sales orders, open deliveries, open invoices, or open accounts receivables. This selection is similar to the one available for credit management in the SAP ERP system. Figure 12.2 shows an example of a credit exposure report. This type of information provides you with a more detailed view. For example, during a credit block, the details help you determine whether to release the transaction for further processing, temporarily increase the credit limit, or reject the transaction.

Credit Exposure

Partr	Cr.Seg	BP Message	Name of Cr. Exp. Cat.	Seg Expi	Curre...	Cr. Expos.	Mess...
CMS1	0000	CMS0000001	Open Orders	23,173.84	EUR	28,768.00	USD
		CMS0000001	Open Items from FI	5,799.90	EUR	7,200.00	USD
		CMS0000001	Delivery Value	5,373.43	EUR	6,670.58	USD
	0000			**34,347.17**	**EUR**	**42,638.58**	**USD**
	3000	CMS0000001	Open Orders	28,768.00	USD	28,768.00	USD
		CMS0000001	Open Items from FI	7,200.00	USD	7,200.00	USD
		CMS0000001	Delivery Value	6,670.58	USD	6,670.58	USD
	3000			**42,638.58**	**USD**	**42,638.58**	**USD**
CMS1				**34,347.17**	**EUR**	**85,277.16**	**USD**
				42,638.58	**USD**		
CMS2	0000	CMS0000002	Open Items from FI	24,971.81	EUR	31,000.00	USD
		CMS0000003	Open Items from FI	13,291.45	EUR	16,500.00	USD
		CMS0000010	Open Orders	73,370.85	EUR	73,370.85	EUR
		CMS0000010	Open Items from FI	168,358.31	EUR	209,000.00	USD
		CMS0000011	Open Items from FI	10,472.05	EUR	13,000.00	USD
		CMS0000012	Open Items from FI	233,607.22	EUR	290,000.00	USD
	0000			**524,071.69**	**EUR**	**73,370.85**	**EUR**
						559,500.00	**USD**
	3000	CMS0000002	Open Items from FI	31,000.00	USD	31,000.00	USD
	3000			**31,000.00**	**USD**	**31,000.00**	**USD**
CMS2				**524,071.69**	**EUR**	**73,370.85**	**EUR**
				31,000.00	**USD**	**590,500.00**	**USD**

Figure 12.2 Credit Exposure Report

Other credit management reports in FSCM Credit Management provide you with an analysis of credit profiles, credit segments, and credit limit use by business partners. Detailed logs and extracts also help you understand the system response based on the transactional information received from other components. Before closing the discussion on Credit Management, let's compare the FSCM Credit Management functionality with the credit management functionality in the standard SAP ERP system.

12.1.4 Comparison of functionality

Table 12.1 provides a comparison between the two components.

	SAP ERP Credit Management	FSCM Credit Management
Master data	Customer account in AR	Comprehensive functionality of SAP Business Partner
Financial data	Only from AR	From AR, contracts accounting, and others
Monitoring of credit exposure	For a simple one FI and one SD system	Across multiple FI, SD, and CRM systems
Customer scoring and rating	Not available	Credit rules engine
External credit rating information	Only through third-party, partner products	Support for any XML-based service
Rule-based definition of credit limits	Not available (you manually assign credit limits to customers)	Credit rules engine
Support for SAP Business Workflow	Only in SD system	SAP Business Workflow capability for any credit event
Analysis capability	Customer fact sheet and other SAP ERP reports	Credit Manager Portal, including support for SAP NetWeaver BW
Connectivity to non-SAP systems	Not available	Connectivity possible through SAP NetWeaver PI Server

Table 12.1 Comparison of Credit Management Functionality

As you can see in the table, instead of credit segments, SAP ERP Credit Management uses credit control areas to subdivide credit management from an organizational point of view; the credit rules engine isn't available, so you have to maintain credit rating and credit limits individually for every customer. Instead of complex checking rules, you have to choose from limited options that meet most basic credit checking requirements.

The next section discusses Dispute Management.

12.2 Dispute Management

A customer dispute can arise at any stage, including order processing, order fulfillment, invoicing, or later. The dispute can be for any reason, such as late delivery, quality issues, or to force resolution to other issues. The dispute may be communicated in any form such as calling customer support, sending a complaint letter, or withholding invoice payments. In this section, we'll only focus on using SAP Dispute Management to manage and monitor customer issues and disputes based on payment deductions. However, the case management features of SAP Dispute Management are so generic and flexible that you can use it for other types of issue managements as well. For example, a product development company can use it to track product-related issues that are identified internally by employees or externally by customers.

12.2.1 Dispute Case and Role Assignment

At the core of SAP Dispute Management are completely flexible and fully customizable dispute case templates that you can use to efficiently create dispute cases relevant for your business. SAP Dispute Management offers several pieces of information that you can include, record, calculate, or reference in a dispute case (see Figure 12.3).

You can enter business partner information and contact information directly in a dispute case or let the system automatically copy it from AR. To effectively manage cross-departmental coordination for dispute resolution, a dispute case in SAP differentiates among the three roles of a processor, a coordinator, and a person responsible, which all can be different from an employee who creates a dispute case. A *coordinator* is the central contact person and is responsible for resolution of the dispute case, for example, a customer support representative. A *person responsible* is typically the person that is impacted financially if the dispute hasn't been resolved, for example, a cost center manager. Whereas a *processor* is typically the person responsible for processing or carrying out an activity and can change as dispute resolution moves through different stages.

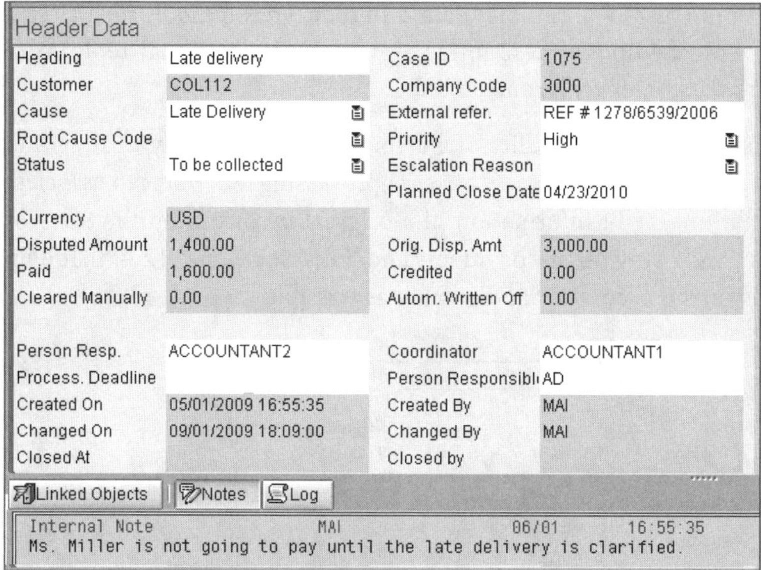

Figure 12.3 Information in a Dispute Case

Example

For a dispute about shipping charges for a delayed shipment, a coordinator may first assign a member of the shipping department as a processor, who confirms that the shipment was delayed; followed by an account manager as a processor, who decides that credit for shipping charges should be given; and lastly someone in AR as a processor to process credit to the customer.

Other unique characteristics of dispute cases include the following:

- For easy auditing, reconciliation, and communication, you can track several different amounts associated with a dispute case such as original dispute amount, current disputed amount (which can be different if the dispute has been partially resolved), amount paid, amount credited back to the customer, amount adjusted (cleared) manually, and amount written off.
- You can carry out powerful root cause analysis by assigning root cause to a dispute case in addition to a reason for dispute. For example, dispute reasons can be late delivery, but the root cause of this problem may be supplier or transportation issues.

- With every dispute case, you can maintain different types of notes such as customer description, additional description, internal note, internal reply, concluding remark, customer reply, and so on.

Another extremely useful functionality of a dispute case is its ability to store and link all relevant documents and objects for case processing. So, you can associate customer information, credit information, the original invoice from the Sales or SAP CRM system, and many other documents and links (see Figure 12.4) that help you process a dispute as accurately and quickly as possible.

Record Entry	Element Type	Visibility
Linked Objects		
Business Partner		All Roles
COL112 (Customer)	Customer	All Roles
Disputed Objects		All Roles
3000 1409 (Residual Items)	Acc Doc Line Item	All Roles
Credit	Acc Doc Line Item	All Roles
Partial Payment	Acc Doc Line Item	All Roles
Resolved Objects		All Roles
Residual Item	Acc Doc Line Item	All Roles
3000 1866 (Invoice)	Acc Doc Line Item	All Roles
Credit	Acc Doc Line Item	All Roles
Partial Payment	Acc Doc Line Item	All Roles
Items Assigned during Clearing		All Roles
Partial Payment	Acc Doc Line Item	All Roles
Credit	Acc Doc Line Item	All Roles
Other Objects		All Roles
Dispute Case	Case	All Roles
Customer	Customer	All Roles
Invoice	Acc Doc Line Item	All Roles
Accounting Document	Accounting Document	All Roles
Billing Document	CRM Billing, Billing Doc	All Roles
Account Statement Item	Account Statement Item	All Roles
Other Objects	All Element Types	All Roles

Figure 12.4 Linked Objects in a Dispute Case

In the next section, we'll discuss processing a case.

12.2.2 Processing a Dispute Case

Processing a dispute case is largely controlled by its processing status. SAP provides you with the status management functionality that you can customize to determine the routing and processing of a dispute case in different stages. For example, a utility company may use a status management process that routes a customer complaint through the processing stages of new, information requested, waiting for response, under investigation, closed or voided, confirmed, and so on. Status management also controls which actions you can take depending on the status of a case. So, you can decide, for example, whether a case that has been "voided" can be reopened by changing its status back to "in-process."

You can simplify dispute case processing even further by combining it with SAP Business Workflow, which enables you to automatically and electronically notify the appropriate employee. For example when a case coordinator assigns an AP person as a processor, he automatically receives an email indicating that his action is required on a dispute case. After the necessary action is completed (e.g., credit posted to customer account), he can update the status and return the case back to the case coordinator. Sometimes, a dispute case needs to be escalated because either a case processor isn't responding to the action request, an irate customer calls repeatedly, or case resolution is taking longer than an internally established benchmark.

Regardless of the reason, in SAP Dispute Management, you can assign an escalation reason to a dispute case to inform the supervisor, manager, or other employees that a dispute case has reached a critical stage. Similarly, you can add or modify new customers, business partners, open invoices, disputed items, and information while processing a case. Depending on the dispute case template you're using, you can customize which functions are available while processing a dispute case.

Different actions taken on a dispute case generate different types of external and internal correspondence. SAP provides the powerful Post Processing Framework (PPF) that works behind the scenes to manage the processing of relevant correspondence activities. Necessary correspondence for a dispute case update can be triggered automatically, or the processor, coordinator, or person responsible can initiate it manually. The template associated with a dispute case type controls several factors relevant for correspondence such as available types of correspondence, whether they are triggered automatically, what triggers the correspondence, how they are processed (e.g., fax, printout, email, SAP Business Workflow), and so on. Typically, as part of day-end processing, you can collectively process all correspondence requests.

Because the Dispute Management functionality primarily focuses on customer issues that are translated into payment deductions, it's fully integrated with the SAP AR component.

12.2.3 Integration of Dispute Management

The strength of Dispute Management is evident in its integration with SAP AR Ð particularly, the ability to automatically create dispute cases from AR items and the ability to update and take action on open dispute cases based on activities in a customer account. In its simplest form, this integration enables you to create a dispute case directly from commonly used AR programs such as while processing an open line-item list, a customer account clearing, and incoming payments. Similarly, from a dispute case, you can access open items in a customer account and insert their reference to the dispute case.

Additionally, SAP provides a highly sophisticated program that can automatically create dispute cases in Dispute Management based on residual items created in AR. Typically these residual items on a customer account are created as a result of payment activity such as incoming payments, lockbox processing, bank statement processing, and electronic check processing. The criteria, logic, and default values for dispute cases are determined based on a custom interface integrating AR with Dispute Management and default parameters (case type, reason, priority, etc.) specified in the system configuration.

Another helpful functionality is the automatic write-off of dispute amounts. The logic and criteria used by this write-off program can be influenced using custom development. For creating an accounting entry for write-off, the program determines the corresponding GL account based on the reason assigned to a dispute case and the corresponding cost center based on the person responsible assigned to a dispute case. Similarly, a custom development can be used to automatically close dispute cases that meet certain criteria, for example, cases that are in the status "customer reply requested" for more than 60 days.

Note

As you may have noticed by now, you do have to carry out custom development to effectively use Dispute Management functionalities that automate and integrate dispute case processing.

Whereas Dispute Management assists you in managing your receivables after recognizing a customer dispute, Collections Management helps you with proactively initiating contacts for due or overdue receivables.

12.3 Collections Management

Collections Management supports the evaluation and prioritization of receivables based on collections strategies to help you follow up with customers for payment reminders and record their response in the system for follow-up actions. Collections Management uses freely definable and customizable collection strategies to automatically prepare daily work lists with relevant information for all collection specialists, that is, employees responsible for follow-up with customers and collections. Because collection strategies are at the core of Collections Management, let's dig deeper.

12.3.1 Collection Strategies

Collection strategies (see Figure 12.5) primarily consist of collection rules that are used to select, evaluate, and prioritize customer receivables and create work lists for collection specialists.

Overdue Periods | Due Date Periods

Overdue Period 1	[ ]	1	To	30	Days
Overdue Period 2	[ ]	31	To	60	Days
Overdue Period 3	[ ]	61	To	90	Days
Overdue Period 4	≥	91	To		Days

Assignment of Rules

Collection Rule	Val	Name of Prerequisite	Name of Condition
CR0000002A	25	Risk Class A , B	Total of all items overdue since 30 days: Total amount larger than 5,000.00 USD
CR0000002A	25	Risk Class C , D , E	Total of all items overdue since 15 days: Total amount larger than 2,000.00 USD
CR00000003	20		Individual items overdue since 30 days: Amount larger than 1,000.00 USD
CR00000013	15		Broken Promises to Pay: Total amount larger than 10.00 USD
CR00000018	5		There is a resubmission due for the customer

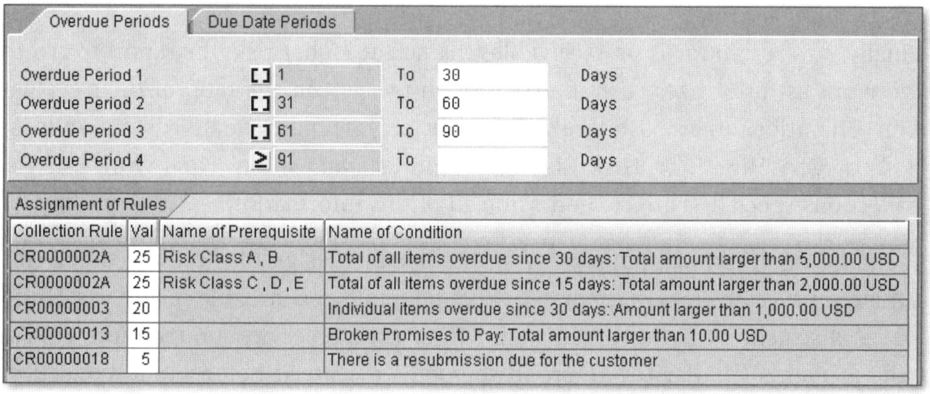

Figure 12.5 Collection Strategies

Collection rules reflect the reason a customer is to be contacted. A collection rule formulates the prerequisites and conditions that a customer must fulfill to be included in the collection processing. SAP delivers various collection rules based on the following:

- Total of all items overdue since "n" days
- Amount of individual items overdue since "n" days or due within "n" days

- Total amount to be collected
- Customer has paid less than minimum amount since "n" days
- Customer has items in legal dunning procedure

Customer receivables are selected for further processing if they satisfy one or more of these rules. You can even use rules as prerequisites for evaluating other rules. For example, you can prepare a rule that selects an item overdue for five days, only if the corresponding customer is also deemed a high credit risk. The process than evaluates selected items and assigns valuation points, which represent a number assigned by you to indicate the weight associated with a collection rule. Additionally, to avoid abnormally skewing the final results, you can specify the maximum valuation points that a collection strategy can assign to a customer.

Tip

A collection strategy can be customized so that it factors in payment terms offered to customers (10% in 10 days, 5% in 20 days, Net 30 days) while evaluating and reporting amounts to be collected.

Finally, so you can focus on receivables that are at higher risk, the report to create the work list prioritizes customers based on the percentage ratio of their evaluation. The priorities are also freely definable, so you can evaluate customers as A, B, C, or Very High Risk, High Risk, Medium Risk, and so on. Final work lists for collections specialists are created using all of this information.

From an organizational point of view, the flexible design of the Collection Management processes makes them easily configurable and scalable regardless of the size and structure of your organization. Your companies are grouped into collection segments (similar to the credit segments discussed before), and collection segments are grouped into one or more collection profiles. Similarly, collection specialists are grouped into collection groups, which are in turn associated with a collection profile. Thus a collection profile provides a common element that links collection specialists to the collection segments.

While preparing work lists for collection specialists, the report determines the default collections group based on the collection profile associated with a company. All specialists in a collection group collect open receivables with the same collection strategy, which helps collections managers ensure that the performance of all specialists in a group is evaluated using the same basis. Let's discuss the collections work list and activities in more detail.

12.3.2 Collections Work Lists

Work lists are created based on a default collections group and collections specialists associated with a collections profile. An easy maintenance program enables you to assign a substitute collections specialist if the main collections specialist is unavailable for any reason. Additionally, you can use the distribution method enhancement to allocate unassigned receivables items to collection specialists who have fewer numbers of items in their work list or who have a work list with a lower evaluation score and thus possibly quicker, easier interactions with customers. From work lists, collections specialists can easily branch out to a detail screen (see Figure 12.6) that shows them all relevant customer information and supports various collection activities. The details include customer contact information, past payments, open invoices, and due as well as overdue receivables conveniently grouped into different time periods (< 5 days, 5 – 15 days, 15+ days, etc.).

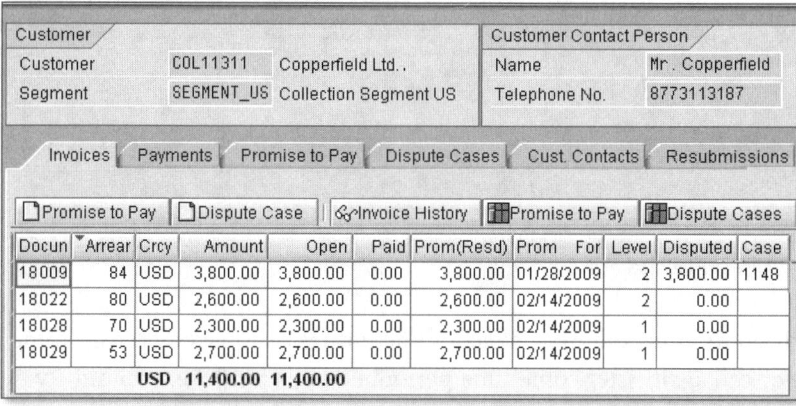

Figure 12.6 Collections – Detail Screen

Collection activities and their outcome can take different forms. For example, a collections specialist may not be able to reach the customer, or a customer may request later follow-up, highlight a dispute, or promise to make payment by a specific date. SAP Collections Management provides support for recording, managing, and reporting different types of custom-defined collection activity results such as customer contact not necessary, customer could not be reached, message left on voice mail, promised to pay, customer dispute, and so on.

12.3.3 Collections Activities

If a customer responds by promising to pay one or more invoices, you can create promise-to-pay records with the promised amount and promised date of payment. Even if you enter the promise information for multiple invoices, Collections Management tracks it at the individual invoice level. The strong integration between AR and Collections Management ensures that when incoming payments from customers are processed, promise-to-pay records are updated with the appropriate status depending on whether the promised amount was paid in full (status = kept), in part (status = partially broken), or not at all (status = broken). By using appropriate collection rules, you can make sure that partially broken or broken promises show up on the collections work list again. Figure 12.7 shows an example of entering a promise-to-pay record.

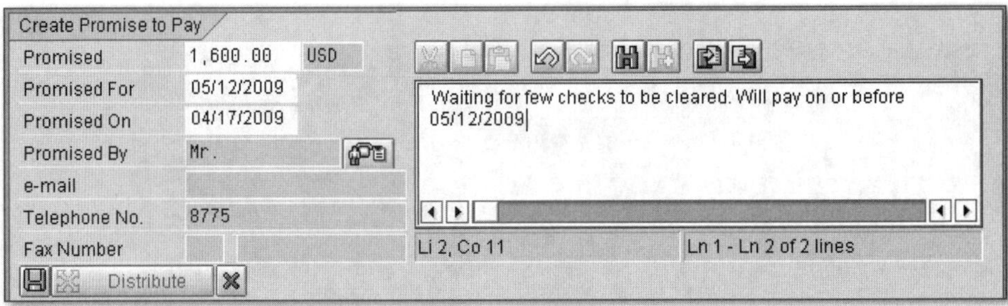

Figure 12.7 Promise-to-Pay Record

Another fairly common result of a collections activity is a request by the customer to follow up or call again after some time period. For this purpose, you can create resubmission requests and specify the date when the item should be included in the collections work list again. Similarly, you can record any customer disputes by creating dispute cases and any other information in detailed notes with each collection activity. A processing screen presented to a collections specialist always shows all details, including priority, outstanding amount, amount to be collected, amount promised, amount broken, amount under dispute, amount already dunned, last dunning date, last payment date, last contact date, and so on.

Apart from these activities carried out by collections specialists, processes are also available for collections managers. Because creation of an appropriate collections work list is completely dependent on the accurate definition of collection strategies, collections supervisors can tweak the strategies from time to time to adapt to customer payment patterns. Similarly, a supervisor can analyze the performance of collection specialists in his group by using a work list statistics report that shows daily open items, successful customer contacts, attempted customer contacts, and so on for each collections specialist.

In the next section, we'll explore integration of the Collections Management component with other SAP components.

12.3.4 Collections Management Integration

Similar to other SAP components, Collections Management is also fully integrated with other relevant SAP components. We already discussed how, because of this integration, incoming payments in AR automatically update promise-to-pay records created in Collections Management. For this integrated process to work seamlessly, SAP provides you with a program that can be enhanced to synchronize customer data in AR with business partner data for Collections Management. Similarly, a mass change program lets you update collection profiles in business masters. Other customer master data that is available in Collections Management include dunning levels to exclude customers from collections processing if legal proceedings have already been initiated against them, payment authorization to exclude those customers from collections processing who have authorized direct debit of their bank accounts, and so on.

Collections Management is also linked with Credit Management and Dispute Management. We already discussed how a collections specialist can create a dispute case while processing a collections work list. Similarly, in Dispute Management, if a dispute is unjustified, and the amount should be collected from customers, you can set the status of that dispute case as "to be collected."

This integrated functionality is evident in the definition of collection strategies, which can consist of collection rules based on the following:

- AR data such as open items, dunning and payments information, customer master information, and so on
- Dispute Management data such as the status of a dispute case and the disputed amount at the individual invoice level
- Credit Management data such as risk class, credit limit, use of credit limits, and so on
- Collections Management data such as promise-to-pay amount, contact data resubmission data, and so on

In conclusion, Credit Management, Dispute Management, and Collections Management components of SAP ERP FSCM provide you with many features and functionalities to improve the efficiency of your cash management. As mentioned at the beginning of this chapter, the purpose of this chapter is to provide you with an overview of FSCM functionalities.

- Using the advanced credit rules engine, you can automatically evaluate, calculate, and maintain credit scores and credit limits for business partners.
- You can control credit risk via real-time credit allocation to operational transactions, ongoing monitoring, and flexible reporting to evaluate credit exposure based on different internal and external criteria.
- Optimize, streamline, and accelerate cross-departmental dispute resolution, and use root cause analysis to uncover flaws in existing business processes.
- Using the Collections Management functionality, you can increase the share of collected receivables, avoid or reduce write-offs, and increase on-time payments.
- Using efficient Dispute Management and proactive Collections Management, you can reduce your average DSO, increase customer profitability, and improve the working capital forecast.

12.4 Conclusion

Hopefully, you are reading this after making your way through at least a few chapters of this book. As mentioned earlier, this book is an attempt to fill a void that may exist between business requirements of those who use, implement and support SAP system and the existence of corresponding features in the areas of

Accounts Receivable. However, I must acknowledge that as sizable as this book is, it only focuses on core Accounts Receivable processes in generic SAP installations. You may want to keep the following points in mind while evaluating information presented in this book.

Some of the core Accounts Receivable processes in your SAP system may provide more features than are presented in this book. For example, these core processes may have been enhanced in your SAP system, if you have implemented any SAP Industry Solutions or any SAP Country-Specific versions. You may even use entirely different SAP processes for some areas of Accounts Receivable. For example, it is not uncommon for companies with high transaction volumes and an extremely large customer base to use Contracts Accounting. Even though the underlying concepts remain the same, the receivable processes in Contracts Accounting is somewhat different from what has been discussed in this book.

Another aspect to keep in mind is the interaction and integration of Accounts Receivable processes with other SAP components that you may have implemented. For example, sale of a fixed asset in Asset Accounting can directly create receivables in Accounts Receivable, or settlement of an employee expense report in Travel Management may result in receivables posted to an employee account for any personal charges. The legendary integration capabilities of SAP makes it possible for processes in other SAP components to directly integrate with processes in Accounts Receivable. However, practical constraints make it difficult to include all possible combinations in a single book like this.

As always, I will appreciate your feedback on this effort, and thank you for purchasing and using this book. If you have questions, concerns or comments, please feel free to reach out to me via SAP Press or through my LinkedIn profile.

Appendices

A Technical Overview

This appendix is intended to provide a conceptual overview of the technical details mentioned at the end of each chapter in this book. In particular, we'll discuss the following topics in this appendix:

- Customer enhancements
- Business Transaction Events (BTEs)
- Business Add-Ins (BAdIs)
- Business Application Interfaces (BAPIs)

The intent of this appendix isn't to provide in-depth information on how to carry out different types of enhancements in the SAP system. Instead, this appendix should be used to get a high-level overview of technical details. Enhancements and modifications to the SAP system require considerably advanced technical knowledge and experience. All enhancements should be ideally implemented by your SAP technical team or at least after very close consultation with your SAP technical team.

A.1 Enhancements

Application enhancements in the SAP system allow customers to enhance their application functions. Some of the characteristics of these enhancements include the following:

- These enhancements are preplanned and predelivered in the SAP system.
- In a typical system, these enhancements are delivered in inactive status. As necessary, you can complete and activate the enhancements.

Figure A.1 shows different types of program enhancements available in the SAP system. For the purpose of this discussion, enhancement refers to customer exits. In subsequent sections of this appendix, we'll discuss other options such as Business Transaction Events (BTE) and Business Add-Ins (BAdIs).

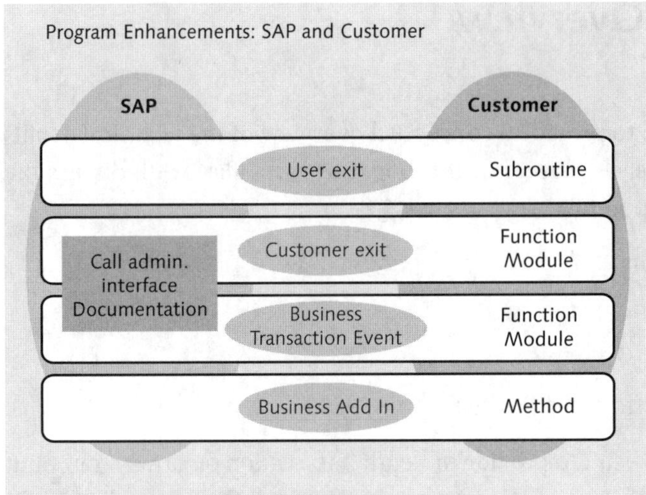

Figure A.1 Program Enhancements

You access enhancements transactions through menu path SAP MENU • TOOLS • ABAP WORKBENCH • UTILITIES • ENHANCEMENTS.

A.1.1 Enhancement Definition

As discussed previously, enhancements are predefined in the SAP system. One of the advantages of a properly documented enhancement is that you can implement it without carrying out an in-depth analysis of source code. That isn't to say that the implementation doesn't require proper knowledge and analysis. However, enhancement implementations make it easier to identify and enhance only a small part of a business process, without having to analyze the source code of an entire business process.

You can review available enhancements using the enhancement definition transaction (Transaction SMOD). This transaction presents you with an option to display, change, and test one of the predefined enhancements. For each enhancement, you can access the following information:

- **Attributes**: This screen provides basic information about enhancement such as description, creation, and modification details, and the technical package that contains the enhancement.

- **Documentation**: This screen provides any documentation that the SAP system programmers may have provided for an enhancement. A well-documented enhancement can certainly help ease its implementation.
- **Components**: This is the main screen that contains the technical components of the enhancement. For example, Figure A.2 shows a definition of enhancement `SDVFX009`.

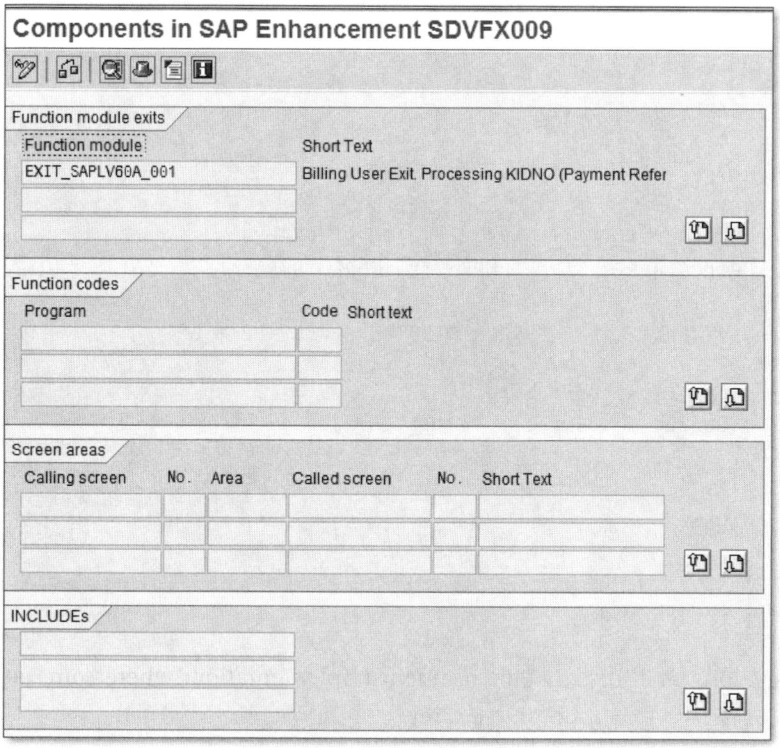

Figure A.2 Enhancement Definition

We discussed this enhancement in Chapter 5, Incoming Payments. It's used to influence the value of payment reference number in a customer document. This is a simple example of enhancement that contains only one function module. Some enhancements may contain multiple function modules. For example, the enhancement `V05I0001` discussed in Chapter 3, Customer Billing, contains two function modules: one for order-related billing and another for delivery-related billing.

Note

This appendix only discusses enhancements used for influencing application logic. However, a similar process is used to carry out enhancements to menu areas and screens in the SAP system. Depending on the type of enhancement, you use function codes or screen areas to carry out enhancements.

You can access the code for a function module by double-clicking on its name on the components screen. Following is an example of a code definition for the function module EXIT_SAPLV60A_001:

```
FUNCTION EXIT_SAPLV60A_001.
*"----------------------------------------------------
*"*"Local Interface:
*"     IMPORTING
*"         VALUE(XVBRK) LIKE  VBRKVB STRUCTURE  VBRKVB
*"         VALUE(LOC_BKPF) LIKE  BKPF STRUCTURE  BKPF
*"     EXPORTING
*"         VALUE(XVBRK) LIKE  VBRKVB STRUCTURE  VBRKVB
*"     TABLES
*"         LOC_BSEG STRUCTURE  BSEG
*"----------------------------------------------------


  INCLUDE ZXVVFU09.


ENDFUNCTION.
```

In the next section, we'll discuss enhancement implementation, where some of the elements of this code will become clearer.

A.1.2 Enhancement Implementation

At a high level, the process for enhancement implementation involves the following steps:

1. Create an enhancement project using Transaction CMOD (enhancement project management).
2. Assign the required enhancements to the enhancement project. By the nature of its definition, one enhancement project can consist of multiple enhancements.

3. Add the necessary code to the include of an enhancement component. This is where you specify custom application logic to carry out the required processes.
4. Activate the enhancement project. Activating an enhancement project activates all of its components.
5. At least for the sake of those who will maintain this enhancement, document your modifications.

The step about adding necessary code to an enhancement component requires some explanation. The enhancements are predefined in the SAP system. Components of an enhancement are also predefined as function modules in the SAP system. You shouldn't modify these function modules to add your code. Instead, you should add the code to the `INCLUDE` referenced in a function module. Figure A.3 nicely summarizes this process.

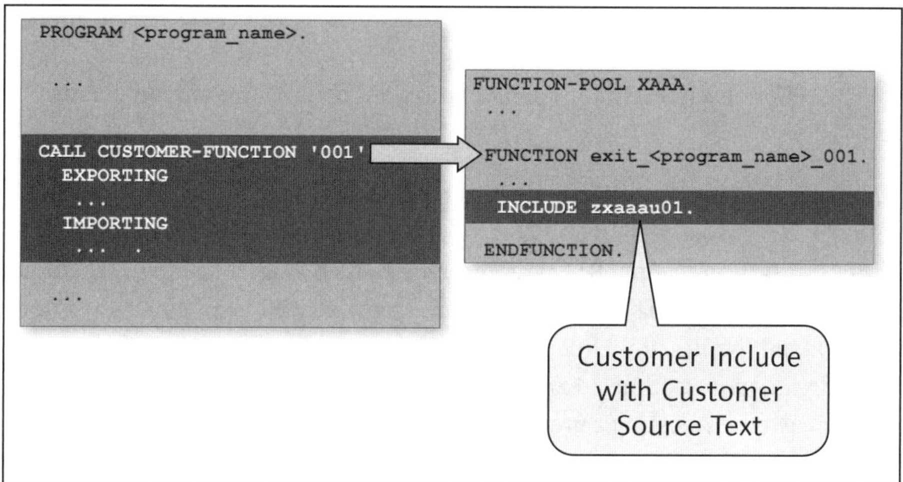

Figure A.3 Enhancement Implementation

For any enhancement, `CALL CUSTOMER-FUNCTION` is part of the standard program code. However, it's executed only if the enhancement project is activated. The naming convention of all function modules of a program is `EXIT_<program name>_nnn`, where `nnn` refers to a sequential number.

The standardized naming convention of function modules provides a relatively easy way to determine whether a program provides any enhancements. First you find name of a program by selecting SYSTEM • STATUS from a transaction screen. Subsequently, you search for an enhancement by searching for function modules starting with EXIT_<program name>.

Before moving on to the next type of enhancement, let's see a list of available transactions for managing this type of enhancements.

A.1.3 Enhancement Transaction List

Table A.1 provides a list of transactions relevant for enhancement implementation.

Transaction	Usage
SMOD	SAP enhancements
CMOD	Management of SAP enhancements
SE37	Function builder

Table A.1 Enhancement Transactions

The next section discusses the implementation of business transaction events.

A.2 Business Transaction Event (BTE)

Business Transaction Events (BTEs) represent the Open FI enhancement technique developed in the Financial Accounting component. A BTE is an event for which you can extend the functionality of an SAP system without affecting its programming using function modules. Examples of such events in AR processes are creating a new customer, posting a credit memo, or initiating a dunning run.

By using BTE, you can attach an external application developed by an SAP partner or custom developed for your company via a function module. You can add an interface at any of the following layers depending on the available BTEs:

- Other SAP components such as components from SAP Financial Supply Chain Management (FSCM)
- Function modules from software partners such as Dun & Bradstreet
- Custom function modules developed specifically to meet your business requirements

You'll find BTE-related configuration under SAP IMG • FINANCIAL ACCOUNTING • FINANCIAL ACCOUNTING GLOBAL SETTINGS • TOOLS • CUSTOMER ENHANCEMENTS • BUSINESS TRANSACTION EVENTS (Transaction FIBF). The first thing you may notice when you start this transaction is that there are two types of BTE interfaces.

A.2.1 Types of BTE Interfaces

The SAP system provides the following two types of BTEs:

- Publish and subscribe (P/S) BTE
- Process BTE

A P/S type of BTE informs that a certain event has occurred in the standard SAP system, and corresponding data is available to the receiving component or function module. The external, receiving components in this case don't return any data back to the SAP system. This type of BTE can be used to start a business workflow, generate or change additional custom data or documents, or print reports, notices, and other correspondence or reference documents. For example, the P/S type of BTE is used to publish credit account information to external systems or to print additional dunning notices.

A process type of BTE, on the other hand, enables you to replace the standard process of a SAP system. You can use a process type of BTE to carry out actions such as change data values of fields, change process calculations, and suppress specific processes in a standard system. For example, you can use the process type of BTE to influence DSO calculations or dunning charges calculations.

Tip

BTEs support multiple, simultaneous client-specific implementations, which enables you to use the same business event in different clients, if necessary even multiple times, for different purposes.

The P/S BTE has the advantage that you can carry out simultaneous implementations of the same business event. These implementations can carry out different processes in response to the same business event, independent of each other. For example, in response to a credit management BTE that publishes credit account information, you can have two external products carry out different processes independent of each other. However, because a process type BTE replaces the standard processing of the SAP system, you can have only one active implementation for this type of BTE.

Let's consider the implementation of a BTE in more detail.

A.2.2 BTE Implementation

Figure A.4 shows sample implementations of P/S BTEs for application components. As is evident in the figure, the same BTE can be implemented differently for different countries or different applications.

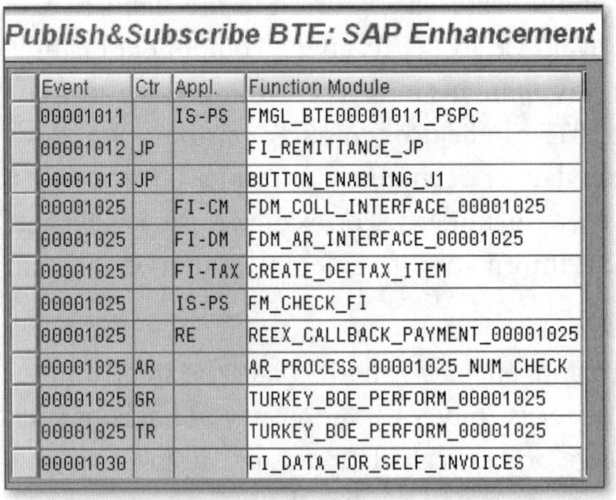

Publish&Subscribe BTE: SAP Enhancement

Event	Ctr	Appl.	Function Module
00001011		IS-PS	FMGL_BTE00001011_PSPC
00001012	JP		FI_REMITTANCE_JP
00001013	JP		BUTTON_ENABLING_J1
00001025		FI-CM	FDM_COLL_INTERFACE_00001025
00001025		FI-DM	FDM_AR_INTERFACE_00001025
00001025		FI-TAX	CREATE_DEFTAX_ITEM
00001025		IS-PS	FM_CHECK_FI
00001025		RE	REEX_CALLBACK_PAYMENT_00001025
00001025	AR		AR_PROCESS_00001025_NUM_CHECK
00001025	GR		TURKEY_BOE_PERFORM_00001025
00001025	TR		TURKEY_BOE_PERFORM_00001025
00001030			FI_DATA_FOR_SELF_INVOICES

Figure A.4 P/S BTE Implementation

Consider BTE 00001025, which represents the event signifying that all final checks for posting a document have been completed. As shown in the figure, this BTE has the following different implementations simultaneously:

- Different applications
  - **FI-CM:** Collections Management
  - **FI-DM:** Deduction Management
  - **FI-TAX:** Sales and Use Tax
  - **IS-PS:** Public Sector Industry Solution
  - **RE:** Real Estate Solution

- Different countries
  - **AR:** Argentina
  - **GR:** Greece
  - **TR:** Turkey

Implementation of a BTE involves creating, assigning, and activating a custom-built function module in the configuration. If the BTEs you want to implement are part of a partner application or a product, then that company will provide you with more implementation details. Otherwise, your SAP implementation and support team will provide you with more details on BTE implementations. You may want to first check BTEs that are already available in the standard SAP system.

To display a list of available BTEs, start Transaction FIBF. By selecting ENVIRONMENT • INFO SYSTEM (P/S) OR INFO SYSTEM (PROCESSES) in the transaction, you can display a list of available P/S BTEs or process BTEs. From this list, you can branch to display active component definitions or sample function modules.

ACTIVE COMPONENT DEFINITION will show you all application indicators, partner products, and customer developments for which the selected interface is already implemented. Whereas, the SAMPLE FUNCTION module will take you to the function module maintenance, which displays the sample code for the selected BTE. You can use this sample code to create your own function modules for implementation. The following is an example function module definition for P/S type BTE 00001025 available in the standard SAP system.

```
FUNCTION SAMPLE_INTERFACE_00001025.
*"----------------------------------------------------
*" Local Interface:
*"   IMPORTING
*"     VALUE(I_BKDF)LIKE BKDF STRUCTURE BKDF OPTIONAL
*"   TABLES
*"     T_AUSZ1 STRUCTURE  AUSZ1    OPTIONAL
*"     T_AUSZ2 STRUCTURE  AUSZ2    OPTIONAL
*"     T_AUSZ3 STRUCTURE  AUSZ_CLR OPTIONAL
*"     T_BKP1  STRUCTURE  BKP1
*"     T_BKPF  STRUCTURE  BKPF
*"     T_BSEC  STRUCTURE  BSEC
*"     T_BSED  STRUCTURE  BSED
*"     T_BSEG  STRUCTURE  BSEG
*"     T_BSET  STRUCTURE  BSET
```

```
*"       T_BSEU  STRUCTURE  BSEU     OPTIONAL
*"----------------------------------------------------


* You can add here custom logic for processing
* additional data and update other tables before
* AR documents are saved


ENDFUNCTION.
```

As discussed previously, this BTE provides the P/S interface for AR documents (Chapter 2, Accounts Receivable Transactions) before they are saved. As you can see from the definition, you have access to all of the FI document tables so that you can carry out additional data processing and table updates in this function module.

You implement and activate this BTE with the following steps:

1. Create a customized function module containing requisite validations and processing logic.
2. Create a customer product definition using Transaction FIBF • SETTINGS • PRODUCTS • OF A CUSTOMER.
3. Assign the function module to a BTE process by selecting Transaction FIBF • SETTINGS • PROCESS MODULES • OF A CUSTOMER.
4. On the subsequent screen, specify the link among the BTE, the function module, and the customer product.

Note that although BTEs aren't available for all components in all areas of SAP ERP Financials, new BTEs are continuously added to the SAP system. If available, BTEs provide you with an easy-to-implement and easy-to-maintain technique for making enhancements to the SAP system.

The next section provides a list of transactions relevant for implementing BTE technique enhancements.

A.2.3 BTE Transaction List

Table A.2 provides a list of transactions relevant for BTE implementation.

Transaction	Usage
FIBF	SAP Business Framework: BTEs
BERE	P/S BTE InfoSystem
BERP	Process BTE InfoSystem
BF31	P/S BTE: Implementation for application modules
BF32	P/S BTE: Implementation for partner products
BF34	P/S BTE: Implementation for custom development
BF41	Process BTE: Implementation for application modules
BF42	Process BTE: Implementation for partner products
BF44	Process BTE: Implementation for custom development

Table A.2 BTE Transactions

Now let's move on to another type of enhancement technique called Business Add-Ins.

A.3 Business Add-Ins (BAdIs)

BAdIs bring an object-oriented development approach to the SAP system enhancements. If it's been awhile (or never) since you interacted with computer programming, consider this approach as one of the most modular and manageable approaches for controlled implementation of SAP system enhancements. Similar to BTEs, BAdIs also allow multiple, simultaneous, and independent implementations.

The BAdI implementation logic has changed considerably as of the SAP NetWeaver 7.0 release. BAdIs introduced prior to this version are referred to as classic BAdIs. Classic BAdIs can still be accessed using transactions in the area SAP MENU • TOOLS • ABAP WORKBENCH • UTILITIES • BUSINESS ADD-INS. However, the discussion and the figures in this section only refer to the implementation of new BAdIs.

> **Note**
>
> The example discussed in this section refers to the enhancement of application logic. However, you can also use BAdIs for enhancing the SAP system menus and the SAP system screens.

Let's divide the BAdI discussion into two parts: BAdI definition and BAdI implementation.

A.3.1 BAdI Definition

You access BAdI definitions using SAP MENU • TOOLS • ABAP WORKBENCH • OVERVIEW • OBJECT NAVIGATOR • <CONTEXT MENU FOR A PACKAGE> • ENHANCEMENTS. Figure A.5 shows the definition of the `FI_LIMIT_CURCONV` Business Add-In.

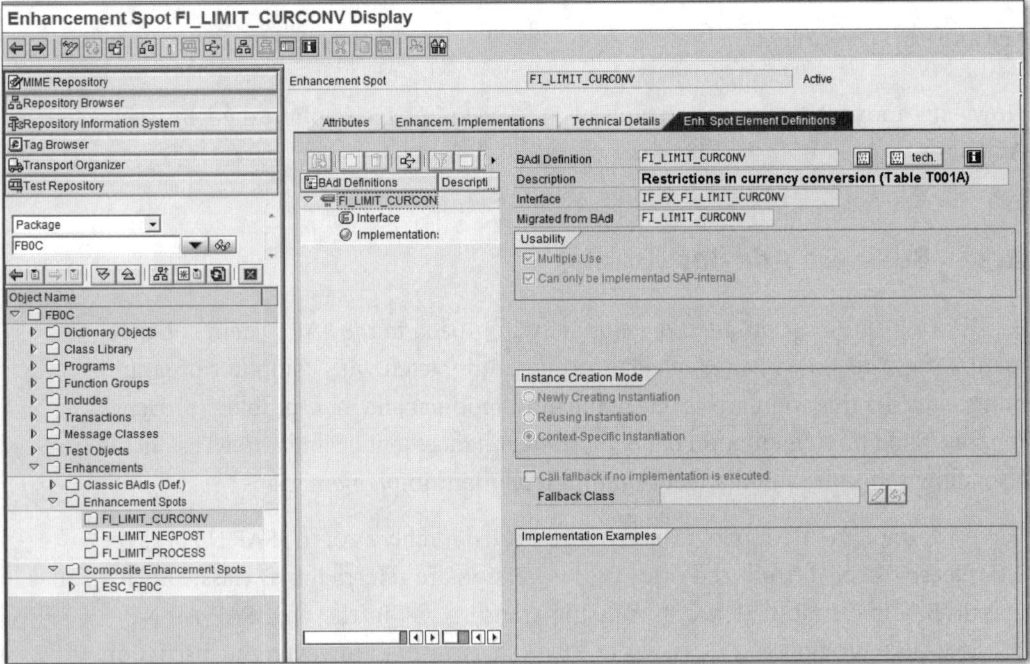

Figure A.5 Business Add-In Definition

We discussed this BAdI briefly in Chapter 2, Accounts Receivable Transactions. It's used to influence currency conversion while posting customer data to a company code. In the overall schema of technical implementation, this BAdI is part of development package FBOC (Financial Accounting – Customers).

Note the following BAdI definition displayed in the preceding figure:

- ENHANCEMENT SPOT refers to the so-called "container," which contains information about enhancements such as BAdIs.
- The BADI DEFINITION and DESCRIPTION fields refer to the name and description of a BAdI.
- If the MULTIPLE USE indicator is set, the BAdI can have multiple active implementations at the same time.
- The CAN ONLY BE IMPLEMENTED SAP-INTERNAL indicator is self-explanatory. However, you can use a BAdI specified as internal use only as a reference to create new BAdIs to meet your business requirements.
- The TECHNICAL DETAILS tab provides information about the reference interface as well as any implemented interfaces.

The INTERFACE describes methods available for the corresponding BAdI. You can double click on the INTERFACE link to display a list of available methods. Double-clicking on a method takes you to the screen shown in Figure A.6.

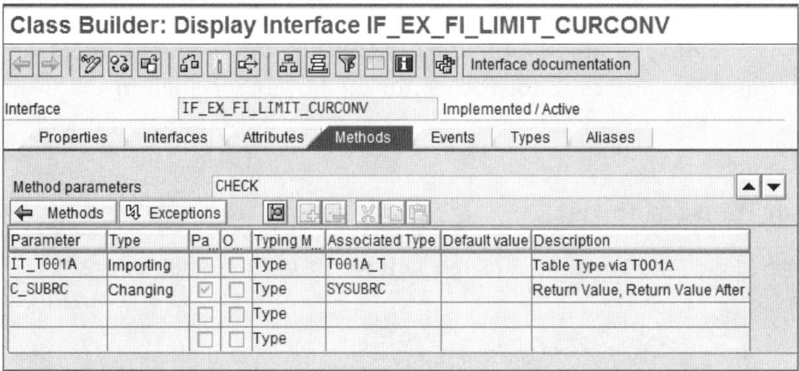

Figure A.6 BAdI Interface

This is a detailed class-builder screen on which you can specify import/export parameters and exceptions for a method. Figure A.6 shows details for a method

CHECK associated with interface IF_EX_FI_LIMIT_CURCONV. This method imports Table T001A that contains currency translation parameters, and returns status code back to the calling program.

Now let's see an implementation of a BAdI.

A.3.2 BAdI Implementation

The BAdI discussed in the previous section is marked for internal SAP use only. However, the following is an example of a code snippet that you would use to access a BAdI. The relevant commands are GET BADI and CALL BADI.

```
*"--------------------------------------------------------
... ... ...
... ... ...
DATA: bd_handle TYPE REF TO badi_name.
... ... ...
... ... ...
GET BADI bd_handle FILTERS <flt> = <val>.
... ... ...
... ... ...
CALL BADI bd_handle->method_name
... ... ...
... ... ...
*"--------------------------------------------------------
```

You specify any filter conditions in the GET BADI statement. Subsequently, in the CALL BADI statement, you access individual BAdI methods with the necessary parameters. Obviously, the code for each BAdI method is specified in the BAdI definition.

A.3.3 BAdI Transaction List

Table A.3 provides a list of transactions relevant for BAdI implementations.

Transaction	Usage
SE18	Create BAdIs (Classic)
SE19	Implement BAdIs (Classic)
SE80	Object Navigator

Table A.3 BAdI Transactions

The next section discusses implementing Business APIs.

A.4 Business APIs (BAPIs)

From a strict technical viewpoint, the SAP system BAPIs don't fall in the same category as the other topics discussed so far in this appendix. The enhancements techniques discussed so far are used to modify and influence the application processing logic of the SAP system, whereas BAPIs are used to exchange business data among SAP components and non-SAP components. However, because this appendix provides an overview of technical details discussed in every chapter, let's also look at BAPIs and their significance in a SAP system.

In the previous section, we discussed how BAdIs provide an object-oriented approach to enhancement of the SAP system. BAPIs extend this object-oriented system architecture by providing interfaces that can be used to access and process business objects in the SAP system. Customer, SalesOrder, and BillingDocument are all examples of business objects in the SAP system. BAPIs provide interfaces that create, change, display, and carry out other processes on such business objects.

You'll find BAPI-related transactions under the menu path SAP MENU • TOOLS • BUSINESS FRAMEWORK. Under this menu area, BAPI Explorer is one of the most commonly used transactions.

A.4.1 BAPI Explorer

You access BAPI Explorer using Transaction BAPI. It provides an easy-to-use, hierarchical interface to explore all BAPIs available in the SAP system. Figure A.7 shows a sample screen of BAPI Explorer.

As shown in the figure, the left window of the BAPI Explorer transaction provides a hierarchical or alphabetical view of available BAPIs. Every business object is shown as a node under the appropriate functional area. Figure A.7 shows the expanded nodes of the Accounts Receivable area under Financial Accounting. DEBTOR/CREDITACCOUNT, ARACCOUNT, and CUSTOMER represent the business objects available in the Accounts Receivable area.

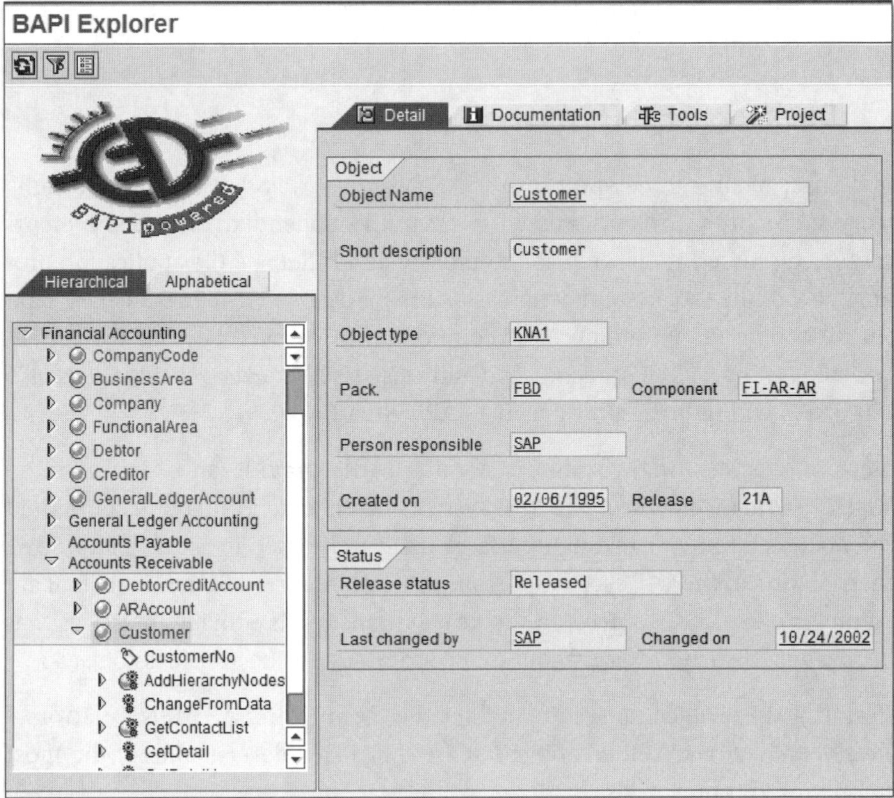

Figure A.7 BAPI Explorer

The right window of the BAPI Explorer transaction shows more details of the selected object. In this case, the figure shows details of business object "Customer." For every object, information is displayed on following tabs:

- DETAIL: This tab provides information such as the SAP COMPONENT, OBJECT STATUS, and most importantly the BUSINESS OBJECT TYPE (e.g., KNA1).
- DOCUMENTATION: This tab provides documentation for the business object, including information about the object structure and object integration.
- TOOLS: This tab provides links to branch out to different tools that are useful for BAPI implementation. You can access the ABAP Dictionary, function builder, business object builder, and BAPI list generator from this tab.
- PROJECT: Using this tab, you can create an implementation project for a BAPI. Later, we'll discuss this project in more detail.

In Figure A.7, all of the nodes below an object represent BAPI methods that are used to access and process the business object. Create, delete, and display are all examples of methods available for an object. Each method in turn is associated with a function module. Table A.4 shows some of the methods and corresponding function modules for customer business objects.

Method	Function Module	Description
Create	BAPI_CUSTOMER_ CREATE	Create customer master.
Edit	BAPI_CUSTOMER_ EDIT	Change customer master.
Display	BAPI_CUSTOMER_ DISPLAY	Display customer master.
Delete	BAPI_CUSTOMER_ DELETE	Delete customer master.

Table A.4 BAPI Methods

You'll find other methods and corresponding function modules in Chapter 1, Customer Master Data. By double-clicking on the function module name, you can display the associated ABAP code.

Tip

You can use the test function module option to test function modules associated with BAPI methods.

Following is the ABAP code for function module BAPI_CUSTOMER_ DISPLAY.

```
FUNCTION BAPI_CUSTOMER_DISPLAY.
*"----------------------------------------------------
*"*"Lokale Schnittstelle:
*"      IMPORTING
*"              VALUE(CUSTOMERNO) LIKE  BAPICUSTOMER_ID-CUSTOMER
*"        EXPORTING
*"              VALUE(RETURN) LIKE  BAPIRET1 STRUCTURE  BAPIRET1
*"----------------------------------------------------


  CALL FUNCTION 'BAPI_CUSTOMER_EXISTENCECHECK'
       EXPORTING
            customerno  = customerno
*           COMPANYCODE =
       IMPORTING
            return      = return.
```

```
  IF not return is initial.
    EXIT.
  ENDIF.

  SET PARAMETER ID 'KUN' FIELD CUSTOMERNO.

* S/G-Parameter für Buchungskreis und Vkorg löschen, sonst
Fehlermeldung
  SET PARAMETER ID 'BUK' FIELD space.
  SET PARAMETER ID 'VKO' FIELD space.
  SET PARAMETER ID 'VTW' FIELD space.
  SET PARAMETER ID 'SPA' FIELD space.

  CALL TRANSACTION 'XD03'.

ENDFUNCTION.
```

A.4.2 Using BAPIs

BAPIs enable integration between multiple SAP systems, as well as between SAP and non-SAP systems. You can use Internet portals, XML, and a range of other technologies with SAP BAPI function modules.

In an over-simplified technical realm, BAPIs are similar to remote function calls (RFC). So you can call BAPIs similar to the way in which you would call function modules in other SAP systems. However, the actual implementation is decidedly more complicated and too technical for the scope of this appendix.

You may want to refer to other resources for details on BAPI implementations.

Let's end this appendix by listing transactions relevant for BAPIs.

A.4.3 BAPI Transaction List

Table A.5 provides a list of transactions relevant for BAPI implementation.

Transaction	Usage
BAPI	BAPI Explorer
SE19	Implement BAdIs (Classic)
SE80	Object Navigator

Table A.5 BAPI Transactions

B SAP Authorizations

In this appendix, we'll discuss authorizations, which are used to control and limit user access in the SAP system. The authorization concept in the SAP system allows you to control user access to a transaction, a field on a transaction, or even a value of a transaction field. In this appendix, we'll only scratch the surface of the SAP authorization concept. However, depending on the business and statutory requirements, you can make SAP authorizations as simple or as complicated as you want. Obviously, you have to strike a balance between having the most restrictive authorizations versus the practical aspect of running a day-to-day business.

You will find authorization-related transactions under SAP MENU • TOOLS • ADMINISTRATION • USER MAINTENANCE • ROLE ADMINISTRATION. A simplified process of maintaining user authorizations is summarized as follows:

1. Identify authorizations required for a user.
2. Identify the standard SAP role that contains as many required authorizations as possible.
3. Create a copy of the SAP role to a custom role.
4. Add other authorization objects to the custom role as necessary.
5. Maintain the values for the authorization fields to implement the required access.
6. Generate an authorization profile for the custom role.
7. Assign the custom role to the user.

Of course, this process isn't scalable for a large company with thousands of worldwide users using hundreds of SAP transactions. For that, you use composite roles, user groups, and other advanced authorization concepts and tools. However, for the purpose of this appendix, the process just described captures the essence of the SAP authorization concept. Let's focus on two important elements of the SAP authorization concept: authorization objects (step 4) and authorization profiles (step 6).

B.1 Authorization Objects

An authorization object in the SAP system enables you to define complex authorizations by grouping up to 10 authorization fields to check whether a user is allowed to perform a certain action.

> **Note**
>
> Toward the end of every chapter in this book, you'll find a section that lists important authorization objects relevant to the functionality discussed in that chapter.

You can list available authorization objects by using any transaction under SAP Menu • Tools • Administration • User Maintenance • Information System • Authorization Objects. Figure B.1 provides a sample list of authorization objects for the AR component.

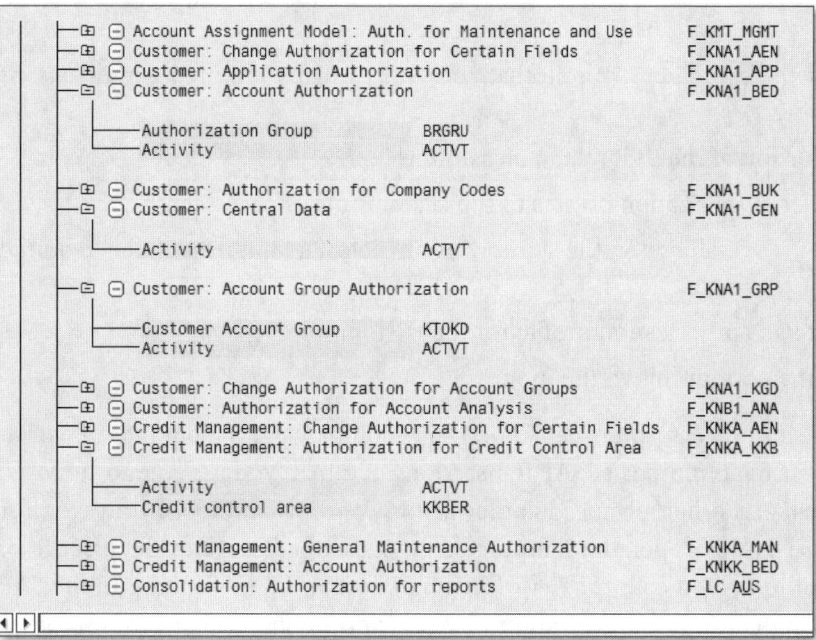

Figure B.1 List of Authorization Objects

In Figure B.1, F_KNA1_AEN, F_KNA1_APP, F_KNA1_BED, and F_KNA1_BUK are examples of authorization objects. The fields listed below each authorization object correspond to the associated authorization fields. So the authorization object F_KNA1_KKB includes authorization fields Credit Control Area and Activity. The authorization object F_KNA1_GEN contains only one authorization field: Activity. You can display details of an authorization object by double-clicking on its name.

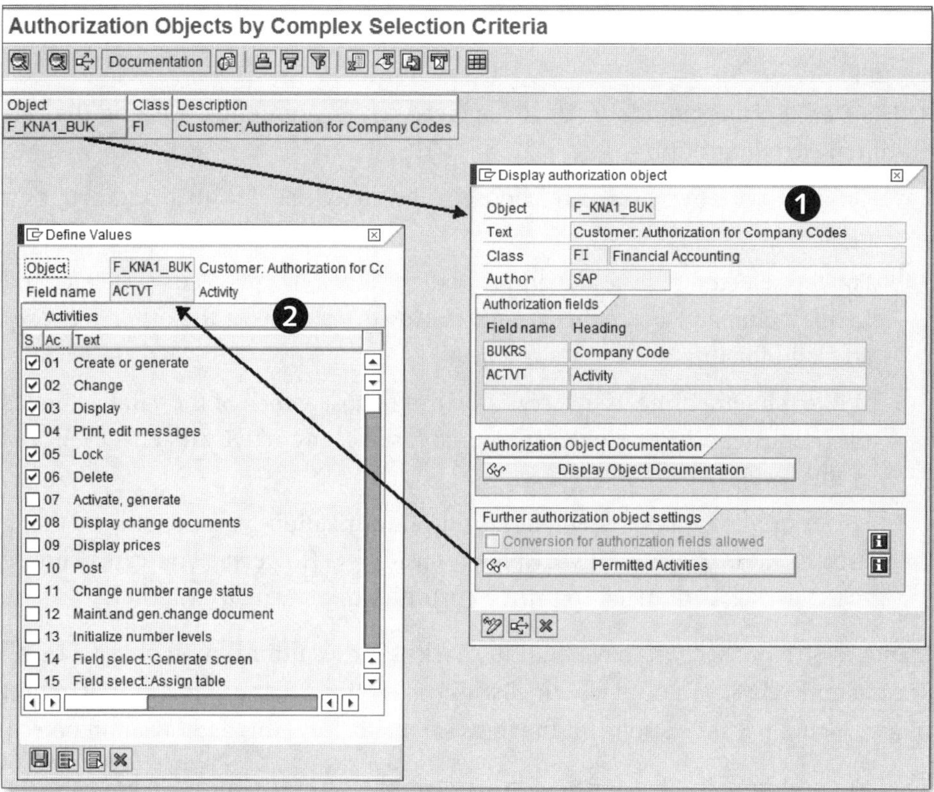

Figure B.2 Authorization Object

Figure B.2 shows the details underlying authorization object F_KNA1_BUK. As the description indicates, this authorization object is used to implement user access to customer accounts by company codes or legal entities. The figure shows two levels of details:

- The Display Authorization Object window (❶) is displayed when you double-click on the authorization object.

- It shows the Authorization Fields that are part of the authorization object. In this case, fields "BUKRS" and "ACTVT" are the authorization fields for which you can maintain access values.
- Using Display Object Documentation, you can display documentation associated with the authorization object.
- Permitted Activities provides the list of activities permitted for this authorization.

- The Define Values window (❷) is displayed when you double-click on the Permitted Activities button.
  - On this window, you can choose valid activities for this authorization object.
  - For the selected object, activities Create, Change, Display, Lock, Delete, and Display Change Documents are valid. However, none of the other activities are valid for this authorization object.
  - While implementing user access, you can choose which of the valid activities the user can perform. However, you can't select any activity that isn't selected at this level.
  - For example, while implementing this authorization, you can choose that a user is authorized to only display a customer. However, you can't choose that a user is authorized to print a customer or activate a customer.

Standard SAP transactions have built-in checks for the authorization objects. Using Transaction SU24, you can view the list of transactions that use this authorization object. Figure B.3 shows some of the transactions that use this authorization object.

The Proposal field in Figure B.3 indicates whether a user is provided access to a transaction and whether the default value for the authorization object is added to that user authorization profile (discussed later). As you may expect, all transactions that access company code customer master data (Transactions FD01 to FD05) have this value set as "yes." The transactions that post customer invoices (Transaction FB70) and customer credit memos (Transaction FB75) do as well. So if these transactions are assigned to a user, by default, the system will also add authorization checks using this authorization object. You can change the Proposal field value to change this default behavior of the SAP system.

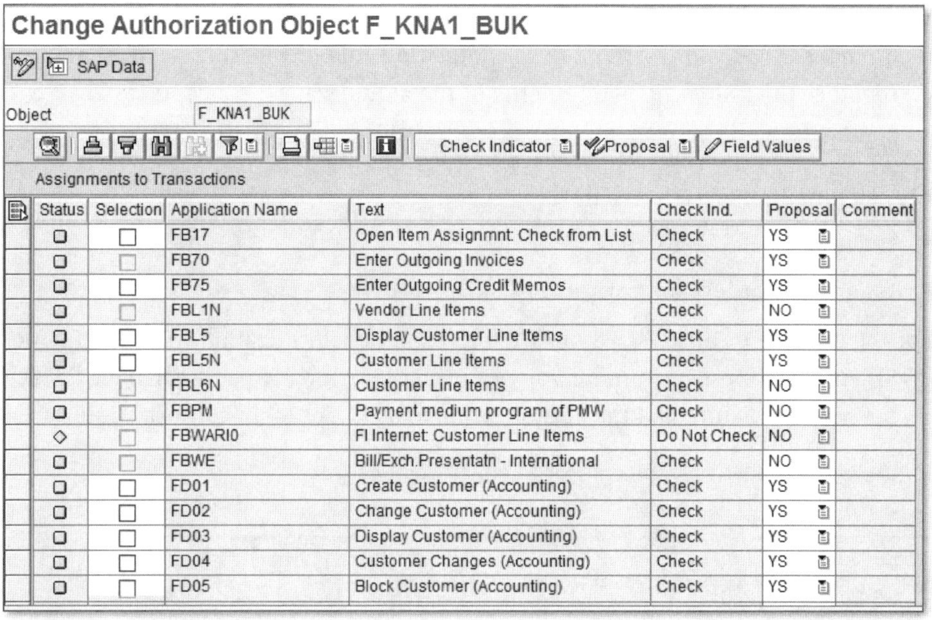

Change Authorization Object F_KNA1_BUK

SAP Data

Object F_KNA1_BUK

Check Indicator | Proposal | Field Values

Assignments to Transactions

Status	Selection	Application Name	Text	Check Ind.	Proposal	Comment
		FB17	Open Item Assignmnt: Check from List	Check	YS	
		FB70	Enter Outgoing Invoices	Check	YS	
		FB75	Enter Outgoing Credit Memos	Check	YS	
		FBL1N	Vendor Line Items	Check	NO	
		FBL5	Display Customer Line Items	Check	YS	
		FBL5N	Customer Line Items	Check	YS	
		FBL6N	Customer Line Items	Check	NO	
		FBPM	Payment medium program of PMW	Check	NO	
		FBWARI0	FI Internet: Customer Line Items	Do Not Check	NO	
		FBWE	Bill/Exch.Presentatn - International	Check	NO	
		FD01	Create Customer (Accounting)	Check	YS	
		FD02	Change Customer (Accounting)	Check	YS	
		FD03	Display Customer (Accounting)	Check	YS	
		FD04	Customer Changes (Accounting)	Check	YS	
		FD05	Block Customer (Accounting)	Check	YS	

Figure B.3 Authorization Check

Another important element of the SAP authorization concept is the authorization profile. You use the profile generator to generate authorization roles and authorization profiles.

B.2 Profile Generator

An authorization profile contains authorizations that provide users access to the SAP system. A profile contains authorization objects and associated authorization field values. If an authorization profile is assigned to a user, the user is assigned all of its authorizations. Authorizations themselves don't have any meaning. They are meaningful only when associated with an authorization profile.

In earlier versions of the SAP system, you had to maintain authorization profiles manually. However, in the new SAP system, it's highly recommended that you use the profile generator to maintain, generate, and assign authorization profiles to SAP system users. You access the profile generator using SAP MENU • TOOLS • ADMINISTRATION • USER MAINTENANCE • ROLE ADMINISTRATION • ROLES (Transaction PFCG).

When you start the profile generator, you're presented with authorization role maintenance. You can consider an authorization role as one of the elements that tie together the following components of the authorization concept:

- The SAP system menu structure
- Assignment of SAP transactions
- Assignment of SAP users
- Assignment of SAP authorizations

For the purpose of this discussion, we'll look at the authorization role SAP_FI_AR_POST_ENTRIES (post customer invoices and credit memos). In particular, we'll focus on the menu structure and the authorization assignment to an authorization role.

Figure B.4 shows the Menu tab of an authorization role.

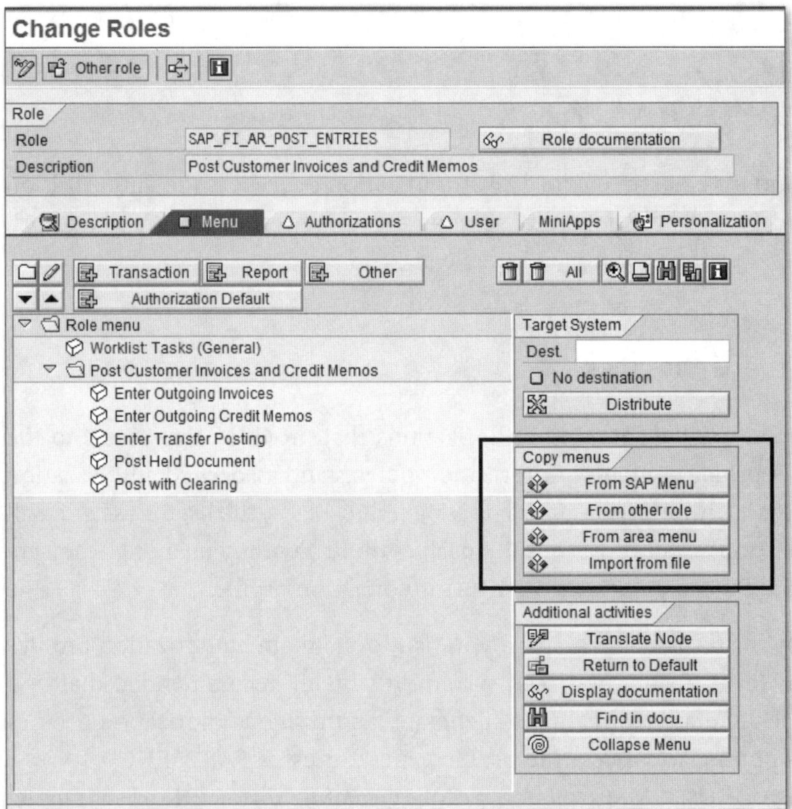

Figure B.4 Authorization Role

Note the following.

- The window on the left shows the authorization Role Menu. This is the menu presented to a user who is assigned this authorization role.
- Using the options under COPY MENUS (highlighted area in the figure), you can add to a role menu from an SAP menu, from an area menu, or from other authorization roles, or you can import the menu from a file.
- Menu additions to an authorization rule automatically associate corresponding SAP transactions to the role. Using the +TRANSACTION option, you can also add other SAP transactions directly to this authorization role.
- The +REPORT option can be used to add custom reports and queries to the authorization role.
- Using +OTHER, you can even add other objects to a menu such as a web URL, documents, or other reference links.

You may recall from the previous discussion that all standard SAP transactions include authorization objects and corresponding authorization checks. So let's look at the Authorizations tab of the authorization rule.

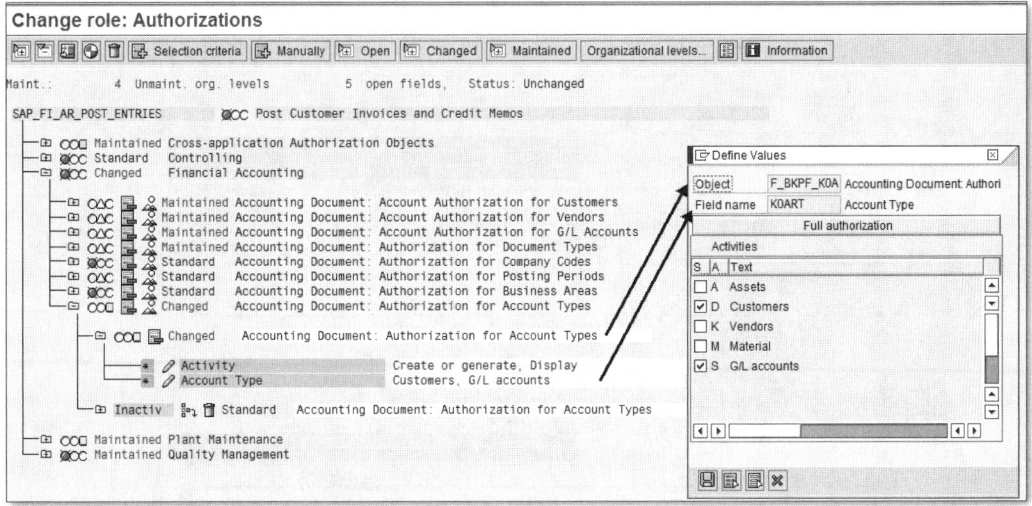

Figure B.5 Authorization Maintenance

Figure B.5 shows the authorization maintenance screen of the authorization role SAP_FI_AR_POST_ENTRIES. You reach this screen from the AUTHORIZATIONS tab by selecting Change Authorization Data option. Take note of the following points about this screen:

- The screen shows the expanded hierarchy of authorization objects grouped under authorization object class such as Controlling, Financial Accounting, Plant Maintenance, and so on.
- The display hierarchy consists of Authorization Role • Authorization Object Class • Authorization Object • Authorizations • Authorization Fields.
- In the example shown here, the authorization consists of two fields: activity and account type.
- Available values for the authorization field activity are determined based on the definition of the authorization object.
- Other authorization field values can be either selected from a predefined list for fields such as Account Type, or they can be entered manually for fields such as Company Code or Sales Organization.

After you've maintained the authorizations, you can add users on the User tab. This assignment updates the role information in the user master (Figure B.6). Finally, you have to carry out the process of user master data reconciliation (Transaction PFUD), so that user master records are updated with relevant authorization profiles.

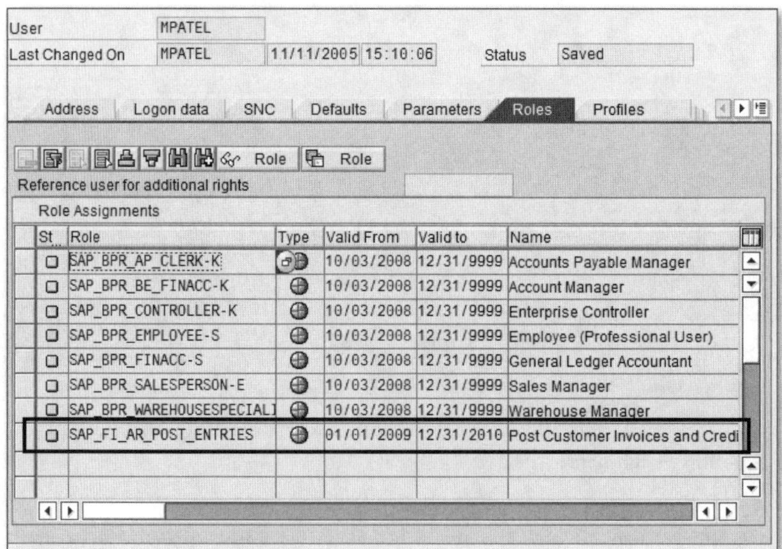

Figure B.6 Authorization Role Assignment

The next section provides a list of standard SAP authorization roles.

B.3 Authorization Roles

This section provides a quick reference to all standard SAP authorization roles for the functionalities discussed in this book. You can use these roles as a starting point to research, analyze, and create roles relevant for your business.

B.3.1 AR Roles

Table B.1 lists Accounts Receivable roles in the standard SAP system that are relevant for the functionalities discussed in this book.

Role	Description
SAP_FI_AR_BALANCE_CARRYFORWARD	AR: balance carry forward
SAP_FI_AR_CHANGE_LINE_ITEMS	Change customer line items
SAP_FI_AR_CHANGE_PARKED_DOCUM	Change parked document
SAP_FI_AR_CHANGE-REVERSE	Change/reverse AR postings
SAP_FI_AR_CLEAR_OPEN_ITEMS	Clear customer line items
SAP_FI_AR_CREDIT_MASTER_DATA	Credit Management master data
SAP_FI_AR_CUST_DOWN_PAYMENTS	Process customer down payments
SAP_FI_AR_DISPLAY_CREDIT_INFO	Display credit data
SAP_FI_AR_DISPLAY_CUST_INFO	Display customer information
SAP_FI_AR_DISPLAY_DOCUMENTS	Display customer documents
SAP_FI_AR_DISPLAY_MASTER_DATA	Display customer master data
SAP_FI_AR_DISPLAY_PARKED_DOCUM	Display parked customer document
SAP_FI_AR_DUNNING_PROGRAM	Dunning program
SAP_FI_AR_INTEREST_CALCULATION	AR interest calculation
SAP_FI_AR_INTERNET_FUNCTIONS	Internet functions for AR accounting
SAP_FI_AR_KEY_REPORTS	Key reports for AR accounting
SAP_FI_AR_MASTER_DATA	Maintenance of AR master data

Table B.1 AR Authorization Roles

Role	Description
SAP_FI_AR_PARK_DOCUMENT	Park customer documents
SAP_FI_AR_PERIOD_END_PROCESS	AR closing operations
SAP_FI_AR_POST_ENTRIES	Post customer invoices and credit memos
SAP_FI_AR_POST_MANUAL_PAYMENTS	Post incoming payments manually
SAP_FI_AR_POST_PARKED_DOCUMENT	Post parked customer document
SAP_FI_AR_PRINT_CORRESPONDENCE	AR correspondence
SAP_FI_AR_RECURRING_DOCUMENTS	Recurring customer documents
SAP_FI_AR_SAMPLE_DOCUMENTS	Sample customer documents
SAP_FI_AR_VALUATION	Valuation of AR items

Table B.1 AR Authorization Roles (Cont.)

B.3.2 SD Roles

Table B.2 lists Sales and Distribution roles in the standard SAP system; that are relevant for the functionalities discussed in this book.

Role	Description
SAP_LO_SD_BILLING_BATCH	Process billing by batch
SAP_LO_SD_BILLING_DISPLAY	Display billing documents
SAP_LO_SD_BILLING_PROCESSING	Billing processing online
SAP_LO_SD_BLOCKED_BILLING_DOC	Release blocked billing documents
SAP_LO_SD_CREDIT_MANAGEMENT	Credit management in sales documents
SAP_LO_SD_OUTPUT_PROCESS	Output process
SAP_LO_SD_PRICING_DISPLAY	Display pricing
SAP_LO_SD_SALES_DISPLAY	Display sales information

Table B.2 SD Authorization Roles

Finally, the next section provides a list of transactions relevant for functionalities discussed in this appendix.

B.4 List of Transactions

Table B.3 lists the SAP system transactions relevant for the authorization management functionality.

Transaction	Use
PFCG	Role maintenance
PFUD	User master data reconciliation
SUPC	Generate profiles for roles
SU24	Check indicators for authorization objects
SU02	Edit authorization profiles manually (use PFCG instead)
SU03	Edit authorizations manually (use PFCG instead)
S_BCE_68001404 to S_BCE_68001409	Authorization profiles: Information system by different criteria
S_BCE_68001410 to S_BCE_68001413	Authorization objects: Information system by different criteria
S_BCE_68001414 to S_BCE_68001417	Authorizations: Information system by different criteria
S_BCE_68001418 to S_BCE_68001424	Roles: Information system by different criteria

Table B.3 Authorization Transactions

C The Author

Manish Patel is a senior SAP professional with almost 15 years of experience in the IT industry. After graduating from Bombay University, Manish worked at an Indian software company on various financials projects in the Asia Pacific region. During his tenure at this company, he gained experience as the finance lead responsible for implementing the company's indigenously-developed ERP system. Over last ten years, he has worked on variety of SAP projects in a number of different industries. He has also conducted several successful SAP trainings at various SAP America facilities. This breadth of assignments has honed his abilities to successfully perform different roles in an SAP project, ranging from system configuration to project management. He is currently working as a Senior SAP Solutions Consultant in Northern California.

He is also the author of bestselling books *SAP Account Determination* and *Discover SAP ERP Financials*, published by SAP PRESS in English and in German. The account determination book is targeted at the technical and consulting community. The book explores vital design elements that carry out automatic determination of GL accounts from business transactions in various SAP components. The Discover series book describes functionalities of 19+ SAP Financials components. It is primarily targeted at decision makers and project managers. However, it is also useful for technical people who want to understand business logic underlying available functionalities.

Manish enjoys working through the challenges and complexities that are inherent in the implementation of such a full-featured enterprise-wide system. He is keenly aware of the potential constraints and other non-technical aspects that limit scope of initial SAP implementations.

Index

D

E

P

R

S

T

U

V

W

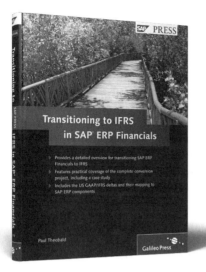

www.sap-press.com

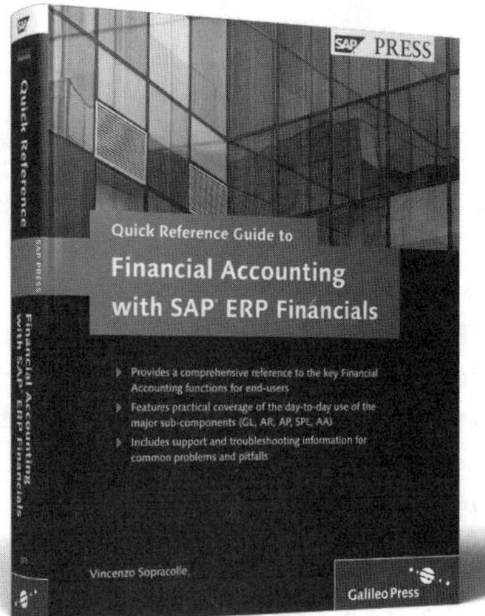

- Provides a comprehensive reference to the key Financial Accounting functions for end-users
- Features practical coverage of the day-to-day use of the major sub-components (GL, AR, AP, SPL, AA)
- Includes support and troubleshooting information for common problems and pitfalls

Vincenzo Sopracolle

Quick Reference Guide to Financial Accounting with SAP ERP Financials

If you use SAP ERP Financials on a daily basis, this definitive, comprehensive guide is a must-have resource. You'll find practical, detailed guidance to all of the key functions of the Financial Accounting component, including troubleshooting and problem-solving information. You'll find easy-to-use answers to frequently asked questions in the core areas of the SAP General Ledger, Asset Accounting (AA), Accounts Payable (AP), Accounts Receivable (AR), Banking (BK), and Special Purpose Ledger (SPL). In addition, the book includes quick-reference material such as lists of Transaction Codes, Tables, Codes, and Menu Paths.

approx. 650 pp., 69,95 Euro / US$ 69.95
ISBN 978-1-59229-313-1, May 2010

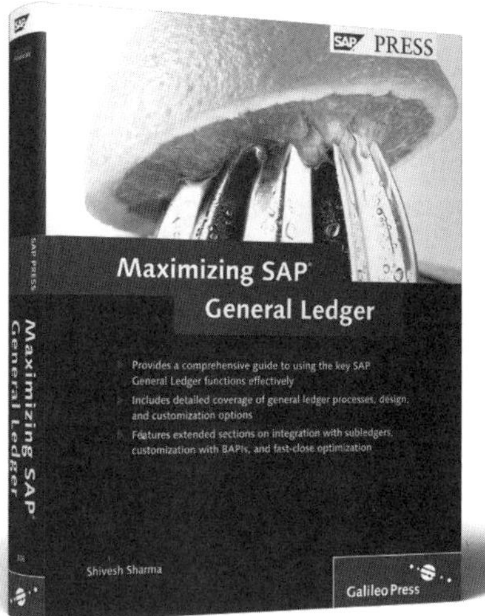

Provides a comprehensive guide to using the key SAP General Ledger functions effectively

Includes detailed coverage of SAP General Ledger processes, design, and customization options

Features extended sections on integration with subledgers, customization with BAPIs, and fast-close optimization

Shivesh Sharma

Maximizing SAP General Ledger

Successful integration of the SAP General Ledger into an existing infrastructure can make a significant impact on the ROI of an ERP Financials upgrade. Many users, however, lack the guidance necessary to sort through the integration and customization options available, particularly as consulting budgets are being slashed around the world. This book provides implementation teams, functional and technical teams, and end-users with a roadmap for the maximum utilization of the SAP General Ledger. This book focuses using the General Ledger in real-world situations and details how to customize and optimize it for specific business processes, and it teaches how to and integrate it with other SAP components. It will also help readers develop knowledge and strategies for enhancing the SAP General Ledger and integrating it with other SAP services and components.

540 pp., 79,95 Euro / US$ 79.95, ISBN 978-1-59229-306-3

>> www.sap-press.com

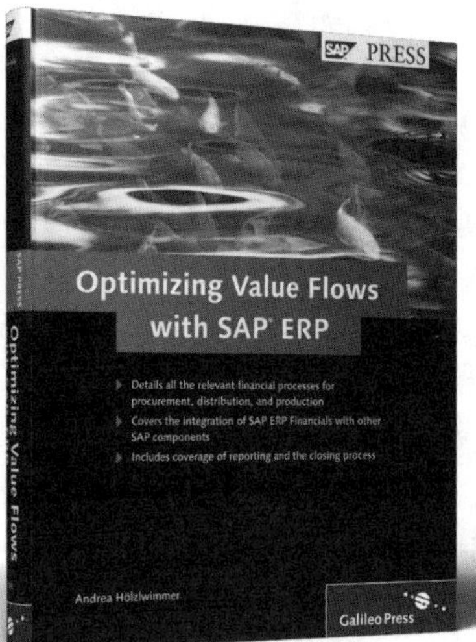

Covers all Finance-related processes, from purchasing and production to distribution

Teaches how to integrate Financial Accounting and Controlling with MM, PP, and SD

Details financial statement preparation and reporting

Andrea Hölzlwimmer

Optimizing Value Flows with SAP ERP

This book is written to teach financial consultants, IT managers, and integration consultants how value flows can be enhanced across an organization's entire finance and logistics chain. The book takes a process-oriented approach to the problems presented by non-integrated value flows in an organization and explains the solutions available in the SAP system. With this book you'll understand integrated value flows and learn about the important integration concepts, such as management of master data. You'll explore the central processes of purchasing, production, distribution accounting, and reporting, and you'll understand the impact of system settings and integration points as they relate to the overall process.

441 pp., 79,95 Euro / US$ 79.95
ISBN 978-1-59229-298-1

>> www.sap-press.com

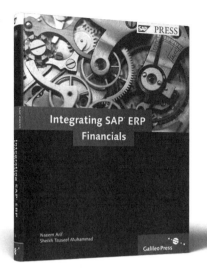